30408
√94

D1483244

THE DIARIES OF
EDWARD R. STETTINIUS, JR.,
1943-1946

THE DIARIES OF
EDWARD R. STETTINIUS, JR.,
1943-1946

edited by
THOMAS M. CAMPBELL
Florida State University

and
GEORGE C. HERRING
University of Kentucky

NEW VIEWPOINTS
A Division of Franklin Watts, Inc.
New York 1975

Library of Congress Cataloging in Publication Data

Stettinius, Edward Reilly, 1900–1949.
  The diaries of Edward R. Stettinius, Jr., 1943–1946.

  Includes bibliographical references.
  1. Stettinius, Edward Reilly, 1900–1949. I. Campbell, Thomas M., ed. II. Herring, George C., 1936–
ed.
E748.S836A33   973.917'092'4   74-9660
ISBN 0-531-05362-8
ISBN 0-531-05570-1 (pbk.)

Copyright © 1975 by Thomas M. Campbell and
George C. Herring
Printed in the United States of America
6 5 4 3 2 1

FOR

Julie, Tom, David, and Billy

AND

Nancy

CONTENTS

ACKNOWLEDGMENTS

During the years in which we have been working on this volume, we have incurred numerous debts which can never be fully repaid but must be acknowledged, however inadequately, in this space. The Florida State University Committee on Faculty Research Support and the University of Kentucky Research Foundation provided generous financial support which greatly facilitated the travel and extensive duplication of materials necessary for undertaking this project. Edmund Berkeley, Jr., Curator of Manuscripts and his colleagues in the University of Virginia Library, enthusiastically assisted us from the outset; furnishing convenient and comfortable workspace on our frequent visits to Charlottesville, helping us in the location and duplication of documents and, through his gracious hospitality and unflagging encouragement, making our task both easier and more enjoyable. While efficiently discharging her responsibilities as departmental secretary in the University of Kentucky history department, Dorothy Leathers somehow managed to type an exemplary manuscript from a mass of pasted pages and handwritten insertions, all in time to meet a publisher's deadline. Clifford Solway has taken a personal interest in our work and has assisted us in a variety of ways beyond the requirements of his position as Executive Editor of New Viewpoints.

Several long-standing personal acknowledgments are worthy of special note. Since we began working with the Stettinius Papers in 1962, Wallace and Joseph Stettinius of Richmond, Virginia, have given support and encouragement without in any way attempting to influence our assessments of their father's career. To Edward E. Younger, Professor of History in the University of Virginia, we can only express our deepest appreciation for over a decade of assistance. More than a teacher and adviser, he has given unsparingly of himself on our behalf from our days as graduate students throughout our subsequent careers. We can only hope that our work as historians will be worthy of his faith in us.

THOMAS M. CAMPBELL
Tallahassee, Florida

GEORGE C. HERRING
Lexington, Kentucky

INTRODUCTION

Such are the strange and fascinating twists of history that Edward R. Stettinius, Jr., an industrialist with only scant background in international relations, was thrust into the center of foreign policy making during one of the most critical periods in United States history. From September, 1943 to June, 1946, Stettinius served as undersecretary of state, secretary of state, and U.S. representative to the United Nations. While holding these posts, he played an important part in the negotiations which accompanied the triumph and ultimate breakdown of the Grand Alliance, and his work at Dumbarton Oaks, Yalta, and San Francisco, gives him solid claim to the title of architect of the United Nations.

Stettinius entered the world of diplomacy after a meteoric rise to the top echelons of American business. The son of Edward R. Stettinius, a leading industrialist and partner in the Wall Street financial house of J. P. Morgan & Company, and Judith Carrington, of an old and established Virginia family, he was born in Chicago in 1900. Along with his older brother and two sisters, he grew up in moderate wealth and moved freely through the top social circles of New York and Virginia, enjoying such elitist pastimes as polo and horseback riding.

The elder Stettinius sought the best education for his children, sending Edward Jr., to the prestigious Pomfret School in Connecticut, and later to the University of Virginia. Much to his father's disappointment, the young man did not achieve academic distinction in either place. He entered the

University of Virginia on probation and lacked sufficient credits for graduation when he left in 1924. However, he did take an active part in extra-curricular affairs, demonstrating the drive, social consciousness, and missionary zeal that would stamp his later career in business and government. He reorganized the listless campus YMCA, led missionary treks to rural areas in the nearby Blue Ridge Mountains, and developed an employment bureau in the University which attempted to locate jobs for students in Charlottesville businesses. This pioneering program was eminently successful and won for the young student recognition in the University's *Alumni News*. [1]

Stettinius wanted to enter the ministry, but lacked the degree required. Under the urging of his father, who regarded his interests as "socialistic," he agreed to consider a business career. Armed with introductions arranged by his father through General Motors president Alfred P. Sloan, Jr., he visited Detroit and talked with GM executives. Nothing excited him until he went to the company's headquarters in New York and talked with vice-president John Lee Pratt. An alumnus of Virginia himself, Pratt had been impressed by Stettinius's imagination in setting up the employment bureau. He outlined the opportunities for creative work in labor and public relations, and his promise of a "congregation" of thousands sparked the young man's interest. [2]

After holding a series of jobs which exposed him to the problems of assembly line workers, Stettinius joined Pratt in New York. He convinced Pratt and Sloan of the need for a company-paid life insurance program and, working with Metropolitan Life Insurance executives, came up with the largest group life insurance program in U.S. history. In 1930, Sloan appointed him assistant to the president in charge of employee benefit programs and public relations. In this capacity, Stettinius sought to persuade the public of GM's progressive outlook toward social problems and its advances in technology through sponsorship of a radio show and the publication of a *General Motors Magazine*.[3]

By the early 1930s, the nation was engulfed in the Great Depression, and Stettinius devoted much of his time to combating the problem of unemployment. He helped to develop the "back-to-the-land movement," an experiment in subsistence homesteads sponsored by General Motors. He also directed the "share-the-work campaign," a program sponsored by the federal government and implemented by private industry, which aimed to reduce unemployment by limiting work hours and spreading jobs among more workers. Neither of the projects was particularly successful, but through them Stettinius did secure his first introduction to New York Governor Franklin D. Roosevelt.[4]

After Roosevelt became president, Stettinius went to Washington to work with the National Recovery Administration, the New Deal's first organized attempt to promote economic upturn. As liaison between the Industrial Advisory Board, composed of businessmen, and the NRA, his chief assignment was to get representatives of business, labor, and government to draft codes which would regulate the operations of each individual industry. It was a challenging and frustrating undertaking. "My experiences here are immensely interesting," he wrote a friend in 1933, "but I have come to the definite conclusion that 'big corporation life' is a bed of roses compared with Government service." Stettinius demonstrated a talent for getting the various interest groups to sit down together, and by December, 1933 some 570 codes had been drafted. But the NRA became a political liability and by the end of the year, Roosevelt had all but abandoned it.[5]

Stettinius's work with NRA did open to him a new and exciting opportunity. His abilities had impressed Myron Taylor, chairman of the board of United States Steel, and in November, 1933, Taylor invited him to become vice-chairman of the company's finance committee with primary responsibility for developing plans to revitalize and modernize the giant of American industry. Stettinius eagerly accepted the challenge and in 1934, left General Motors for U.S. Steel.

By this time, he had assumed heavy family responsibilities. His father had died in 1925, his mother and older brother were in poor health, and he had to handle family financial and personal matters. He had also married Virginia Wallace of Richmond, a woman of keen intelligence and beauty, whose graceful charm complemented his own intensity and drive. The couple lived in New York with their three young sons until 1940, but in 1934, Stettinius had acquired the home of his dreams—a 579-acre estate set in the rolling foothills of the Blue Ridge Mountains in Orange County, Virginia. Throughout the rest of his life, "Horseshoe" was an oasis for rest and relaxation, and turkeys and hams bearing its mark were a sign of Stettinius's friendship and generosity to people throughout the world.

Over the next four years, Stettinius occupied himself with the reorganization of U.S. Steel. Working with the industrial engineering firm of Ford, Bacon, and Davis, and traveling to most of the corporation's major plants, he gained a firsthand knowledge of operations and personnel. He developed an efficient staff system to handle the vast data accumulated. He showed an uncanny knack for organizing the talents of men and getting them to work together, and he impressed Taylor and others with his quick grasp of problems and his recommendations for solutions. He developed a comprehensive plan for cutting out inefficient operations and making new capital investments. Most significant, he helped to persuade Taylor to come to terms with organized labor. In the spring of 1938, U.S. Steel recognized the Congress of Industrial Organizations, agreed to increase wages by ten percent, and accepted the principle of the forty-hour week.[6]

When Taylor retired in 1938, Stettinius succeeded him as chairman of the board. It was a critical period for the giant industry. A serious recession was underway, and production of ingots, the major indicator of steel prosperity, had dipped to one-fourth capacity. The Justice Department had launched an investigation of the corporation's alleged monopolistic practices. Stettinius confronted these problems effectively. By the late summer of 1938, business had picked up and profits increased. Instead of stubbornly opposing the government investigation, Stettinius worked with the Attorney General's office, and he simultaneously won public approbation by engineering a ten percent price reduction without cutting wages.[7]

Stettinius's career had been blessed with exceptional good fortune, but a more important ingredient in his rise to the top of American business leadership was his unflinching commitment to the new industrial order emerging in the 1930s. He brought an open mind to corporate problems and used his talents of persuasion to convince others to seek fresh approaches. He intuitively sensed the importance of changing relationships between business, labor, and government. Infused with a deep strain of social consciousness, he sought to make industry more responsible to the public upon which it ultimately depended. While many of his colleagues bitterly fought the New Deal, Stettinius adapted to changes which he felt were inevitable and even desirable. His positions won him a standing among New Dealers accorded few businessmen. He developed a close personal friendship with Secretary of Commerce Harry Hopkins, and was known among anti-New Deal businessmen as one of Hopkins's "tame millionaires." Secretary of Labor Frances Perkins expressed to him her gratitude that U.S. Steel was "in the hands of one who has consistently used both his mind and his conscience, his total personality, to help him in determining the wise course in the development of business." [8]

Stettinius's tenure at U.S. Steel was destined to be brief. The outbreak of war in Europe appeared imminent in the late summer of 1939, and concern mounted about the nation's defenses. On August 9, President Roosevelt established a War Resources Board and named Stettinius to head it, charging him with the responsibility for developing a comprehensive plan for industrial mobilization. The board completed its deliberations by October, but it had attracted sharp criticism from labor and New Dealers because it was composed almost exclusively of businessmen, and Roosevelt shelved its report and terminated its activities. [9]

Stettinius returned briefly to U.S. Steel, but in June, 1940, Roosevelt again called him to Washington. By this time, Germany had conquered much of Europe and war with Japan appeared possible, and the administration had quickened its efforts to mobilize for defense. Roosevelt revived the old Advisory Commission to the Council of National Defense and appointed Stettinius Commissioner of Industrial Materials. After a reshuffling of the defense agencies in January, 1941, Stettinius became Director of Priorities in the Office of Production Management. His primary task in both positions was to help expand industrial output to meet the growing defense needs.

It was an impossible assignment. Raw materials were in short supply, business refused to convert to defense production as long as the United States was not at war, and the operation was plagued by bureaucratic warfare between dollar-a-year men and New Dealers, and conflict between business and labor. In this frantic atmosphere, Stettinius at first made significant contributions. Roosevelt accepted his recommendation that a federal coordinator be appointed to oversee all government defense purchases, eliminating much duplication of effort and time-consuming competition among federal agencies. Stettinius also set in motion a change in tax law to allow businesses to depreciate defense-related capital investment over a short period of time, encouraging conversion to defense production.[10]

In other matters, however, he was less successful. His industrial materials group badly miscalculated the available supplies of several vital raw materials, including aluminum which was essential for the production of aircraft. Even as contractors warned of shortages, Stettinius assured reporters that "no serious difficulties are expected." His committee took no measures to limit civilian production, curb speculative buying, or assign priorities for the use of available supplies. By the spring of 1941, an aluminum shortage was holding back defense production, and Stettinius had to accept responsibility.[11]

He was also unable to set up a workable system of priorities for the use of raw materials. His division developed a "preference rating system" to ensure that the most important defense contracts received first attention, but the deluge of applications far exceeded the ability of OPM to process them. Stettinius did not anticipate this bottleneck, and though he could impose controls on military procurement he lacked authority to restrict civilian purchasing. The entire priorities system became bogged down in red tape, and defense mobilization became hopelessly snarled.[12]

Roosevelt rescued Stettinius from this nightmare in the autumn of 1941. In March, the President had deepened the U.S. commitment to embattled Britain, securing passage of the Lend-Lease Act which enabled him to turn over war materials to any nation whose defense was considered vital to the defense of the United States. He had originally entrusted administration of Lend-Lease to his confidant, Harry Hopkins, but he preferred to conserve Hopkins's limited energy for policy making. In addition, by the summer of 1941, Lend-Lease was under fire from those who felt that inefficient administration was restricting aid to the anti-Hitler forces and from others who suspected that the "big spender" Hopkins would exhaust the federal treasury. On August 28, 1941, Roosevelt appointed Stettinius Lend-Lease Administrator, authorizing him to transfer supplies under the Lend-Lease Act. Shortly after, he established an Office of Lend-Lease Administration and appointed Stettinius to head it. It turned out to be the most successful undertaking of Stettinius's career, and led directly to his appointments to major diplomatic posts.[13]

His first task as Lend-Lease Administrator was to untangle the bureaucratic snarls which had stymied the program in its early months. Requests for assistance had to pass through a maze of offices before approval, and each order had to be signed individually by the president. It took an estimated ninety days to process an order and many more days before items could be procured and loaded aboard ship. Stettinius gathered about him an able staff and working in an unfinished apartment building amidst exposed telephone wires and scurrying painters, they streamlined and simplified the Lend-Lease procedure and established mechanisms for long-range planning. Working in close coordination with other departments and agencies, OLLA had, by December, 1941, reduced to seventy-three hours the time required to process an application.[14]

Throughout his first months in office, Stettinius also fought a continuing battle with the military for supplies. American industry was not producing enough to satisfy the needs of Lend-Lease nations and U.S. rearmament, and the Army and Navy deeply resented the dispersal across the globe of equipment they desperately needed. Backed by the president and Hopkins, Stettinius pressed the military relentlessly to meet the legitimate requests of Britain, Russia, and other Lend-Lease claimants. The volume of assistance increased from $60 million in May to $338 million in December, and by the time the United States entered the war, Lend-Lease was firmly established as an instrument of global warfare.[15]

The civilian-military struggle for control over the arsenal of democracy intensified after Pearl Harbor, and OLLA emerged with restricted powers. Suddenly caught in a two-front war, the Army and Navy insisted that they must have control over the allocation of military supplies and in early 1942, Roosevelt agreed to place the handling of munitions under a Munitions Assignment Board, chaired by Hopkins but composed primarily of military officials. Henceforth, OLLA was responsible only for allocating non-military supplies.[16]

Undaunted by this loss of authority, Stettinius went about his work with characteristic zeal. He and his staff worked tirelessly to find raw materials, foodstuffs, clothing and machinery for allied nations and to break the logistical bottlenecks that restricted assistance. They came to view Lend-Lease not only as an instrument of global warfare but also as an experiment in international cooperation. "It is a living thing," Stettinius told a British audience in 1942, "with a heart and soul, ready to give its energies to the forces and peoples of the United Nations." During 1943, aid to the Allies totaled more than $10 billion, and Lend-Lease had indeed become a "weapon of victory." [17]

Stettinius's administration of Lend-Lease attracted much attention in a wartime Washington, characterized by pervasive inefficiency and debilitating bureaucratic warfare. He brought into OLLA many talented men, including Scott Paper Company president Thomas McCabe, lawyer-historian Bernhard Knollenberg, and such prominent future diplomats as George W. Ball and Eugene Rostow, and they worked together with an elan rare in government agencies. Despite its great responsibilities and the vast sums of money spent, OLLA remained a simple, compact agency which won plaudits from that perennial watchdog of the treasury, Senator Harry F. Byrd of Virginia. During its lifetime, OLLA was engaged in many struggles, with the Army, with Henry Wallace's Board of Economic Warfare, and with the State Department. More comfortable in the clean administrative lines of big business, Stettinius did not enjoy such in-fighting and was not particularly effective at it. Despite several bitter defeats, he refused to air his grievances publicly. "Always tactful, always earnest, always willing," the columnist Marquis Childs observed, "Stettinius has tried to do his job with a minimum of incidental friction and that fact alone sets him apart in contentious Washington." [18]

Stettinius's greatest contribution in Lend-Lease was in public relations, an area where he felt quite at home. Through a series of magazine articles, press releases, and radio broadcasts, he sought to get across to a skeptical public that the United States was rendering effective aid to the Allies and getting substantial assistance in return through reverse Lend-Lease; that Lend-Lease was not draining off American resources and causing domestic shortages, but was saving American lives by enabling the Allies to fight more effectively; and that the program was not an act of charity but of "enlightened self-interest." OLLA never overcame the deeply entrenched suspicions of foreign aid, but the consistent support which Lend-Lease commanded throughout the war suggests the effectiveness of its publicity campaign. [19]

Stettinius was especially successful in dealing with Congress. He took great pains to respond to every congressional inquiry regarding the Lend-Lease operation. In hearings before House and Senate committees, he prepared the administration's case with the utmost care and presented clear, hard-hitting arguments. He patiently and thoroughly answered questions, even petty or contentious ones, and at night after the hearings had ended he wrote letters providing additional details. "His willingness to spend time with a congressional committee, his willingness to hear complaints and investigate them," the conservative Ohio Republican John Vorys remarked, "were so different from the typical Washington bureaucrat, and so refreshing that I feel it my duty to make special mention of him." [20]

By the summer of 1943, Stettinius had established a reputation as one of the most effective administrators in Washington. Only forty-two years old, strikingly handsome with silver hair, dark, heavy eyebrows, and a warm flashing smile, he radiated youth and vitality. A man of action rather than ideas, he was nevertheless able to grasp quickly the essentials of complicated problems, and he brought a prodigious energy to every task he undertook. With Lend-Lease, he had shown particular adeptness in using the talents of his subordinates and in developing public and congressional confidence in his work. The aid program was no longer controversial, *New York Times* columnist Arthur Krock observed in 1943. "But less wise and able management might have made it so." [21]

Thus when Undersecretary of State Sumner Welles was forced to resign in 1943 under the cloud of a personal scandal and after a long feud with Secretary of State Cordell Hull, Stettinius emerged as a logical choice as his successor. To be sure, he had no diplomatic experience, and he himself had qualms about accepting the offer on these grounds. But Roosevelt and Hull selected him in the hopes that his administrative abilities and his flair for public relations might revamp the creaking apparatus of the department and repair its unfavorable public image. The president and secretary also appreciated the excellent relations Stettinius had established with Congress, and felt that this might be of considerable value when the administration went to secure endorsement of an American commitment to an international organization.

Neither Roosevelt nor Hull could have foreseen that in a little more than a year, Stettinius would assume the nation's highest diplomatic post. In October, 1944, Hull had to be hospitalized for a serious illness, and one month later he resigned. Again, Stettinius appeared the logical choice. He did not have strong party identification, an advantage when the administration was attempting to construct a bipartisan foreign policy, and he lacked the political liabilities of other strong candidates such as Henry A. Wallace and James F. Byrnes. Roosevelt appreciated Stettinius's loyalty to the administration, and recognized that, while he would administer the department effectively, he would not challenge presidential leadership in foreign policy. He had begun the all-important work of negotiations on international organization at the Dumbarton Oaks Conference in the fall of 1944, and it seemed natural to allow him to continue to completion. His good standing in Congress would continue to be helpful. Thus in December, 1944, Stettinius assumed the post of secretary of state.

Stettinius would be in the Department of State from the fall of 1943 until July, 1945. It was a critical period, spanning the time from the Italian surrender and the Teheran Conference to V-E Day and the conclusion of the San Francisco Conference, and Stettinius was deeply involved in the formulation and implementation of foreign policy. As undersecretary and secretary, he devoted great effort to making the machinery of the department more responsive to America's expanding role in world affairs. He carried out two major reorganizations, attempting to clarify lines of authority and create organs for long-range planning. He worked vigorously to improve communications with the White House and to coordinate policy making with the War and Navy Departments.

Building on his work with lend-lease, he attempted to influence public opinion on foreign policy issues and to develop better relations with Congress.

Throughout his tenure in the State Department, Stettinius was particularly concerned with the creation of an international organization. He headed a top-level diplomatic mission to London in the spring of 1944 to sound out the British on postwar plans. He chaired the Dumbarton Oaks Conference outside Washington in the summer of 1944, and did much to bring these four-power talks to a successful conclusion. At Yalta, he persuaded Churchill, Roosevelt, and Stalin to accept a compromise which insured further negotiations on an international organization. He immediately flew off to Mexico City to secure Latin American adherence to the proposals developed by the Big Three nations. From April to June, 1945, he headed the American delegation to the San Francisco Conference and played a vital role in the negotiations which brought forth the United Nations Charter.

Stettinius's work at San Francisco marked the apex of his career in public service, and ironically, even while he was negotiating the UN Charter, President Harry S Truman was arranging for his replacement. Truman had assumed the presidency after Roosevelt's death on April 12, 1945, and from the beginning he wanted James F. Byrnes to be secretary of state. He encouraged Stettinius to remain in the post until the San Francisco negotiations had been completed, but once the conference had ended he accepted Stettinius's resignation.

Truman immediately appointed Stettinius U.S. representative to the United Nations, a natural move considering his earlier involvement with the world organization, and he would serve in that capacity until June, 1946. He headed the U.S. delegation to the London Preparatory Commission which assembled in the fall of 1945 to make arrangements for the first meetings of the United Nations. In the stormy sessions in New York in early 1946, he played an important role in the laborious discussions on establishing a permanent headquarters for the UN and in the negotiations on the Iranian issue, the first battleground of the Cold War.

Increasingly, however, he became disenchanted with his work. As the Cold War set in, the Truman administration paid less attention to the United Nations, a trend which greatly disturbed him. More important, his own position became untenable. President Truman and Secretary Byrnes ignored him in making policy and appointing personnel, even where the UN was concerned, and Byrnes insisted on personally handling major negotiations during the Iranian crisis. As a consequence, Stettinius resigned his post in June, 1946, and retired to private life.

Stettinius's diaries fully document his three years at the center of American foreign policy. He began keeping a personal record of his activities when he went to Washington in 1940, apparently as a safeguard against a future congressional investigation of defense mobilization, but his notes are fragmentary and of uneven value up to the time when he became undersecretary of state. Conscious of the significance of the events in which he was then participating, he began to keep more systematic records, dictating at the end of each day his "calendar notes," his own personal summaries of the various meetings and conferences in which he had taken part. Stettinius used the telephone to a much greater extent than his predecessors, and he also kept verbatim transcripts of most of his calls, assigning a stenographer to listen in on the conversations and take shorthand notes. The "calendar notes" and transcripts of phone conversations comprise the "diary" for most of Stettinius's tenure at the State Department and UN. From these notes, however, he and his aides compiled formal diaries for his major diplomatic missions, such as the London trip of 1944 and for the conferences at Dumbarton Oaks, Yalta, Mexico City and San Francisco. He also assigned several assistants to put together the "Record," an account of his work as secretary of state compiled from the calendar notes, official documents, and newspaper clippings.

A diary naturally reflects the personality and needs of the man who compiles it. Stettinius intended his diary primarily as a record of his official activities, not as a source of intellectual satisfaction or emotional release. Hence it is confined largely to public matters and tells little about his private life. The diary sometimes offers sensitive and perceptive comments on public affairs in World War II, but in general it takes a cautious, even uncritical approach, reflecting the cautiousness of Stettinius's personality and his concern for the reputations of the men around him. A sometimes insecure man who stood in awe of many of his associates, Stettinius liked people and desperately wanted to be liked, and his diary lacks the candid, frequently acerbic appraisals of men which typify the diaries of John Quincy Adams and Henry Stimson. He deals only sparingly with the power struggles that were going on around him, and indeed plays down his own conflicts with his associates.

Nevertheless, the Stettinius diary forms an important and revealing record of American diplomacy during and immediately after World War II. The summaries of conversations with U.S. officials and foreign diplomats nicely supplement the official documents published by the Department of State. The transcripts of phone conversations are a particularly valuable source, and frequently catch prominent officials in candid, unguarded moments. The diary provides significant information which cannot be found elsewhere, and it reveals much about the manner in which decisions were made in the State Department and the government as a whole. The sketchiness of Franklin Roosevelt's papers and the inaccessibility of Truman's papers leave a large gap in the record of the period which the Stettinius diary helps to fill. The particularly detailed accounts of conversations with the two presidents provide many fascinating insights into their thoughts on major issues.

The Stettinius diaries are voluminous, and in putting together this highly selective volume, the editors have been governed by several considerations. They have attempted to include those entries which deal with the most significant problems Stettinius encountered, provide information not available elsewhere, or are particularly revealing about the men and events of the era. All deletions have been indicated by asterisks. Ellipses within paragraphs generally indicate the elimination of repetitious language. In dividing the initial editorial responsibility, George Herring drafted chapters 1 through 5 while Tom Campbell drafted chapters 6 through 13. However, both editors worked through the entire manuscript in its various stages, and the final product represents their joint judgment in editorial and interpretive matters.

In many studies of World War II, Edward R. Stettinius, Jr., appears only as a peripheral figure, a small man who scarcely affected the great events in which he participated. We hope that this volume, while making available significant new materials on wartime diplomacy, will also encourage a more balanced assessment of the career of a dedicated public servant who gave unsparingly of his talents and energy in the cause of victory and an enduring world peace.

I
UNDERSECRETARY OF STATE
October 1943–March 1944

The appointment of Edward R. Stettinius, Jr., as undersecretary of state in September 1943, was part of a reshuffling of top government personnel and agencies designed by President Roosevelt to counter a growing criticism of his administration's conduct of foreign policy. By the summer of 1943, the fortunes of war had shifted in favor of the Allies. The Red Army had taken the offensive on the eastern front; Anglo-American armies had completed the conquest of North Africa and were near victory in Sicily; the forced resignation of Mussolini from the cabinet on July 25 indicated that an Italian surrender was near. But the uncertain and sometimes contradictory manner in which American diplomats responded to these events suggested to many that U.S. foreign policy was not keeping pace with the accomplishments of Allied arms. "The great overwhelming fact by which we are confronted this week," the *New Republic* editorialized on August 16, "is that we are completely unprepared for a possible victory that may come sooner than anyone has dared to predict." [1]

Critics placed much of the blame for the ineffectiveness of American foreign policy on a cumbersome and divided bureaucracy. The long-smoldering feud between Vice-President Henry A. Wallace and Secretary of Commerce Jesse H. Jones for control over U.S. purchasing abroad had been carried into the public forum and became a source of much embarrassment to the administration. The numerous emergency agencies the president had created to deal with economic foreign policy, the Office of Lend-Lease Administration, the Board of Economic Warfare, and the Office of Foreign Relief and Rehabilitation Operations, openly struggled with each other and with the Army and State Department to dominate relief operations in liberated North Africa.

The State Department itself was singled out for special criticism. In a much-publicized *New York Times* article on August 4, 1943, John Crider charged that "conflicting personalities, lack of a cohesive policy, and a resulting impairment of efficiency," had completely paralyzed the department responsible for shaping the nation's foreign policy. Overlapping jurisdictions resulted in contradictory policies and inefficient administration. Most important, the long-standing and increasingly bitter rivalry between Secretary of State Hull and Undersecretary Sumner Welles exhausted the energies of the department's two top officials and diverted them from their responsibilities. These problems would have to be corrected, Crider warned, if the United States was to develop a "coherent and meaningful" foreign policy at "one of the most critical junctures in its history." [2]

Responding to these charges, Roosevelt in August and September 1943 drastically reorganized the machinery for economic diplomacy and appointed new men to key diplomatic positions. Wallace and Jones were deprived of all responsibility for economic warfare, and their agencies, along with OLLA were soon absorbed into a new Foreign Economic Administration headed by the former Wisconsin banker and utilities executive, Leo T. Crowley. At the same time, Hull used the uproar over the Crider article and rumors that Welles had committed a moral indiscretion to force the president to accept the undersecretary's resignation.

After nearly four weeks of discussion, the two finally agreed on Stettinius as a replacement. Both the president and the secretary had originally preferred other candidates, but

Stettinius emerged as an ideal compromise choice. His background with General Motors and U.S. Steel would satisfy conservatives, while his close relationship with Harry Hopkins, his general support of the New Deal and the president's

Courtesy Cyrus Hungerford, Pittsburgh Post-Gazette

foreign policies, and his work with lend-lease might at least defuse liberal opposition. His reputation as an outstanding administrator would reassure those who had long condemned the State Department for incompetence and inefficiency, and his lack of experience in diplomacy ensured that he would not challenge either Hull or Roosevelt in policy making. Perhaps most important, the excellent relationship he had established with key congressional committees during his tenure with lend-lease would be of great value when the time came to win the support of Congress for the administration's postwar programs.

[The decision was reached while Stettinius was on the west coast surveying operations in ports handling lend-lease shipments to the Soviet Union, and the news that he was being considered for undersecretary reached him on the night of September 24.]

CALENDAR NOTES | *September 24, 1943*
On my tour of the San Francisco Bay area with Lt. Comdr. Watson to inspect facilities for handling lend-lease shipments, I arrived at the Mare Island Navy Yard at 1:45 in the afternoon. There was an urgent call from the Washington office awaiting me. I was informed that Justice Byrnes [3] and Secretary of State Hull both were anxious to talk to me. As . . . there was no opportunity to talk in private, I said I would be in touch later.

When I arrived back at the Mark Hopkins Hotel, there was a message that the White House operator would call at 7:30 that evening and would have Justice Byrnes and Secretary Hull on the line.

I talked to Jim Byrnes first. He asked whether Secretary Hull had called me and I said "No." He asked me when I was coming home. I said, "In a few days, but if it is really important I can fly right back." Byrnes then said, "I've engineered around for you. Hull wanted Armour [Norman Armour, Foreign Service officer, ambassador to Argentina], the president someone else, but now all agree on you for undersecretary of state. Don't tell Hull I told you. The president is at Hyde Park and will be back in the morning. Can he reach you there?" I said, "Yes." Then I asked Byrnes, "Will it be an ordeal? You know the State Department. You think there is . . . ." Byrnes interrupted to say, "Lend-Lease and OEW and OFRRO are all under Crowley. This is a deep new field for you. It takes only honesty and common sense and you have both. It is the best, most important job in Washington. I talked to Harry Hopkins about it too."

When I hung up with Byrnes, the White House operator asked if I would talk to Secretary Hull. He said, "How are you? I need some help—badly. I want you to come over as undersecretary." I told him that I was greatly complimented, and didn't know anyone whom I had more respect for or confidence in than him. He said he was going to London or Moscow and must get a few days away, and asked when I could come. I said, "In a few days." He said, "Two days?" I replied, "No. A few." He said . . . to try to come soon. . . . I asked the secretary what the duties of the position are, and he said, "Act generally as assistant to me—policy determination—prepare matters to take up with me—act as secretary in my absence. We have an assistant secretary in charge of administration. I know your folks—both sides—I have confidence in you and your ability, your character. I would like this association." I said, "Thank you, Mr. Secretary."

After that, I called Mr. Knollenberg, Mr. Pratt, and Gen. Marshall.[4] They were unanimous in their advice that I accept. General Marshall had just arrived at Leesburg. He said, "Let me think." Then he advised me, "I would accept. With what's ahead it is a great opportunity and I'd do it." I mentioned the pitfall of bureaucracy, and he replied, "Well, you are an organizer."

[The following day, Stettinius advised Washington of his acceptance of the appointment, and on September 27, he returned to the capital. During the next few days, he discussed his new responsibilities with Hopkins, Hull, and the president.]

CALENDAR NOTES | *September 28, 1943*
I went to the White House where I was immediately shown up to Harry Hopkins's bedroom (the Lincoln Room). He looked bad, and is still weak from his illness. I had a forty-five-minute visit with him in which he and I discussed a great many matters. Harry was quite emotional about the two-year relationship he and I have had in Lend-Lease coming to an end. He told me all of the background of the discussions relative to my appointment, involving the president, Hull, Douglas,[5] and Armour. . . .

* * *

He mentioned that my first official move should be an important one and that he would speak to the president about this. He recommended that I look into my stockholding situation. I reviewed with him certain ideas I had relative to the State Department, such as reorganization, etc., and he was thoroughly in accord.

The talk was a most satisfactory one and I have a very high regard for Harry Hopkins.

On the way from the Lincoln Bedroom down the hall, I passed the president's oval study. His door was open and his eye seemed to be on the hall. Instinctively we almost waved at each other from hall to study at the same moment. His greeting was "Hi! Come in. When did you get back?" We had a most satisfactory ten-minute visit. . . . He said he wanted to have a long talk with me as he had a thousand things to talk about and might call me for lunch tomorrow or the next day.

[On Saturday morning, October 2, Stettinius visited with the president for nearly two hours. FDR was in a light-hearted mood and talked casually and openly about a variety of subjects.]

CALENDAR NOTES | *October 2, 1943*
The president said his dog, Fala, was interrupted at night, by the rats from the State Department who came across the street and ate up his food. He didn't want me to take that as a symbolic statement.
[He] . . . described the handling of the destroyer base transaction [6] which he and the prime minister worked out together. He said Cordell was fine about the whole thing but the president really had to do it himself.

* * *

He made a comment that he thought that radio talks were the way really to get things across to the country. He seemed in a fine mood and was very relaxed. He talked about his wife having gone to Hyde Park with a load of souvenirs—loot obtained in the Pacific.

* * *

The president commented on ways we can get away from the stiff formality of cutaways, white ties, etc. He is receiving ambassadors in his office informally—putting on his coat to receive them works well.

* * *

The president mentioned to me that after the war he would like to get a 110-foot boat with a couple of small diesels in it and go for a cruise around the world.

* * *

He said he had been trying ever since he had been in Washington to reorganize our foreign service so that these professional diplomats knew something about America. He felt diplomats should be recalled and sent to Tennessee for a year. . . .

[Two days later, on Monday morning October 4, Stettinius went to the State Department for swearing-in ceremonies and for his first day in office.]

CALENDAR NOTES | *October 4, 1943*
I reported at ten o'clock this morning and was shown right in to the secretary. He greeted me in a very warm, affectionate manner. . . . We visited a few minutes. I went into the next office and shook hands with the staff and went back to the secretary's office and had a long leisurely visit.

* * *

I didn't mention bringing any other assistants with me. I pledged to Mr. Hull my loyalty and said I would submit to him in memorandum form every action I had at the White House—president, Byrnes, etc.

* * *

The secretary said he and I must work together in a complete spirit of cooperation and work jointly.

* * *

The secretary also spoke to me about forty-five minutes of the evolution during the past ten years of relations with the White House, Congress, internal troubles. He discussed very, very privately Sumner Welles's situation and the whole personal situation—certain things he had given to the press and his relations with the press and a very personal private situation surrounding Sumner Welles.[7]

During my visit Mr. [Breckinridge] Long [Assistant Secretary of State] was there part of the time and said unless we revamp things pretty quickly, the Department is likely to disintegrate. Long said, "Ed has the organization experience and we can rely on him." The secretary agreed. I said, "There are a lot of things to be revamped." The secretary said he had thought that Welles was following the administration of the State Department, but found out he wasn't. . . .

At eleven o'clock we went into the conference room to take the oath of office—assistant secretaries were there, newsreels with sound. I took the oath on a bible. Then there were fifteen to eighteen still cameras and then I had to go through again for newsreels and sound and then took sound with Mr. Hull and me at the table.

[Just three days after Stettinius took the oath as undersecretary, Hull departed for Moscow to meet with the foreign ministers of Britain and the Soviet Union. During his absence, Stettinius served as acting secretary. One of the first major problems he confronted—relations with Congress on international organization—was in a sense prophetic, for during his entire service in the State Department much of his attention was devoted to securing congressional endorsement of a new League of Nations.

The problem arose in the Senate, and ironically it was not with those who opposed United States involvement in a new international organization but rather with those who thought the Senate leadership was not going far enough in that direction. On October 14, the chairman of the Foreign Relations Committee, Tom Connally [D.-Texas], had introduced a resolution pledging the United States to "join with free and sovereign nations in the establishment and maintenance of international authority with power to prevent aggression and to preserve the peace of the world." The resolution was quickly approved by the committee, but when it moved to the floor of the Senate, a bipartisan group of internationalist senators vowed to fight for amendments to strengthen it. Connally, fearing delay and an angry floor fight, immediately called upon Stettinius for assistance.]

TRANSCRIPT OF TELEPHONE
CONVERSATION | *October 27, 1943*
Connally: I wanted to get hold of you while you were there. We have this resolution bill you ought to have an interest in. There is no doubt about its passing, we are going to vote it with an overwhelming vote, but they are deliberately staging a filibuster until next week. . . . They think they are going to create a public upheaval to make us adopt that plan. This meeting is going on at Moscow. They don't know at Moscow that this represents just a shirt tail of votes—there is a real division here in the Senate. Hill and Hatch [8] ought to be amenable to State Department influence. The press has told me that Secretary Hull wanted it passed right now just as it was written. I told them I couldn't confirm anything like that—I don't know whether he has or not. If he has he ought to tell somebody about it. They are going on until next week Thursday if we don't have word.
Stettinius: If the president would tell Lister [Hill] and Hatch promptly . . .

Connally: That would end it.
Stettinius: I will go to work immediately.

[Stettinius contacted Justice Byrnes at the White House, but Roosevelt's adviser, himself a former senator, recommended caution.]

TRANSCRIPT OF TELEPHONE
CONVERSATION | *October 27, 1943*

Stettinius: I am sorry to bother you. I have just come back from 2½ hours upstairs and I hate to go back on an emergency. Tom Connally phoned and said he was in a jam— they were going to filibuster about the foreign resolution bill—and couldn't we get a message from the president that it is important to pass it immediately.

Byrnes: That isn't practical.

Stettinius: He said that if the president would send word to Lister and Hatch he could put it through promptly.

Byrnes: I know Tom. Whenever he gets any bill, and he doesn't get many, he wants the president immediately to interfere and put his bill through for him. There is a whole lot in that. My first reaction would be that it would be unwise for the president to do it. His group of fellows who are first class fellows—strong supporters of foreign policy like Ball and Burton, Hatch and Hill, and Pepper,[9] they have a right to discuss it. Of course Hill happens to hold that view. They came down to see me, wanted to discuss it, about two weeks ago— whether the president would consider trying to get Connally to put through a real resolution with teeth in it, or even the Fulbright[10] [resolution] and the president was friendly to the Fulbright resolution. I mentioned it to him one day and in view of his feeling I feel it wouldn't be wise for him to mix up in a thing like this. There isn't any reason. The men on the floor of the Senate want to talk about it—fifteen or sixteen of them. My reaction is to stall on him. Tell him the president is not well and you will send him a message.

Stettinius: Wouldn't it be satisfactory for me to call Tom and say I have sent word to the president?

Byrnes: Say he is sick, but you have sent a message to him and let it go at that. It is a damned unreasonable thing.

Stettinius: I know it is absurd.

Byrnes: Barkley [11] is away and he therefore wants to put pressure on Hill to stop people from speaking. It would be a hell of a thing. Hill and Hatch and Ball haven't had a chance to speak. Mr. Connally filibustered for two months last year—he would go to the roof on anything he wanted to. He is one of my closest friends but when he gets on the floor of the Senate he considers it a personal matter.

[As Connally had predicted, the internationalist senators challenged his resolution, arguing that it should include a commitment to the use of force. For over a week the debate droned on, and then on October 30, word reached Washington that the conferees at Moscow had agreed on a declaration committing the United Nations to establish "at the earliest practical date a general international organization . . . for the maintenance of international peace and security." The insurgent senators saw this as an opportunity to strengthen the Connally resolution, and on November 1 recommended that it be returned to committee for revision.

Just as it appeared that the internationalist forces might be split by the battle, Senator Carter Glass [D.-Virginia] proposed a way out of the impasse, suggesting that the Connally resolution be amended to include certain key phrases from the Moscow Declaration. The

State Department was sympathetic to the idea, and Stettinius consulted Byrnes about handling Connally.]

TRANSCRIPT OF TELEPHONE CONVERSATION | *November 3, 1943*

Stettinius: Breck Long feels that somebody should go up and talk to Tom and hold his hand and explain the Moscow thing and find out what is on his mind for the next move. Do you have any objection?

Byrnes: No, I told him I had talked to Tom. I told Breck that I knew him so damn well and that God alone might be able to get Tom to change a sentence in the Connally resolution. He would change the whole resolution of Stettinius, Byrnes, and Long, or anyone else, but I knew of no power on earth that would get him to change that resolution. If Breck can by any means get him to do it, it would be all right.

Stettinius: I will tell Breck he can go up this morning and have a talk with Tom and see where he gets.

Byrnes: Fine. They say the day of miracles is past, but maybe not. . . .

[Byrnes was too pessimistic. Administration officials quietly lobbied for the amendment, and Connally, probably realizing that further opposition would gain nothing, agreed to the proposed changes. The resolution, including phrases from the Moscow Declaration, passed the Senate on November 5 by an overwhelming 85 to 5 vote. It was an ambiguous document, and the nature of the American commitment was unclear, but contemporaries attached great significance to the vote. "The Senate yesterday undid a twenty-four-year-old mistake," the *New York Times* affirmed. After a cabinet meeting on November 5, Roosevelt told Stettinius that he was "pleased" with the resolution and he "thought everything was going smoothly." [12]

On November 10, a triumphant Cordell Hull arrived back in Washington with the Moscow Declaration. The following day, Roosevelt, Stettinius, and the secretary met at the White House to discuss the results of the foreign ministers' conference.]

CALENDAR NOTES | *November 11, 1943*

I went to the White House today at noon. I met Mr. Hull in General Watson's [13] office where he was . . . going over the Moscow papers. Mr. Hull and I had a personal talk while the president finished having a private visit with the vice-president, Barkley, McCormack, and Rayburn. [14] I told Mr. Hull everyone realized the conference would not have succeeded if it had not been for him. He said he did not feel a great spirit of elation; it had taken him ten days to work through the Chinese matter. [15]

We joined the president at 12:15 and were with him until 1:10. Mr. Hull, Mr. Hopkins, and I were present. Mr. Hull reviewed in great detail all the intimate dealings and background relative to the meeting—his various private talks with Stalin, and Molotov, in which he emphasized to Stalin mutual frankness and trust. He and Molotov had talked on a very friendly, cooperative basis, and Molotov was willing to discuss anything that was brought up by the Americans. This was not true of other items.

We discussed the makeup of the European Advisory Commission [16] at length with the president quizzing the secretary thoroughly. The secretary was definite in his view that the commission would be only advisory and would have to refer to their governments questions before taking action.

* * *

The question was raised as to whether or not those three [the foreign ministers] had referred matters for discussion to the other three [the Big Three] and he said apparently there were no specific questions. The president said he is very anxious to see one man [apparently Stalin] alone. While we were there a very vital and important message from Russia was handed to the president which he read aloud.[17]

[One of Stettinius's primary charges as undersecretary was to make the State Department more efficient and better capable of dealing with America's expanding diplomatic problems. In one of their first meetings, Hull had given Stettinius a free hand in reorganization and in hiring new personnel, provided he avoided "extremists" and did not "bring in any leftists." [18] Stettinius made some preliminary studies of reorganization and in late November he again discussed his ideas with the secretary.]

CALENDAR NOTES | *November 27, 1943*
We discussed the organization charts for about a half an hour. The secretary was amazed to see how loose things were in the State Department from the standpoint of organization lines and when I showed him the new recommendation, he was most enthusiastic and thought that something should be done very promptly to increase efficiency within the department and to bring the department into a satisfactory light. There has been a great deal of unjust criticism of the department in the past and this could be, to a large extent, eliminated by the proper organization. We also mentioned the efficiency of the department and he wants me to move and do anything that is necessary in the direction of modernizing systems, methods and procedures within the department.

[The reorganization, completed in December and announced in January, attempted to eliminate overlapping jurisdiction, to set clear lines of authority, and to allow more attention to policy making. It created twelve line offices to handle day-to-day administrative matters in order to free top officials for policy and two major committees to work on current and postwar problems. In addition, it established an Office of Public Information to analyze public attitudes toward foreign policy and to influence opinion on important issues.

Stettinius's revamping of the department improved both its efficiency and its public image, but it did not resolve all of the problems. As contemporary critics pointed out, organizational changes meant little when the top echelon personnel remained the same. And it would take more than structural changes to recoup the loss of influence the department had suffered since the first years of Franklin Roosevelt. Throughout the remainder of his career in the State Department, Stettinius sought to attract new personnel into the department and to restore its prestige and influence, but with only limited results.[19]

As wartime expenditures mounted to unprecedented heights, conservative Democrats and Republicans in Congress, many of them long-time critics of the administration's spending policies, began to challenge the president openly. In October 1943, five senators, headed by the powerful Georgian Richard Russell, returned from a world tour and charged Roosevelt with squandering American resources across the globe. Shortly afterward, the Senate Appropriations Committtee served notice that it was through voting "blank check and lump sum" appropriations and warned that henceforth it was going to be a "tough job" to get money out of Congress. Thus when the administration in November submitted a proposal for American participation in the United Nations Relief and Rehabilitation Administration, an international agency to distribute relief funds in liberated areas, it encountered strong opposition. Stettinius discussed the handling of the UNRRA legislation with Republican Representative Charles Eaton of New Jersey on December 13.]

CALENDAR NOTES | *December 13, 1943*

Congressman Eaton came in to discuss with me privately the matter of the appropriation for UNRRA. He says that there is a tremendous amount of suspicion on the part of the Republicans. The Republican members of the Foreign Affairs Committee are meeting privately as a body this afternoon. He wondered if we would be willing to have the amount appropriated to the State Department because they questioned appropriating it to FEA and they also would prefer not to appropriate the money directly to the president if there is any other way to do it. I advised him personally that it was my opinion that it would be best to appropriate the funds to the president just as Lend-Lease funds had been appropriated and that the president would then in turn select the agency best qualified to administer the funds. In this case, it would be our opinion that FEA was the only agency existing at the present time that was set up in such a manner that they could with efficiency handle the funds and act as the American supply agency for UNRRA.

[The president's opponents nearly succeeded in getting UNRRA funds appropriated to the State Department rather than the White House. An amendment to that effect passed the House on January 24, but was reconsidered the following day and defeated by a 217–175 vote. The joint resolution authorizing participation in UNRRA passed both houses in February 1944.

In the meantime, President Roosevelt had returned

from an extended visit in the Middle East where he had met personally with Generalissimo Chiang Kai-shek at Cairo and with Churchill and Stalin at Teheran. No formal agreements resulted from the conferences, but the Teheran meeting seemed to draw the major Allies closer together. Churchill and Roosevelt pledged to open a second front in France in 1944 and Stalin agreed to enter the war against Japan once the war in Europe ended. The three vowed to work together to keep peace, and the president's private discussions with Stalin convinced him, as he told the American people in a Christmas Eve radio broadcast, that "we are going to get along very well with him [Stalin] and the Russian people—very well indeed." [20]

Roosevelt returned to Washington after Christmas, and in a conversation with Stettinius and President Alfonso López of Colombia on January 17, he reviewed some of the developments at Teheran and ranged over a variety of other matters.]

CALENDAR NOTES | *January 17, 1944*
I went to the White House and was presented to the president of Colombia and Ambassador [Don Gabriel] Turbray. We had a pleasant visit and in about five minutes were shown up to the president's upstairs study. We greeted the president at his desk.

The president of Colombia presented his credentials and President Roosevelt gave him the letter of response. I then reminded the president that the United Nations Agreement [21] had to be signed. I presented this agreement for signature. The president told the interesting story of how he and the prime minister had arrived at the words "United Nations" early one morning in the prime minister's bedroom in the

White House. He also stated that the second signing of this agreement, it was Sunday and they could not get the documents so they had to use White House letterhead. The president thought it would be interesting to have a picture taken of the documents.

The president said Chiang Kai-shek doesn't want Indochina back. The president has discussed a trusteeship.

The president told us one incident in connection with the meeting at Teheran. Stalin offered a toast to the shooting of 50,000 Prussian army officers and said unless this many were shot, we would have another war in a year. The prime minister said the Empire would never agree to this. The president offered a toast and said that he agreed with the prime minister that it would be all wrong to shoot 50,000 Prussian army officers—the number should be 49,000. The president gave a detailed description of both Churchill and Stalin which was most interesting.

The President of Colombia expressed a definite feeling that we would have peace in the Pacific at the time of peace with Germany. President Roosevelt was not sure that this could be done, but thought that wholesale bombings might bring about complete panic on the part of the Japanese. The general feeling was that the war would not go on in the Pacific as long as people were talking about.

The president described the last dinner in Teheran at which there were nine present—the Big Three, [Anthony] Eden [British secretary of state for foreign affairs], Hopkins, [V.M.] Molotov [Soviet commissar for foreign affairs] and three interpreters. He did not mention [W. Averell] Harriman [U.S. ambassador to Russia.] The only matter with which they had difficulty was the disposition of the Baltic states.

*　　*　　*

[After the Colombian president had departed, Roosevelt conferred privately with Stettinius.]

The president spoke about Henry Morgenthau [secretary of treasury] being terribly upset. The president said he used to get upset when he first came to Washington, but he had learned not to get upset.

* * *

The president said that the plan of organization of the State Department was very good and that he was very much impressed but there was still much to do.

He then talked about the foreign service officers that should be retired.

The president thought it was very essential that I go to England just as soon as possible for a month for many reasons. This is something I will have to speak to the secretary about. The president wanted me to become familiar with the personalities of the Foreign Office and another important matter would be to clear up the terms of surrender.

* * *

The president thought the Lend-Lease book was good. He said the publicity was wonderful—that we were getting more publicity for a dull subject than anybody ever got for a dime novel.[22]

[The European neutrals posed one of the greatest problems for American wartime diplomacy, and of these nations none was more important or more difficult than Spain. Strategically situated at the gateway to the Mediterranean, Spain was also a major producer of wolfram (tungsten), a material essential in the making of high-grade steel for armaments. Its leader, Francisco Franco, had old and close ties with the Axis nations, and although he adopted an official position of neutrality when the war broke out he leaned distinctly toward Germany and Italy. From 1941 to 1943, the major goal of the United States was to keep Spain neutral and to limit its role as a supplier of Germany, and it adopted a conciliatory policy, providing the Spanish with substantial quantities of petroleum and purchasing great volumes of wolfram.

When the fortunes of war turned toward the Allies in 1943, Spain made overtures for closer relations with the United States, but it found American officials increasingly unsympathetic. American liberals, who had long despised Franco, expressed great annoyance that the U.S. was providing him with supplies. The Russians, furious that Spanish volunteers were still fighting with Germany on the eastern front, demanded that the United States take a hard line with Franco. The U.S. military deeply resented Spain's continued heavy trade with Germany, especially in wolfram, and pressed for economic sanctions. Relations between the U.S. and Spain worsened when the Spanish government sent a letter of congratulations to Jóse P. Laurel, a Filipino installed by the Japanese as puppet governor of the Philippines. As the Army and State Department discussed the possibility of putting an embargo on oil shipments to Spain, U.S. officials treated Spanish diplomats with a studied coolness.]

CALENDAR NOTES | *January 20, 1944*
The Spanish ambassador [Juan Cardenas] called upon me at his request, and (a) called to my attention Page 7 of the attached copy of the Information Bulletin published by the Soviet Embassy. He said that he thought this was unfair propaganda. He wanted this article called to the attention of the department. I received the document courteously and made

no comment; (b) he left with me the attached clipping from the *New York Times* of January 16 which was a despatch from London. He said this carried a complete misstatement of fact.[23] He had received a cable stating the exact facts and the corrections in ink on the attached are the true facts. He inquired as to whether or not it would be possible for this government to call this inaccuracy to the attention of the *New York Times*. I assured the ambassador that we would carefully study the matter. The ambassador then asked me whether any discussion relative to Spain had taken place in the Cairo and Teheran conferences. I stated those conferences were of a military nature and I was not informed as to whether or not any questions relative to Spain had been discussed; (c) the ambassador stated that he had had an appointment with the president that had been cancelled. He had a very handsome set of books that he has had for quite some time and he would like to present them to the president and he was hopeful that an appointment could be arranged for him . . . at an early date. I told him the president was recovering from quite a severe attack of the flu and I did not believe that an appointment could be arranged at any time in the near future. He seemed perfectly satisfied and understood why it was not possible for him to see the president promptly. He further stated that Franco had sent the president a New Year's greeting to which no reply has been received.

[Within the Western Hemisphere, Argentina, which Hull would later describe as the "Bad Neighbor," caused the most serious problems. Despite repeated U.S. protests, the Argentine government had refused to break relations with the Axis and had allowed German agents to operate within its borders. The State Department was certain, moreover, that Argentina was undermining U.S. influence in neighboring countries, and when the Bolivian government was overthrown in December 1943, presumably by rebels who had contact with Argentine and German agents, it determined to take strong action. State Department officials decided that the new Bolivian government should not be recognized; a statement would be released denouncing Argentina's complicity in the coup; Argentine funds in the United States would be frozen; Ambassador Norman Armour would be recalled for "consultation." Just as the department was making final preparations to take these steps, however, word arrived from Armour that Argentina was on the verge of breaking relations with the Axis. A meeting was called immediately to decide what to do in the light of these most recent developments.]

CALENDAR NOTES | *January 24, 1944*
It was the consensus of those present that, at least pending the break in relations, the proposed action vis-à-vis Argentina, which was to have been taken at 12:30, should be postponed.

* * *

The delay in these steps was in accordance with Ambassador Armour's recommendation and was also consistent with the indication of the Argentine Foreign Minister to the effect that we should avoid any action which would appear to involve pressure on the Argentine government in order that the latter might be able to carry out its intention to break with Germany and Japan.

* * *

It was also decided that the only action to be taken immediately was the issuance of a statement to the effect that for the present the Bolivian revolutionary junto would not be recognized and that Ambassador [Pierre] Boal was being recalled to Washington.

[Immediately after the meeting, Stettinius called Secretary Hull, who reluctantly agreed to delay action pending the approval of the president. The undersecretary then contacted Roosevelt at Hyde Park.]

TRANSCRIPT OF TELEPHONE
CONVERSATION | *January 24, 1944*
President: What's this all about?
Stettinius: I am sorry to bother you.
President: You caught me right in the midst of my bath.
Stettinius: Are you having good weather?
President: It is perfectly beautiful up here—about 35 degrees—bright sunshine.
Stettinius: We have had a 'phone call from Armour. He has been authorized to say that the country would break relations with Germany before Saturday noon. They will take that action provided nothing is done to indicate they are acting under pressure. That raises the whole question about how to proceed.
President: We sent the thing yesterday.
Stettinius: We can hold the freezing and the release for the time being. In the next ten minutes we can reverse ourselves completely. Armour says his judgment is to postpone the Argentine freeze and go ahead and act on Bolivia. I have talked to Hull and Henry [Morgenthau]. Hull wanted me to talk to you due to his sore throat. We have our gang assembled and we wanted to give you a flash and get your hunch.
President: You saw the dispatch from Churchill?
Stettinius: I know about it.
President: In which he pleads to do nothing to cut off their food supply.[24] I think he is right. I would feel the same way if I

were a Britisher. They don't get any food from Bolivia—it comes from Argentina. It would save the British position. They won't go along with us.

Stettinius: No—not diplomatically or economically.

President: I believe it is a pretty good solution.

Stettinius: How about Bolivia?

President: We would still want to shoot on Bolivia and send the statement we discussed.

Stettinius: And recall the minister to Bolivia—we have to go on with them.

President: I think that is pretty good—it is the right thing.

Stettinius: Just to hold off the freeze.

President: Let Armour stay and take forty-eight hours to await developments.

Stettinius: And then take the action later on. They have stated they are carefully studying the Japanese problem and will break with them if they can find evidence of espionage.

President: They are a damned bunch of crooks anyway.

Stettinius: Then you would not act?

President: No. You might reply to the ambassador from me and send it up here and I will see if it is all right.

[While official Washington troubled over relations with Argentina, representatives of other governments sought assurance about U.S. policy on postwar issues.]

CALENDAR NOTES | *January 24, 1944*
The minister of Lithuania called at his request this afternoon and stated that he wished to have a general discussion relative to Lithuanian problems.

He stated that his people were anxiously following the Polish matter. They feel it is a test case; and it is their opinion that whatever treatment the Russians finally give Poland will also apply to their country. He further stated that he felt it was vitally important that his people be given some assurance, or at least a hint, that they would be treated fairly by the Russians as it is possible that otherwise when the Russian army marches through Lithuania, the people in desperation might resist and cause great suffering and bloodshed. I asked if he had ever taken this specific matter up with the department. He replied that he had not but was planning to do so in the form of a note. I made no comment whatsoever but listened patiently. At the end of the conversation the minister referred to the Moscow declaration on Austria [25] and said he hoped some such declaration as that could be made relative to Lithuania.

[The Polish problem was much more than a test case for the Lithuanians: by 1943 it had become one of the most difficult and potentially divisive political issues confronting the Grand Alliance. The USSR had made clear its intention to hold territory seized from Poland in 1939, and in April 1943 it had broken relations with the Polish government-in-exile in London. The London Poles, on the other hand, insisted on the return of all land taken from Poland in the Nazi-Soviet partition, and claimed to be the only legitimate government of Poland.

Both Roosevelt and Churchill perceived that the clash over Poland could jeopardize Allied collaboration during and after the war and attempted to work out an amicable settlement. Aware that the Red Army might soon be in a position to dictate the terms in Poland, they encouraged the London government to compromise with Russia on the territorial dispute and to restore diplomatic relations. Without relenting from their demands, the London Poles agreed to discuss the issues with the Russians, but only if the United States and Britain would act as intermediaries. Roosevelt in particular was reluctant to go this far for fear of antagonizing Stalin. Thus in early 1944, the Polish ambassador in the United States, Jan Ciechanowski, pressed for an appointment with the president to try to pin down his views and Roosevelt carefully evaded him.]

CALENDAR NOTES | *February 18, 1944*

I then discussed with him [the president] the matter of his seeing the Polish ambassador. He was definitely opposed and couldn't be moved. I then said it would be essential that I see the ambassador and be authorized to make some statement to him. He . . . said that was satisfactory. He then went on and commented that he felt I should make it clear to the Polish ambassador that it was a bad start in the days ahead for any country to make too much of an issue about a border question and also that perhaps the Poles had not fully realized the suspicion with which the Russians had looked upon the refugee questions. He thought perhaps the wise course was the course that had been followed by the king of Norway—as soon as the country was liberated the country would be turned over to the people to have a new election. The president did not instruct me to say this to the ambassador, but he thought it would be a good thing to get this across—that in his views it would be smart for the present Polish government to make plain to the world that they would have an election and the present refugee government would retire as soon as hostilities came to an end.

[The same day, Stettinius talked with Ciechanowski, but his deliberately vague statement, instead of encouraging the Poles to compromise, may have convinced them that the United States would provide friendly support for their position.]

The Polish ambassador called upon me . . . at my request. . . . I had previously obtained permission from the president to state the following to the ambassador in his behalf:

> *That you regret very much that you are unable to see him at this particular moment before he leaves for London, and assure him that our interest in an amicable and satisfactory solution of the present difficulties is deep and abiding, and that this government is doing, and will continue to do, everything it properly can within the framework of our interest in the larger issues involved.*

The ambassador was most appreciative. He was deeply touched and seemed to feel that this message was almost as satisfactory as if he had seen the president personally. I then arranged for transportation facilities for the ambassador to fly by U.S. Army plane to London next Wednesday.

[Failing to get the Spanish to stop exports of wolfram to Germany, the United States in late January had suspended further shipments of oil to Spain. Dependent upon American oil yet still anxious not to effect a complete break with Germany, the Franco government desperately sought a way out of its dilemma.]

CALENDAR NOTES | *February 22, 1944*
Señor Don Juan Francisco de Cardenas met me at my apartment this afternoon at his request. . . .

The ambassador had with him a long cable and a page of handwritten notes. He said he wished to approach the Spanish difficulty with me and thought that he and I, as two men of good will, might be able to find a solution. He was very emotional. He stated that he was a friend of the United States, that his personal prestige was jeopardized, that Spain was trying to be neutral, and that he thought the United States was taking a very unjust point of view.

After he had finished, I repeated that our position was the same as had been made clear to him on a number of previous occasions—that nothing short of complete stoppage of all exports of wolfram to Germany was acceptable. The ambassador then stated he was sure his government wanted to settle the matter and he was willing to go to the extreme, and asked only that we give him some way to save face, such as starting oil shipments in March and relying on their honor to reduce shipments of wolfram to Germany.

I told the ambassador that I had discussed the entire matter with the president this morning and he was definite in our position on wolfram. The ambassador then asked if I would review the entire matter and see if a new solution could be found. I told him I would continue to study the matter.

[The United States subsequently agreed to a compromise proposed by the British in which Spain, without making a formal commitment, would cease wolfram shipments for six months. Negotiations with the Spanish government on this proposal got nowhere, however.

In the meantime, the Argentine situation, apparently on the verge of settlement just weeks before, once again required urgent attention. On February 15, a group of army officers, "reputed" according to Secretary Hull, to be "more pro-Axis and anti-American" than the existing government,[26] overthrew that government and installed General Edelmiro Farrell as chief of state.

The State Department quickly determined to take a firm response. Latin American experts within the department recommended that after consulting with other South American governments, the United States should announce publicly that its ambassador had been instructed not to have official contacts with the new Argentine government. They also urged consideration of other possible moves, including the freezing of Argentine assets and a show of naval force in neighboring areas. On February 29, Stettinius discussed these proposals with Secretary Hull, who was vacationing in Florida.]

CALENDAR NOTES | *February 29, 1944*

At one o'clock I called the secretary and reviewed with him the latest Argentine developments. While the secretary made it clear that we should proceed here as we saw fit and that he would back us up in anything we did, his feeling was that we should obtain the reaction of other American republics to the statement about Ambassador Armour not having official dealings with the new regime before making an announcement. He had in mind such countries as Mexico, Chile, Colombia, and Venezuela.

He also felt that as only a few days had elapsed since the events took place we could afford to spend more time to get to the bottom of the entire situation and obtain the support of the other American republics.

He had no definite feeling one way or the other as to the visit to the waters adjacent to the Argentine of an American cruiser but he felt that the country of the port of call should be first consulted.

He thinks the freezing of funds could take place any time and that we should proceed with preliminary arrangements, but he thinks the best procedure would be to take all action simultaneously.

[After consulting with the president and getting a favorable response from a number of Latin American governments, Stettinius on March 4 instituted the proposed policy. He issued a public statement that the United States would not have official relations with the new Argentine regime. A cruiser was dispatched to Montevideo, which, according to the president's instructions, was to drop in for a few days to refuel. There then began a period of waiting to determine whether the Argentine government would continue the gradual drift away from the Axis initiated by its predecessor.

In the meantime, Stettinius began preparations for his first major diplomatic assignment. On the suggestion of the president, he had agreed some weeks before to visit England in the spring of 1944 for a series of informal discussions with top British officials. Secretary Hull had endorsed the mission, but as the day of departure approached he became increasingly fearful of its domestic political implications. Since the Moscow Conference, journalists and congressmen had pressed the administration to outline its policies on major postwar issues. Roosevelt's and Hull's refusal to respond led some to speculate that secret deals had been concluded at Moscow and Teheran; others, including Arthur Krock of the *New York Times*, feared that the administration's lack of a concrete policy would permit the USSR to dominate postwar Europe. In March, a group of Republican congressmen publicly demanded a clear statement of the principles of U.S. foreign policy. Hull feared that Stettinius's visit to London might provoke further reaction in Congress and the country.²⁷]

CALENDAR NOTES | *March 16, 1944*
I had a long talk with the secretary. He was concerned about a growing groundswell—Arthur Krock's articles, communications from twenty-five Republican congressmen, etc., asking "Where is our foreign policy?" The secretary must call on the Foreign Relations Committee in connection with this matter. The first question they are going to ask him is what is Stettinius and his mission going to do in England. The secre-

tary said he is happy that we are going and it is for a great many reasons and particularly because of the misunderstandings that have arisen. The secretary feels that he must make a clean breast of things before the Senate committee. He wants a few sentences on each subject that we will discuss at London so that he will be in a position of indicating that he does know the kind of questions we are going to bring up.

[That same day, Senator Joseph O'Mahoney [D.-Wyoming] called Stettinius to express further concern about the ambiguity and drift in American foreign policy. O'Mahoney had just read a story in the *Baltimore Sun* that the United States was going to release Great Britain from its earlier pledges not to re-export Lend-Lease supplies in competition with American manufacturers, and he feared that concessions of this sort would undermine America's attempt to end political and economic imperialism.]

TRANSCRIPT OF TELEPHONE
CONVERSATION | *March 16, 1944*
Stettinius: I am keeping my promise to call you back to prove I am an honest man.
O'Mahoney: The A. P. sprang the story today and that was one of the things disturbing me.
Stettinius: What was that?
O'Mahoney: Paul Ward's story in the *Baltimore Sun* on the front page? About Lend-Lease. The proposal now is that Britain be granted an opportunity to export Lend-Lease materials. This is going to create a lot of hullaballo.
Stettinius: It is wrong, Joe.
O'Mahoney: You had better read that.
Stettinius: There is nothing to it—the White Paper Eden agreed to is still in effect.[28]

O'Mahoney: I am glad to hear that. The press is carrying it today. It might be well for you to have somebody take cognizance of that.

Stettinius: I will look at it right away. I am leaving Washington tomorrow—but not leaving for London right away.

O'Mahoney: I had a talk with the chief down there and let me say this to you: I am a firm believer in the fundamentals of the Atlantic Charter [29] and I have every reason to believe that a great deal of progress has been made with respect to fixing that in the minds of a lot of our people who are working with us in this terrible situation, but there is also the great danger that the people with whom you are about to talk may not wish to proceed. Of course the representatives of that country have been traveling around the United States talking about the necessity of maintaining the cartel system. I don't have to tell you of my own basic belief that the cause for all this has been the failure to protect the economic independence. Unless we do that we are laying the basis for a new war. I believe in individual liberty against imperialism. I know the troubles that shape up in Asia are due to opposition in China and Moscow. An imperialistic policy is to continue after this is all over. No salvage for the world and no permanent peace unless we have economic independence—that means no cartels.

Stettinius: You have worded it very well and I am delighted to have it before I go.

O'Mahoney: Thank you for ringing me. If this isn't done, this whole bloody thing will have to be done over.

Stettinius: I will see you after I return. I am not going to agree to anything—you know what I mean.

O'Mahoney: Say hello to all of my ancestors over there.

[O'Mahoney's fears of British imperialism were shared by many Americans, including the president and the secretary of state. The whole question of imperialism was indeed one of the most troublesome issues in Anglo-American relations, and was given special attention by Stettinius and his advisers as they completed final preparations for their discussions with top British officials.]

II

MISSION TO LONDON
March–April 1944

The Roosevelt administration publicly minimized the importance of Stettinius's mission to London. The undersecretary, Hull explained in a press release of March 17, was simply "repaying" earlier visits by top British diplomats to the United States.[1] In fact, the White House and State Department designed the mission with much more tangible objectives in mind. Despite close collaboration on military and economic matters and the unique camaraderie established by Roosevelt and Churchill, the United States and Britain had differed sharply on many issues from the beginning of the war. As they completed final preparations for the cross-channel invasion these differences were accentuated on each side by growing uncertainties about the other's postwar intentions.

Some of the problems in Anglo-American relations arose from differences over the conduct of the war. The United States wished to tighten the pressure on neutral nations such as Spain and Portugal, which still carried on an extensive trade with Germany, and on pro-Axis governments such as the Farrell regime in Argentina. The British, who had important interests in these nations, tended to be more cautious and conciliatory. The Churchill government, on the other hand, wished to work closely with the French National Committee of Charles de Gaulle during the invasion and liberation of France, while President Roosevelt, who despised de Gaulle personally and doubted that the committee was representative of French opinion, wished to keep the general and his group at arms length and to leave open for a future election the question of a government for liberated France.

More significant differences concerned the political and economic principles that would govern the postwar world. Secretary Hull and the State Department were determined to combat economic nationalism and preferential trading agreements, and since 1941 they had pressed the British to commit themselves to liquidate the Imperial Preference system at war's end. The Churchill government had stubbornly refused without reciprocal commitments of postwar economic aid and lowered tariffs which the United States would not give. The United States also sought self-determination and equal commercial opportunity in colonial areas, and throughout 1943 American officials grew increasingly fearful that Britain was using the exigencies of war—even American Lend-Lease supplies—to extend its political and economic influence in the Middle East at the expense of U.S. ideals and interests.

Leaders in both nations agreed that Anglo-American cooperation was an essential cornerstone for a stable postwar world, but by early 1944 there was growing concern on both sides that differences on political and economic questions might jeopardize this goal. At the same time, the approaching invasion of Europe made it increasingly urgent to harmonize positions on surrender terms for Germany and the methods by which governments would be established in nations liberated from the Axis. The State Department had culminated years of work in December 1943, by drafting a plan for postwar international organization and was especially eager to find out where the British stood before the opening of formal international discussions.

Thus it was decided, apparently upon the suggestion of President Roosevelt, that Stettinius should go to London in the spring of 1944 to conduct informal exploratory talks with the prime minister and the Foreign Office. As the undersecretary himself explained it, "We would discuss . . . a very wide range of subjects of current mutual interest to our two governments and inform ourselves as completely as possible about the British trend of thinking on these subjects. We would exchange views fully and frankly, but would make no commitments or agreements." [2]

By mid-March Stettinius had completed preparations for the trip. He chose four State Department officials to accompany him: Dr. Isaiah Bowman, a geographer of some distinction, president of Johns Hopkins University, and a member of Wilson's Inquiry of 1918–1919, was selected to consult with the Foreign Office on international organization; John L. Pratt, a former General Motors executive and an old friend of the Stettinius family, was to handle Anglo-American economic problems; Wallace Murray, director of the State Department's Office of Near Eastern and African Affairs, would deal with Middle East issues; and H. Freeman Matthews, deputy director of the Office of European Affairs, would concentrate on European matters, particularly surrender terms. During late February and early March, the members of the mission held frequent meetings, prepared an agenda and position papers, and consulted with Secretary Hull. They decided to leave the United States on March 30, and to travel by ship to allow some time for rest and reflection before their meetings began.

[On March 17, St. Patrick's Day, Stettinius's group met with the secretary of state and the president for the last time before departing for London. Both men stressed the importance of confronting the British on imperialism. Hull complained that the British and French were "taking great amounts of wealth" out of the Middle East and leaving "very little for the people themselves." The policy of the United States, he concluded, should be to "work for a more equitable economic system." [3]

The mission then crossed the street to the White House. Roosevelt and Stettinius joshed about the president's green-tweed suit and green tie.]

DIARY | *March 17, 1944*

* * *

After a few minutes of such joking, I opened the discussion by saying that we are going to London to listen to the British express their views . . . and in turn to set forth the American views in a very informal, exploratory manner. I stressed that we would make no commitments or agreements.

"Well," the president said, "You know, of course, that the senators and congressmen, the newspapers and everyone else will immediately accuse me and the secretary and all of you going to London of making all sorts of secret deals with the British. They are sure to say that it is all underhanded and illegal and even unconstitutional. But we always have to put up with that."

* * *

Dr. Bowman asked the president his wishes about our discussing the whole world issue of colonial trusteeship.

"That is something I have discussed many times" the president said, "and I have not been able to get very far with it. It is a subject in which I have been interested for some while. Back in 1936, for instance, the secretary and I proposed it for a little island in the Pacific—Canton Island. Pan American Airways needed it for an air base in the hop to New Zealand and Australia. We sent a little group down there to establish a base, and the British sent a cruiser down and asked

our people to get off because the island was a British possession. The head of our group asked how they figured that out.
The British officer produced a map. 'Well'? our man said. 'It is
shown in red on the map', the British answered. Apparently
anything shown as red anywhere on a map belongs to the British."

Later, the president said, the British ambassador to the
United States, Sir Ronald Lindsey, had raised the question
with him. The president quoted Sir Ronald, imitating his English accent: "Well, now, Mr. President, this is a British island. You simply can't do this." The president replied with a
broad English accent, "But, Roney, I've done it."

The president said that he and Secretary Hull cooked up
an exchange of letters by which the issue of sovereignty over
Canton was to be postponed for a period of fifty years—until
1987. . . . The system so far has worked beautifully, and
there has been no further disagreement.

The president indicated that he believed there is no reason why the same system could not work successfully for
much larger areas in other parts of the world.

Dr. Bowman said at this point, "Well, Mr. President,
you stated that you had not gotten very far with the British on
this issue. Do you want us to bring it up again?"

"Yes, by all means," the president said, "It is something I
think we should discuss with them at every opportunity."

The president pointed out that he had discussed the question of a trusteeship for French Indochina with Generalissimo
Chiang Kai-shek at Cairo. The French have badly mis-
managed the country and the people, the president said, and
the country is worse off than it was a hundred years ago. The
white man's rule there is nothing to be proud of. The president said that the French have always been poor colonizers
and a trusteeship is the only practical solution. When the president asked Generalissimo Chiang Kai-shek what he thought,

the generalissimo replied that China had no designs on Indochina, and that the Chinese did not want that country united with theirs because its people and the country as a whole were completely different from their own. He thought a trusteeship would be an ideal arrangement.

When the president told Churchill that China does not want Indochina, Churchill replied, "Nonsense!" The president had said to him, "Winston, this is something which you are just not able to understand. You have 400 years of acquisitive instinct in your blood and you just don't understand how a country might not want to acquire land somewhere if they can get it. A new period has opened in the world's history, and you will have to adjust to it." The president then said that the British would take land anywhere in the world even if it were only a rock or sand bar.

* * *

"But we are still going to have a tough time with the British on this issue," the president said. He pointed out that the British suspect that if they give in on any one colony or another country, we will ask them to do the same with other places which are possessions of the British—for example, Burma and the Malay Peninsula.

* * *

The meeting concluded at approximately 1:30 with the president wishing us a good trip and remarking that he wished he could go along with us.

[On March 30, Stettinius and his advisers boarded the *Queen Elizabeth* in New York. The former luxury liner, converted into a troop ship upon the outbreak of war, was making a regular run between New York and Glasgow, carrying 13,000 soldiers in addition to a handful of civilian passengers and a crew of 1,000. The vessel departed New York harbor on the afternoon of March 31, and after an uneventful seven-day voyage, anchored in the river Clyde on April 6. The next morning the Stettinius mission boarded a Flamingo transport at Prestwick Air Base and flew to London where they were greeted by officials of the British Foreign Office and the U.S. Embassy. From there they were taken to Claridges Hotel, their base in London, and spent the remainder of the day in informal conversations with Ambassador John G. Winant and Admiral Harold Stark, commander of U.S. naval forces in Europe. The following evening, Stettinius began a heavy schedule of conferences.

His first meeting was not with the British but with King George II of Greece. Like the leaders of many of the "exile" governments, the king had fled his country when the Axis moved in and now as the day of liberation approached he looked toward the future with growing anxiety. In Greece, as in other satellite nations, internal resistance groups had been formed to fight the Germans and these same groups had developed political programs and organizations to block the restoration of the prewar status quo. Many of the resistance parties contained strong communist elements, and the exile leaders feared that the Soviet Union might give them diplomatic and military backing. Thus in 1943 and 1944, these men desperately sought British and American support against those who would prevent their return to power.

The position of King George was especially tenuous. While he had been in exile in Cairo, the resistance parties, including the communists, had coalesced into the EAM (National Liberation Front) and had established the political machinery to make themselves a force in the government of liberated Greece. On March 3, the EAM had demanded a voice in the Cairo government, and the peremptory rejection of the demand provoked a crisis in the king's cabinet and a mutiny in the army in Egypt. The mutiny broke out less than a week before Stettinius arrived in London, and when the king encountered the American diplomat at Claridges, he had immediately asked for an appointment.]

DIARY | *April 8, 1944*

Mr. Pratt and I received King George of Greece in my sitting room at the hotel at 6:30. The king is very much concerned with communistic activity in Greece which he feels was organized by the Germans in Sofia to create disunion among the Balkan countries. He stated that it was later picked up by some British agents in Greece. These communistic activities have resulted in disloyalty among the Greek troops in Egypt which makes it necessary for him to return there.

King George stated that he hopes that when the pressure on Germany from the east and west becomes greater, the Germans will have to withdraw the eight or ten divisions which he estimates they now have in Greece. He stated that if they do withdraw it will be necessary to send in a small army of reoccupation to restore order so that an election can be held to decide who will rule Greece. He stated that the communists are trying to seize the government and put themselves in a position where they can say there is no need for an election.

The king stated that he had seen Mr. Churchill yesterday and that they had a very satisfactory talk. He feels that if the local British officials will only carry out the wishes of the prime minister, he will be able to straighten everything out when he gets to Cairo. . . .

[The following morning, Stettinius and Ambassador Winant drove to Churchill's country home, Chequers, for a series of conversations. After a warm greeting by the prime minister and his wife, they were joined at lunch by Stanislaw Mikolajczyk, head of the Polish government-in-exile. The conversation soon turned to American politics, a subject which obviously fascinated and concerned Churchill.]

DIARY | *April 9, 1944*

* * *

During lunch Mrs. Churchill asked me a great many questions—about Willkie,[4] about Harry Hopkins's health, about the president and his health and Secretary Hull. I was very much impressed with the way Mrs. Churchill asked me about all the matters which the prime minister obviously wanted to know about. He paid close attention to my answers, without talking very much. It was an example of teamwork between the two of them which was very impressive.

The prime minister said that he was thinking of asking Willkie over perhaps in June. He said he thought that this would possibly be of some assistance to the president. In discussing the coming campaign, Churchill said there was one man who was his choice but he could not say who that was. He was very much afraid of becoming involved in American political affairs. He thinks that the Polish prime minister should go over to the United States sometime this summer. He said that this might have a considerable influence on the Polish vote.

I discussed the recent attacks on Secretary Hull,[5] and the prime minister said that he hoped the secretary would make clear the meaning of the Atlantic Charter since this was of the utmost importance in the European situation.

The prime minister talked frankly to the Polish prime minister at great length. He said that Britain and the United

States would never stand for any infamous deal and that we would insist on a strong and vigorous Poland. He said that he had pressed the Russians on the necessity for reaching a fair solution, but that up to two weeks ago they seemed to be at a complete deadlock. He said that he had had many exchanges on this with the president.

* * *

There was much general talk during lunch. The prime minister mentioned the invasion and said that he had been against it twice before. Now, however, our troops are thoroughly equipped. I gathered that he was still not tremendously enthusiastic about it but that he was firmly committed to it and was going forward with all his energy. He stated that there would be dreadful losses. At one moment when talking of the state of world affairs he said, "The world is a wounded animal."

* * *

[Churchill had "an extraordinary number of brandies and ports" after lunch, Stettinius noted in his diary, and then retired for his customary afternoon nap. Following dinner that evening, the two men settled down for an extended private discussion. The prime minister immediately turned to the question of British dollar balances, one of the most troublesome issues in Anglo-American relations. The United States had initiated Lend-Lease in 1941 because the British had run out of dollars to purchase American supplies. Britain's cash reserves remained precariously low throughout the first half of 1942, but then began a steady rise because of the massive expenditures of U.S. military forces in the United Kingdom. By the beginning of 1943, they had risen to $1 billion and the United States was providing billions of dollars worth of supplies on Lend-Lease. The Roosevelt administration, fearing a reaction in Congress, began to take steps to reduce Britain's dollar balances, proposing that the British should purchase by cash many items formerly provided under Lend-Lease. The British naturally resisted, arguing that the rise in dollar balances was not indicative of their very unfavorable overall economic position. In their conversation at Chequers, Churchill attempted to explain to Stettinius why Britain could not afford to make the concessions insisted upon by the United States.]

The prime minister talked at great length about the British financial position. He said that you cannot understand the financial condition of Britain by just examining the dollar position. The whole world financial position . . . must be considered. He stated that they were building up a tremendous debit balance. It is true that the British have more dollars now than they had two years ago but their overall world position is much worse. The prime minister said it is as if a man two years ago had ten thousand dollars in the bank and five dollars in his pocket, whereas now he has one hundred dollars in his pocket but he owes the bank several thousand dollars. If you only look at the cash in his pocket he is rich compared to what he has.

The prime minister said over and over again that they are going to end this war the debtor of the world. He does not feel that the British should be dealt with more harshly than other nations which have large balances in the United States. As to the possibility of manipulating the British dollar balances in order to make them appear not so large, he felt that this would simply not be honest. It would be a subterfuge which would come back to embarrass both the British and the United States. It was simply no good.

[Later in the conversation, Churchill turned to the problem in Greece. He fully shared King George's appraisal of the difficulties, and indicated his own firm commitment to upholding Britain's longstanding interests in the Mediterranean.]

When we turned to the Greek situation, the prime minister said that 40,000 British soldiers were killed or tortured in the attempt to defend Greece. He spoke of the mutiny in the Greek forces and said that it looks like we may have to do some shooting to bring some order out of the chaos there. Three divisions of Greek troops which had been ready to sail to Italy recently to fight with our forces there had to be disarmed because of the communistic difficulties.[6]

* * *

[Their conversation continued through dinner until two o'clock in the morning. Stettinius remained awake in his room making notes for another hour. The next morning he and Churchill resumed their conversations.]

DIARY | *April 10, 1944*
The prime minister said that he thought our Mission to London would be of the utmost importance in preparing the president for the next meeting. He stated that the American representatives at the meetings were always very well prepared on military topics but that they were not equally well prepared on the political and diplomatic topics. He hoped that as a result of this visit, the American delegation would be more completely documented on the political side the next time.

[Stettinius returned to London after lunch and spent the rest of the day reviewing with his advisers the weekend discussions with Churchill. The following morning, he drove with H. Freeman Matthews to Binderton in Sussex, the country estate of British Foreign Secretary Anthony Eden. Much of the conversation that followed centered on the role of the European Advisory Commission and the schedule for talks on the international security organization. Anglo-American differences were particularly pronounced on the former. Since the creation of the European Advisory Commission at the Moscow Conference in October 1943, the British had sought to enlarge the area of its responsibility, making it into a political counterpart of the combined chiefs of staff that would formulate positions on all issues related to the peace settlements in Europe. The Roosevelt administration, on the other hand, still preferred to delay formal discussions of political problems, and feared that the assignment of broad powers to a body located in London might arouse the isolationists at home. As a consequence, it had insisted that the commission concern itself solely with issues related to the surrender and occupation of Germany. Eden raised the matter with Stettinius at the outset of their talks.]

DIARY | *April 10, 1944*

Mr. Eden then said that the question which was uppermost in his mind was that of the European Advisory Commission. He outlined at some length the British view concerning the scope of the commission's activities and he stated that his view was also shared by the Russians. He explained in detail the view that the scope of the EAC's activities should be considerably enlarged.

In reply I set out the American position at some length explaining that the surrender terms seemed to us to be fully occupying the commission, and that moreover our military feels very strongly that conferences concerning the purely operational period cannot be held up for discussion and approval by the European Advisory Commission.

It was left that I would explore this subject further with [Sir Alexander] Cadogan [British undersecretary of state for foreign affairs]. . . .

I then turned to the procedures for discussing the World Security Organization. Eden said that he was anxious to move as rapidly as possible and that he felt very encouraged by the Russian attitude. He said that he was perfectly prepared to hold the discussions on this subject as well as any other postwar subjects in Washington if we wished this, but that he thought it would be very helpful if we held some of the talks in Moscow. I said that I would try if possible to determine the date and place for the security talks while we were in Britain so that this could be announced as a result of our meetings.

Eden said that this was fine. He thought that late this summer, he, Hull and Molotov should get together. At that time, they might be able to announce the preliminary outline of the World Security Organization.

* * *

On the Argentine question, Eden was most cooperative. He stated that they would go along with us on any action we thought necessary provided the supply problems could be solved. He said that the British did not want to have to use economic sanctions but that they would do so rather than create a rift between Britain and the United States. . . . Eden's apparent desire to back up the United States was . . . most encouraging.

* * *

Eden appeared to be very tired and obviously in need of a rest which his doctors have ordered him to take. . . . My overall impression . . . was that he was an efficient, quick, frank, attractive fellow. I liked him much better than when I saw him in Washington last summer.

[The next day, Stettinius visited the headquarters of the Allied Expeditionary Force and talked with General Dwight D. Eisenhower and his chief of staff, General Walter Bedell Smith. The main topic of conversation was Germany. At Teheran and later in discussions in the European Advisory Commission, proposals had been submitted to divide Germany into separate British, American, and Russian zones of occupation. Eisenhower felt that it would be simpler and more practical to establish a single Anglo-American zone. He and Smith also proposed a modification of the unconditional surrender statement, agreed upon by Roosevelt and Churchill at the Casablanca Conference in January 1943, in order to encourage German resistance to Hitler.]

DIARY | *April 12, 1943*
Eisenhower has a fairly small and very neat office. There was a coal fire burning in the grate. There were pictures of the president, the prime minister, and General Marshall. The office gave the impression of being very efficient and not at all swanky. . . .

The most important subject which Eisenhower raised with me concerned the zones of occupation in Germany. He has a deep conviction that there . . . should be . . . a single Anglo-American zone. He feels that the armies of the two countries have now been united in a completely integrated fighting force and that it will be very difficult to separate them when Germany surrenders. He also feels that . . . it would be very difficult and tremendously wasteful to attempt to set up . . . independent supply systems to service the two separate zones of occupation. He said that we have combined boards and combined agencies dealing with all the problems of the invasion and it just does not make any sense to suddenly attempt to split all this the moment Germany surrenders. He asked me to do everything I could to impress this point on Mr. Hull and the president. . . .[7]

Eisenhower said that the prime minister is up and down in his feelings toward the invasion. This tends to confirm the impression I had at the weekend at Chequers. . . . They said also that our friends are always thinking of the Empire in everything they do.

* * *

Bedell Smith spoke to me at great length about the desirability of some document or memorandum which could be used for propaganda purposes defining unconditional surrender. He is thinking in terms of a statement to the German people over the heads of Hitler and the Nazi party saying that the Germans will receive humane treatment. Bedell said that the morale of the army and air force in Germany is very high. The morale of the civilians seems to be somewhat lower, but the Gestapo has complete control over them. . . .

[Later in the morning Stettinius met with Cadogan and British Minister of State Richard Law at the Foreign Office. Cadogan struck the undersecretary as "calm, intelligent [and] . . . very quick on the trigger." [8] They discussed the scope of EAC, finding no common ground. They quickly agreed, however, on the need to begin formal talks on international organization as soon as possible.]

* * *

. . . Law said that Congressman [J. William] Fulbright [D.-Arkansas] had spent the weekend with him recently and had said that Congress was now in a mood to authorize participation in an international organization. If the Republicans are victorious and secure a majority in Congress next winter, they may easily block the international program. Fulbright had therefore urged all possible haste.

I told Cadogan and Law that I had been urging all possible speed on our side. I said that the tentative schedule of holding conversations in May was even later than I should like to see them. I said that if we discussed international security in May and report back to our government in June, it cannot be put up to Congress until early fall and it would be impossible to get the thing through before the middle of the fall. I asked them if they had any suggestions as to how this matter could be speeded up.

Law stated that the British already knew exactly what they want in the way of an international security organization, and he asked us if we did not already have a pretty good idea of what our proposals would be. . . . It appeared to all of us that as a matter of fact we were . . . very close together. It was therefore agreed that Dr. Bowman and Richard Law should immediately exchange information on our international security planning to see how close our views are. If we are already very close together, we may very well speed the whole thing along and hold a conference in London now to plan for the overall security conversations in the near future. It might even be possible to bring the Russians into the meetings here and get them to agree to an early date for the talks. . . .

[On Thursday, April 13, Stettinius received representatives of the Greek and Yugoslav governments-in-exile, both of whom expressed grave concern about Soviet designs on the Balkans. The following day was spent going over papers for weekend conferences with Churchill and Eden, and on Saturday, April 15, the undersecretary returned to Chequers. After a lunch of roast beef and the customary port and brandy, the Americans drew the prime minister into a discourse on preserving peace in the postwar era. Churchill's ideas differed significantly not only with those being formulated by the State Department but also with those held by the British Foreign Office.]

DIARY | *April 15, 1944*

. . . The prime minister asked a few questions about our mission and this enabled us to talk about some of the items on our list concerning world organization. Dr. Bowman introduced the subject tentatively and mildly, since we had been forewarned by the Foreign Office and by Ambassador [William] Phillips, who had described Churchill's bridling and indeed his violent talk when Phillips tried to discuss India with him.[9] Churchill said that he could not discuss world organization at this period of the war when we had great operations in prospect and when infinite attention had to be given to military details. We had to see the war through first and take up world organization afterward. Moreover, we did not know just what "the war situation" would be at its close, and its relations to peace. He said that he might not be present at the peacemaking. He had no assurance of life and he could not tell when the war would end.

During this conversation Dr. Bowman met him on his own ground of interest and thus brought the conversation back to the theme of world organization through the use of the military at the close of the war and in dealing with Germany under the surrender terms. . . .

In describing the world organization that he had in view, the prime minister referred to "the tripod upon which peace depends." Taking the sheet of paper on which the seating list had been prepared by Mrs. Churchill, he drew a tripod with a head on which stood the three powers and China. He said that he did not refer to China and the three great powers as "The Four Great Powers." He could not bring himself to do that. What China is now and what she may become are two different things. She is not a great power now. He thinks the generalissimo is a strong man and "the generalissima," as he called Madame Chiang Kai-shek, is a charming woman. But China is not a great power. There is no unity, and there is much communism. For thirty-five years we have had in China unstable government and division. It is nonsense, he said, to talk about China as a great power. . . .

He referred to the Chinese as "the pigtails." This accords with the president's statement and his warning to Anthony Eden that he must get his skipper to change his thought about the Chinese. It led me to remind him that the president was anxious that China fifty years from now should be a world power and have a friendly attitude toward other powers. "But," he replied, "I have little confidence in the pigtails, first as to their power to unite and second as to their worth in the future. Japan was friendly at one time and then she armed and became an enemy." He emphasized the fact that in none of his speeches had he ever used the phrase "The Four Great Powers"—he couldn't bring himself to use it. "It is a misrepresentation of facts, and plain facts at that. The Chinese are disunited and weak and are actually not a great power. Likewise, France is needed for a peaceful and happy Europe, but France must be reconstituted and what will she be? Eventually she will be very critical of all English speaking peoples, sensitive and very difficult to deal with. In fact, she has already given us no end of trouble."

Underneath the head of his "tripod of world peace" is the Supreme Council, suspended from and acting under the authority of the three great military powers. This council is the main show. It possesses the force to act in the interest of security. From it everything depends and all orders issue. Then he drew three circles below the Supreme Council to indicate the regional councils and their subsidiary position and authority. The object of these councils is to have regional affairs settled regionally and thus avoid having every nation poking its finger into every other nations' business the world over.

When he started discussing world organization, Churchill said: "You young fellows will have to make it work. I may not be here. It will not work if there is no will to make it work. The machinery may be the combined chiefs of staff, but whatever the doubts about world organization and the regional councils, we must try to make them work. Tennyson's line is apposite. We must 'faintly cling to the larger hope.' " He went on to say that if he seemed to be "less warm than some enthusiasts," he would remind the enthusiasts that in England "for a while we held the baby," referring to the situation following Dunkirk. He also referred in the conversation to the fact that half of the personnel of the British merchant marine has been lost.

* * *

[Stettinius left Chequers at five o'clock and arrived at Eden's home for a late dinner. The two men stayed up until after midnight and had a most frank, satisfactory talk about administration of the Foreign Office. The next morning Stettinius and Winant resumed talks with Eden and Richard Law.]

DIARY | *April 16, 1944*

We had a detailed discussion on world organization. Winant described what the prime minister had said yesterday, and then Winant, Law, and Eden got down to details on the assembly and the council. Eden took issue with the prime minister on the regional councils and said he thought that this was a mistake. The general feeling was that the British view and our view are pretty close and that we would have very little difficulty in reaching an agreement.

Eden and Law both feel we ought to speed up the conversations just as fast as possible. . . . We finally agreed that these conferences should start in Washington about May 20th. We discussed the matter of some convenient place outside Washington, where there would not be so much confusion—and such bad heat. Winant and Law had the same reaction about the bad publicity at the Food Conference and the bad association of ideas if Hot Springs were chosen. . . .[10]

[When the talks turned to economic matters, the different approaches of the two nations became obvious. Stettinius again pressed the British to open negotiations on mutual lowering of tariffs; Eden and Law emphasized Britain's fears of a postwar economic collapse.]

On the Article 7 talks,[11] I hit it hard and said that we want those talks to go on in the near future. Law said that the prime minister is not too anxious. I took up with Law the two cables of the president to the prime minister on economic organization, and told him it was important that we must have some kind of an answer. He said that he would try to get up one while I am here.

We had a long talk about some mechanism to pick up immediately when Lend-Lease stops at the end of the war.

There will inevitably be a period before normal commercial trade gets started when credits of some kind will be needed.

Eden explained Britain's need for large exports after the war, and spoke of Britain coming out of the war as a debtor nation. He said that exports will be the one way for Britain to become solvent again.

* * *

Eden feels that we have made very good headway in London, and these visits are very worthwhile. Winant likewise is outspoken on the fact that things are working out much better than he had hoped.

[On Monday, April 17, Stettinius was received by King George VI in Buckingham Palace. The talk quite naturally turned to Anglo-American relations.]

* * *

The king asked me how I felt about the prospect of the British and ourselves sticking together in the difficult days ahead. I replied I thought we still had quite a public relations job to do at home but that I was very confident the American people would authorize participation by the United States in a world organization, and that after that, it was up to the British and us not to let anything happen that would cause any disagreement. I said that they would have to give up certain things and change their customs in certain regards and that we would have to do likewise. We would have to deal with each other as blood relations in the next generation or two, and no matter what each of us had to give up, the future of the world depended on an Anglo-American alliance. He was very much interested in the world organization discussions and was delighted to hear we were making such good progress.

* * *

[Two days later, Stettinius resumed his conversations with top British officials, meeting with Churchill at 10 Downing Street and with the chancellor of the exchequer, Sir John Anderson, in his cottage at Westminster.]

DIARY | *April 19, 1944*

The prime minister was dressed in his pull-over suit and appeared rested and in good form. The Cabinet Room with its high ceiling and large windows looking onto the garden, the great table running the length of the room, the bookcases, and portraits, was a very dignified and impressive room. . . .

The first topic the prime minister took up was the definition of unconditional surrender. . . . He doesn't share the view . . . of his own Foreign Office as well as our military that there should be a definition of surrender terms at this time. The prime minister takes the view that it is better to make a landing and be on our way toward Berlin before making any definition. He said the matter had been thoroughly discussed at Teheran, and that Stalin had certain definite views, I gather in favor of defining unconditional surrender. I stated at this point that I had received a message from the president last night stating that he did not wish the matter pressed at this time. The prime minister was heartily in accord with this, and said that matters should stand as they are. This is not the moment to define anything, he said.[12]

* * *

I left 10 Downing Street at approximately 1:45 and proceeded to Sir John Anderson's house at Lord North Street, Westminster.

* * *

We discussed many intimate matters during lunch. Sir John said that Anglo-American relations are the hope of the world. He was apparently rather unoptimistic relative to the Russian relationship, feeling that anything might happen. He stated that he thought the prime minister had great confidence in the forthcoming [invasion] operations. He hoped with all his heart that they would work out well. . . . I told him that I thought relations between the British and Americans were better than a year ago. He said, "Yes, except for a few top irritations."

* * *

[The discussion then turned to Britain's financial position.]

Sir John asked me what the American view was. I stated in very plain language that in 1938 they had three billion dollars. They have received ten billion dollars under Lend-Lease, and now their dollar balances are beginning to rise again. The farmer from Kansas just can't understand why the British are not rich. Anderson said that they fail to take into account the world view of the British Empire. He said, "When you read this [a memo on Britain's financial position] you will find that we will come out of this war with debts of fifteen billion and assets of one billion."

I asked Sir John if there were difficulties in putting over the British view in Washington whether it be agreeable for me to tell the president and Morgenthau that he would be willing to come to America. He said that of course this was impossible during the budget matter and the forthcoming operations, but along in the summer he would be open to such a suggestion.

[Stettinius returned to 10 Downing Street at 3:00 P.M. for further discussions with Churchill. Once again, the talks brought out sharp differences between the prime minister and the Foreign Office on the timing of a conference on international organization and the structure of the proposed world body and between Britain and the United States on economic problems.]

Cadogan came in to discuss with us the world security organization. I stated that Winant, Eden, Law, and I had a most satisfactory conversation over the weekend and that there seemed to be very little difference in our views. I said that we should press for early agreement between our two governments and that I was hopeful that the U.S. would have a proposal to present to our Congress this autumn so that the U.S. could be authorized to participate in a world organization before elections.

The prime minister did not seem impressed with this. He interrupted at one point in the conversation to state that of course his position was that it was best for the war that the president should be elected again. This was a private view and officially he remains strictly out of American affairs. Of course, if there were an upheaval in our affairs it would be his duty to cooperate with Dewey or Willkie or whoever would be elected.

At this point, I stated that there was one feature of our discussion in connection with world security organization which needed clarification and that was the provision for regional councils. The prime minister said, "You have my map that I drew."

I said, "I have, with the pigtails hanging over the end."

He said, "What is the point?"

I said, "During the weekend conversation with Eden and Law it wasn't clear in my mind that all the members of your government have the same view relative to world organization. They seem to think that the European, Asian, and

American Republics regional councils could all go in the assembly." This set off a firecracker. The prime minister stamped around and said he would not stand for it for a moment. I fortunately did not let the cat out of the bag and speak specifically of Eden. I just said "some of your officials."

Cadogan spoke up and said he didn't think there was any fundamental difference in point of view and that we could go along to an agreement. There is, however, a fundamental difference between the prime minister and Eden.

I then mentioned the fact that our conversations with the Foreign Office had been a great success, and that Eden and I were planning to make a joint statement of some kind. I said that we were considering making some reference to having agreed on a date for formal conversations on world organization. The prime minister's reaction was negative. He said that politically he thought it might be bad both in the U.S. and England. People are thinking about fighting now, and he thought it would be bad to interrupt the psychological trend of war and start thinking about the future peace of the world. When he dictated his notes to take up with the War Cabinet, however, he talked about the desirability of getting on with the security discussions sometime within the "next few months."

On the continuation of economic conferences, the prime minister asked whether we meant Article 7. I said, "Yes, in part, but there still remains outstanding and unanswered a wire from the president regarding the future of the Combined Boards. You might want to take that up with the War Cabinet and see if they are agreeable to follow it up." [13]

. . . I sense he is not interested in pressing to have the economic conversations carried on anytime in the near future. The note he dictated on this also mentioned getting on with the conversations sometime in the "next few months."

The prime minister, in a further discussion on Article 7

talks, said that his position is that nothing can be committed in joint discussions at this time. He said that he had made a speech in Parliament recently saying that there would be no binding commitments, just discussions in connection with Article 7 during the next few months.

At one point the prime minister stated, "I must make clear to you, as I have to the president, that we aren't going to repay the Lend-Lease debts. That will have to be adjusted someplace else along the lines of utilizing bases, Empire preferences, tariffs, etc."

[From April 20 to April 23, Stettinius and his advisers took a brief respite from their heavy schedule of conferences. On Thursday and Friday, they toured a number of U.S. Army installations in England, observing training sessions of the paratroopers of the 101st Airborne Division, watching army engineers constructing pontoon bridges and clearing mine fields, and viewing demonstrations of German tactics and operations. Upon returning to London, the diplomats spent a quiet weekend in preparation for their last round of discussions with the British.

On Monday, April 24, Stettinius again met with Eden. The first topic on their agenda was the long-standing difference over the role of de Gaulle's French National Committee in the invasion of Europe. The British wished to establish close liaison with the committee during the invasion and to see it installed as the government of liberated France, but President Roosevelt would not go along. In a directive of March 15, he had empowered General Eisenhower to determine how and when civil administration should be established in France. And to facilitate the forming of civil authority, he had advised the general that "you may consult" with the French National

Committee. Consultations were not to be limited to that group, however, and the directive should in no way be interpreted to imply recognition of the committee. But several weeks later, in a much publicized radio address, Secretary Hull stated that he and the president were "disposed to see the French Committee of National Liberation exercise leadership to establish law and order under the supervision of the Allied commander in chief." The British felt that Hull's speech signaled a change in U.S. policy, and sought to use it to effect a more flexible American position toward the French committee.] [14]

DIARY | *April 24, 1944*
We discussed the French directive at length. Eden still takes the view that there is a great difference between Secretary Hull's speech and the president's directive. . . . Eden read to us his speech in Parliament on September 22, 1943, in which he stated that the British would recognize and deal with the French committee. He feels that he is in a very difficult and embarrassing position as a result of this public commitment, and he said that he did not know of any way of getting out of this commitment at the moment. Eden stated that he would discuss the matter with the prime minister this evening. He seemed very pessimistic about the entire situation, however, and said that he was at a loss to know what the next move should be. He simply recognized the fact that we are still at a deadlock over the matter and he did not commit himself in any way as to what Britain would do about it.

[At their last conference on April 16, Stettinius and Eden had agreed to push ahead with discussions on international organization, and to announce that formal talks would begin shortly. Secretary Hull had flatly rejected this approach, however, and Stettinius attempted to explain Hull's reasoning.]

The second item on the calendar was the world security organization conversations. I explained to Eden that the secretary felt very strongly that no public announcement about these conversations could be made until he had progressed further in his talks with the congressional leaders. I stated that Mr. Hull had informed us that it would be fatal both domestically and in our relations with the Soviets if there were any intimation whatsoever that we had discussed the world security organization while in London. Eden seemed quite disappointed. . . . He seems to be genuinely anxious both to get along with the discussions as quickly as possible and also to secure the public approbation which he thought would be the result of such an announcement. . . . He asked me to impress on Mr. Hull the importance to the British of proceeding in the near future and the great desirability of a meeting between Hull, Eden, and Molotov sometime in the latter part of the summer. I assured Mr. Eden that I had already passed this word along to the secretary in one of my personal messages.

[In a cable of April 18,[15] Hull again turned down the British proposal to expand the authority of the European Advisory Commission. Eden continued to protest the American stand.]

When we turned to the European Advisory Commission, Eden showed obvious concern over the reiterated stand of the State Department. . . . He stated that this position did not fit in at all with the agreements reached at Moscow and that as a result of our attitude the commission will not achieve the importance which was intended for it when it was created [and]

. . . will have no chance of success. He seems to feel that
. . . we have a desire to whittle down the authority originally
granted to it.

* * *

[In the afternoon of April 25, Stettinius again visited
General Eisenhower and his staff. SHAEF was preparing
to receive unofficial representatives from the French National Committee, and the generals expressed regrets
about the committee's appointees and skepticism about
establishing a satisfactory working relationship.]

DIARY | *April 25, 1944*

Throughout the conversation . . . Generals Eisenhower,
Smith, and [Julius C.] Holmes [Civil Affairs Officer, SHAEF]
made it clear that they have little confidence either in the committee itself, in its appointees, or in its intention to give real
cooperation. As General Eisenhower put it, however, "We are
going on the principle 'If you can't lick 'em, join 'em.' "

* * *

General Eisenhower said that he has every intention of
working with the committee and that while he knows the task
would be full of headaches there is no alternative. He added,
however, that he could not be bound to the extent of adversely
affecting his military operations. . . . He said: "Suppose
there are a crowd of Frenchmen in Bordeaux who say they
will be glad to turn over the city to us, but they will have
nothing to do with the people appointed by the committee.
Do you think I am going to tell them I won't take Bordeaux
under those conditions but will insist on their accepting the
committee and thus slow up my military operations? That
would be stupid and the answer is 'No.' "

[The following day, April 26, Churchill escorted Stettinius to the House of Commons where the undersecretary was to make a brief, off-the-record statement. Before the two men entered the House, the prime minister "became emotional and had tears in his eyes . . . when talking of the future of the world." In his speech, Stettinius also talked about the future, particularly stressing the importance of Anglo-American cooperation. He noted his own personal commitment to friendship with Britain and recalled his family's intimate connections with British-American relations: his father's work as purchasing agent for the Allies in 1915–1916, his own work with Lend-Lease, his visit to London in that connection in 1942, and his current mission. He sought to reassure his listeners that the United States would not retreat into isolation after this war as it had after World War I. "We have all learned the bitter lesson of disunity," he concluded. "Henceforth, we know that only by working together can we maintain our freedom and progress toward great horizons of opportunity for all men." [16]

By April 1944, however, some men were already expressing skepticism and cynicism about the goals so eloquently stated by Stettinius in the speech to the House of Commons. The undersecretary spent most of April 27 talking with officials of the exile governments in London. The complaints of each were the same: the great powers were ignoring the wishes of the small nations and making decisions of vital importance to them without prior consultation.

The Polish prime minister, Stanislaw Mikolajczyk, strongly protested the pressure the British were placing on the Poles to surrender territory to the Soviet Union.]

DIARY | *April 27, 1944*

. . . Mr. Mikolajczyk said that it was not really a boundary question between Poland and Russia. The question involved was how to rule Europe. Poland was a test case. He said that five persons from the Polish Underground had recently come out of Poland, including a representative of the deputy prime minister in Poland, and they had reported that the people there could not understand why they should be asked to give away nearly half of Poland's territory and 11 million of its population. . . . Mr. Mikolajczyk said that it was his own opinion that the Soviets were desirous of communizing Poland but that they would not succeed.

[After Mikolajczyk departed, Stettinius was visited by Dr. E. N. van Kleffens, minister for foreign affairs of the Netherlands. Van Kleffens also expressed concern that the small nations were not being consulted by the great powers on postwar issues.]

Dr. van Kleffens said he felt these matters should not be left exclusively to the three Big Powers. The small powers should be given an opportunity to present their views. There were certain questions that affected them directly and if matters were left as they were, there would be great difficulties. Dr. van Kleffens mentioned the experience of UNRRA. After the four big powers had agreed on the preliminary draft, the smaller powers were told time and again when they wanted to suggest changes, "We have had so much trouble, do not raise the point." If the armistice terms were not satisfactory the government would be asked by the Dutch people, "Why did you accept them?" and it would only be able to answer, "We were not consulted."

[On April 28, the mission's last full day in London, Stettinius and his colleagues paid a farewell call on Eden, then went to 10 Downing Street. There, Stettinius introduced everyone to Churchill. The prime minister, attired in his famous air-raid suit and smoking one of his huge cigars, "was most cordial." After a short chat Churchill and Stettinius went into the Cabinet room for a private discussion. They both concluded that the mission would lead to closer relations between the State Department and Foreign Office, and Churchill observed that the British "were most happy and felt that our trip here had been important."

The two men next took up the problems that had dominated Stettinius's discussions in London. The undersecretary urged the prime minister to join with the United States in demanding that Spain stop all wolfram shipments to Germany. He advised Churchill that a date could not be set for the tripartite talks on world organization until Secretary Hull gave the word. The prime minister then raised the matter of a conference on trade and economic problems.]

The prime minister asked what our views were on the economic talks. I told him that we had had lengthy conversations with Richard Law, Sir John Anderson, and others on this matter, and that we were anxious that the talks get on just as soon as possible. He said this was a matter of embarrassment because he had a very difficult political situation here that we must recognize. He then commented that Anderson was not a politician and knew nothing about the political angles of these matters. . . . He further stated that Law, while a member of the Conservative party was in the progressive wing of that party—"he was flirting with the Left," as he put it—and that in the event of a change of government he would be on his ear in a moment. Therefore it would not do to put too much weight on any part that Law might play. Chur-

chill then added that it was necessary to have an all-out conference with the prime ministers of the Dominions on all economic matters first, and that it was impossible for him to give
me an assurance that the economic conversations could be
resumed at any definite time. I repeated the hope that these
conversations could go along on the expert level at the same
time that the monetary talks start. He was doubtful but assured me that he would give the matter his attention and see
what could be done. I repeated it was important to us at home,
particularly during the coming six months to get on with the
economic conversations, Article 7, and all related matters.

* * *

On the French directive, Churchill said, "I have the following formula now on the French directive and I propose to
make a speech on it next Tuesday. . . . I am going to say that
the British government's position . . . is exactly as outlined in
Mr. Hull's speech. I propose to say that Eisenhower and
members of his staff are already in conversation in an informal
manner with a French general whose name I will not mention.
If I am asked about the famous directive we have heard so
much about, I will say that that is a private matter between
two governments in the prosecution of the war and not a concern of Parliament or the press. I think that formula will satisfy the situation here in England and I do not propose to communicate with the president again."

At this point I interrupted and told the prime minister
that Bedell Smith had shown me and Mr. Matthews a copy of
the communication addressed to the combined chiefs of staff
by General Eisenhower relative to the matter of having conversations with the French, and reminded the prime minister
that he had shown me the reply of the combined chiefs of staff
to General Eisenhower a few days ago, in which they stated it
was satisfactory for Eisenhower to proceed with informal con-

versations on the clear understanding that they were on a "tentative" basis. I emphasized the word "tentative" to the prime minister, and explained to him that this could not be final. I said that Eisenhower would have to receive something else from the combined chiefs of staff before we could say the matter has come to a close, and that therefore his merely putting the whole question to sleep with his little formula did not check up completely in my mind. I am sure he understood the point I was making . . . , but he did not give any indication of what he might do about it.

* * *

Churchill told me at lunch today that Representative Fulbright had urged him to say publicly that he was convinced that there was no difference in the views of the president or Dewey or Bricker [17] relative to international affairs. The prime minister's reaction was that this would probably be unwise to do and that it might be a bombshell. He said it would look too much as if he were meddling in American politics. I agreed with him and took a firm position pleading with him not to take any position whatsoever in connection with American politics.

* * *

The other members of the mission then joined us and we went out on the terrace for a group picture. . . . The prime minister showed us the recent bomb damage. He walked back into the house with us, warmly bid us farewell, and wished us a good journey.

[The Stettinius mission to London did not produce specific agreements or immediate tangible results. In May 1944, the United States, Britain, and Spain finally worked out a compromise under which Franco agreed to curtail drastically, though not to cut out altogether, wolfram shipments to Germany. But this was the product of negotiations in Madrid and Washington, and was not affected by Stettinius. The one area that promised concrete results—the setting of a date for the opening of talks on world organization—was undercut by Hull's insistence that he must wait until his discussions with Congress had reached a more advanced stage.

On most of the immediate issues under dispute, the United States and Britain were as far apart when the undersecretary departed from England as when he arrived. The two nations continued to disagree on the proper function of the European Advisory Commission, and continued American indifference to its work ensured that it would not play an important part in postwar settlements. In like manner, the mission failed to resolve Anglo-American differences on France. As before, the British refused to accept Roosevelt's March 15 directive and the United States was unwilling to accept anything less. SHAEF was left to improvise policy on an ad hoc basis. Despite Stettinius's persistent urging, the British still refused to enter formal discussions on postwar commercial policy, and in fact these talks would not begin until after V-J Day, when Britain's desperate economic situation left no choice but to go along with the United States.

Still the mission was not without constructive results. It had not been designed to negotiate agreements but rather to develop closer working relations with the British at the lower diplomatic levels and to determine more accurately the British viewpoint on important postwar matters. In both of these areas it succeeded. Stettinius won the confidence and respect of Eden, Cadogan, and other Foreign Office officials, and opened up impor-

tant personal contacts that would contribute greatly to
the success of the Dumbarton Oaks, Yalta, and San Francisco conferences. The extended and often frank exchanges of view during April 1944, pointed up differences that had to be reconciled, but the mission
discovered, sometimes to its surprise, that British and
American positions ran parallel on many matters. On international organization, Stettinius reported to Roosevelt
and Hull, "British thinking" was "very similar to our
own," and he expressed confidence that when formal negotiations began "we and the British will find ourselves in
substantial agreement." Even on the touchy question of
colonialism, Stettinius and his staff found the British and
Americans "much closer in our thinking at the end of our
talks than we could have hoped." At the very least, most
British officials seemed to agree that the question of "dependent peoples," as they referred to it, would be discussed at the international level, and this, at least at the
time, seemed of great importance.[18] Thus as the State
Department set out to complete its postwar planning in
the summer of 1944, there was renewed optimism that
the dream of international cooperation could be made a
reality.]

III

TRANSITION FROM WAR TO PEACE
May–August 1944

During the three months after Stettinius returned from London, the Allies launched massive offensives against Hitler's Fortress Europe. On June 6, 1944, in the greatest amphibious operation in the history of warfare, the United States and Britain landed 176,000 troops on the beaches of Normandy. Two weeks later, the Red Army initiated a series of attacks along an 800-mile line south of Leningrad. By the end of July, U.S. forces had broken out at St. Lo, opening the battle for France, and the Russians had driven to the outskirts of Warsaw; Allied armies advanced so rapidly in both the east and west that it appeared by late summer that Germany might collapse before the end of the year.

As the armies of the Grand Alliance pressed on toward Berlin, the attention of diplomats focused increasingly on the problems of the peace. Aware that the United States might have a decisive influence on postwar settlements in Europe, officials from large nations and small came to Washington in the summer of 1944 in search of American backing. The Poles and Greeks sought protection against their Russian neighbor; the British continued to press for American economic assistance to protect them against the economic disaster they saw ahead.

In most cases they were disappointed. Roosevelt and especially Hull harbored a deep fear of a resurgent isolationism at home, and they were unwilling even to consider the sort of secret commitments they were certain had destroyed

Woodrow Wilson. The campaign of 1944, which got underway with the Republican convention in June, provided an additional reason for caution. The president and the State Department listened patiently and sometimes sympathetically to the pleas of foreign diplomats, but they adamantly insisted that political and territorial settlements must await the end of the war. The State Department preoccupied itself with immediate problems such as Argentina and with long-range planning for an international organization that would be capable of resolving issues unsettled at the end of the war. It continued to be obsessed with its own public image, which officials felt had to be improved if the American people were to be converted to internationalism.

[Despite Stettinius's attempts to refurbish its image, the State Department continued to suffer a bad press during much of 1944. The columnist Drew Pearson, a long-time adversary of Hull, was particularly critical, and in a column of May 12, he revived old charges of dissension among the department's top officials. According to Pearson, Hull had insisted that Stettinius not talk to the press on his return from London, and when the undersecretary had held an off-the-record press conference the secretary would not release his remarks. This incident had added to the bad feeling that had already developed, Pearson alleged, and the two men were "in about the same pistol-drawn position as Hull was with former Undersecretary Welles." [1]

Pearson's column stirred up much concern in the State Department, and Stettinius met with his aides to decide how to respond.]

CALENDAR NOTES | *May 18, 1944*
This meeting was held to discuss the Drew Pearson article on the secretary not wishing me to have a press confer-

ence on my return from London. After considerable discussion Mr. [Michael] McDermott [State Department public information officer] is going to recommend to the secretary that we ignore the Pearson article; that neither the secretary nor I should write the publisher of his column and that I should not make any statement to the press saying it is false. To do any of the foregoing would be pouring fuel on the fire. We would be apt to lose from it rather than benefit by such action. McDermott will recommend to the secretary that sometime soon at a press conference a question will be raised and the secretary will say "It happens that Mr. Stettinius is handling this. Let me call him in and have him tell you personally." This gesture of team work will make an impression as it has never been done before. Also McDermott is to recommend to the secretary that Arthur Krock [*New York Times* columnist and a close friend of Hull] be given the job of writing a special article telling the truth, i.e., that there is a wonderful relationship between me and the secretary.

[The following day, Stettinius pursued the matter further.]

CALENDAR NOTES | *May 19, 1944*
I talked with Arthur Krock and he said he would do something about Mr. Hull and I working harmoniously. McDermott is going to talk to Mr. Hull some time in the next few days and tell him the whole thing is buttoned up and to forget it.

Mr. Hull said to me, "I think the way to handle this is for you to write a letter to the 600 newspapers in which Drew Pearson's column appears, and say this is a lie. Talk to the boys and whatever you decide is all right with me."

I have talked to Mac. He is against it. [Cecil] Gray [special assistant to the secretary] is against it. Krock is against it. [Robert] Lynch [Stettinius's secretary] is against it. I spoke to the press conference instead, and Krock is now going to do something else.

> [Next to Drew Pearson, the still unrecognized govern-
> ment of Argentina provided the greatest headaches for
> the State Department. In commemoration of its indepen-
> dence day, May 25, the Farrell regime planned an elabo-
> rate celebration including a *Te Deum*, a banquet, and a
> gala performance at the Colon Opera, and apparently as a
> means of securing tacit diplomatic recognition it invited
> representatives of other governments to attend. The State
> Department authorized Ambassador Norman Armour,
> who was still in Buenos Aires although not officially ac-
> credited to the government, to attend the *Te Deum* on the
> grounds that it was a religious ceremony and U.S. ab-
> sence might be an affront to the church and the Argen-
> tine people. But it adamantly opposed his attending the
> other functions, which would be presided over by Argen-
> tine government officials, and it also placed great pressure
> on its Latin American allies to follow this line of policy.
> Through various intermediaries, the Argentines worked
> to change the American position.]

CALENDAR NOTES | *May 23, 1944*
The Mexican ambassador . . . stated that the Argentine ambassador this morning had asked that he endeavor to per- suade his government to authorize the Mexican ambassador in the Argentine to attend not only the *Te Deum* but the banquet as well . . . and also urge the State Department to authorize Ambassador Armour to attend the banquet. I stated that we had authorized Armour to attend only the *Te Deum* and he would not be authorized to attend the banquet. The Mexican ambassador stated to me that he thought this was entirely the

right course and he said he was recommending to his government that the Mexican ambassador be authorized to attend neither.

* * *

[Shortly afterward, the Spanish ambassador came to the State Department with a message from Argentina.]

Señor Cardenas called on me this afternoon at his request and left with me a memorandum relative to a communication that his government had received from the Argentine urging that we participate in the ceremonies relative to their independence day on May 25. I explained . . . that Ambassador Armour had been instructed to attend only the *Te Deum*. The ambassador was somewhat embarrassed in presenting this note and he admitted that he had no personal interest whatever and was merely performing a routine diplomatic function.

[The United States persisted in its firm stand, and when Uruguay threatened to break the united front of American nations, Hull dispatched a strong note to his ambassadors in Latin America urging them to make plain the importance of avoiding even implied recognition of the Farrell regime. Most of the governments followed the United States's lead, and with obvious satisfaction, Armour reported from Buenos Aires on May 26 that the independence day celebration lacked its "usual sparkle." [2] Since the beginning of 1944, the Polish government-in-exile had been trying to enlist the support of the United States in its dispute with the Soviet Union and to secure a private meeting between its prime minister, Stanislaw Mikolajczyk, and President Roosevelt. The president had put the Poles off, fearing that a meeting with Mikolajczyk might cause a break with Moscow and stir up Polish-American organizations that were already agitating against the USSR in the United States. Roosevelt finally agreed to see Mikolajczyk in June, however, on the condition that the prime minister make no public speeches and establish no contacts with Polish-Americans. Mikolajczyk arrived in Washington on June 5, and for the next nine days held a series of conferences with the president and State Department officials. Hull was on vacation for much of this time, and Stettinius, as acting secretary, held primary responsibility for the talks. The Poles' unrealistic approach toward the USSR was evident from the outset. In his initial conference with Stettinius on June 6, Mikolajczyk stressed that his government would not make concessions on territorial matters and expressed optimism that in time the Russians would have no choice but to settle on Poland's terms.[3]

The following evening, Stettinius took Mikolajczyk to the White House where the president gently encouraged him to compromise with the USSR.]

CALENDAR NOTES | *June 7, 1944*

After the White House dinner in honor of the Polish prime minister, Stanislaw Mikolajczyk, the president invited the prime minister, the Polish ambassador [Jan Ciechanowski], Mr. Stanislaw Tabor [the general second in command of the underground forces], and myself to join him in his upstairs study. We went up there at 10:00 p.m. and remained with the president until 11:45 p.m.

The president opened the discussion by saying that, while he had had a most satisfactory hour with the prime minister that morning, he was now interested in having a frank discussion with General Tabor relative to the underground movement in Poland.

The general presented the underground movement in a most dramatic fashion, speaking in Polish, with the Polish ambassador acting as interpreter. The general spoke from maps and memoranda, showing the president the damage that had been done in the way of destroying bridges, highways, derailing German munition trains, and other like matters. The president seemed very favorably impressed and several times during the discussion he spoke of the fact that it was a great pity that a closer liaison relationship had not been established between the Russians and the Polish army. It was perfectly clear from the discussion that no formal relationship in this regard does exist, although the Polish military officials in London are reporting their accomplishments daily to the Allied military authorities in London. However, the Poles have no way of knowing whether or not this information is being given to the Russians.

* * *

The president then stated he thought it very important that the Polish prime minister go to Moscow and have a conference with Stalin and Molotov. He was convinced that this would be very useful. The Polish ambassador asked how this could be arranged. The president at first stated that he was not quite sure what steps should be taken to bring this about, but later in the discussion, in response to a request of the Polish ambassador, stated he would be willing to send a cable to Stalin suggesting he invite the prime minister to come to Moscow for a frank discussion.

During the conversation, the president referred to their morning's conversation with the Polish prime minister, and gave the reasons again why it was impossible for him, as an individual, to take an active part in ironing out Soviet-Polish relations during the "American political year of 1944." There was a lengthy discussion on this point, and the president referred twice to his statement to Stalin at Teheran at which he explained the "American political year of 1944" and the delicacy of the Polish situation.

The president stated he did not feel that they could rely on Mr. Churchill being able to come forward with a helpful solution and that he had had his "fingers burned" once and didn't feel he could try again at the present time inasmuch as all his time and energy were now being devoted to present operations in France.

The president asked General Tabor in what direction he felt the Russians would move across Poland. The general replied that there were two alternatives—the southernly route or the middle route, which he referred to as the "Napoleonic route." The general also stated that it was very difficult for him to plan their underground operations without knowing what the Russians' plans were, and that if they knew more about the direction in which the Russian troops would move, it would be possible for them to cooperate more intelligently and be of greater assistance. The president replied that they would never get this information. As a matter of fact, he said, it was impossible for us to obtain such information. The president then referred to a wire he had received from Stalin yesterday in which he had congratulated the president on the capture of Rome, the landings in France, and reassured the president that he would keep his word he gave at the Teheran Conference, and that in the next few days he would start a grand offensive.[4] The president emphasized that he had no idea what this offensive was or where it would be, and neither did any other Allied leader.

The president stated that they must win Russia's confidence as he had been able to do partially. The president said he felt the Russians trusted him more than they did Churchill, but they don't even trust him completely.

Throughout the discussion, the Poles showed a lack of confidence and a lack of trust in the general situation. Several times during the evening they spoke of the fact that they felt the salvation of Poland rested in American hands. To this, the president replied that perhaps a little later he could take a vigorous stand, but again referred to the "American political year of 1944."

The president stated that the Poles must recognize the fact that they would have to make certain definite changes in their leadership in order to create a working arrangement with the Russians, and this was a point he hoped they would not be stubborn about.

* * *

The . . . prime minister asked the president whether or not he felt the Russians would wish to permanently dominate adjoining European countries and the Balkans. The president stated that the Russians had their own political problems and he felt that they were already so large and unwieldy that they would not wish to take on additional burdens. The president stated that they would wish to cooperate with the other United Nations in having strong, independent adjoining states friendly to them.

The president inquired if there was any way in which we could help the Polish underground movement. General Tabor replied that what they needed most in the way of supplies was small arms. The president stated that he thought it was a possibility of our being of assistance in this regard now that we are shuttling bombers between England and Russia and between Italy and Russia, since the bombers would be flying over Polish territory. He said he could easily see that when a bomber left England on a bombing mission over Germany, it could continue on over Poland and drop say, 1,000 rifles or 100 machine guns at a designated place. If this were arranged, it would, of course, have to be done with the consent of the Russians because of the fact that our planes would eventually land in Russian territory. This matter was not pursued nor was there any agreement raised in the conversation as to what steps would be made to make the arrangements.

* * *

[In a conversation with Stettinius the following afternoon, a worried Mikolajczyk objected to the president's suggestion that he go to Moscow for talks with Stalin.]

CALENDAR NOTES | *June 8, 1944*

The prime minister said he was somewhat disturbed from the president's remarks last night regarding his going to Moscow. He was particularly anxious to know whether that was a carefully thought out plan on the part of the president or whether it was a spontaneous and impulsive thought. I advised the gentleman that the Department, in analyzing the Soviet-Polish relations, had thought of the possibility of the prime minister going to Moscow, but that we had made no suggestions to the president specifically.

My impression was that it was a thought which had occurred to the president earlier that morning during the discussion.

The prime minister then stated that he thought [Eduard] Beneš [chairman of the Czechoslovak National Committee in London] had gone much too far, and the formula would not be acceptable to his government.[5] He hoped that he would not be asked to go to Moscow and be presented with a formula which he could not accept. On the other hand, he saw great merit in going to Moscow promptly in order to work out military collaboration.

At this point I stated that the prime minister had made a favorable impression on Churchill and the president, and I thought he should take advantage of the first opportunity of seeing, face to face, Stalin and Molotov, because if they could have the same faith in the present leader of Poland as Churchill and the president have, I thought it would help the situation a great deal. The matter was left that they would continue to study the situation. . . .

[After a cabinet meeting the following day, Stettinius spoke privately with the president about Mikolajczyk's proposed visit to Moscow, and found Roosevelt now reluctant to get involved.]

CALENDAR NOTES | *June 9, 1944*

The president has made up his mind that it would be a mistake for him to "mix in" with the question of the Polish prime minister going to Moscow. He has come to the conclusion that Stalin would misunderstand this in view of the president's statement to Stalin at Teheran that this was a political year. The president has authorized me to tell the Polish prime minister that he cannot send the message to Stalin but for me to make the suggestion that the Polish prime minister make arrangements to go to Moscow through President Beneš of Czechoslovakia.

[Stettinius relayed Roosevelt's suggestion to Mikolajczyk later in the afternoon. The prime minister, who thought Beneš had given up too much in a treaty he had signed with the Russians in December 1943, firmly opposed his playing the role of intermediary. It was then suggested that Roosevelt and Churchill make a joint approach to

Stalin proposing the desirability of bringing about close military collaboration between the Red Army and the Polish underground. Mikolajczyk remained suspicious.]

The prime minister thought that perhaps an approach might be made at this level, but he wondered whether, if the approach was made at the military level, the Soviet authorities might accept with alacrity military collaboration, but as their armies advanced, they would go ahead independently on the political level and organize the administration in Poland along their own lines without consultation with the Polish government-in-exile. No final decision was made as to the advisability of making this second approach.

[On Monday June 12, Stettinius arranged for Mikolajczyk to meet with Secretary Hull, who had just returned from vacation, and with the president. Both men stressed the need for compromise with Russia.]

CALENDAR NOTES | *June 12, 1944*
This morning I presented the Polish prime minister, accompanied by the Polish ambassador, to Mr. Hull. We had a twenty-five minute discussion at which time there was a very frank exchange of views. . . .

The secretary made a comprehensible and excellent appeal to the prime minister on the matter of working with one's neighbor no matter how difficult it might be.

We spent forty-five minutes with the president this morning. He was very sympathetic.

* * *

The president stated that he felt Poland and Russia were at an impasse at the present moment, and the sooner the Polish prime minister returned to Poland with his government, and went to Moscow for conferences, the better.

The president spoke of the fact that Queen Wilhelmina [of the Netherlands] and King Haakon [of Norway] had both agreed to return to their countries at the first moment possible. Furthermore, they had agreed to select new members of their cabinets from their countrymen who had remained at home during the war and had gone through the terrible suffering.

The president at this point stated that he felt it was important for the Polish prime minister to make the changes in his government which the Russians were demanding,[6] for after all, it was only four people and it might be the deciding factor. The Polish prime minister did not agree with this, saying it would be misunderstood and that he would be losing face.

The prime minister spoke of the commitment that had been made in December 1939 by his country, to hold an election the first three weeks of liberation so that the people could decide what kind of government they wanted and who their leaders would be. The president stated that he remembered this, but thought it had been forgotten, and said it would be a good thing to have restated at this time.

The president said he was convinced the Russians were sincere in their desire for a strong independent Poland, and indicated that he thought they could trust the Russians to give them fair treatment.

The Polish prime minister indicated that he could trust America to give them fair treatment politically and economically, but did not trust Russia.

The president said that he was not worried about territorial matters, that they would get East Prussia and Silesia, and if they had to give up a little something somewhere else, he thought it was a pretty good exchange.

The president said he did not agree on the formula based upon the old Curzon line.[7] He did not feel the Russians would insist upon this. Further, the president stated, he did not feel that Stalin would insist upon Koenigsberg, and that he felt Stalin would be willing to have Koenigsberg as a "shrine for the world," inasmuch as the city controlled Danzig and was an important locality. The president recalled Stalin having referred to it as the "Home of the Teutonic Knights."

* * *

The Polish prime minister was most frank, most cordial, and there is no question in my mind that the president and the prime minister have established a complete faith between the two men.

[Despite the generally cordial atmosphere of the talks and Stettinius's optimism, the extent to which the United States would support the Polish government-in-exile in negotiations with the USSR remained unclear. This problem occupied a central place in the discussions during the last two days of Mikolajczyk's stay in the United States.]

CALENDAR NOTES | *June 13, 1944*

The prime minister asked if we had had time to examine the Polish record of the . . . conversations here and the conclusions which he had drawn from them. In reply to my inquiry, Messrs. [Charles] Bohlen [chief of the State Department's Eastern European Division] and [Elbridge] Durbrow [State Department's Eastern European Division] said that they had examined the document carefully, and it appeared to them to be a faithful and accurate account of the conversations.

There was one suggestion, however, which could be

made in regard to the conclusions and that was that instead of saying that the prime minister could count on the moral support of the president in Poland's efforts to reach a settlement with the Soviet Union, it would perhaps be more accurate to state that the president's moral support would be given towards their efforts to reach a solution mutually satisfactory to Poland and the Soviet Union. Mr. Bohlen pointed out that he felt that this would be a more accurate statement of the president's attitude since it would avoid any implication that this government was taking a positive stand against the Soviet government.

The prime minister then said that he wished to have as clear an indication as possible to take back to London as to exactly what the president meant by moral support, and he had therefore put forth in the document three questions to the United States government to which he would like to have a reply before leaving. These questions related to possible forms of moral support under certain contingencies that might arise if direct negotiations were started between the Polish and Soviet governments. I said that I thought it would be a mistake to try to pin down the president too definitely as to future action in view of what the president had said of the difficulties of intervening in the Polish-Soviet dispute during the present year.

The prime minister said that he fully understood this and was not asking for any definite commitment but merely an indication as to whether the American government would give consideration to some form of moral support in the three contingencies mentioned. Mr. Bohlen pointed out that in effect the president's willingness to lend moral support covered the situation and that obviously the time and manner would have to be left up to him.

After some further discussion I said that the best method would be to put the matter up to the president and he could give his views to the prime minister when he called to say goodbye tomorrow. I suggested therefore that the Polish ambassador consult with Mr. Bohlen and Mr. Durbrow with a view to presenting to the president the questions on which the prime minister desired clarification.

* * *

[In a memorandum to the president, June 14, 1944,[8] Secretary Hull raised the questions alluded to by Mikolajczyk, and at their final meeting on the same day, Mikolajczyk again pressed Roosevelt for an answer.]

CALENDAR NOTES | *June 14, 1944*
The prime minister asked the president if he had any comment on the memorandum which had been sent yesterday relative to possible future interest of our government in Polish problems. The president stated he had not had an opportunity to read the memorandum. He then turned to me. I stated that the important point was that the prime minister wished a verbal assurance from him, the president, that if he failed in his discussions with the Russians, he could feel free to come back to discuss matters with the president again. The president stated, "Of course, my door is always open." This seemed to satisfy the prime minister and although this doesn't go thoroughly into the matters raised by the prime minister, there was no other way to handle the situation in the few moments that were available in view of the fact that the president had not read the memorandum submitted to him by Mr. Hull.

* * *

[This final exchange between Roosevelt and Mikolajczyk illustrates the extreme delicacy of the Polish problem. The president was unwilling to intervene directly in the

Soviet-Polish dispute at a time when the Allied offensive in Europe depended upon the advance of the Red Army in the east. On the other hand, he was sympathetic to the principle of self-determination for Poland, and he was unwilling to abandon the Poles altogether for fear of domestic political repercussions. He tried to persuade Mikolajczyk that it was possible to work with the Russians and encouraged him to compromise in hopes that the issues might be resolved before he had to commit himself. But he kept holding out the possibility that he might back the London Poles at some future point, and this undermined his efforts to get them to compromise with Stalin.

While Stettinius hosted visiting diplomats, rumors of tensions between the undersecretary and Hull continued to circulate in the press and among Washington gossips. In a private conference on June 21, the two men discussed the rumors and how to deal with them.]

CALENDAR NOTES | *June 21, 1944*
The secretary said that Harry Eaton [editor of the *Whaley-Eaton Newsletter*, a business periodical] came in the other day and said he was talking in great privacy—Mr. Eaton said there were an increasing number of stories around about friction between the secretary and me. He said he was telling both of us as a friend, that he was disturbed about it. The secretary asked him if this had come from within the administration or outside. Mr. Eaton said he thought it was coming from within the administration from people who are unfriendly to me. Mr. Hull then stated—"Well I have never had a more satisfactory relationship with anybody. The relations between Stettinius and myself have been 100 percent plus ever since he arrived in the department—it couldn't be more satisfactory." I then stated that I thought one thing he ought to know was the fact that some of the gossip about trouble between him and

myself had started by his saying, in a rather irritated way, in Morgenthau's and Crowley's ⁹ presence, when the question came up as to whether or not I was going to discuss the British dollar position when I went to England, "I don't know what Stettinius is going to discuss"—this gave the impression to those present that he was a little bit irritated. He said "that's perfectly absurd—I approved your going—I approved what you were going to do. That's preposterous." I said the seed of the personal gossip about trouble between him and myself emanated from that incident.

. . . I said that the time had arrived when the secretary should say something publicly about the satisfactory relations—this might be the time to do it in connection with these world security conferences.¹⁰ He could say in a few words that he had asked me to head up this delegation because of his confidence in me. If he would do that on some such occasion I thought it would put to sleep all these malicious rumors. He said "I shall do that and will take advantage of the first opportunity." He repeated again that his relations had been 100 percent plus. . . .

[By the time of the invasion of France, relations between the United States and de Gaulle's French National Committee had deteriorated into what one Frenchman described as a "hideous mess." U.S. officials had not taken the French into their confidence on the details of the invasion. The French had refused to go along with General Eisenhower's attempts to work out a stopgap arrangement for the administration of liberated areas, and de Gaulle would not agree to make a D-Day radio broadcast to the French people until late in the afternoon of June 6. Tempers on both sides became strained, the French resentful that they were not being consulted about matters relating to the liberation of their country, the Americans certain that the French were obstructing military progress. At a social meeting with Jean Monnet, representative of the French Purchasing Commission in Washington, top U.S. officials unloaded their anger against the committee.]

CALENDAR NOTES | *June 22, 1944*
I spent the evening aboard the secretary of navy's yacht, "Sequoia," with the secretary of the navy, Admiral [William D.] Leahy [the president's chief of staff], Mr. [John] McCloy [assistant secretary of war], and Jean Monnet. . . . We spent several hours together in a most intimate and frank discussion. Early in the evening, Mr. McCloy gave a rather detailed report on General Marshall's reaction relative to events in England, France, and Italy. The General, confident and hopeful, is returning to Washington with a high heart. As we already know, however, he was very discouraged with the political situation relating both to the British and French. . . .

Secretary Forrestal and Admiral Leahy were brutally frank with Monnet about De Gaulle and the French situation. They "let him have it with both barrels," emphasizing . . . that if the American public knew the truth about the deplorable manner in which de Gaulle and the committee had handled affairs, there would be a definite breach between this country and France that would take a generation to get over.

Admiral Leahy went into great detail reviewing the history of our relationship with the French committee over the past two years. He stated with great force that from the start they had hampered our war effort, and had caused us difficulty and embarrassment at every turn. The admiral placed emphasis on the fact that they had practically placed the former governor of Dakar in a prison and that he had been friendly to our cause. Now, they had imprisoned [General

Henri] Giraud [commander of French troops in North Africa and a rival of de Gaulle for leadership of liberated France]. The admiral also stated that while the French troops were useful in Italy, they were not fighting under the conditions laid down by the Allied military leaders. It was indicated that the French seemed to be doing everything possible to make matters difficult and that, while we were confident of winning the war in France, they were being of little or no help. Meanwhile, their great leader was "sulking" in London.

* * *

Monnet made a rather feeble attempt to defend the French situation, but his argument lacked force and carried little conviction.

* * *

[At the same time, the government of Greece continued to try to arouse American concern about possible Soviet designs in the Mediterannean.]

CALENDAR NOTES | *June 23, 1944*
The Greek ambassador called upon me at his request this morning. He stated that he had been away from Washington and was sorry that he had not had an opportunity of calling upon me since my return from England.

He stated that he had received a full report of my discussions in England with the king of Greece and the Greek ambassador to England. He was very appreciative of my interest in Greek problems.

He stated there was great concern on the part of the Greeks as to the attitude of Russia toward their country and problems. They felt that Russia would perhaps exert influence that would not be welcome. I told the ambassador that I thought he and his people should have confidence and faith in the future and that I, personally, was hopeful that a solution of Greek problems could be found that would be fair and just.

* * *

[The British had long been aware that they would face serious economic problems at the end of the war, but in the summer of 1944 they began to see the full magnitude of the approaching crisis. During the war, the United Kingdom had accumulated external liabilities almost five times its prewar totals. The liquidation of most of its foreign assets and the loss of the export trade left it without any means to service its debts or to pay for the imports upon which Britain depended. Officials estimated that the nation would enter the postwar era with liabilities fifteen times greater than available reserves and would incur an annual deficit of $1 billion in the first years after the war.

British Minister of State Richard Law, in Washington on other business in July 1944, discussed these problems and their political implications in a private conversation with Stettinius. The undersecretary, like many other Americans at this time, was unsympathetic.]

CALENDAR NOTES | *July 18, 1944*

The first matter that Mr. Law raised was the question of postponing the agreement on the so-called White Paper [11] until large issues were thought out. He stated that he felt Sir John Anderson [chancellor of the exchequer] would be coming to Washington sometime probably in August and he hoped our government would not press an agreement on re-export of Lend-Lease material until after Sir John Anderson had had an opportunity of explaining the overall financial condition of the Empire to the president, Mr. Hull, and the secretary of the treasury. I assured Mr. Law that I would take the matter up with the proper officials and that I did not think there would be any difficulty in postponing these decisions until that time.

Mr. Law again referred to the serious financial condition of the Empire and referred also to the difficulty that the British would have in accepting interest bearing obligations. I frankly told Mr. Law that this view was making a very unfavorable impression in Washington—that after America had spent 12 billion dollars seeing them through, to think now that we would have to treat the British as pensioners for an indefinite period, extending them aid perhaps from two to three billion dollars a year without repayment, would react unfavorably with the American public.

While I considered this matter in detail, I could not accept this statement that with the vast resources of the Empire they could not find some way to service a debt of somewhat in the neighborhood of five to ten billion dollars over a thirty year period at 2 percent, say.

Mr. Law saw the point and sympathized with my point of view. He continued, however, by saying that we must realize that the British people have gone through five years of, as he put it, "hell;" that they felt they were in the home stretch; that the flying bombs had been terrifically difficult for them to take when they thought they were now safe from anything like that; that if the British population of four or five million people were told, at the end of this long period of suffering and sacrifice, that they could not have some of the niceties of life such as adequate food, new clothes, radios, gasoline, tires, etc., they were apprehensive as to the social reaction, feeling there would be a distinct possibility of an extreme left swing that might take the form of some totalitarian system and might be led by a man such as Shinwell, the left wing socialist, who has been raising so much trouble in Parliament in recent months. Mr. Law said it was just as important to us as to them to see England through in the middle-of-a-road course, and eventually to bring her into a state of solvency. I assured Mr. Law that I was tremendously interested in hearing his story and told him that I thought before this matter was reported officially to our government that it would be best to have Sir John Anderson present this story himself when he came over in August.

*   *   *

Mr. Law did not think that the present labor leaders of England such as Bevin and Citrine [12] would go all the way to the left in the way of a socialist state, or totalitarian, unless they were forced to, and that anything could be expected. He thought that Attlee, Morrison, and Cripps [13] would stay in the middle of the road. Mr. Law feels that in the postwar period it would be so serious that some of the conservatives might go all the way to the left in order to save the situation.

There is no question but that the British are apprehensive relative to a social upheaval in the postwar period and that they expect to be able to return to a high standard of living which is going to be impossible as a result of their indebtedness and the long period it will take to build up their export trade.

[While the British were preeminently concerned with economics, Americans were preoccupied with politics and the upcoming presidential election. It was assumed that Roosevelt would run again and be nominated, and among Democratic politicians the most intriguing questions surrounded the vice-presidency. The names mentioned most frequently were those of Vice-President Henry A. Wallace and Director of War Mobilization James F. Byrnes, but there were numerous others, including Stettinius. The undersecretary had some support among Virginia Democrats and friends in Congress, and on July 18, the day before the Democratic convention opened in Chicago, Supreme Court Justice Robert H. Jackson sounded him out on his availability.]

TRANSCRIPT OF TELEPHONE CONVERSATION | *July 18, 1944*

Mr. Jackson: This situation out in Chicago is a wide open proposition. Some of these gentlemen whose names are more prominent at the moment are likely to kill each other off. I had a talk with Frank Hague [New Jersey's Democratic "boss"] and he is very favorable to you. Indirectly he asked me to ascertain just what the situation was. Is Virginia going to do anything about your name?

Mr. Stettinius: No. They are not going to do anything. They aren't going to make any move. They are friendly and receptive but I haven't taken this thing seriously and haven't wanted any of my friends to stir anything up.

Mr. Jackson: Of course, I feel a real friendship for you. After talking with Frank about the situation he said "He would be the best bet of all of them. What is anybody doing?" I wanted to talk with you and see just what the situation is.

Mr. Stettinius: I don't think anybody is doing anything. I have told my friends that I had come into the government to help my country in the war and I just didn't have any ambitions. Of course, naturally, if anybody wants to say nice things, a fellow appreciates them.

Mr. Jackson: This is going to be a very close race and they have to get out every last vote and they have to present a ticket which appeals to every last possible voter. Jimmy is an able fellow but South Carolina doesn't mean a thing and he is a Catholic. Alben [Barkley] is a good fellow, but Alben has been all around the map and [Robert] Kerr [Governor of Oklahoma] is an unknown. They have to get the vote in New York State. If Dewey carries New York, we will have a devil of a time winning. If we carry New York, he can't possibly win. Those things reduce themselves to a very simple equation.

Mr. Stettinius: Yes, I know. I think you will not find that anybody is going to do anything.

Mr. Jackson: I will talk to Frank on the phone tonight. He is a lot better fellow than his reputation makes him out to be.

Mr. Stettinius: I appreciate your calling. You know I am just a good citizen trying to help.

[The Stettinius boomlet did not get underway, and the Democratic convention nominated Senator Harry S Truman of Missouri for vice-president. Shortly after the convention, Stettinius discussed politics and diplomacy with *St. Louis Post-Dispatch* columnist Marquis Childs.]

CALENDAR NOTES | *July 28, 1944*

Mr. Childs came in to pay a personal visit. He told me of his interesting time in Chicago and that Wallace had come out of the convention with real stature and had made the best speech at either convention.

Mr. Childs thought that Senator Truman would probably get a few more votes but not many.

Mr. Childs is going west with Dewey. He says Dewey's plan is to make an attack on eight top members of the government, beginning in October. I volunteered that the two oldest men in the United States government were the two most efficient and well liked—Mr. Hull and Mr. Stimson—and that it would be most interesting to see whether Dewey threw any bricks at these men who had the full confidence of the world. Marquis Childs thought this was a good point.

[On June 15, Roosevelt had announced that the United States would host a conference in August to discuss with Britain, Russia, and China the framework of a new international organization. Hull had subsequently named Stettinius to head the U.S. delegation, and the undersecretary busied himself preparing for the conference. Journalists, naturally curious about American plans for the meeting, began probing for details. Stettinius would reveal nothing.]

CALENDAR NOTES | *July 28, 1944*

Mr. Metcalf of *Time* came in and said he wanted to discuss the Argentine situation and asked whether or not we were prepared to go all out [on] economic sanctions. I told him that that was an unfair question and that he was just trying to get a scoop. I told him with a smile, "No comment. I'm a diplomat."

He then asked several questions about the postwar discussions. I told him there was nothing to be said other than we were going to have the discussions and that I was going to head up the American group.

[Stettinius gave essentially the same response to *New York Times* correspondent James Reston.]

Mr. James Reston came in for general background discussion.

He asked if we had made up our minds as to the partitioning of Germany. I said that that was something under discussion and study and I could see nothing gained by discussing this matter in the American press.

He then asked about the new ambassadors to be sent to exiled governments. I told him that matter was "moving along," but that there was nothing I could say on the subject at this time.

Mr. Reston then said that lately he seemed to be getting very little satisfaction from me, or any help or guidance. I told him frankly that I felt he was misusing his past friendship with me to obtain inside information pertaining to the State Department, and that it was totally impossible for me to discuss any subjects on this basis. I told him that if he intended to use our friendship for "exclusives," or if he were to write on anything like that, I was the last person to come to. I told him I was his friend, but was not going to give inside information to him because of it.

He left with a smile, saying, "OK, I'll have to operate on my own and give up hope of getting any guidance from the State Department." [14]

I said, "Scotty, you might as well give up the idea of getting 'exclusives.' "

[Three days later, however, Stettinius was much more open with the columnist Walter Lippmann, revealing to him a considerable amount of detail about the forthcoming conference and the State Department's proposals for an international organization.]

TRANSCRIPT OF TELEPHONE
CONVERSATION | *July 31, 1944*
Mr. Stettinius: I promised to call you. Walter, if you have time this afternoon or tomorrow to drop by, I think it might be helpful.
Mr. Lippmann: I can do it this afternoon. I am leaving tomorrow morning.
Mr. Stettinius: Why not blow in this afternoon and we will have a little talk.
Mr. Lippmann: What time?
Mr. Stettinius: Any time you come I will come out. I am loaded to the hilt. What time can you come?
Mr. Lippmann: If you are very rushed, don't bother. It would

not be worthwhile. I don't want to take your time. I realize how awfully pressed you must be.

Mr. Stettinius: I would like to see you and I think there may be a few little things that we could throw out that would be helpful.

Mr. Lippmann: Let's let it go until I get back.

Mr. Stettinius: O.K. Of course, we will be pretty well through things then. Unless you would like to talk on the phone a few minutes now and give [get?] a few ideas of how we will approach the matter.

Mr. Lippmann: All right.

Mr. Stettinius: One. We are going to meet and start these conferences in about two weeks time. The definite dates will not be announced for another two or three days. Cadogan will head the British delegation with about eight or ten of their specialists. The Chinese will send a group of four or five and the Russians will send a similar group. The British, the Russians, and ourselves will all meet together and then when we finish that, we and the British will meet with the Chinese. That last item of the Russians not meeting with the Chinese has to be kept awfully cozy for a little while.

Mr. Lippmann: That has been printed.

Mr. Stettinius: Only in a speculative way.

Mr. Lippmann: Yes. Not officially.

Mr. Stettinius: The Chinese are still a little upset about it. We approach the thing in an informal exploratory way—the British, Russians, and ourselves—bringing our researches to the table for general discussion to see if we can get a meeting of the minds on a general international plan for security. We think that will take about two or three weeks. I am heading the American delegation with a group of 17 experts to draw on including Army and Navy and political people. We are very well prepared with definite ideas as to a plan. We don't however know as to how they will differ from the ideas of the Russians and the British. The general framework of our business you already know—about having the Executive Council with a chairman, a General Assembly with a president, and a director general over the whole thing. The Executive Council would meet constantly and the Assembly would meet for about a month a year in some given permanent location. There is provision for an International Court; it provides for the Executive Council to use the armed forces of any participating country but no international police force. The decision of the Executive Council will really be supreme in all matters of security. The matter of security will not be referred to the Assembly.

Mr. Lippmann: What kind of agreement? Is it an agreement to agree?

Mr. Stettinius: When he joins he agrees to agree.

Mr. Lippmann: There is no commitment to act by majority vote? In other words, each state has to agree at this time that it will be willing to use force before force can be used. Then what about the enforcement of the German treaty? Is that separate from this?

Mr. Stettinius: The German surrender terms?

Mr. Lippmann: The enforcement of it.

Mr. Stettinius: That would all come within this machinery. Of course, we have the surrender terms that the Russians and the British and ourselves will agree to very well thought out.

Mr. Lippmann: Yes, but how does the machinery of enforcing the terms get moving? Does the council have to agree that it is necessary to use force in Germany or do the signatories of the German treaty do that?

Mr. Stettinius: The signatories of the German treaty. The provision for the enforcement of the German treaty is a separate document.

Mr. Lippmann: That's very crucial.

Mr. Stettinius: It is set up so we can jump in either direction. We have a satisfactory arrangement with the Russians and the British to take care of Germany for a generation which would be satisfactory to the American people. That's crystal clear.

Mr. Lippmann: What has been worrying me is whether the two things would come up for ratification in one document.

Mr. Stettinius: No. They won't.

Mr. Lippmann: That's a crucial point in my mind. If we make that point, we probably are sure of ourselves.

Mr. Stettinius: As far as keeping Germany unarmed and demobilized, that is taken care of in the surrender terms in which the Russians, British, and ourselves are involved only.

Mr. Lippmann: The French and Poles will not be brought into that?

Mr. Stettinius: Not at this moment.

Mr. Lippmann: They will have to help do that.

Mr. Stettinius: We are in touch with them but it has taken us five months to get the other two to agree.

Mr. Lippmann: The point where [Woodrow] Wilson went wrong was in not separating those two things.

Mr. Stettinius: I think we are on safe ground.

Mr. Lippmann: I am glad to hear that. I was worried, especially after reading Sumner's book.[15]

Mr. Stettinius: Of course, Sumner used some of the State Department stuff but he went off on his own in a lot of ways that did not represent the official thinking here. As a matter of fact, most of this has been developed within the last six months and Sumner has been gone a year. The surrender term business has really been done since I was in London. That whole thing has crystallized since April. What else comes to your mind?

Mr. Lippmann: That's the point I am most concerned about. The rest—the mechanics—seem to me interesting but not vital.

Mr. Stettinius: It is the substance that you are concerned with.

Mr. Lippmann: And particularly the enforcement of the two treaties—Japan and Germany.

Mr. Stettinius: Let me assure you again that the surrender terms they sign and we sign with them take care of that and if the enforcement was transferred to the international body and that was not acceptable, we would not have to agree to it. We will watch that every turn of the road and the mistake that was made the last time.

Mr. Lippmann: That's very interesting.

[As Stettinius's conversation with Lippmann makes clear, State Department planning for the upcoming conference on international organization was well advanced by the end of July. The remaining three weeks before the Dumbarton Oaks conference opened were spent in intensive final preparations for the meeting that would lay the foundation of the United Nations and would provide for Stettinius the sternest test he had yet faced in his new career in diplomacy.]

IV

THE DUMBARTON OAKS
CONFERENCE
August–October 1944

On August 21, 1944, thirty-nine delegates from the United States, Great Britain, and the Soviet Union assembled at Dumbarton Oaks, the magnificent Georgetown estate formerly owned by career diplomat Robert Woods Bliss, to begin the arduous task of framing a new international organization. In deference to Russia's sensitivity to its neutrality in the war against Japan, it had been agreed that the conference would meet in two separate stages—the United States, Britain, and the Soviet Union participating in the first and China replacing the USSR in the second. Stettinius headed the American delegation, his friend Sir Alexander Cadogan the British, and the youthful, newly appointed ambassador to the United States, Andrei Gromyko, the Russian.[1]

Much preparation had been done before the Dumbarton Oaks meeting opened. In December 1943, a special State Department committee had submitted an outline for an international organization, and its ideas were subsequently refined in numerous meetings within the department. The United States's proposals, which were completed by the early summer of 1944, borrowed features from the defunct League of Nations but also sought to correct some of the flaws that were felt to have caused the ultimate failure of the league. American plans stressed the importance of providing the organization with powers adequate to its responsibilities, and assigned to the Great Powers a central role in preserving the peace. Like the League of Nations, the new structure would be composed of an assembly of all "peace-loving" nations and an executive council. But the assembly would be little more than a deliberative body that would debate problems and make recommendations, while much greater power was lodged in the executive council, on which the four major powers would hold permanent seats and which would have primary responsibility for peacekeeping. American planners disagreed among themselves on the procedures under which the council would operate, but initial drafts upheld the principle of Great Power unanimity by assigning to the permanent members an absolute veto. The United States also envisioned an active and positive role for the new organization, creating economic and social agencies to deal with the root problems of war and to promote international cooperation and broadening the powers of the world court so that it could function more effectively.[2]

The State Department submitted its "Tentative Proposals for a General Organization" to the British, Russians, and Chinese in mid-July. They responded with their own proposals which followed the American outline in most particulars but differed on a number of significant points. The Russians felt that the organization should not dissipate its energies and resources on social and economic activities but should concentrate exclusively on security. They also proposed the establishment of an international air force, under the authority of the council, which could act swiftly to deal with breaches of the peace.[3]

A more important difference loomed over the veto in the executive council. Recalling the internal divisions that had wracked the League and undoubtedly concerned about preventing action against themselves, the Russians insisted that the permanent members of the council must have an all-inclusive veto. The British argued that such power would emasculate the council, however, and proposed that it be qualified by preventing a member of the council from voting in a dispute to which it was a party. American planners were divided. The State Department had initially supported a position close to that of the Russians, but just two days before the conference opened Secretary Hull had decided that the British argument was fair and sensible and had committed the United States to it. The issue was of the greatest significance, since its outcome would determine the manner in which the council functioned and the extent to which it would be controlled by the great powers. Even before the conference opened, the lines were drawn on this most difficult problem.[4]

The conference opened with formal ceremonies in the spacious music room of the Dumbarton Oaks mansion on the morning of August 21. Secretary Hull presided over the opening session, and in brief speeches, he, Cadogan, and Gromyko all stressed the significance of the work being undertaken. The three men agreed that the new organization must be established quickly, that it must be given sufficient authority to preserve the peace, and that its charter should respect the rights of all nations. As Stettinius noted in his diary, however, there were important differences of emphasis. "Mr. Hull especially stressed the necessity of justice to all nations while Ambassador Gromyko placed especial emphasis on the greater responsibility of the Great Powers in maintaining peace and security. Sir Alexander's remarks followed a middle course between the views just mentioned."[5]

The delegates then quickly settled down to their task. Stettinius was elected permanent chairman of the conference on a motion offered by Cadogan and seconded by Gromyko. The United States had originally planned that most of the work should be done in meetings of the full delegations, but Gromyko preferred smaller, more intimate sessions, and the Americans and British deferred to his wishes. As a consequence, most of the top-level negotiations were conducted in a

Joint Steering Committee, composed of the heads of delegation and their most important advisers. The Joint Steering
Committee created four subcommittees to consider general
principles related to the various spheres of international organization and two formulation groups to draft specific proposals from the agreements reached in the subcommittees.
Within the American delegation itself, the major decisions
were reached in a committee made up of Stettinius; James C.
Dunn, chief of the Office of European Affairs; Edwin C. Wilson, director of the Office of Special Political Affairs; Leo Pasvolsky and Green Hackworth, special advisers to the secretary
of state; and Admiral Russell Willson and General George
Strong representing the Joint Chiefs of Staff.

> [Before the conferees could get down to serious delibera-
> tions, they were diverted by a clash with the American
> press. The State Department had decided that the dele-
> gates could not function under the glare of publicity, and
> after permitting reporters and newsreel photographers to
> attend the opening session, it had placed a tight security
> clamp around the estate, allowing only accredited diplo-
> mats to enter. The cries of outrage began immediately
> and from this point on, Stettinius noted, the State De-
> partment was "plagued" by complaints from the press.[6]
>
> The protests grew louder on August 23, when James
> Reston of the *New York Times* revealed from "unim-
> peachable sources" the details of the proposals brought to
> Dumbarton Oaks by the three delegations.[7] Editors and
> reporters from papers across the country denounced their
> exclusion from the conference and demanded information
> about the proceedings.
>
> Stettinius took up the problem with his press aide,
> Michael McDermott, on August 23.]

DIARY | *August 23, 1944*

I then called Mac to tell him that both Gromyko and Cadogan were complaining about the press leaks. Mac said that as a result of the Reston article all of the other correspondents were catching hell from their editors and were absolutely on the warpath and that he did not feel they would be satisfied unless they could be told officially of the substance of the plans of the three governments. Mac said the correspondents wished to form a protest committee of from five to

Courtesy The Washington (D.C.) Star-News

seven people to call on the three chairmen to present their views. I told Mac I would arrange a meeting of the three chairmen with the press representatives of the three groups at 2:45 for a thorough discussion of our press policy.

* * *

[After discussing the matter with Gromyko, Cadogan, and with President Roosevelt, Stettinius again talked with McDermott.]

After meeting with the president, I immediately called McDermott and told him that we should issue releases as promptly as possible. We first planned to do it that evening, probably from my apartment, but as we were unable to get Gromyko, in fact he did not call me until 11 that night, it was decided that we would postpone it until the following morning and issue it at 10:15. Gromyko's position on this matter was in favor of a very short statement. Cadogan took the position that a statement should be added indicating that the press could not expect texts at the close of the meetings as we would be obligated to submit the final conclusions to our governments and to the other United Nations before making them public.

[At 10:15 the following morning, Stettinius, Cadogan, and Gromyko met with the protest committee established by the angry journalists.]

DIARY | *August 24, 1944*
The committee handed us a statement urging a change in our press policy and . . . charging us with secrecy, referring to the article (in the *New York Times*) summarizing the three plans and quoting from the British plan and pointing out that this policy would result in a "vacuum of ignorance" which would lead to bad guesses and half-truths of rumor. The state-

ment urged the day-to-day release of substantive information.

We replied by a statement stressing the informal and exploratory nature of the conversations. The British denied the [*New York*] *Herald-Tribune* story [alleging that Cadogan had been willing to release information but the United States had refused]. We promised to give serious consideration to the points made by the correspondents.

The meeting did little to correct the fundamental problem as nothing but a complete reversal of our press policy would have satisfied the correspondents. It did some little good, however, in that the correspondents could tell their editors that their committee had met with the chairmen of the three groups.

[Whatever good it might have done, the meeting did not placate the press. Reston continued to print authoritative reports and other newspapers continued to fume.

Later that afternoon, the undersecretary met with the president to review the U.S. plans for international organization. Roosevelt expressed a particular interest in the name that should be given to the new body and to the location of its various organs.]

It developed that the president favors the name "The United Nations" and that he feels strongly that Geneva should not be the headquarters. He expressed the opinion that the permanent secretariat would require some fixed seat but that the council and the assembly could hold its sessions at different places, pointing to the experience of Pan-American conferences in this regard. He mentioned the Azores and Hawaii as possible places of meeting where ideal climates could be found. He referred to the Pentagon and Empire State buildings as places where the permanent secretariat could be housed and did not seem to feel there would be too much difficulty in holding meetings in different places with the secretariat not located in the same city. He made inquiry as to the ownership of the World Court Building at the Hague, which we were unable to answer specifically, but we could tell him that it had proved to be adequate. The president expressed the opinion that the history of the court was good. Opinion toward it was favorable and he felt that continued association of the court with the Hague would be desirable.

[The Joint Steering Committee held its first meeting on Friday, August 25, and after a brief, exploratory session, many of the delegates adjourned for a weekend of sightseeing and entertainment in New York City. They were escorted through Rockefeller Center, viewed the floor show at Billy Rose's Diamond Horseshoe, attended the current Broadway hit *Oklahoma*, and toured New York harbor aboard the yacht of the commanding general of the Port of Embarkation. "It was very evident from the spontaneous reaction of all the delegates on their return," Stettinius noted, "that the trip had been an impressive exposé of the best New York had to offer in the way of entertainment and sightseeing; it did much to bring about a spirit of camaraderie which contributed in no small measure to the informal atmosphere that subsequently characterized the Dumbarton talks." [8]

The conference resumed on Monday morning, and at a Joint Steering Committee meeting the diplomats confronted for the first time the issues that would cause the most serious difficulties. Gromyko raised one of them when he proposed that each of the sixteen Soviet republics be given a vote in the assembly. The Russians had brought this up before, in February 1944, but had not mentioned it since, and Gromyko's initiative caught Stettinius and Cadogan by surprise.]

DIARY | *August 28, 1944*

The Joint Steering Committee met in my office in the downstairs library at 11:00. This was the meeting at which our Soviet friends dropped the bombshell in the form of bringing up the famous X-matter, during a discussion of the initial membership of the organization. Sir Alexander said he had no comment to make on the matter but he thought this was a subject which his government would have to talk about with the Soviet government generally. We indicated that we would have to think about the ambassador's statement. This was to become rather an explosive subject for the balance of the conversations and we made every effort to keep the matter secret, only two or three of our group knowing of it. We always referred to it as the X-matter and kept it out of the regular minutes which were circulated, keeping a special file of a secondary set of minutes with references to it carefully guarded in my safe. Outside of this matter, there seemed to be general agreement without thought that the initial membership should consist of the united and associated nations.[9]

[Later in the same meeting, discussion turned to the composition of the Executive Council and the voting procedure it would follow. When Stettinius set forth the United States's position Gromyko immediately objected.]

I indicated that at some later stage of the conversations we might wish to propose [increasing] the number of permanent members of the council to provide for some Latin American countries such as Brazil. Sir Alexander said he would inform his government of this but doubted if they had contemplated the possibility of such a proposal and said he felt if the permanent members were increased beyond five, there would be considerable confusion. It was obvious the Soviets also felt there should be only five permanent seats.

There seemed to be general agreement that a permanent seat should be reserved for France regardless of whether they had a formally recognized government by the time the organization is established.

There appeared to be general agreement for six nonpermanent members of the council. . . .

We reported that we had reached the conclusion a state involved in a dispute should not vote on matters affecting that dispute and carefully explained our reason. We were supported strongly at all points in the discussion by the British. The Soviets, however, said they considered this to be in violation of and a retreat from the principle that major decisions of the organization should be reached on the basis of unanimity among the Great Powers. They held to the provision in our original document which stated a special procedure should be worked out and suggested that a specific Soviet proposal on this might be made later.

[At five o'clock that afternoon, Stettinius went to the White House for a conference with the president. Roosevelt once again expressed an especial interest in the location of the organization, and he was particularly disturbed by the Soviet request for sixteen votes in the assembly.]

The president was alone and in a relaxed mood. I told him I could cover my business in five minutes but he raised various questions and I stayed with him from 5:02 until 5:20. I first presented him with our summary memos covering the proceedings for the fifth and sixth days. He glanced over these and seemed satisfied and said he would read them carefully tonight. He made the observation that these were an excellent record for him to have covering the conversations for the future. He asked me what open items were of the most importance. . . . I mentioned:

(1) The status of France and told him of the private indication I had that Sir Alexander might request at an early date that France be given a seat immediately. The president said he could not agree to this but was perfectly willing to have a seat reserved for France on an "if and when" basis that France had a government justifying it, and if and when the council duly elected France to take her place at the table on a permanent basis. He expressed the hope that I could work out some general language on this which would leave the matter flexible.

(2) Brazil. I reported to the president that we had raised the question of a permanent seat for Brazil this morning and both the British and Soviets had been negative. I expressed the opinion that if he wishes us to press this hard now it would be more difficult. The president considered this carefully and finally said personally he would be willing on the initial draft not to name Brazil but that he wished a general provision incorporated in the proposals which would leave the door open so that he, possibly working with the prime minister and Stalin at a later time, could bring this up with them before the organization was actually launched.

(3) X-matter. I then informed the president . . . of the X-matter. The president said, "my God," and went on to instruct me to explain to Gromyko privately and personally and immediately that we could never accept this proposal. He said to tell the ambassador this might ruin the chance of getting an international organization approved by the United States Senate and accepted publicly in this country. He then drew a comparison between the organization in this country and the Soviet Union and the British Empire and the possibility of creating new dominions in the empire out of colonies, islands,

etc., and that I should spell all of this out for Gromyko. I promised to do so immediately and added that at a later date we might ask him to communicate with Stalin.

(4) Votes of members involved in a dispute. I explained again our position that members of the council who are parties to a dispute should not be allowed to vote on matters affecting that dispute and that the British stated this view but the Soviets feel it violates the principle of unanimity of the Big Four. The president reiterated he felt our position was entirely correct and that we must not depart from it. He asked me to explain to Gromyko that this was a matter on which we would have to be consistent and that we hoped his government would find it possible to agree with us.

* * *

I then told the president we were still under fire by the press on the question of secrecy. He said he had not heard anything about it around the White House but I told him the criticism was not only in the press but in publications such as the Kiplinger and Whaley Eaton letters,[10] and that even Senators Connally and George [11] had made critical remarks. I told him that we would have to do something about it and that the three chairmen were planning to meet the press tomorrow morning. He thought this was satisfactory. He referred to the secrecy surrounding the Constitutional Convention and I told him we were considering making a release referring to that and other instances of this type.

* * *

The president then inquired whether we had discussed location. I told him only privately to date in informal discussions. He said he had been thinking more about this and continued to hope we would agree on the assembly meeting in different places from "hemisphere to hemisphere. . . ."

At this point I expressed the view it would be a mistake to separate the secretariat from the permanent headquarters of the council. . . . I also said we were afraid his suggestion of having the secretariat located in America would not be acceptable to the other nations. At this point I spoke in favor of Geneva. . . . The president said he would not object to the permanent secretariat being located there but that he would object strongly to the assembly or the council having official meetings there.

[The following morning, August 29, Stettinius, Cadogan, and Gromyko held a press conference, the purpose of which, as Sir Alexander put it, was to "tell the press that we weren't going to tell them anything." [12] Shortly afterward, Stettinius met privately with Gromyko to discuss several of the most difficult issues facing the delegations.]

DIARY | *August 29, 1944*
The ambassador stated he was concerned and wished to discuss several points with me. The question of the two-thirds vote,[13] the ambassador said, he and his colleagues in Moscow had been greatly pleased with the proposal in the American document with a simple majority vote and that he was now very discouraged over the fact that we had retreated . . . to a two-thirds majority. He was afraid this would cause great difficulty with his government and hoped we could reconsider our position. I assured the ambassador we would give the matter further study. He then talked about the voting issue when big powers were involved in a dispute, and stated that . . . the unanimity of the four powers must be preserved and he hoped it would be possible for us to reconsider our position on this matter. I explained . . . this was a question to which we had given great study . . . and that only last night the presi-

dent had asked me to explain to him that it would cause great difficulty in presenting the plan to the American public if it provided that a party involved in a dispute could vote on its own case. The ambassador then replied that it was clear this would be a point of actual disagreement but that perhaps we could find some general language to cover it so that it could be dealt with at a later date and that a definite position would not have to be arrived at during these conversations. . . .

The ambassador then said he had two other points. . . . The first was the matter of the international air force. . . . He said that they visualized each of the four powers placing at the disposal of the council airplanes and forces which could be used very promptly without the delay of many days which the procurement of authorization from a government would cause. . . . I told him that on the question of the authority of the council to utilize these forces on a moment's notice we would have to study further because by the terms of our Constitution, Senate relations are involved in that position. He replied he understood that and knew we were studying the entire matter.

The ambassador then stated he was impressed by our arguments relative to an economic and social council and would be available to discuss it in more detail at any time at my convenience. At the close of the conversation, I told the ambassador I had discussed his statement on .the X-matter both with the president and secretary. I told him . . . that pressing the point at this time might jeopardize the success of the conversations. I said it . . . should more properly be presented to the international organization in due course after its creation. The ambassador was most cooperative and indicated that he . . . would agree in the present meetings at Dumbarton Oaks there should be no further reference whatsoever to the subject. . . .

[Despite their differences on important problems, the heads of the three delegations remained optimistic about an early completion of the talks. After the conclusion of the Joint Steering Committee, Stettinius, Cadogan, and Gromyko talked over tea in the garden and agreed that they might complete their discussions by the middle of next week.]

Gromyko then stated the only points he could see that were really open and might cause difficulty were the question of the two-thirds vote; the question of voting when a big power was involved in a dispute; the international air force; the economic and social council; and the military committee.[14] He admitted that he had heard from home on all these points but said it was taking him about three days to get an exchange of views between Washington and Moscow.

Cadogan and I both talked very frankly with the ambassador on the question of a country voting when it was involved in a dispute. Among other things we stressed that such a procedure would be entirely unacceptable to the small nations. The ambassador refused to recognize the validity of that point or of our other arguments.

*   *   *

[Gromyko had helped to smooth the course of the proceedings by agreeing not to raise the X-matter—the request for sixteen votes in the assembly—again at Dumbarton Oaks. Roosevelt was still most perturbed by the request, however, and asked Stettinius to draft a personal message for him to send to Stalin urging him not to press it further. The undersecretary gave the draft to the president on August 31, and discussed this and other related matters with him.]

DIARY | *August 31, 1944*

I then presented to the president the proposed wire for him to send to Marshal Stalin on the X-matter. The president seemed very pleased with the message and signed it while I was there. He added one sentence, "This would not prejudice later discussion of the question after the organization has been formed and the assembly would have full authority to deal with the question at that time." [15]

I handed the president the memorandum on Brazil. . . . The president read this very carefully and I had quite a struggle with him. . . . At first he was not impressed but finally swung around and said it would be satisfactory . . . that we not press at this time for a permanent seat for Brazil.

I then presented to him the memorandum on France, recommending in effect that a seat be reserved for France which she could take on a permanent basis at the appropriate time. He immediately approved this procedure but stated that he wanted it to be thoroughly understood that any one of the Big Four would have a veto power in the matter. . . .

As the president is leaving tonight and will not be back until Tuesday I will not see him for further reports until next Tuesday or Wednesday. He said, "I hope by that time you will have a draft."

[Optimism about early completion of the talks turned out to be premature. Little progress was made during the remainder of the week, and at the Joint Steering Committee meeting the following Monday, Stettinius began to see that some of the major issues could not be easily resolved.]

DIARY | *September 4, 1944*

The Joint Steering Committe met in my office at 11:30. Generally the progress was much less satisfactory than we had made at previous meetings. Ambassador Gromyko was much more insistent than he had previously been in preserving intact the exact language contained in the Soviet document even though his representative in the formulation group had previously agreed on modifications.[16]

* * *

I again emphasized the great importance which we attach to the proposal that a party to a dispute should not vote in connection therewith, pointing out that if agreement could not be reached on this vital question the whole project might be endangered. Sir Alexander strongly supported this position. Ambassador Gromyko, while he agreed on its importance, added in a rather unyielding manner that he had no other proposal to make on it.

[In a private conversation later that day, Stettinius and Cadogan agreed upon a strategy to try to break the deadlock. The British and Americans would make concessions on major problems, and, as Cadogan put it, "we can then say to Gromyko, 'Where are yours?' "] [17]

After Gromyko left, I talked further with Cadogan and he told me that he was now prepared to yield on three or four points which the British had been pressing for and asked my advice as to whether we ought to start doing this tomorrow. I told him that it was psychologically important for him to do this. . . . Cadogan said he had inquired from his government as to whether the Economic and Social Council should be in or out of the general organization. I expressed the hope that they would not back away from us on this important matter. Cadogan thought there might be difficulty on the international air force. . . . He said he was ready to agree on the language of the expulsion provision [18] and that he would also agree on a majority vote rather than a two-thirds vote in the Security Council. But he continued to place great emphasis on the need for agreement that a country involved in a dispute should not vote.

[Before the strategy could be put into effect, Leo Pasvolsky advised the American steering committee that the Russians had set forth another disturbing proposal.]

DIARY | *September 5, 1944*
Mr. Pasvolsky then raised for discussion a knotty question which had been put forward by the Russians. They desire to have a provision stating in substance that if a nation did not possess sufficient armed forces to carry out the action recommended by the council they could be called upon to furnish bases or facilities under the control of the council or of one of the members of the council. This proved to be a very difficult point in our negotiations with the Russians. We were against it from the start as their proposal seemed to include the transfer of sovereignty over such bases, and it was a proposition which would never be accepted by small states. It would also be in the form of an obligation to furnish such bases. Most of the members of the group seemed to feel the Russians are putting this forward with the idea in mind of getting bases for their use in neighboring countries, such as Finland or Korea. Admiral Willson [19] and I pointed out that the question of bases was being emphasized in view of the fact that by far the greater portion of these that would be needed would be in existence at the end of this war. Our group seemed to feel that some formula by which bases were leased rather than turned over outright might offer a channel of solution. Several alternative solutions were brought forward by different members of the group for discussion. . . .

[Despite this troublesome new matter, Gromyko, at a luncheon later that day, privately indicated that he was prepared to make concessions.]

Gromyko entertained the top members of the three delegations at lunch at the Soviet Embassy this noon. Messrs. Dunn, Pasvolsky, and I attended from our group. Gromyko told me at luncheon that he felt the time had arrived when . . . each of us would have to concede on some points. He told me in a low voice, "I am ready to start to concede but I want you to know that we attach big importance to the voting procedure both on the matter of majority and the matter of dispute." I replied that the question of voting when involved in a dispute was the aspect of the question that disturbed us most. The ambassador concluded by saying, "I will be ready tomorrow to start getting down to cases."

[Stettinius hurried from the luncheon back to the State Department for a press conference. The insistent demands of newspapermen for more information had forced him to agree to hold the conference, and it turned out to be an unnerving experience for him.]

I met with the press at 2:30 and stayed with them for an hour and ten minutes. They asked me exhaustive and searching questions and it was a grueling experience. On several different questions they pinned me down and made me say more than I had wanted to tell them, but I do not think any great harm has been done. At the beginning, there was a little debate as to whether the conference should be "background" or "off the record." At the wish of the correspondents, it was made background, although I explained to them that I could not be as frank as I could by speaking off the record. They said if it was off the record they could never use what I might say even if they developed the information from other sources. They asked me direct questions, such as the composition of the council, the treatment of France, whether the plan when completed would be sent to Congress as a treaty. [John] Hightower [A.P. correspondent] in particular questioned me at great length on our schedule for the future and made quite a point about the necessity of allowing sufficient time for proper debate of the issues in this country. Hightower was apparently stressing this point as the secretary had said in his press conference earlier in the day that he hoped a United Nations conference could be held in the autumn and Hightower did not believe that schedule would provide sufficient time for a public debate. Reston in particular stressed the question of congressional approval. I left the conference feeling none too comfortable about things, but no real damage had been done.

[Just when it appeared that Gromyko was willing to clear up some of the major outstanding issues, the British began to offer resistance. Cadogan's request to give way on a number of matters had been only partially approved by the Foreign Office, and Prime Minister Churchill, who had just looked over the Dumbarton Oaks papers for the first time, appeared to be quite enthusiastic about the Russian proposal for an international air force. Stettinius and Cadogan discussed these new developments at an afternoon conference on September 6.]

DIARY | *September 6, 1944*
I had a long conversation with Sir Alexander at three o'clock this afternoon. He had received a cable from London which had just been decoded and he was quite disturbed because it didn't free his hand to any great extent. However, he felt he would have enough to make a meeting of the Steering

Committee worthwhile and I called one for ten o'clock the following morning. He stated that Churchill was now on his way to the meeting [with Roosevelt at Quebec] [20] and that as he did not arrive in Canada until the following Monday he might not hear on the international air force question until the middle of next week. I commented that a delay of this type would not fit in very well with his plan of going home next week. I asked him if he must delay what he would think of recessing the Soviet phase and dealing with the Chinese. He did not respond very enthusiastically to this suggestion saying that he didn't think Eden would particularly like it but if we wanted to do it he would go along. He said his instructions were to stand pat on the voting question when a great power is involved in a dispute. He said that while his instructions were not too specific he thought he had enough authority to go back from a two-thirds to a simple majority on council voting if it was necessary to do so. He said he could definitely clear the brackets from the suspension and expulsion clauses and let the Soviet proposals on these matters stand. Also I was encouraged when he said that he had definite instructions to support our position that the Economic and Social Council should be made part of the framework of the general organization. . . .

He also said that Eden was thinking along the line of it being desirable to hold a meeting of foreign ministers to settle the voting procedure question if it could not be handled at Dumbarton Oaks. . . .

[Later that afternoon, Stettinius and Hull went to the White House to consult with the president before his departure for Quebec.]

* * *

I . . . took up . . . the question of an international air force. We had some little difficulty in explaining this so that the president completely understood it. But after we had stressed that he had already gone on record against an international police force and recommended to him that we stick to our guns on this question, he finally agreed. . . .

* * *

I then presented the memorandum on bases. . . . At first I could not get the settled interest of either [FDR or Hull] on this question but when I explained it was a matter of the council being given authority to demand territory or bases they both had violent objections, feeling this whole performance should be voluntary and that it would be a great mistake at this time to place any compulsion on a small nation to furnish a base or facilities. . . .

We then reviewed the question of the next step. I said we hoped to finish within two weeks and that we felt the demand in this country from the public for the plan . . . and the demand from the smaller nations to get it would be so great that it would be most embarrassing not to send out the memorandum to the United Nations just as promptly as possible and that it would be ideal if we could . . . send it to the other governments the latter part of September, simultaneously inviting them to attend a United Nations full dress conference in the interior of the United States in the latter part of October. I said we had been thinking of French Lick, Indiana. At first the president thought this would be too early but then after he had grasped the idea of having it in the interior, isolationist part of the United States he said it was a magnificent idea. . . . The president then talked on the political aspects of the matter, saying that he previously had in mind not having the conference until after the election. He and the secretary talked in some detail as to the effect of holding it before the election. The secretary made a strong plea that we had a sound plan and that we should do the courageous thing by presenting it to the world and having the president and this administration identify themselves immediately with it. At first the president argued against it, feeling that many of the isolationist senators would come out against certain features of the plan and would commit themselves in the campaign and then would not be free to change their opinion in January when the matter came up to vote. He said that after all two-thirds of the senators were carried over and only one-third changed. Finally, the president swung around. He mentioned the decision he had made in the 1940 campaign on the draft despite Jim Farley's [21] argument that it was not an expedient thing to do but that he had done it the courageous way and it had worked well. He agreed on an immediate presentation to the United Nations and to aim for October 25th at French Lick.

* * *

Before I joined the president I told the secretary very frankly that it seemed to me that prompt action was advisable if the administration should be changed. Otherwise there would be the possibility of the president and the secretary not getting appropriate credit for what they had done in this field. In discussing this with the president I did not talk as frankly but I think he understood the point. I expressed to him . . . that no one could forecast the turn of events and it was important for both him and the secretary, particularly for him personally, and important historically for us to move rapidly in this field and not leave the matter for the future.

* * *

We then discussed the question of voting in the council and I explained that they had both instructed . . . that a two-thirds vote was preferable. I reported that the Russians were insisting on a majority and that this was another matter on which we thought it might be wise to yield, particularly for trading purposes. . . . I received authorization along those lines.

I then raised the difficult question of voting on the part of a great power when it was involved in a dispute. Although this had been raised previously with the president on several occasions this time he seemed confused on the issue and both Mr. Hull and I had to explain the matter in some detail before it was clear to him. Mr. Hull said that the Russians would be practically unanimously voted down on this issue at the United Nations conference and that in their own self-interest they should see that point now and agree to the other procedure (Mr. Hull, while driving to his apartment after leaving the White House, advised me to stress this point strongly when talking to Gromyko in the morning). I told the president this question might be the one big point on which we could not reach agreement at Dumbarton. The president then spoke up and said there might be a second—whether that might be the one of the use of force without the approval of our Senate. Mr. Hull and I both replied to this, saying we thought it was pretty well in hand and it was something he could follow through politically on a sound basis. The president indicated clearly that he realized that this question of the immediate use of force is a key point of the whole plan, saying that if we had to go to the Senate in each case as it arose, the plan would not be any good. Mr. Hull in explanation said that of course if the council used force and if the Senate later disapproved through failure to authorize appropriations, etc., we could always withdraw. This approach was new and apparently of interest to the president.[22]

I then said that Sir Alexander Cadogan had received instructions today that he could settle on a majority vote but that he must stand pat on the larger issue of a great power voting when involved in a dispute. I reported . . . that Eden felt the issue was of such prime importance, and that if it could not be settled at Dumbarton, consideration should be given to having it settled at a meeting of foreign ministers. The president and Mr. Hull felt that was unthinkable and that having foreign ministers devoting the two, three, or four weeks time, which would be necessary for that would be widely misunderstood. The president added that he saw no reason why this should not be left open for settlement at the United Nations conference. I explained that it was doubtful the Russians would agree to going into that conference with the point open; and also that as it would look as if we had not reached agreement on such a big point it might arouse suspicions of the Soviet Union on the part of smaller nations and in that way perhaps jeopardize the possibility of success of the big conference, or of some of the smaller nations attending it. That did not impress the president or the secretary and it was left that if we could not agree we would attempt to find some very general language to hold the matter over for discussion at the later United Nations conference. Practically, this means that I am now instructed by the president and the secretary to stand firm against the Soviet position. I then reviewed generally the progress of the discussions. Both the president and Mr. Hull were amazed to find that the British were causing a delay, observing that that was usually done by the Russians. I told them this might be due to the fact that Eden had been sick and the prime minister had been out of the country.

* * *

I then raised with the president the importance of his having political advisers with him at meetings such as the forthcoming one at Quebec, in the event that political questions would be discussed. The president agreed that this was sound and important but said the forthcoming meeting would be of a military nature. He did, however, promise to send for Mr. Hull if the discussions took a political turn. I later asked Mr. Hull if he thought I had spoken out of turn and he said no, that it was wonderful.

*   *   *

During our conversation with the president he said that he hoped we would do everything within our power not to allow the X-issue to become public and he quizzed me in some detail on how we stood. I reviewed the matter with him, mentioning the cable to S[talin], etc.

[The Joint Steering Committee meeting, twice delayed because of Cadogan's lack of instructions, finally convened on September 7, but it got nowhere. The Russians agreed to drop their proposal for expulsion powers, but on other major issues—voting in the council, the economic and social organizations, bases, and the international air force—the three sides were still far apart. At lunch that day, the three men discussed their differences frankly.]

DIARY | *September 7, 1944*

We then had a long discussion on the general progress of the conversations viewed in the light of this morning's Joint Steering Committee meeting. Gromyko seemed discouraged. He told me privately that he was ready to act on all matters. He put it this way, "I am 99 percent sure I could clean up everything except the voting procedure and this is a serious matter to us." Cadogan and I both stressed to him that a document with this matter unsettled would be weak. . . . After some little talk, Gromyko seemingly came around to the position that it was necessary to settle the voting question at this time and not refer it to a general United Nations conference. I then asked whether he felt there was a possibility of agreement at this meeting on the Economic and Social Council and he replied that he felt it should be settled at Dumbarton.

[The talk with Gromyko confirmed what Stettinius had already suspected, that the voting question was the major roadblock to completing the conference. When he arrived home that evening he pondered how to break the impasse.]

After reaching my apartment late in the afternoon, I . . . came . . . to the conclusion that the voting question was the crux of the problem and that we . . . should call out our biggest and last remaining gun. . . . The success or failure of the conference depends upon this one point. I then telephoned Mr. Hull and . . . told him I had reached the conclusion that bold action was now in order. . . . I reviewed various possibilities . . . such as Hull phoning Molotov, the president sending a wire to Stalin, our requesting Harriman to see Molotov, or the president sending for Gromyko for a private talk. Mr. Hull immediately responded that he felt the most effective step would be to have the president see Gromyko, but warned that in presenting the matter to Gromyko, I should do it in a rather personal way, asking if he would be willing to discuss the matter with the president and not put it on the basis of the president sending for him.

* * *

[Stettinius subsequently arranged the appointment, and early the following morning he and Gromyko met with Roosevelt for a half hour in the president's bedroom.]

DIARY | *September 8, 1944*
. . . At the beginning the president warmed the atmosphere by telling Gromyko some of his plans for his trip to

Quebec to meet Churchill. In this connection, he spoke of the desirability of having another conference of the three chiefs of state as early as possible. The president also spoke briefly of the war, that our forces in the west as well as the Soviets in the east had gone beyond their respective supply lines and that this was a period of pause for consolidation on the part of both. The president told Gromyko how delighted he was with the way things have gone on both fronts. He then read to him a wire from General Pat Hurley [23] in which Hurley had said that Molotov had told him that the Soviets were not interested in the Chinese communists, that they were not really communists anyway. The president commented that they were agrarians.

. . . The president finally came around to Dumbarton Oaks and said that he understood there was only one fundamental point remaining open. Gromyko said that there were others and I then nailed him down on the others and it turned out that only the one point is really difficult. Gromyko indicated pretty clearly that he would be able to yield on everything else except the voting question, specifically mentioning that he could approve our economic and social council proposal. He also seemed perfectly open minded on the question of the international air force. . . . Gromyko told the president . . . that if we seriously objected to the term international air force, or the proposal as originally submitted by the Soviets, they would . . . drop it. I said I was confident we could write a provision in simple language which would accomplish the aim which all of us sought. . . .

The president then told Gromyko that we would be prepared to accept a majority rather than a two-thirds vote in the council if that would help him at home. He then went on into the major issue, opening this part of the discussion by saying that traditionally in this country, husbands and wives when in trouble never have the opportunity to vote on their own case, although they always have an opportunity to state their case. The president told a beautiful story tracing the development of this American concept of fair play back to the days of our founding fathers. He then stressed the difficulty which we would have in our Senate with the Soviet proposal, saying at the same time that he felt the issue of the quick and immediate use of force could be met successfully in the Senate.

Gromyko did not seem at all depressed by what the president said. He accepted the remarks gracefully, asked a number of questions . . . and discussed the way in which he could explain our position clearly to his people at home.

At this point I asked him if it would be helpful to him if we sent a message on the matter to Marshal Stalin. . . . Gromyko said he would leave that to our judgment. I then handed to the president the draft cable which Chip Bohlen had prepared, which referred to the president's talk with the ambassador, outlined the difficulty we faced on the voting question, referred to the traditional American concept that parties to a dispute never vote on their own case, and we said that American public opinion would neither understand nor support a plan of international organization in which this principle was violated. It also indicated that we felt that other nations, particularly the smaller nations would feel as we did. It ended with an expression of hope that Stalin would be able to instruct his delegation to meet our point on this issue. The president thought the cable was excellent but wanted us to add a reference to his husband and wife simile which he had made earlier in the conversation, and stress more the probably adverse reaction . . . of the smaller nations and the difficulty we would have in getting their plan through our Senate. The president asked that the cable be redrafted to incorporate his suggestions and be sent to Miss [Grace] Tully [Roosevelt's secretary] for transmission. . . .[24]

* * *

The president said . . . that he wanted to have this whole matter finished up by the end of next week when he would be returning to Washington. He said, "I want at that time the document signed and a report from you that great success was achieved. This is an order to you." During this conversation, Gromyko squirmed a bit in his chair as I did in mine. . . .

> [Roosevelt's lecture evidently had some effect, for at a Joint Steering Committee meeting later that day agreement was reached on several outstanding issues. Gromyko accepted the American proposal for an Economic and Social Council; Stettinius and Cadogan agreed to reinstate the expulsion provision which the Russians had pressed for; and Stettinius indicated his government's willingness to accept a majority vote in the council. The conferees had made "excellent progress," Stettinius reported to Hull, and he felt "more encouraged" than at any previous time in the conference.[25]
>
> The committee reconvened at 3:00 P.M. and worked through until midnight, but this time the progress was negligible. The Russians and British took exception to a statement on human rights and freedoms drafted by the American delegation, there was disagreement over the name to be given the new organization, and some old and vital issues could not be resolved.]

* * *

No progress was made on the question of voting in the council. It was also not possible to reach final agreement on the issue of sites for bases and the international air force, although we continue to feel that it is quite unlikely that these issues will prevent final agreement. We also are hopeful that we can obtain acceptance of some provision providing for assistance to states carrying out measures decided upon by the council.

[On Sunday, September 10, Stettinius escorted the British and Chinese delegations on an all-day tour of northern Virginia. They motored down the Skyline Drive and then visited the University of Virginia in Charlottesville, where Stettinius, according to Cadogan, held forth "on the beauties of the scenery as if he not only owned it but had painted it." The delegates then toured Monticello, the home of Thomas Jefferson, and proceeded on to the homes of James Monroe and James Madison. They finished out the evening at Stettinius's home, Horseshoe, where they were served mint juleps and a ham and chicken dinner and serenaded by a black quartet. "What a day!" Cadogan exclaimed to his wife, "and what extraordinary people—quite charming and kind to an extraordinary degree, in some ways rather like ourselves but (as you can see) so utterly different." [26]

The conference resumed the following day, and in the initial sessions substantial progress was made. At the Joint Steering Committee meeting on Tuesday, Gromyko accepted the name "United Nations," and agreed to withdraw the Soviet proposals for an international air force and the assignment of bases to the international organization. At a meeting the next day, however, the Soviet ambassador brought the proceedings to a halt.]

DIARY | *September 13, 1944*
Towards the end of the meeting, Ambassador Gromyko said that he must inform us that on the basis of instructions he had received from his government his position on the question of voting in the council is unchanged. I attempted to ascertain if Gromyko felt these instructions were final and the ambas-

sador seemed to think that they were. In his discussion, he stressed that the British position, which we had been supporting, in the opinion of his government flatly violated the principle of unanimity, which, to them, is of highest importance. I replied at some length on the importance . . . of the position we had been advocating. . . . I went so far as to say that in view of the almost certain strong and vigorous objection to the Soviet position on the part of the smaller nations, that I could hardly see how we could expect to have a general conference if that position continued. Sir Alexander at that point stated that he did not believe a single one of the British dominions would join an organization if the Soviet principle were adopted, and seconded what I had said as to the smaller nations. . . . We all agreed to consider what should be done in the light of this development. . . .

This brings the whole conference to a climax. We are deadlocked . . . and the success of the whole undertaking lies in the balance on this one point.

* * *

[Stettinius instructed the American delegation to find a way out of the impasse, and late that afternoon they produced a compromise formula that would allow the great powers a veto in cases calling for enforcement action but not in matters pertaining to the pacific settlement of disputes. Gromyko and Cadogan agreed to refer the proposal to their governments, and Hull directed Stettinius to pass it on to the president at Quebec.

Before the compromise proposal could be studied, however, the undersecretary's hopes were further dampened by other developments. While talking to Harry Hopkins, he learned to his horror that before leaving for Quebec the president had received a cable from Stalin pertaining to Dumbarton Oaks. Roosevelt had not for-

warded the cable to the State Department. Hopkins was not familiar with its contents "but he did say that the president thought it said "No with a loud bang. . . .'"
Hopkins secured for Stettinius a copy of the cable, which was a response to Roosevelt's message of September 1 on the X-matter. The undersecretary immediately consulted Hull.]

I called on Mr. Hull at 3:30 to tell him about the contents of the message from Stalin, which was on the X-matter and which was discouraging. . . .[27] They are going to bring it up later, perhaps at the general conference. Mr. Hull was discouraged. . . . We agreed that if the Soviets continued to be sticky about questions such as the X-matter that it was going to be difficult to work things out.

* * *

Today was the low point of the conversations. . . . An impasse has been reached and we cannot tell whether we will be able to work out of it . . . or whether the conference will blow up. I am much encouraged by remarks made by old hands at international negotiations, such as Joe Grew and Ed Wilson,[28] who said there never has been a conference which did not look as if it had completely broken down at one stage or another.

[The next few days brought more discouraging news. On September 15, Stalin's response to the president's cable on voting procedure arrived in the White House map room. It offered little ground for optimism. The Soviet premier expressed hope that the conference could be "brought to a successful close," but emphasized that the voting issue was vital to the success of the international organization and that it was "essential that the council should base its work on the principle of agreement and unanimity between the four leading powers on all matters. . . ." The original American position was "sound." Any deviation from that would reduce to "nought" the principle of unanimity agreed upon at the Teheran conference.[29]

Before Stalin's cable could be fully studied, Stettinius and Hull were further disturbed to learn that Roosevelt and Churchill had rejected the compromise on voting prepared on September 13. On September 16, Stettinius called on Cadogan and the British ambassador, Lord Halifax, to consider the dilemma they faced and to search for a way out.]

DIARY | *September 16, 1944*
Lord Halifax then inquired what was going through my mind as to a possible solution. I told him . . . I was convinced we could not let this dream for a world organization collapse at this stage. I emphasized that their [the British] relations and our relations with the Soviet Union are too important from the standpoint of the prosecution of the war to allow a collapse to occur. I said we must find a way over this hurdle . . . and that I had been thinking this afternoon something along the following lines.

1. Commence conversations at Dumbarton with the Chinese on say, Tuesday and finish about Friday.
2. On Saturday disband and have a joint communiqué issued by the chairmen of all four delegations, stating they were returning home to report to their governments, that they had been able to agree on a wide range of subjects, but there were some subjects still open. I said we would publish what we had . . . and state that after our governments had had an

opportunity to study and review them they would agree on a time for another meeting to resume the discussions. . . .

* * *

Before leaving I made a very strong point that we must all realize that we were heading rapidly into the zero hour and that the demand from the American press would soon be too great to hold off and that every hour we delay we are toying with dynamite. . . .

[On the recommendation of Secretary Hull, Stettinius called another meeting of the heads of delegation to try to break the impasse. The results only reinforced the gloom in Washington.]

DIARY | *September 18, 1944*

As soon as I left the American meeting, I tried to get Gromyko and Cadogan, but could not reach Cadogan as he was down town shopping. He joined us for the last part of our meeting. In talking with Gromyko alone, I first emphasized to him, as the secretary had reasserted, the very serious consequences which he foresaw both for the creation of the international organization and for the Soviet Union itself which might result if the conversations were terminated without agreement on the voting procedure. I then asked him if he felt his government would be willing to consider a new formula on voting. He replied that the position of his government is final and would not be changed whether the conversations were prolonged for a week or a year. He emphasized that the Soviet government would never consider joining an organization in which a major power involved in the dispute did not have the right to vote on it. During the course of the conversation, he said that it was his personal view rather than the official view of his government that the Soviet government would never agree to attend a general United Nations conference until an agreement had been reached with the other Great Powers on the voting question. He promised to ascertain his government's official view on that point. He then asked me if I felt there was any possibility of the British changing their position on voting and I replied that my personal opinion was that there was no likelihood of such a change in the reasonably near future. I later repeated this conversation to Sir Alexander Cadogan. He said he felt his government also would not attend a general conference until the four powers participating at Dumbarton Oaks were in full agreement on all basic issues. He agreed to try out on his government, however, the idea of holding a general conference with the issue of voting open for consideration. . . .

* * *

I told Gromyko that we felt failure to reach agreement on voting would seriously jeopardize the acceptance of the plan by the American people and ratification of it by our Senate. In elaborating on the possible consequences to the Soviet Union, I told him that in our judgment if their position became known there would be a serious attack on them by the small nations over the world and also considerable anti-Soviet discussion in the American press. I told him in view of our happy relations with his government that we would like to see both avoided. Gromyko took the position that if there had to be a break among the Big Four on this issue they might as well have the break right now rather than at some later conference. The ambassador assured me that not only he but his government as well understood the serious implications of this situation and that the whole international organization was at stake. . . . He asked me if I was familiar with the message Stalin sent to the president and . . . he said that that was the final word and spoke for itself. . . . I inquired how long he thought it would take to hear from his government on the proposed procedure for winding up the talks and he thought certainly not before tomorrow and possibly not before Wednesday. . . . I sounded him out informally on whether he thought our foreign ministers or chiefs of state could find a way out and he received this suggestion rather negatively. He then said, "You can't have an international organization without us. We can't have one without you. And there has to be unanimity between us and the other powerful states. The moment this principle of unanimity breaks down there is war, and it seems to me in view of that realistic situation that all this discussion of one or another solutions to the voting question is purely 'academic.' "

[The talks with Gromyko and Cadogan produced near despondency in the American delegation. Military representatives feared that the collapse of the conference might jeopardize Soviet-American collaboration at a critical stage of the offensive in Europe. Others were certain that the inability to agree on voting procedure would convince the American people that Dumbarton Oaks had been a "complete failure." The political consequences on the eve of a national election were all too obvious, and it was also feared that public acceptance of the international organization might be doomed. Despite the general pessimism, Secretary Hull counseled the American delegation to be patient and optimistic.[30]

Meanwhile, a number of American delegates, spurred by Assistant Secretary of State Breckinridge Long and including the military representatives, had devised a plan to break the impasse. Sympathetic to the Russian position on voting and especially concerned with the possible consequences of a complete breakdown of the talks, their memorandum warned of "long and short-term adverse military consequences" if the conference collapsed. They advised a final effort to work out a compromise and if that failed to concede to the Soviet point of view.[31]

Over the next few days, American diplomats heatedly debated various compromise proposals. Hull, supported by Pasvolsky and other members of the delegation, angrily rebutted Long's contention that the United States had reversed its position on voting, arguing that it had never committed itself to the Russian view. More important, the secretary continued to hold a "firm and definite position that under no circumstances should a party involved in a dispute be allowed to vote on that dispute." That would "amount to one-man rule as one man could enforce his will . . . on the rest of the world."[32] The delegation was also split on the wisdom of making another appeal to Stalin, some fearing that it would be unwise to press him too hard and that it would be much preferable to recess and meet again in several months.

As the debate wore on, Stettinius began to grow more optimistic.]

DIARY | *September 19, 1944*
I have formed the impression that some of the American group have become panicky, if not hysterical, and have reached the stage where they are not thinking straight on the problem. Personally, I am not discouraged. While it looks as if we will not have a 100 percent victory, I think it will be at least 75 percent and there is no reason to think it is as bad as some of our people think.

[At a meeting later that day, Hull took the same line, again pleading for calmness and restraint.]

He first told of the interest to him in recently viewing the motion picture *Wilson* [33] in view of the remarkable similarity in conditions which then faced the leaders and those which are now facing us. He then spoke directly of the present conversations and stressed the need for patience and of taking a friendly attitude in dealing with our friends from the Soviet Union. He said that he had returned from Moscow [in November 1943] convinced that the Soviets had directed their course along the path of international cooperation and that he still felt that. He said that he felt all the Russians' interests would cause them to take that course as it would be only through international cooperation that she could advance her general economic interests, her industrial development, and her social welfare.

The secretary pleaded at some length for a patient attitude . . . and that the main job was to get an organization established even if it took time to do that. He referred to Senator Vandenberg's [34] statement to him that he could carry all but six Republicans with him in opposition to the use of force without specific congressional approval. He referred to other questions which would require patient handling, such as possible disappointment on the part of small states, particularly Latin American seats, under the proposed makeup of the Security Council. He referred to the Latin American nations who were associated but not united nations and of the disappointment they would feel if they were not invited to the general conference and were not initial members of the organization. They would feel that they had been put in the same class with Argentina. He referred to the fact that they might attribute the fact that they had not declared war to certain utterances of American officials. In closing, the secretary said that he had been well informed of the compromise formulae on voting and realized that it would possibly take time to work this out. He referred to his scheduled meeting within the next day or so with the president and said that any members of our group who wished to do so were welcome to present their particular views on this subject to the president. He stressed that everyone had full freedom of action in this respect.

[Perhaps inspired by Hull's statement, Stettinius now decided that the only feasible alternative was to end the work at Dumbarton Oaks "in some graceful way as promptly as possible," leaving the open questions for future negotiations. It was subsequently agreed that after the conference had been terminated, a document would be submitted to the other governments for approval and a communiqué would be published listing the items agreed upon and those left for later settlement.

The undersecretary was optimistic about this solution. He felt "more and more," as he advised the American delegation, "that failure to reach agreement on all points should not and would not be regarded as a body blow to our establishing an international organization, and that it would not be construed as defeat or failure." He was confident that adjournment would not threaten Soviet-American relations. "All indications during the conference had been to the contrary. Our relations had been good, a cordial feeling had prevailed, and I saw no cause for alarm." [35]

After some vigorous exchanges, Stettinius brought the members of the American delegation around to his point of view, and on the morning of September 21, President Roosevelt gave his endorsement.]

DIARY | *September 21, 1944*
The president immediately commented that he did not think there were serious domestic political implications in the matter. He said this was in reality a preliminary working

paper and that it was natural that it should take considerable time to work out such an important matter, and that it would naturally need to be reviewed in detail by the chiefs of the other major powers. He added that the whole subject was one to which Churchill had not yet given his attention and that he knew, from his recent conversations with him, that he would take some time to make up his mind on some of these issues. . . .

[In fact, there was a lull of six days while Cadogan and Gromyko waited for instructions. Finally, at 9 A.M. on September 27, the Soviet ambassador phoned Stettinius at home to advise him that a cable had been received from Moscow. "I said I hoped the news is good," Stettinius ventured, and Gromyko replied: "I always have good news. I am ready to have my final conversation." [36]

The Joint Steering Committee met for the last time at 10:30 that morning. Agreement was quickly reached on a number of procedural and substantive matters, but in closing Gromyko again went to great lengths to make clear the Soviet Union's firmness on the issues it considered of greatest importance.]

DIARY | *September 27, 1944*

I called the meeting to order shortly after 10:30 and immediately afforded Ambassador Gromyko the opportunity of reporting to us on the nature of his instructions.

He indicated that his government was generally agreeable to the publication of the full text as agreed upon at Dumbarton Oaks. He also said his government accepted the chapter on amendments which was accordingly inserted in the document. He then reported his government approved the insertion of the provision relating to the promotion of human rights and fundamental freedoms at the end of the first sentence in

Chapter 9 on economic and social arrangements. He then indicated that his government agreed to the British proposal for
the insertion of a paragraph providing that the section on pacific settlement of disputes should not apply to matters of
domestic jurisdiction.

Agreement was then reached that in addition to the statement in the body of the text, the question on voting procedure
in the council is still under consideration. There should be ap-
pended to the document as published a brief note indicating
that several other questions were also still under consideration.

* * *

During the course of the meeting Ambassador Gromyko
said he wanted to make it clear that the agreement of his government to participate in a general United Nations Conference on world security at a later date is contingent on the British and American governments meeting the Soviet proposals
as to voting in the council and on the X-matter. On the voting
question he said his government wished to reaffirm that it considers the principle of unanimity of the four Great Powers
must be carried out unconditionally.

[The Russian phase of the conversations ended with a
plenary session on September 28, and the Chinese phase
began the following day. Since the United States had
consulted frequently with Chinese diplomats during
negotiations with the Russians, the second stage of Dumbarton Oaks proceeded smoothly and brought no major
changes. Negotiations were completed by October 7, and
the Dumbarton Oaks Proposals were published on October 9.[37]

This document provided the framework around
which the United Nations was later built. It called for the

early establishment of an international organization to maintain peace and security and to promote international cooperation. The new body was to contain a General Assembly in which all member nations would have one vote and which was empowered to discuss questions relating to the maintenance of peace and to undertake studies and make recommendations for the promotion of cooperation in social and economic matters. Primary responsibility for keeping the peace was lodged in an eleven-member Security Council on which the five Great Powers (including France) would have permanent seats. The council was authorized to investigate international disputes, to call upon the parties to settle their differences peaceably, and in the event that failed to employ "any other measures," including diplomatic or economic sanctions and military force, that were necessary to prevent war. Member nations were obligated to furnish armed forces to the council upon request and these would be employed under the direction of a Military Staff Committee composed of officers from the countries that were permanent members. The Dumbarton Oaks Proposals also provided for the creation of an Economic and Social Council, an International Court of Justice, and a permanent Secretariat that would be the administrative arm of the General Assembly.[38]

United States officials expressed great satisfaction with the results of Dumbarton Oaks. "All in all, it is pretty good," Stettinius told the American group on the final day of the Russian phase of the conversations. The delegates had agreed on 90 percent of the issues, President Roosevelt advised a press conference, and "that is what we used to call in the old days a darn good batting average." [39]

Such statements and the official communiqué released at the end of the meetings glossed over the significant issues that remained to be settled. Russia's request for sixteen votes in the assembly—still a closely guarded secret—threatened acceptance of the United Nations by the American public and by the small nations that would comprise a majority of the membership of the organization. The inability of the conference to resolve the vital issue of voting in the council left unanswered critical questions about how the organization would function and by whom it would be controlled. Hull's postponement of

Courtesy The Washington (D.C.) Star-News

the question of congressional authority over commitment of troops to the United Nations, while politically
expedient, left unresolved a vital Constitutional question that had doomed American participation in Wilson's
League of Nations in 1919.

Dumbarton Oaks did represent an important
achievement, and Stettinius, who had taken a leading role
and handled the negotiations with considerable skill
could take justifiable pride in it. But much remained to be
done, and the undersecretary could not have imagined, as
he brought the gavel down on the final session on October 7, the crucial part that he would play in the completion of plans for the United Nations in the months
ahead.]

Edward R. Stettinius, Jr.

Stettinius and Anthony Eden at Binderton, April 1944

Molotov greeting Stettinius at Saki air base in the Crimea February, 1945. Ambassador Harriman is at right.

The delegates to Dumbarton Oaks.

ttinius and Cordell Hull at Dumbarton Oaks, August 1944

V

ACTING SECRETARY
October–November 1944

On October 2, 1944, his seventy-third birthday, Cordell Hull left the Department of State never to return. Seriously ill, exhausted from years of wearying struggles within the Roosevelt cabinet, frustrated by the president's increasing tendency to bypass him on important matters, Hull remained in his apartment for the next eighteen days, and on October 20 was admitted to Bethesda Naval Hospital for rest and treatment of a severe throat ailment. One month later he submitted a letter of resignation and insisted that the president accept it. Hull's absence from the department during these weeks left Stettinius acting secretary of state and moved him from the comparatively narrow sphere of planning for world organization and Anglo-American relations into the entire array of foreign policy problems confronting the United States.

During the two-month period that Stettinius served as acting secretary, allied military forces tightened the vise on Nazi Germany. U.S. troops crossed the border on September 12, and on October 21 took Aachen, the first German city to fall to the United Nations. In the meantime, the Red Army had penetrated deep into Central Europe. Bulgaria and Rumania capitulated in early September, and Soviet forces entered East Prussia on October 20, the same day combined Russian and Yugoslav units liberated Belgrade. Increasingly stubborn resistance dampened earlier hopes that the European phase of the war might be concluded by the end of the year, but the defeat of Germany was still only a matter of time.

The approach of victory quickened the tempo of political activity within the alliance. As Soviet forces swept across Europe, the USSR's relations with the liberated German satellites became a matter of growing concern to British and American officials. On September 20, 1944, Ambassador Harriman expressed to Washington his fear that the Soviet Union intended to establish a sphere of influence in the Balkans. "It can be argued," he added, "that American interests need not be concerned over the affairs of this area. What frightens me, however, is that when a country begins to extend its influence by strong arm methods beyond its borders under the guise of security it is difficult to see how a line can be drawn." [1] Churchill was so alarmed by the intrusion of Russian power into the Balkans that he journeyed to Moscow in early October to work out with Stalin an agreement on the disposition of British and Soviet influence.

Early discussions on a policy for the treatment of defeated Germany had raised divisions not only among the Allies but also within the United States government. The acceptance by Roosevelt and Churchill of the punitive Morgenthau plan at Quebec in September had produced bitter conflict within the president's cabinet. The State and War Departments opposed the plan in principle. They objected that it was politically inexpedient, and if word leaked out that it was being considered, German resistance would be intensified. They also greatly resented Morgenthau's influence with the president and their own exclusion from the Quebec decision. In the months after Quebec, State and War struggled with the Treasury to determine a final U.S. position on the fate of the Reich.

More familiar problems also demanded the attention of the acting secretary of state during October and November. The State Department began preparations for an arduous campaign to sell the Dumbarton Oaks Proposals to the Congress, the American public, and a number of smaller nations that had not been invited to the conference. In October, moreover, a top-level British delegation, headed by the distinguished economist John Maynard Keynes, arrived in Washington for negotiations on American economic assistance for the United Kingdom after the end of the war against Germany.

Despite the press of these urgent matters, American foreign policy was characterized by extreme caution in the last months of 1944. As acting secretary in Hull's absence, Stettinius undoubtedly felt reluctant to take decisive action. More important, the president and his advisers felt compelled to move quietly until the election was over. To avoid damaging his political position at home or restricting his freedom of action abroad, the president clung stubbornly to the policy of postponement adopted early in the war.

[In a conversation with Stettinius and Denis Cardinal Dougherty, Archbishop of Philadelphia, Roosevelt on October 13 admitted the importance of domestic politics in his foreign policy calculations.]

CALENDAR NOTES | *October 13, 1944*
Friday afternoon, the thirteenth, when I was with the president, the president told Cardinal Dougherty that he could do much more after the election, particularly in regard to Poland. This is particularly significant.

[Domestic politics also influenced the administration's decisions on Lend-Lease to Great Britain during Stage II (the period between the defeat of Germany and the defeat of Japan). At Quebec in September, Roosevelt had agreed to provide Britain with $3.5 billion in munitions and $3 billion in nonmunitions during the first year of

Stage II and to release the British from their earlier pledges not to re-export Lend-Lease supplies. By the time Lord Keynes and a British Treasury delegation had arrived in Washington to work out the details, however, substantial opposition to the Quebec arrangement had developed within the president's cabinet. The State and War Departments linked the deal on Lend-Lease to British acceptance of the Morgenthau plan for Germany. Secretary Hull deeply resented that the British had not been required to make trade concessions in return for Lend-Lease. Stettinius feared the possible political repercussions of Roosevelt's promises, and on October 18 he discussed his reservations with Keynes.]

CALENDAR NOTES | *October 18, 1944*
Lord Keynes called on me this afternoon at his request. We had a very long visit and discussed Stage II of Lend-Lease very thoroughly. He stated he had seen Mr. Acheson last night at dinner and had talked with him.

He particularly wanted me to look up Section III [of the British proposal for Lend-Lease] as he thought that presented a convincing . . . [picture] of the British financial position.

He said Lord Halifax would come tomorrow for the meeting and I gave him the point that Admiral [Joseph M.] Reeves [U.S. Navy member of the Munitions Assignment Board] had given me about the difficulty the Army and Navy would have putting on a protocol [2] and eliminating all screening. I also told him that exporting commodities and then having them re-exported would cause political embarrassment in the United States. . . .

Lord Keynes had an amazing grasp of the Dumbarton Oaks conversations. Apparently he had studied Cadogan's cables very thoroughly. He stated he was appalled at the Russian suggestions, at first, on voting in the council, but is now swinging around, thinking that they are perhaps being more realistic.

Lord Keynes referred me to a cable that Clark-Kerr [Sir Archibald Clark-Kerr, British ambassador in Moscow] had sent to the Foreign Office regarding a talk he had had with Molotov in which Molotov had put up a convincing argument. . . .

[On October 18, Arthur Hays Sulzberger, publisher of the *New York Times*, candidly discussed with Stettinius the upcoming presidential election.]

CALENDAR NOTES | *October 18, 1944*

* * *

He talked about the decision of the *New York Times* to go for the president. Originally, he said, they were for Dewey, but they had written the editorial on Monday as a trial balloon and it had read so well they decided to publish it. As he and his wife put it, it was better to put up for another four years of mismanagement of a country than . . . with another world war, and this was their choice—the Republican record was so bad . . . that they would not be able to handle world affairs, and as bad as they thought this administration was from the standpoint of domestic things, etc., they were going to plug for the president.

[The delicate relationship between domestic politics and foreign policy during an election campaign at the height of a global war was clearly revealed by an incident that occurred in late October. In a speech to the *New York Herald-Tribune* Forum on Current Problems, the Republican candidate, Governor Thomas E. Dewey of New York, sharply criticized the president's "personal secret" diplomacy, and in a blatant appeal for the East European ethnic vote singled out for special attack FDR's failure to secure Soviet recognition of the Polish government-in-exile in London. The speech evoked an immediate response within the administration.]

CALENDAR NOTES | *October 20, 1944*

Wednesday night after Dewey spoke, I returned to my apartment at the Shoreham from Lord Halifax's dinner and at 11:00 P.M. the White House telephone rang and Judge Rosenman said he was disturbed about Dewey's attack on the Soviets. He asked whether or not consideration could be given to telling the Soviets somehow that it would be very unfortunate for the president if they attacked Dewey as they did Willkie.[3]

I told Judge Rosenman that this was a very delicate matter but I would discuss it with Mr. Hull.

The next day I told Mr. Hull of the suggestion. He said there was no objection if it wasn't done in an official way and not done by him or myself. However, if some other friend of the president wished to make it, it was entirely proper.

At Mr. Hull's suggestion I talked to Mr. Joe Davies [ambassador to the USSR, 1936–1938, who maintained close contact with the Soviet Embassy in Washington] and pointed out the situation to him. He immediately grasped the matter and said he would be delighted to immediately have a conversation pointing out that he, as a private individual and a friend of the president, felt that any editorial comment unfavorable to Dewey would not be helpful to the president.

[The Morgenthau plan for Germany had set off a bitter debate within the Roosevelt cabinet, and when the details of the proposal leaked out it raised a great stir in the press as well. Morgenthau interpreted much of the opposition as personal, and on October 24 he complained about it to Stettinius.]

CALENDAR NOTES | *October 24, 1944*
Secretary Morgenthau called me on the phone at night and said if he had been rude he was sorry—the attacks on him are terrific from all sides and he is getting burned out and says things he doesn't mean.

[Drew Pearson, syndicated columnist and gadfly of Washington officeholders, was partially responsible for Morgenthau's problems, having printed several columns about the plan from inside information. Pearson had also been highly critical of Stettinius and the State Department, and on October 25 he discussed his columns and a number of other matters with the undersecretary.]

CALENDAR NOTES | *October 25, 1944*
. . . He sat at my desk and I sat beside him. When I came in he stood up and smiled warmly, said I was looking fine and that he was delighted to see me again. He said, "My brother, Leon, gave me your message about six weeks ago about your having said, 'You had better tell Drew that I have no political ambition whatsoever, I am in Washington for war service only, so it doesn't make much difference to me whether he destroys me or anybody else—I am doing a war job only.' " He said he wanted to apologize to me for the rotten article, how it had gotten by him he would never know, that it was hitting below the belt and he raised hell with his assistant who wrote it. I smilingly made no comment. He then stated that the reason he hadn't come to see me before in the last year was the fact that when he used to come to see Sumner

[Welles] it got Sumner in trouble. . . . . He said he had a friendly feeling toward me so therefore he had not come to see me.

He then said, "Sumner is singing your praises, he thinks you are doing a wonderful job in a tough spot. I thought you ought to know that. . . . He said, "If I see you, I think Mr. Hull will be offended. . . ." I said that my policy was to receive any member of the press, whoever he is. . . .

He then stated that he thought the president had done a magnificent job on Saturday night. He said he thought it was a magnificent speech [4]—that the gossip around town was that the president had a little cocktail and that of course it wasn't true—but Drew said he did know he had a brandy and soda while he was making the speech.

He then asked how things had gone between Churchill and Stalin.[5] I said that I thought they had made very good headway and that it was a great success. He asked if it was true that Churchill had not had an agenda—that it was a goodwill trip. I said that was my understanding that he had handled himself magnificently and that tremendously constructive results had come out of the meeting.

He asked about activity in the Balkans. I said that a statement on that would be that as long as any country set up a friendly community that was not anti-Soviet that Stalin would not take any steps or would not meddle. For example, such a country as Czechoslovakia has set up a satisfactory government and I would think it would be fair to guess that Churchill is accepting that.

He asked if it were true that the Russians had withdrawn their influence from Greece and I said that I was not fully informed on that matter but my feeling was that Greece would have a chance to work out its own problems in its own way.

* * *

I said, "Drew, how about Dumbarton Oaks, how did we do?" He said, "I think you did wonderfully. I realize what a tough job it was for you." He said he thought we had a chance for world organization. He thought it had been handled well politically and he said, "I think you are on your way to a great success." I asked him about isolationists. He said of course there was some isolationist thought in Wisconsin and Illinois but he didn't think it was going to cause us any trouble.

He asked me how things were going in Latin America. I said things were improving. I had met with them on Columbus Day and was having a meeting again on Thursday at 5 o'clock to answer their questions on Dumbarton Oaks. He said, "That's interesting." He said that of course since Sumner had been gone—they used to like Sumner and of course Larry [Duggan] and Phil [Bonsal]—no one was left that they really knew. He said they liked me but I didn't understand their problems and couldn't speak their language. . . . He said what we ought to do is to get some great specialist in Latin American Affairs who is the best man in America and put him in charge. . . .

He then left, thanked me ever so much for letting him come in, and said he thought I was doing a wonderful job.

[The following day, Morgenthau complained further to Stettinius about the treatment he was receiving within the cabinet and attempted to defend himself against charges that he had maneuvered around the State and War Departments to secure the president's approval of his plan.]

CALENDAR NOTES | *October 26, 1944*
I lunched with Secretary Morgenthau at his office today at his request. He was dejected and depressed. Morgenthau stated that after the Cabinet Committee [established by the

president on August 25 to consider a policy for Germany] had been appointed, composed of Stimson, Hull, and himself, they had many meetings both in his office and the president's office at which Harry Hopkins was present. On September 6, a week before he went to Quebec (he was there from the thirteenth to the fifteenth) he sent copies of his so-called control of Germany plan to the president, to Hull, and to Stimson. At no time did Mr. Hull express dissatisfaction. In one letter Morgenthau spoke of his being gratified that Mr. Hull thought the plan was good. Morgenthau stated that at a White House meeting Mr. Hull nudged him and said, "Henry, go on and present your plan." Mr. Hull's attitude had always been friendly and at no time had he shown any dissatisfaction. Morgenthau stated that he also knew that Mr. Hull was sore because he was presiding over the present Lend-Lease discussions. . . .

Morgenthau feels he is being unfairly treated. He was asked to do this by the president and somewhere between the War Department and State Department there is a coordinated attack on him that he feels [is] unfair and anti-Semitic. He says he has never undertaken any of these things without instructions from the president. He was called by the president on the Germany memorandum and ordered to Quebec—he didn't ask to go and didn't know what he was going for. . . .

Morgenthau stated the president had asked him to preside at the meeting covering Lend-Lease discussions with the British and that had already been leaked to the ANA [NAM?] and elsewhere.

* * *

[In October, the long-simmering dispute between the Polish government-in-exile in London and the USSR assumed critical proportions. Churchill and Stalin had invited Stanislaw Mikolajczyk, the prime minister of the

London government, to join their discussions in Moscow, and the profound differences among the various parties quickly became evident. Mikolajczyk insisted that he must choose the new government of Poland from among representatives of existing political parties. Stalin and Boleslaw Bierut, leader of the Polish Committee on National Liberation, demanded that the Lublin faction should have a majority in any new government. Joined by Churchill, Stalin also pressed Mikolajczyk to agree to the Curzon line as the boundary between Poland and the Soviet Union. The premier at first objected that his government could never agree to this, but under intense pressure from Churchill he finally agreed to try to secure the approval of his colleagues.

Back in London, however, Mikolajczyk found his government still adamantly opposed to the Curzon line, and he immediately appealed to President Roosevelt for assistance. He warned that the Polish nation "would feel itself terribly deceived and wronged if . . . it were faced . . . with the loss of nearly one-half its territory on which are situated great centers of its national and cultural life and considerable economic values." He begged Roosevelt to "throw the weight of your decisive influence and authority on the scale of events" in order to save for Poland the city of Lwow and the oil fields of Galicia.[6]

Mikolajczyk's cable arrived in the State Department on October 27, and three days later Stettinius and Ambassador Harriman met with the president to decide upon a response. After a long discussion on Polish affairs Roosevelt directed that the State Department should simply send Mikolajczyk a cable saying, "I think that everything will be composed satisfactorily in the end and I will send you another message in about a week's time."[7]

As the struggle for Europe entered its final stages,

the United States intensified its economic warfare against Germany, applying increasing pressure on neutral nations to cease trade with the enemy. Months before, the State Department had offered Sweden important trade concessions if it would cut back its shipments of strategic items, such as ball-bearings, to Germany. The Swedes had accepted the American offer, but they did not reduce their trade enough to satisfy the United States Army and Navy. Under pressure from Secretaries Stimson and Forrestal, Hull had demanded in the summer of 1944 the cessation of all trade with Germany. The Swedish government had refused, and the State Department began to consider the imposition of economic sanctions.]

CALENDAR NOTES | *November 8, 1944*
Dunn [James Dunn, director of the Office of European Affairs] and Cumming [Hugh Cumming, chief of the Division of North European Affairs] met with me this morning and we discussed trade relations with Sweden and agreed that I should take a very firm stand with the Swedish minister, saying to him that if they expected to get aid from the U.S. now in the way of synthetic rubber or anything else they must stop all aid to the enemy. This I did and I have reported the conversation with the Swedish minister.[8]

[In November 1944, the volatile Palestine question assumed a central place in American politics and diplomacy. Throughout 1943 and into early 1944, Zionist leaders and congressmen with Jewish constituencies had pressed the administration to commit itself to the establishment of a homeland in Palestine for Jewish refugees, and resolutions had been introduced in both Houses of Congress approving such a move.

The administration was sympathetic to the plight of

the Jews and sensitive to the political implications of inaction, but countervailing pressures forced it to hold back. The army warned that premature steps could spark open conflict in the Middle East, forcing a diversion of Allied troops when all resources were required for the invasion of Europe. At the same time, the United States was attempting to secure oil concessions from a number of Arab states, and the response of Arab leaders to the mere introduction of the congressional resolutions indicated that a definite American commitment to Palestine would have serious consequences. Thus the president, while expressing sympathy for Jewish aspirations, opposed congressional action on the grounds of military expediency and convinced congressional leaders to withdraw the resolutions.

By November 1944, however, Zionist leaders found reasons to reopen the issue. Both political parties had included in their platforms planks favoring the creation of a Jewish state. More important, Secretary Stimson in a letter to Senator Robert Taft of Ohio had withdrawn the military's earlier objections to congressional action. Agitation again began in Congress, and on November 9, two days after the election, Jewish leaders visited the State Department to renew their quest for administration backing.]

CALENDAR NOTES | *November 9, 1944*
Dr. Wise, Dr. Silver, and Dr. Goldman [9] called on me today at their request.

Dr. Wise stated he hoped it [the Palestine resolution] could be introduced in this session of Congress. . . . I advised him this was a matter I wished to discuss with the president. . . .

The gentlemen then asked whether or not I had heard

anything relative to the partitioning of Palestine. I said no. They asked me if I would inquire from the British. . . . I assured them that the British knew nothing about partitioning. Dr. Wise then stated he hoped that if the president met Prime Minister Churchill it would be possible for him to take along an expert on Palestine with him. . . . They wished to recommend somebody to us who was an expert and neutral to be used on the trip.

Dr. Wise then stated that they thought it would be possible for them to get the terrorists in Palestine under control. I said I thought that the assassination of Lord Moyne [British Minister of State in the Middle East] would be a setback for the movement and public opinion in England would be against Palestine efforts and the rabbi stated he realized this was tragic and serious. He said a very small group of young men who had a fanatical point of view were responsible.

* * *

[On November 7, 1944, the American people returned Franklin D. Roosevelt to the White House for an unprecedented fourth term. The president won an overwhelming victory in the electoral college, the Democrats strengthened their position in both Houses of Congress, and several leading isolationists, including Senator Gerald P. Nye, had been defeated.

Nevertheless, the election did have certain sobering implications for the administration. Roosevelt's popular majority was the smallest of his four elections and the smallest of any victor since Wilson's narrow victory over Charles Evans Hughes in 1916. Congress was still dominated by the coalition of conservative Democrats and Republicans that had obstructed the president on domestic matters since 1938. Even though the election had encouraging results, it did not convincingly answer the question whether the American people were prepared to give full and unqualified endorsement to active participation in a postwar international organization.

Despite these doubts, the initial reaction of the president and his advisers was one of relief and reassurance. On November 10, Roosevelt returned to Washington and received a warm welcome from the cabinet.]

CALENDAR NOTES | *November 10, 1944*

I . . . finished up some work in the car on the way to the Union Station to meet the president who was coming in at 8:30 from Hyde Park in his special train.

The sky was overcast and it was raining fairly hard when we got there. I went into the train to greet the president. All members of the cabinet were there, together with the heads of many of the agencies.

The car was surrounded by radiomen, MP guards, and a host of Secret Service agents.

After greeting the president, I got back into my car and waited for the procession to begin. . . .

At exactly 9:00 the first car left the station loaded with Secret Service agents in their armoured car. The second car contained the president, and seated with him in the back of the car were Vice-President Elect Harry S Truman, and Vice-President Henry A. Wallace. The only other occupant of the car, beside the driver, was Johnny Boettiger, the president's grandson. The next five or six cars contained newsmen, and following them were the greeting committee of cabinet members and so on. We were about the tenth car.

The procession stopped at Columbus Memorial fountain where Commissioner John Russell Young extended to the president Washington's official homecoming welcome. The president responded with a few minute's talk on how glad he was to be back, but that he didn't hope to make Washington his permanent home.

CABINET MEETING

The president entered the room at 2:10 P.M., and the entire cabinet rose and clapped. The president was very cheerful and looked well. The president said he was like the old man Dante wrote about, who had gone to Hell four times.

The president said the past campaign had been the dirtiest one in his entire political career.

The president turned to me and said he had been out of touch with foreign relations and was there anything new. I told the president there was much I would have to report to him and hoped to have a private talk promptly; stating to him that we had met with the Latin American ambassadors yesterday and that we had made good progress and I was sure we would get their full support on the world organization. I told the president that we had taken them to the Blair House afterward. The president asked whether we served liquor, and I said, yes, but always after five o'clock. He then said, "You must invite me over some time!"

I then told the president that there had been some differences of opinion and viewpoints in the Army, Navy, State, and FEA on shipments of certain supplies to Sweden—whether or not we should send rubber before or after. The president was very dissatisfied in the way Sweden had acted in the war and thought that by all means they ought to cut off all trade before anything was sent. I warned the president that the Swedish minister would appeal to him over our heads. The president then said, "I hope that he does—I'll have plenty to say to him."

The president then called me "Eddy" a number of times during the cabinet meeting.

The president turned to Secretary Morgenthau and asked for his report. Morgenthau stated that the next War Loan Drive would be announced on November nineteenth and would start on the twentieth. The banks would not participate this time, and they were hopeful the drive would be a success.

(The president interrupted here and said he didn't know what his plans were, frankly, but he wanted to meet Stalin and Churchill, but that Stalin would not make a long trip and he, the president, did not want to go through the Black Sea to Odessa as it was filled with disease, and there would be difficulty in getting a battleship through the Dardanelles. The president mentioned Malta, Rome, and Cairo. The whole thing is still up in the air and nothing has been decided up to the present time.)

*   *   *

The president then stated that he had heard over the weekend of Dewey's proposed cabinet, and they were to include Aldrich [Winthrop Aldrich, president of the Chase Manhattan Bank], who was telling everybody that he would be secretary of the treasury, Dulles [John Foster Dulles, Dewey's foreign policy adviser], secretary of state, and Wilson [Charles E. Wilson, General Motors executive], attorney general.

Regarding leaks to the press during the campaign, the president said, in a joking way, of course, that we should handle it like the Russians do, mentioning that Krock and Pearson would then be eliminated.

Secretary Stimson had no business. He volunteered, however, that it would take another week to clean up Antwerp. He said MacArthur was right that the Japs would make a last stand at Leyte and it would be a long hard fight to the Philippines.

*   *   *

There was a discussion at this point about a pamphlet which had been issued by the Republicans, and it was felt it would be a wise matter for some suits to start. Truman might sue in connection with the Ku Klux Klan matter.[10] McNutt referred to letters which had been issued, containing disgraceful language, etc. Biddle referred to a pamphlet of which a million copies were distributed in Philadelphia, in which the president's picture had appeared with four convicts and [Earl] Browder's name mentioned, which said, "If you vote for the president you vote for these people." This was a clear case of libel. The president gave encouragement that they sue. There was some other private talk on this which astounded me and showed the dirty tactics the Republicans used in this campaign, and which I will not put down in this record.

*   *   *

CALENDAR NOTES | *November 10, 1944*
After the cabinet meeting I told the president there were a number of things I would like to tell him about. I asked for an appointment some time soon, and he asked me if I could come back at 4:30 today. Then he changed his mind and said to come in now. I walked into Miss Tully's office and had just started to sit down when I was called right in. The room was quite hot and the president took off his coat and we settled down to work.

I told him the secretary was on the up-grade but that I felt he would have to take quite some time before returning. The president said he and I would probably have to see Mr. Hull some time soon and have a general talk. At this point, I told the president I hoped this could be soon because if the secretary was going to be away for a very long time, it would be necessary for us to be given a free hand in the department to make some necessary changes. I told the president that we have to have some new people, and we have to get rid of some of the deadwood the President said. I mentioned [Will] Clayton and [Lewis] Douglas as good people to have in the department. The president said that Douglas was fine but too many people were against Will Clayton. We can go back on this with the president, I think.

*　　*　　*

Palestine situation—I told the president what difficulty we were getting into and we should discuss the matter with Harriman. I said I would send him a memo on this. . . . The president feels confident, however, he will be able to iron out the whole Arab-Jewish issue on the ground where he can have a talk. He thinks Palestine should be for the Jews and no Arabs should be in it, and he has definite ideas on the subject. It should be exclusive Jewish territory. I told him of my recent talk with Dr. Wise.

(The president asked me about sending Wallace as ambassador to China. After a lengthy discussion we agreed that it would not be sufficiently attractive to Wallace, but it was very important to make an appointment before January 20.)

Indochina and Southeast Asia—I told the president our policy as expressed in the November 3 memo from him. I said it was the Army and Navy who were taking certain action, and he said this was wrong. I told him I was getting up memos for his signature.[11]

Treatment of Germany—We discussed this at great length. We are getting up a memo on this, and I said it was six pages, not a whole volume, and the president said this was fine. I asked whether or not it would be acceptable for me to deal directly with him and not Army and Treasury. He then asked again whether or not the Army and Navy had approved the memo. I said no; but it had been shown to them. I said it would be much more satisfactory for him to take the memo and call Matthews [H. Freeman Matthews, deputy director,

Office of European Affairs] and myself over and instruct us as to what he wanted the policy to be. We then in turn could send it to the Treasury and Army. The president then gave me a long historical record of how the Morgenthau thing had happened and queried me at some lengths on the leaks which had occurred on the Morgenthau plan. He was willing to take the blame himself on the word "agrarian." He said he should not have said it.

I told the president that there were so many leaks that the time had arrived for aggressive action. The president agreed. He said to take an FBI man and put him in the department and give him a job—make a Foreign Service officer out of the agent; let him roam around the place. He was convinced a lot of leaks had come from the State Department. I told him I thought a lot of leaks were coming from the White House itself. The president said after it gets to the file room he doesn't know what happens. He agreed to get into the thing very thoroughly.

[The uncooperativeness of the Argentine government continued to preoccupy State Department officials, and in the fall of 1944 they determined to step up the pressure on the wayward neighbor. The British presented a major obstacle. The Churchill government had throughout the war paid lip service to America's punitive policy, but it had been extremely reluctant to take concrete action against Argentina. Dependent upon the import of Argentine meat products, British officials feared that a complete break with the Farrell regime would leave them without an adequate food supply. At the very time the State Department was considering further reprisals against Argentina, the British government was preparing to sign a contract to purchase large quantities of meat for four years. On November 14, Stettinius discussed with his advisers the delicate problems in this triangular relationship.]

CALENDAR NOTES | *November 14, 1944*
I met with Nelson Rockefeller [coordinator of Inter-American Affairs] and a group of his chairmen from various Latin American countries. The meeting was brief, and in the main we discussed Argentina. It was their general feeling that if the British supported us, we could force out the present Argentine regime in a matter of weeks. However, they did point out that it would be necessary for the British to cooperate with us honestly and not say to the Argentine people, "We are awfully sorry we have to do this, but the United States is forcing us to take this position." These men pointed out that in this way, the United States would be further criticized and be considered a brute, and Great Britain, the poor innocent party to the deal. I assured Mr. Rockefeller and his chairmen of the State Department's whole-hearted support.

[American annoyance with the British was particularly pronounced in Congress. Throughout the war, various senators and representatives had expressed fears that Britain was subverting American ideals, particularly in the liberated areas, and the protests would become louder in December 1944, when the Churchill government forcibly suppressed an uprising in Greece. Massachusetts Congresswoman Edith Nourse Rogers visited with Stettinius in mid-November, and provided a hint of the Anglophobia that was developing in Congress.]

CALENDAR NOTES | *November 15, 1944*
Mrs. Edith Nourse Rogers called upon me at her request to review her recent trip abroad. She has the impression that we are not sufficiently tough with the British—that our mili-

tary authorities are giving in to the British in many ways. I assured her I did not feel this was the case and felt that our military authorities had stood up to the British extremely well, and on all counts.

* * *

[That same day, Stettinius discussed a number of important issues with Hopkins and the president.]

CALENDAR NOTES | *November 15, 1944*

I went over to the White House this morning at 10:45 and I had a solid hour with Harry Hopkins. He seemed strong and said he was going to be able to stop all his medicine soon, and his personal plans had not changed, but he wanted to wait until after Germany [surrendered] and then take a foreign assignment for awhile and follow the plan he discussed with me in the summer.

He stated that the night before last he had a long talk with the president about the department. The president had a complete realization of the need and urgency with the world situation ahead. Various moves were discussed. We discussed Hurley [12] and I told him we were ready to move and he thought this was good.

I then went to the president's office at 11:45. The president was meeting with the vice-president and the speaker and [Senate Majority Leader Alben] Barkley and did not come over until about 12:15. He then saw Frank Walker for about ten minutes and then I was with the president from 12:25 to 1:00.

Poland. The president states there is no purpose of having the Polish ambassador see him at this time. I told him we were drafting a cable to Mikolajczyk which I would send today and I hoped he would discuss it with Harriman today before he got away. [13]

Palestine Resolution. The president feels that putting the resolution through now would just stir things up. He already has received word from Ibn Saud that he would like to see him and he feels confident that he can settle the Palestine question when he gets on the ground. I must therefore call Dr. Wise and Sol Bloom on this.

Argentine Meat. The president desires that we get up a strong cable to Churchill pointing out that while we agree that they must have the meat from the Argentines, that it would work to our disadvantage if they entered into a long contract and, as the president put it, "they should buy from day to day." The president asked me to obtain from Miss Tully a copy of Churchill's message to him on this subject.[14]

[Later that day, Roosevelt visited Secretary Hull in the Bethesda Naval Hospital to discuss further with him his proposed resignation from the cabinet. That evening, Stettinius called Hopkins to report the results of the conversation.]

I called Harry Hopkins at 9:00 P.M. and said, "The president stayed about an hour and a half out there and everything was left up in the air. He didn't get back until late—stayed until about 5:30. Mrs. Hull phoned me. The president wouldn't listen to anything and it was completely left up in the air. He [Hull] wants to see me about the same thing. I can't do it tomorrow but will go out there early next week.

Mrs. Hull told me that the secretary was picking up and feeling better but he knew it would take a long time. The president stayed an hour and a half but left everything up in the air. Mr. Hull is not very happy about not getting things clarified."

[By November 21, 1944, the British and American Lend-Lease negotiators had completed their work, arranging a program of assistance for the first year of Stage II which fell considerably short of British expectations. The program provided for $5.4 billion in Lend-Lease supplies, slightly below the figures established at Quebec, and the United States refused to remove restrictions on re-export of Lend-Lease items although it did agree to relax enforcement of them.

At a meeting on November 21, the president delivered a more serious blow to Britain's hopes for generous aid. Keynes had sought to get from the United States a definite commitment to provide a specified volume of supplies during Stage II. Warned by several of his advisers that such a commitment would be politically dangerous, however, the president refused to go along with the British.]

CALENDAR NOTES | *November 21, 1944*

I attended a meeting in the president's office this morning with Admiral Leahy and Harry White [undersecretary of the treasury] and Secretary Morgenthau. Mr. Morgenthau presented to the president the results of the discussions with the British on Stage II of British Lend-Lease. The president could not understand why it was necessary to make any commitment. He indicated he did not wish to receive a written report.

He thought the procedure followed in the past on Lend-Lease requisitions and appropriations was proper.[15] Mr. Morgenthau pointed out that this would not be following through on the commitment made to the prime minister at Quebec. The president indicated he could straighten that out. He also indicated it was not his desire to have anything made public or any record made that the British would get help in the future as they had in the past. They must rely on our good will. If the British were promised they could get $6 billion of

Lend-Lease next year it would present a very serious political problem. Re-exports were discussed. Morgenthau mentioned the fact of the debate that would start in Parliament on November 29 relative to increasing British exports. Morgenthau and Harry White spoke up and assured the president that the formula they had worked out would be agreeable to him. After the meeting I told Morgenthau to avoid any misunderstanding he better send a copy of the re-export formula to the president. He agreed and said he would do it. I talked to Acheson when I returned to the office. He was disturbed about not giving the British a firm commitment.

I later talked to Lord Keynes and told him I didn't think they could get a written agreement. He said they didn't expect it and felt all along we wouldn't be able to give them a firm commitment but that it was our desire that if supplies were available we could and that we would carry through the best way possible. This seemed to satisfy him.

[After the meeting with Morgenthau, White, and Leahy, Stettinius met privately with the president and discussed other matters, including the delicate situation in Iran. Provoked at being excluded from Anglo-American-Iranian discussions on oil concessions, the USSR had unleashed a harsh propaganda attack against the Iranian government. On November 3, the *charge d' affaires* of Iran had made an emergency call at the State Department and appealed for American support against the Soviet Union.] [16]

Firmer Position with Russia regarding Iran. I told him [the president] I was sending to him a memorandum on this question. He said if he can do it he is interested. He volunteered that when he talked to Stalin and Churchill in Teheran

177 | *Acting Secretary*

he proposed having a free port on the warm water that would be under . . . trusteeship . . . everyone having access to it.

Argentine Meat. The president showed me a cable that he had just received from the prime minister saying he had made various changes on Argentine meat and was having them printed and was sending them to him by air mail. The president said he had not yet received them but he thought I should get up another cable to the prime minister on Argentine meat before we received the prime minister's staff saying that the Fascist regime was to follow [fall?] and to give him a few more months to work things out. I told the president I would review the whole matter, if that was appropriate, and draft a message and send it to him tomorrow.

[Relations with the USSR remained extremely sensitive at the end of 1944, and U.S. officials continued to try to prevent any incident that might inflame tensions, even to the point of considering suppression of a book critical of the Soviet government.]

CALENDAR NOTES | *November 24, 1944*
Eric Johnston [president of the U.S. Chamber of Commerce] called upon me at his request today. He stated he was very disturbed about a situation that had come up relative to Russia.

On his trip to Russia last year, he said, he had taken with him William Allen White, Jr. [actually William L. White], the son of William Allen White, who had been recommended by the *Reader's Digest* and is now to publish a book which is very anti-Russian and is full of misstatements, untrue facts, stories, and incidents which never occurred. Johnston is fearful that this will be damaging to United States–Soviet relations and most fearful that it will be damaging to him personally in the eyes of the Soviets since they will feel he personally is responsible for bring[ing] White with him, and that Johnston is now indirectly responsible for this antagonistic point of view.

In the telephone records there is a conversation I had with Bohlen on this subject in which I asked Bohlen to see Mr. Johnston. I suggested to Mr. Bohlen that he call in Messrs. Hackworth [Green Hackworth, legal adviser to the secretary of state] and Matthews to discuss with Mr. Johnston whether there was any possibility of us taking steps in connection with suppressing the publication of this book.

[White's book, *Report on the Russians*, appeared in condensed form in the *Reader's Digest*, December 1944, and January 1945. Among other things, it compared conditions in the USSR to those in the Kansas State Penitentiary (to the detriment of the former), attacked the "dull unimaginative bureaucracy" of the Soviet Union, and spoke of the "dreary mediocrity" of all facets of Russian life. *Pravda* responded immediately, charging that White had violated the hospitality of the Soviet government and dismissing his work as the "usual standard production of a Fascist kitchen with all its smells, calumny, unpardonable ignorance and ill-conceived fury." [17]

In the evening of November 26, Keynes paid a final visit to Stettinius before returning to London.]

CALENDAR NOTES | *November 26, 1944*
Lord Keynes called me at 6:45 this afternoon after having spent an hour with the president. Lord Keynes stated the president had been most helpful and that he had discussed with him the future of Lend-Lease and the treatment of Germany principally.

On the future of Lend-Lease the president stated that he had received the preliminary report from Messrs. Morgenthau, Crowley and Stettinius and seemed well pleased . . . .[18]

Lord Keynes stated that he had received a private message from the chancellor of the exchequer today relative to Lend-Lease Stage II, and at the end of the message it was stated that the prime minister had sent the president a statement on Argentine meat . . . which . . . would be most satisfying and gratifying to the president. Lord Keynes stated that the president did not mention this at tea this afternoon and apparently had not yet received it.[19]

Lord Keynes stated that the president discussed with him the economic treatment of Germany at length. He said that as he listened to the president it seemed to confirm what Lord Cherwell had told him transpired at the conference in Quebec. He inquired as to whether this meant a complete agrarian economy and he stated, not quite, but it goes pretty far in de-industrializing of the Ruhr and eliminating many of Germany's basic industries. He stated the president emphasized the fact that he did not feel there was any great hurry in reaching a final decision regarding economic treatment of Germany, that we wanted to see what damage our bombs had done and what the general conditions were, and he said he would like to go there himself and take a look before any final definite positions are taken.

Lord Keynes expressed the hope that it would be possible for me to come to England soon for he thought if I did come there would be many things we could accomplish.

He said the ministers in London were quite satisfied with the results of the Lend-Lease discussions. However, they were disappointed in not commencing exports until V-E Day. All in all, Lord Keynes seemed quite happy, very cheerful, and feeling that his mission here had been a success and he felt London was relatively happy. He was particularly complimentary of the way in which the State Department participated in the matter.

[Keynes was much too optimistic about the Lend-Lease negotiations. Roosevelt's refusal to give the Stage II program the status of an agreement rendered it most vulnerable to unforeseen developments, and the president's death in April 1945, left it with no value whatever. Shortly before FDR died, Congress amended the Lend-Lease Act to limit shipments exclusively to items that were essential for military operations. The new president, Harry S Truman, was especially sensitive to his need for congressional support and despite Churchill's urgent appeals refused to violate the letter of the amendment. The Stage II program was never implemented, and on V-J Day Truman abruptly terminated Lend-Lease. Britain was left in desperate straits, facing what Keynes called an "economic Dunkirk."

As Stettinius had reported, Roosevelt's November 15 meeting with Hull had been inconclusive, the secretary expressing a strong desire to resign, the president trying to discourage him. Not dissuaded, Hull on November 21 sent in a formal letter of resignation. Once again Roosevelt tried to persuade him to remain in office, at least until the beginning of the fourth term. Hull seriously considered this proposal, but advised by his doctors that his health would not permit it he saw no alternative to resigning at once. Roosevelt reluctantly accepted it on November 23. Four days later, the president summoned Stettinius to the White House to inform him that he had been chosen to succeed Hull as secretary of state. After months of preparation, the undersecretary would now assume major responsibilities for charting American foreign policy through a stormy and critical period.]

VI
STORM BEFORE YALTA
December 1944–January 1945

On December 1, 1944, the White House announced that Stettinius would succeed Cordell Hull as secretary of state. Roosevelt had considered other candidates, among them Vice-President Henry A. Wallace and Office of War Mobilization Director James F. Byrnes, but he had finally settled on Stettinius as the man he could best rely on to execute his policies faithfully and energetically. The new secretary fulfilled the president's expectations. During his first months in office, he greatly improved communications between the State Department and the White House. He rarely questioned presidential policies, but during his tenure the department was able to regain considerable influence in decision making.

Stettinius assumed his new position at a decisive time in the nation's diplomatic fortunes. During the two months before the Yalta meeting, friction with both major Allies increased sharply, and in the United States optimism about postwar peace settlements declined appreciably. British troops intervened in recently liberated Greece to suppress an insurgency against the royalist government. Churchill set off a political crisis in Italy by vetoing the inclusion in the government of Count Sforza, a leftist he predicted would lead the nation to communism. The American press reacted angrily, charging that the United Kingdom was playing its old imperialist game and halting progressive elements in the liberated areas. Anglo-American relations sank to a wartime low, and

Stettinius found himself caught in a crossfire between American opinion leaders and the British Embassy.

More ominous were signs that Russia intended to impose its will on Eastern Europe. Over British and American protests, the Kremlin set harsh armistice terms for Rumania, Bulgaria, and Hungary, and kept Western influence in these nations to a minimum. Despite Roosevelt's personal pleas to delay any action on Poland until after the Big Three meeting, Stalin announced in late December that he would recognize the Soviet-sponsored Lublin government. Like British actions in Greece and Italy, these Russian moves evoked cries of outrage in the United States. Liberals and conservatives alike deplored the cynical reversion of the Soviet Union and United Kingdom to power politics, and placed much of the blame on an administration that had not used its influence to prevent the betrayal of the principles of the Atlantic Charter.

Beyond these urgent European matters lurked a multiplicity of problems. Their hopes fixed on the creation of a Jewish homeland in Palestine, American Zionists pressed vigorously for official support, threatening U.S. relations with the Arab nations which many diplomats considered a matter of top priority. Policies for the postwar treatment of Germany and for the colonial areas of Asia and Africa remained undefined. The State Department was eager to begin a campaign to secure popular backing for the Dumbarton Oaks Proposals, but administration officials were divided among themselves on the timing for creation of the international organization. The Pentagon, in particular, thought America's military position in the Pacific should be firmly secured and the atomic bomb completed before the United States went ahead with planning for the United Nations.

[Stettinius thus went through a baptism of fire in his first months in office. Even before he could begin to deal with pressing diplomatic problems, he had to fight an extended battle to get Senate confirmation of his nominees for top State Department positions. This accomplished by late December, he worked unsuccessfully to get the president to reassure American opinion by issuing a firm, clear statement on American foreign policy. He spent hours listening to congressional complaints, and worked diligently to repair the rupture in Anglo-American relations. As the time for the Yalta Conference approached, he became increasingly absorbed with preparing position papers for the Big Three meeting. Although he was fully aware of the complexity of the foreign policy problems he would face, he could not have known how challenging his new job would be when he went to the White House on November 27 to confer with the president about taking Hull's place.]

CALENDAR NOTES | *November 27, 1944*
I was shown in. The president had just had a haircut, looked young and fine. . . . He said, "Perhaps, as you have maybe guessed, I have made up my mind and I want you to be my secretary of state. I had three under consideration—Henry Wallace, Jimmy Byrnes, and yourself. It would have killed the secretary [Cordell Hull] to have Henry. As for Jimmy, he has no understanding of geography. Of course in this whole foreign situation I am going to have to work awfully intimately with Stalin and Churchill. Jimmy has always been on his own in the Senate and elsewhere and I am not sure that he and I could act harmoniously as a team." He said, "You and I could have a perfect understanding and complete harmony and work as a team, you recognizing the big things I would have to handle, at your suggestion." I said, "In other words, Jimmy might question who was boss." He said, "That's exactly it. As far as you and I are concerned we will

never have any misunderstanding on who carries what and we will work things out so that everything will fit in properly between the White House and the department" and I said, "Yes, as long as we are kept informed. The past record had not been too good." He said he realized that. He said, "You and I are going to work out a system so we are both kept more fully informed."

[The president then approved Stettinius's nomination of Joseph C. Grew as undersecretary and his recommendations for the assistant secretary posts: William L. Clayton, Economic Affairs; Nelson Rockefeller, Latin American Affairs; Dean Acheson, International Conferences and Congressional Relations; Archibald MacLeish, Public and Cultural Relations; and General Julius Holmes, Administration. Stettinius later proposed James C. Dunn as assistant secretary for political affairs other than Latin America.[1]

After lunch Stettinius returned to the need for closer coordination with the White House.]

I told the president again that we had to do something to strengthen the White House relationship and that there were too many papers and too much stuff going unattended to. For example, the response from [Patrick] Hurley [ambassador to China] this week had been in for nine days and I didn't know about it yet. The president said, "How could you, I had it in my pocket?" I said, "That's what I'm talking about!" He said the idea of having a diplomatic attaché at this moment would offend Leahy and Hopkins but I said let me appoint a liaison officer between the State Department and the White House. I mentioned Chip Bohlen [chief of the Division of Eastern European Affairs]. I said, "You know him and trust him. We'll appoint him as liaison officer and keep everything straight between us on appointments, calls, correspondence, and cables. I'll take Chip to Miss Tully, Early, and Leahy and let him organize to keep everything sweet between us." He said, "Fine, but when you make your announcement say liaison officer between the president and the chief of staff to the president."

[Stettinius had taken pains to emphasize that he regarded his wartime work as nonpolitical, to which the president agreed. Before leaving he discussed his future plans.]

Courtesy The Washington (D.C.) Star-News

During the conversation when I told the president I did not want a political career, I said I wanted him to know what I was going to do after the war. I said I had the swellest set-up. I would have the presidency of the University of Virginia and Twentieth Century Fox had offered me the chairmanship of the board which would carry $100,000 a year and involve nothing other than attending director's meetings. This company is run by Greeks and Jews who wanted a little prestige and class for their company. He said, "That's the damndest thing I ever heard of. My wouldn't it be fun!"

[One day after his appointment was announced, Stettinius faced an upheaval in Congress over the explosive Palestine question. While acting secretary, he had sought without success to get congressional leaders to delay introduction of a resolution in favor of a Jewish state.[2] He had then secured from Sol Bloom, chairman of the House Foreign Affairs Committee, a promise to table the resolution. But Bloom went back on his pledge and the resolution was reported to the House on November 30. Stettinius discussed the many dimensions of the problem with James Dunn on December 2, advising him that Rabbi Wise was pressing to get State Department approval on the Jewish resolution.]

CALENDAR NOTES | *December 2, 1944*
He [Wise] came back a week or so ago and asked whether or not he should agitate and press now for a reintroduction of the resolution for prompt independence of Palestine. I talked with the president. The president said, "Please tell them on the Hill to please give them more time. I am going to take a trip [Yalta] this winter and will see a lot of people. I want to see if I can't unravel this whole situation on the ground." I then told Wise . . . what the president said and he was very

happy about it. Then Wagner [Senator Robert F. Wagner, D.-New York] called me from Atlantic City and he thought this was all right and wouldn't press. I then talked to Connally and he said all right. I talked to Bloom and he agreed. A couple of days ago, Connally had a rumpus in the Foreign Relations Committee in which Wagner reopened the whole damn thing. Connally then called me and said he would have to ask me to testify next Wednesday, December 6, on the whole business. Meanwhile, in the last twenty-four hours, Wallace Murray [chief, Office of Near East and African Affairs] gives me a twelve page statement to make on Wednesday. My judgment is that we can't be drawn into this controversy with the Arabs and Jews—we should send the president a wire now and say that the thing has gotten too hot for Connally to handle, that I have been requested to testify and he didn't think I should, and he should authorize Connally not to have me testify and the president wants a chance to call on the recalcitrant senators to please let it ride over until the president returns from his forthcoming trip in the winter.

[Roosevelt agreed that Stettinius should encourage Senate leaders to drop the Palestine issue, but on December 6 Senator Connally called and urged the secretary to appear before the Foreign Relations Committee.]

CALENDAR NOTES | *December 6, 1944*
Senator Connally stated that if I wanted to take the responsibility and not appear, all right, but the legislation was going to pass if I didn't come. I agreed to come. . . .

* * *

[When Stettinius reached the hearing room the senator immediately came out and said that he "had to carry the ball and that it was completely out of hand."] [3]

* * *

Senator Wagner introduced the subject by saying . . . that the committee felt the resolution should pass and that if the chief executive arm of the government was against it, they felt they had the right to hear that expression, and had appealed for me to come up.

* * *

I said, Mr. Chairman and Gentlemen, this is a highly delicate matter and I hope we may be able to have an understanding that it is completely off the record and I will be able to talk frankly to you and get your pledge that this information will not get out of this room. Senator Connally said that he spoke for the others in saying that we will respect your confidence in us. I said there probably were many newspaper men around and speculation would occur, but it was understood . . . that I was speaking in secret session.

I started off by saying that it was the president's considered judgment . . . that it would not be in the interest of the general international situation at this time to have this legislation pass. I said the president one day will be meeting the chiefs of state of other countries . . . to have some very frank talks on the subject. . . . Action at this time would tie the president's hands and . . . would not be in the interest of what you are trying to accomplish.

Now gentlemen . . . you can say all this does is to endorse the Republican platform and the Democratic platform and the president's letter of the fifteenth of October,[4] but frankly . . . I must tell you that the experts in the department feel that the whole Arab-Jewish situation is one of great delicacy. I am sure you will recall the assassination of Lord Moyne. You have seen the terrorists of this group. I was then asked if they were Jews, and I said yes, they were Jewish bandits.

Clark stated, is this something new since the president's letter of October 15. I said I think Lord Moyne's assassination is something new. . . . I said that I was in a position to say it is an acutely delicate and dangerous situation with nothing to be gained by action by the Congress now.

Gillette spoke for the resolution saying it would be very embarrassing politically if it wasn't passed.

* * *

Vandenberg asked me whether or not the position I was taking had been conveyed to Bloom. I said, privately, senator, to you, Sol Bloom and I have had some personal and private talks on this. He said, does he know your position, and I said yes.

Vandenberg finally said that for him not to press for the passage of this legislation, he would have to have the right to say to the American people that he had not insisted on passage because he had been advised by the chief executive or the secretary of state and that this was unwise from the international standpoint. He led me to believe that on that basis he would not press for action.

Senator White of Maine arose and said he had committed himself to the legislation and that his constituents were depending on him and he must insist that we clarify our position publicly . . . and if this were done in a definite and positive way quickly, he would withdraw and be perfectly willing to not have the legislation pass.

* * *

[While Stettinius was working to hold off congressional action on Palestine, an incident occurred that threatened relations with Great Britain. Responding to public criticism of Churchill's intervention in Italian politics, the State Department, without consulting the British Embassy, had issued a press release affirming that the United States opposed interference in the internal affairs of other nations. The British naturally and correctly interpreted the statement as an attack on their action in Italy, and Michael Wright, counsellor of the British Embassy, immediately visited Stettinius to protest.]

CALENDAR NOTES | *December 6, 1944*
As Michael Wright put it, it was . . . "really a hot one."
He then talked for five minutes, . . . saying that . . . the statement on Italy . . . had caused great embarrassment and that the prime minister and Mr. Eden were aroused; and that a debate would start in Parliament on Friday about Greece and that he called attention to the last words in a certain paragraph of our statement on Italy in which it referred to other liberated areas. Michael feels this is very disturbing as there was great speculation in London as they felt our remarks on Italy also referred to Greece.[5] Michael then . . . read to me a message from Eden. It was one page long. Michael declined to leave the message with me as he said it was very personal. It stated in brief that they had been surprised and hurt that we had made such a statement which had been damaging to their prestige at home and abroad.

* * *

He said that the prime minister and Eden were on a hot spot . . . and it would be most helpful if we could make a statement promptly. . . . We could say we are in close touch with the British relative to the Greek situation . . . and that we are seeing eye to eye with the British on this matter of Greek policy.

*   *   *

I said that of course, Michael, you must understand that all we have done is to reiterate the policy agreed upon between your government and this government at Moscow. . . . Moreover, the big point that I must make in your mind is that . . . if you had consulted us this incident would never have occurred. Michael immediately . . . said of course we should have consulted you but we are fighting a war together and we all make mistakes and let us have our squabbles in private and not in public. . . .

I then explained the American public opinion [sic] had questioned our whole policy and we had many editorials against us on the handling of the Italian situation and there had been adverse comments in Congress. The reception had been good; they said at last we have a clear cut policy.

[Stettinius complied with the British request by arranging for a question on Greece at his December 7 press conference. The secretary concurred with Churchill's statement supporting self-determination in Greece. The Associated Press interpreted this as yet another attack on British policy, and the strain in Anglo-American relations increased rather than diminished.[6]

The next day Stettinius returned to the Palestine problem. He refused Senator Wagner's request for a new presidential statement backing the Zionists and warned him that if the Zionists pushed the resolutions, the State Department would make an official statement condemning congressional action. He pressed this point home in a meeting with Jewish callers. When Zionist leaders, in a conversation with Senator Connally, still persisted in seeking passage of a congressional statement of support, Stettinius ordered a press release expressing "utmost sympathy" for the Jewish people of Europe but stating that "passage of the resolution at the present time would be unwise from the standpoint of the general international situation. . . . " [7]

Several days later, on December 14, the secretary expressed his sympathy to Wise and Goldman.]

CALENDAR NOTES | *December 14, 1944*

I explained . . . privately that we could not issue the statement they suggested and told them I was sorry I could not be at their conference in Atlantic City, but that the president and I were doing everything humanly possible to relieve the suffering of the Jews in the world, and if there was anything they thought we could do which we're not doing, to please let us know.

[Already embroiled in a controversy over the Palestine resolution, Stettinius soon found himself struggling to secure Senate approval of his nominees for the assistant secretary posts. From the beginning, liberals had protested the big-business orientation of the nominees. The delay occasioned by the Palestine problem gave critics time to probe the background of Stettinius's appointments, and Will Clayton emerged as the major target of Senate opposition. The Senate Foreign Relations Committee requested files on Anderson, Clayton & Co., which had worldwide cotton interests, and Attorney General Francis Biddle warned that it would be extremely difficult to secure Clayton's confirmation.]

SUMMARY OF TELEPHONE
CONVERSATION | *December 9, 1944*

Attorney General Biddle called . . . saying that Tom
Connally had requested that he send over the material on
Clayton having to do with exports to Germany and Japan after
they went to war with England, and that Anderson and Clayton had sent shipments of cotton to them up to the end of
1940.

Biddle said he wanted me informed that he was going to
give this material to Connally privately.

I asked Biddle whether or not he thought the president
would have any trouble getting Clayton through and Biddle
said "Yes" and that he thought he would have a very serious
fight. I asked who was behind the fight and Biddle said he
really did not know. . . .

[Other administration officials confirmed that trouble was
brewing. Secretary of the Navy James Forrestal offered
to talk with Senator Claude Pepper [D.-Florida] about
not opposing Clayton, but Stettinius said he would have
Clayton endorse a policy statement by Hull on cartels to
show his free trade devotion. Hopkins was also concerned about Clayton's chances, but Stettinius believed
that his friendship with Connally could overcome any
problem. On the eve of the hearings, he assured his assembled team, "I have full confidence that this thing is
going to go smoothly and easily." [8] The hearings on
Clayton proved that the secretary was correct. There
were questions about his firm's sales to Axis powers in
1940, but Clayton provided satisfactory explanations.
Before the day was out, the publication of secret,
U.S. documents in Drew Pearson's column diverted
Stettinius's attention from the nominations. The indefat-
igable columnist had revealed a report from the American

ambassador in Athens that described orders Churchill had sent to the British commanding general. The report made the British appear bloodthirsty.[9] Upon hearing of the leak, Stettinius called Ambassador Halifax.]

Courtesy The Times-Picayune

TRANSCRIPT OF TELEPHONE
CONVERSATION | *December 12, 1944*

Stettinius: I am terribly disturbed about the Drew Pearson article. I think it is just unbelievably bad. . . . Nothing has happened that has disturbed me more than this. Between you and myself it looks as if it came from somewhere other than the State Department. . . .

* * *

Lord Halifax: . . . What are you going to say to the press when they start in on you? When they start in on you we ought to say the same thing.

Stettinius: We must not admit it is true. We will find a formula of what to say. . . .

* * *

[Such top secret telegrams were circulated only to the White House, Departments of War and Navy, and to the Office of Strategic Services. Preliminary investigation convinced Stettinius that the leak had originated in one of these agencies, and he contacted the president to ask for an investigation. He reviewed his plan with Grew and other key aides the afternoon of December 14.]

RECORD OF MEETING | *December 14, 1944*

Here are the facts, Mr. Stettinius said. In Drew Pearson's column of December 12, 1944, there appeared a paraphrase of a message from Kirk [10] to the State Department covering Churchill's instructions to his general in Greece which said words to the effect, "Don't let anything stand in your way—they will probably put the women and children up front."

* * *

No copy of the paraphrases made was kept or left in the State Department.

The cable published in Pearson's column was the paraphrase which existed with the Army, Navy, or OSS divisions. This immediately indicates that no State Department person was responsible for the leak.

I reported this entire matter to the president in a wire the evening of December 13, . . . asking authority to stop distribution immediately of our secret cables to Army, Navy, and OSS . . . and asking the president's permission to ask the postmaster general to appoint Post Office inspectors to make an immediate investigation of this matter throughout all agencies involved.

[In the midst of this new irritant in relations with Britain, Stettinius met with Catholic archbishops Francis Spellman, Edward Mooney, and Samuel Stritch and listened to their fears about Russia's aims in Eastern Europe.]

CALENDAR NOTES | *December 13, 1944*
They then expressed a concern over the activities of the Soviet Union which was the keynote of their entire discussion. They were apprehensive over the application of the Atlantic Charter in Eastern Europe referring not only to Lithuania and Poland, but to Hungary and the entire Danube Valley including Austria as well. They stated that while they wished to back up the Dumbarton Oaks Proposals and use their great influence among their people to the end of having these proposals accepted, they were reluctant to do so in the light of these Eastern European developments. They seemed to be apprehensive that the Soviet Union would insist on these various countries being communized. They said this whole question presented to them a most difficult problem as throughout the war they had tried to keep up morale, but that

now these developments were shaking the people and that these coupled with heavy casualties lists which were now coming in and the increasing domestic hardships, were creating a situation of lowered morale throughout the country.

I attempted to indicate to them that our experience with the Soviet Union throughout the war had been a good one and that I was not apprehensive over the future. I admitted that right now we could not see the solution to the Polish question but that I was confident that with faith one would be found. I added that they must consider that until June 6, the Russians had been in a particularly strong position but that now that an invasion had been successful . . . we should be in a position to talk much more strongly than we could in the past. I emphasized that they should have confidence in the ability of the president to work these matters out.

> [The nomination fight now changed from Clayton to Archibald MacLeish, whose liberalism and reputation as an intellectual perturbed some senators. Unexpectedly, some New Deal liberals, including Claude Pepper whom Stettinius had always regarded as a good friend, joined the attack on MacLeish. Only by applying pressure on committee members through such intermediaries as Hopkins, Biddle, and Secretary of Commerce Jesse Jones, was the secretary able to secure a 10–10 tie vote on MacLeish. At this point, on December 14, Hopkins suggested that Stettinius call upon the president for assistance. After a successful appeal to persuade Wagner to switch his vote in favor of MacLeish, the nomination was reported out by one vote. Stettinius regarded this as a significant victory, advising Biddle that it was "important from the standpoint of the whole liberal movement to have MacLeish confirmed." [11]
>
> As the nominations moved on to the Senate floor,

Stettinius secured from Roosevelt a promise to resubmit to the next session of Congress any nominee who might be rejected. MacLeish questioned the wisdom of being forced through, but the secretary encouraged him to hold on and everything would "turn out just the way you and I want it to." [12] Just when a filibuster threatened to delay action until after the Christmas recess, Stettinius learned of a split in the ranks of the opposition. Again he wired the president, who was vacationing in Warm Springs, for help.]

STETTINIUS TO
ROOSEVELT | *December 18, 1944*
Senator Connally has just advised that, under the leadership of Pepper and [Joseph] Guffey [D.-Pennsylvania], a filibuster is likely to develop that will delay action on the State Department nominees until there is no longer a quorum present to make possible a vote at this session.

* * *

Bennett "Champ" Clark has left this leadership and is now supporting MacLeish and the whole group. Pepper is saying that these nominations are not, in fact, yours. Senator Connally feels that you must make your position clear and that it is very important that you either wire or telephone Pepper and Guffey . . . pointing out to them that you are behind these nominees and emphasizing the importance . . . of immediate confirmation . . . because of the world situation and the necessity of the new staff at the State Department assuming their important duties immediately.

[The president responded promptly, and by 9:00 P.M. that evening Stettinius called Hopkins to tell him that Connally had handed the message to Guffey on the floor and Guffey had "melted away." Two days later, December 20, the nominations were confirmed by comfortable margins.

During the height of the Senate battle, the Polish question again came to the forefront of Allied diplomacy. With Soviet armies already in Poland, public speculation mounted over the fate of that nation. Speaking to the House of Commons on December 15, Churchill had hinted that Britain was willing to accept changes in Poland's prewar boundaries. Mikolajczyk's resignation as prime minister had weakened the Polish government-in-exile. Meanwhile, the Russians had turned over administration of liberated Poland to the Lublin committee, and signs pointed toward Stalin's recognition of that group as the government of Poland. In an effort to prevent this, Stettinius urged Roosevelt to join Churchill in a plea that Stalin delay any action until the Yalta conference. The secretary devoted much attention to drafting this message on December 16. He then conferred with Halifax about European problems.]

* * *

CALENDAR NOTES | *December 18, 1944*
. . . I told him this whole activity in Greece and Poland was causing great resentment in this country and we should definitely have a private talk rather soon, and I said that the sentiment was going to such an extreme that some of our military people here were saying that Germany had been boxed in now and there was no longer any danger to the United States, and we might just as well turn the whole situation over to England and Russia and . . . go to the Pacific now and win the war there. I told Halifax that this was an extreme view, but that it was the sentiment of quite a few of our military.

[Stettinius found this same view shared by Senator Vandenberg, who took a keen interest in Eastern European problems because of his large Polish constituency in Michigan.]

Senator Vandenberg . . . said he had talked to two high military officers yesterday and they thought the time had arrived when we might as well say to Russia and England, "Well, Germany is pretty well hemmed in, there is no further danger to us, you might as well take things over and we will finish the Pacific war."

Vandenberg said that on Poland, the general sentiment in this country is that the president has completely turned the Polish situation over to Stalin to do anything he wants to do with them. The senator said the president must come out and clarify that issue one way or the other.

Vandenberg thinks there will be a great debate this week on our whole foreign policy situation.

He felt that this whole Polish situation and other new political developments were linked up to the hold-out on our nominees and it was just pouring water on the wheel for these fellows who were trying to make trouble.

[The statement on Poland, released the afternoon of December 18, pledged that "the United States government stands unequivocally for a strong, free, and independent Polish state with the untrammeled right of the Polish people to order their internal existence as they see fit." Territorial questions should be left for the peace conference, but if Russia and Poland reached mutual agreement on frontiers, the United States would have no objection.[13]

The ambiguity on Polish frontiers and the recent friction over British actions in Italy and Greece kept the

American people stirred up. Morale was sinking, and congressional criticism of the administration's handling of foreign policy had increased when Roosevelt returned to Washington on December 19. On December 22 the secretary met privately with the president prior to the cabinet meeting. It was at this point that Roosevelt told Stettinius he would accompany him to Yalta.]

CALENDAR NOTES | *December 22, 1944*
The president then said, "I want you to go." He then gave me a long talk for ten minutes as to dates and places. He did not think that "U" [Stalin] would be willing or able to fly, and that while he had offered Armenia and Sicily, it would probably end up in [Yalta] which is someplace where all the old Russian palaces used to be.

* * *

I then immediately told the president there was another plan that went hand-in-hand with this, and that . . . was the question of the Latin American meeting of foreign ministers. I said that the whole thing was boiling over and with Argentina kicking up a row it was becoming very difficult. I said we should move promptly and boldly today and agree to a meeting of foreign ministers and let [Exequiel] Padilla [foreign minister of Mexico] know so that invitations could go out, without Argentina present, and we could discuss economics and long-range planning as well as world security matters.

The president agreed to this and thought this was fine.

* * *

Voting in the Security Council
I . . . told him we were pressing the Russians and British for an early decision, and that they might come through

any time with a "yes." If so, we would want to send out invitations for a March meeting and the president said, "Of course, this is entirely proper."

[Policy for postwar treatment of Germany remained unsettled in the weeks after the second Quebec Conference. Roosevelt had repudiated the Morgenthau plan, but he had not defined an alternative policy and the secretary of the treasury continued pushing for punitive handling of Germany. He requested access to State Department position papers and pressed Stettinius to include him in his weekly meetings with Secretaries Stimson and Forrestal. Stettinius resented Morgenthau's intrusion in foreign policy formulation, and sought the president's backing in excluding the treasury secretary from discussions on German policy.]

Economic Treatment of Germany
The president said he . . . did not have, as yet, all his ideas completed. I told him, however, that if we didn't send [John G.] Winant [U.S. representative on the European Advisory Commission] some instructions before he (the president) left on the big trip, it would be very embarrassing. . . . The president promised to send us something soon.

I then asked about Morgenthau and how he wished me to handle him. The president stated it was perfectly proper to keep him personally informed, but that this was a matter between the State Department and the War Department.

The president then stated that Morgenthau had made a great mistake in stirring this whole thing up during the campaign, and that the agrarian thing was absurd.

* * *

Palestine

The president said, "Well, you handled that well in my absence and I hope I don't have to hear about it again for awhile."

Saudi Arabia

I told the president about them needing financial assistance . . . and that it would be impossible through Lend-Lease. The president wanted to know what the hell they were doing with all the money. In this connection, the president said that the world seemed to think that we had all the money . . . and the fact was that we were getting to the bottom of our own well. The president said it was about time we began to get tough and not be so liberal with our money.

[During the last week of the year Stettinius directed his efforts toward the twin objectives of smoothing relations with Britain and persuading the president that it was imperative to make a vigorous statement on foreign policy to rally the public's hopes. The secretary met with Halifax three days after Christmas.]

CALENDAR NOTES | *December 28, 1944*

Lord Halifax then stated he had had a most satisfactory discussion on Saturday afternoon with Mr. Dunn and Mr. Rockefeller relative to closer liaison between the department and the embassy. He stated he had just received a message from Anthony Eden asking Halifax to have a talk with me on how closer liaison could be brought about. He spoke of quarterly meetings of foreign ministers, frequent visits by members of the Foreign Office and the State Department to London and Washington, such as my own trip to London last spring, and Sir Alexander Cadogan's trip to the United States in the summer. He then asked me what I thought. I told Lord

Halifax I thought very well of quarterly meetings and hoped that Churchill, Stalin, and the president would agree to such a procedure. I also stated I thought there was much to be gained by frequent visits by the staff of the Foreign Office and the State Department to their opposite numbers in London and Washington. I also stated that he could rely upon me to do everything within my power so that he could be kept fully informed at all times on matters well in advance of action, and that I would follow the course of complete consultation at all times.

[One of the major difficulties hampering better relations with Britain had been leaks of top secret documents, particularly to Drew Pearson. On December 28 Stettinius got a highly slanted report on Pearson's means of operation from journalist Constantine Brown through undersecretary Grew.]

CONSTANTINE BROWN-JOSEPH GREW,
MEMORANDUM OF
CONVERSATION | *December 28, 1944*
As for the leak of the telegram from Ambassador Kirk, Brown said that there was no doubt whatever that the leak had occurred in OSS. The telegram had been sent to the War and Navy Departments, to OSS, and possibly to OWI [Office of War Information] in slightly different paraphrases, and it was the paraphrase received by OSS which had been published textually by Pearson. Brigadier General Carter Clarke in G2 in the War Department, who is a blunt speaker, would confirm this if we should ask him. Brown said that there are a good many very fine men in OSS, but it is a heterogeneous group and comprises many "fellow travelers."

* * *

206 | EDWARD R. STETTINIUS, JR.

Mr. Brown said that on November 9 he had been given a copy of Mr. Morgenthau's plan for dealing with Germany after the war, and that he had at once recognized that if such a plan were published it would give Goebbels the most powerful material for propaganda that he had had in a long time. He had discussed this with his editor, who agreed with his view, and they therefore decided not to use it, although it would have been a magnificent scoop. Shortly thereafter, the plan was published elsewhere and, in Mr. Brown's opinion, it had had a greater effect than any other development in welding the German home front together.

Returning to Drew Pearson, Brown said that Pearson's fundamental thesis is that, in the best interests of the United States, the British Empire must be dissolved, and he visualizes the British as reduced to their home islands and the dominions. This thesis colors all his thoughts and writing. He is constantly trying to organize support of his thesis and as he earns something like $6,000 a week, he has plenty of money for that purpose.

* * *

Brown said that the revolt against the administration now developing in the Senate was based largely on the feeling that whereas we are fighting this war to destroy German and Japanese totalitarianism, what we are really doing is to substitute Soviet totalitarianism. Congress realizes that after the war we shall be called upon to send vast sums of money to the Soviet Union as well as machines and tools, and that these will be used to turn out cheap goods which will undersell American goods in the world's markets. The group in the Senate, which already numbers twenty-seven members, comprises an astonishing cross-section of senators, including both isolationists and reactionaries. Even Senator [Walter F.] George [D.-Georgia] is among them and they are steadily building up their strength. They propose to take the position that American foreign policy should be formulated and carried out only with the advice and consent of the Senate, and they propose to exert their rights in this respect more and more positively as time goes on. State Department officials must expect to be called more and more frequently before congressional committees. . . .

Mr. Brown summed up the situation by stating that the only way out is for us to get back to the Atlantic Charter and stand firmly on its provisions.

[On December 30, Stettinius went to the White House for an extensive review of foreign policy matters. The secretary hoped to persuade Roosevelt to issue a strong defense of American policy in his forthcoming State of the Union Address.]

CALENDAR NOTES | *December 30, 1944*

* * *

The president seemed relaxed and in a good humor and to have benefitted from his stay at Hyde Park. . . . I referred to our memorandum of December 26 entitled "Suggestions." He said he had seen this and generally agreed with the recommendations. He said he felt it went a bit far at this time. . . . The president stated, however, he thought he should say very little in his State of the Union message—that he should primarily say we had gone to war because we had been attacked by aggressors and that it was our desire to end the war and bring our troops home as soon as possible. . . . He did not show in his discussion with me the keen grasp I had hoped he would get from the memorandum we had sent to him.

* * *

I told the president with emphasis that the country was getting quite disturbed over the action being taken by Russia and England and that I thought it was necessary for him and the State Department to clarify its [sic] position before the world just as soon as possible. The president said he hoped to do a part of this in his State of the Union speech but that much of this would have to wait until his return from his Big Three meeting.

I left with the president the poll which he promised to return. I called his attention to the last page which showed that American sentiment in answer to the question, "Are our foreign relations [well] taken care of?" [had been] 64 percent [yes] in June, 53 percent in October, 49 percent in December. In answer to the question "Are others taking advantage?"—24 percent [yes] in June, 32 percent in October, 39 percent in December. . . .

The president was greatly pleased with the poll on American public opinion that I took to him today. We must make a practice of sending such a poll over weekly.

* * *

The president and I had a general discussion on other matters. I pointed out that he must take a position on the Palestine situation as he would be in difficulty on the Hill this spring. He agreed. He understood that Silver and Wise had resigned. I said Silver was through but Wise would end up as head of the Zionist movement. This seemed to please the president. I said Dr. Wise had great confidence in the president and was willing to leave the Palestine situation in his hands.

* * *

I told the president I thought it was very important to have some briefing sessions next week of about a half hour as to what we were going to take up at these meetings [Yalta]. We could come over with a list of the subjects we thought would be raised. He said, "That's good. But hold it down to Harry, Bohlen, and Bowman."

At this point I asked Mr. Bohlen to join us. Mr. Bohlen came in and we discussed the draft of the message from the president to Stalin on the recognition of the Lublin Committee. The president asked a great number of questions which Mr. Bohlen answered. The president finally initialled the cable with the additional sentence added to it. . . . The additional sentence read as follows: "I cannot from a military angle see any great objection to the delay of a month." [14]

*   *   *

He read a copy of a cable he had received from Churchill in connection with the meeting he and Eden had with the king of Greece. In the latter part of the cable he referred to the difficulty we were facing with the Polish situation but Churchill stated that he was standing firm and would not recognize the Lublin Committee and would continue to urge Stalin to postpone recognition of the Lublin Committee until the meeting. I suggested that the president permit us to acknowledge the message from the prime minister, at the same time sending him a copy of the president's message to Stalin on the same question. Mr. Bohlen has done this and it was dispatched about 3:30 P.M.

[Three days later Stettinius returned to the White House for further consultation on the forthcoming Big Three meeting. Roosevelt took this occasion to elaborate his views about the postwar world, particularly the status of China and American overseas bases.]

MEMORANDUM OF CONFERENCE WITH
THE PRESIDENT | *January 2, 1945*

The president said he had a number of topics in mind which he felt would have to be discussed with Churchill and Stalin.

China

The president said that recent reports from Ambassador Hurley and from our military authorities in China seemed to indicate that the British and the French, but more particularly the British, were working to undermine our whole policy in regard to China. He said that apparently the British did not desire to see a strong China after the war and still clung to the idea of white supremacy in Asia. He said this was entirely contrary to his idea and the policy of the United States government. Our policy was based on the belief that despite the temporary weakness of China and the possibility of revolutions and civil war, 450 million Chinese would someday become united and modernized and would be the most important factor in the whole Far East. China would someday assume the leadership in that area which the Japanese had attempted to seize. The president said that he thought it might be necessary to raise the whole question of a divergence of views on the subject of China and Asia in general between the British and ourselves at the tripartite meeting.

The secretary said he would have memoranda prepared for submission to the president giving all available information and our recommendations on this subject.

Pacific Bases

The president then spoke of the question of island bases in the Pacific. He felt that possibly this subject might be raised with Churchill and Stalin. . . .

In reply to the secretary's question the president said that he had in mind for a number of these islands in the Pacific the application of the principle of trusteeship. Mr. Hopkins said there was a distinct difference between the Japanese mandated islands or Japanese territory such as Korea and islands that belonged outright to Allied countries such as France. He said it would be difficult to apply the principle of trusteeship to territories when sovereignty was vested in a friendly Allied country. The president agreed there was a difference but did not pursue that aspect of the matter further.

Bases in Africa

The president said that we were most interested in acquiring a base in West Africa and that there were three possibilities in this area: (1) Dakar, (2) Gambia, and (3) the Canary Islands. . . . He said he had in mind in particular an airfield which would be primarily of use in breaking up any threat of a hostile landing on South America for which he said he had military responsibility.

The secretary said he would also have memoranda prepared on the political aspects of these suggested bases.

Near East

The president said that during this trip he hoped in some place in the Near East, either Syria, Lebanon, or Port Said, to meet with Ibn Saud and discuss with him the Arabian question. The secretary said that he thought this was of the highest importance because sooner or later we would have to take a definite position in regard to the Arabian-Jewish difficulties and to the Jewish national home in Palestine. The president said he desired to take with him a map showing the Near Eastern area as a whole and the relationship of Palestine to the area and on that basis to point out to Ibn Saud what an infinitesimal part of the whole area was occupied by Palestine and that he could not see why a portion of Palestine could not be given to the Jews without harming in any way the interests of the Arabs with the understanding, of course, that the Jews would not move into adjacent parts of the Near East from Palestine.

The president then briefly and without going into any detail spoke of the Italian colonies along the Mediterranean and seemed to favor the idea of returning Italian Somaliland to Ethiopia and taking Tripoli away from Italy. He also mentioned the desirability of taking Djibouti away from France and turning it over to Ethiopia. Mr. Bohlen remarked at this point that he thought if France was to be asked to relinquish some of her colonial territories either for bases or other reasons it would be most important to take France in as a full partner in regard to European matters since, otherwise, considerable resentment would be aroused in France if she felt she was being kept in an inferior position and some of her colonial possessions were being removed.

Indochina

The secretary said that he had received the president's memorandum turning down any idea of a commitment on the part of this government in regard to military operations in Indochina, and he had so informed Lord Halifax this morning.[15] The president asked how Lord Halifax received the news. The secretary replied he had been somewhat disappointed.

* * *

Voting in the Security Council

. . . The president said he was not too worried about the question of voting in the council since, if the shoe were on the other foot, the American people would be very reluctant to see the United States deprived of a vote if it were involved in a dispute with Mexico. The secretary agreed but said that in this case the real issue was whether or not a Great Power could exclude the complaints of a little power from being considered by an international organization, and he personally felt that was quite different from the question of the application of force to compel the settlement of a dispute. The president agreed to make available a time for discussion of this question.[16]

[The urgency of clarifying America's position on European questions weighed heavily on Stettinius because his callers frequently expressed alarm over recent developments. However, he met frustration in his efforts to win presidential approval for a strong statement about foreign policy in the State of the Union Message. The president held to his original intention of talking in generalities, and the press sharply criticized his evasiveness. In contrast, on January 10 Senator Vandenberg made a major speech on foreign policy that won national acclaim for its forthrightness. To many observers it appeared that Roosevelt was pursuing a rudderless foreign policy.

Stettinius endeavored as best he could do to defuse congressional criticism. The president was also worried and directed Stettinius to discuss with Senator Connally a means to head off a congressional debate on foreign policy. Connally suggested that one way to accomplish this might be for the secretary to appear before the Foreign Relations Committee an hour each month.

In order to improve understanding between the White House and Congress, a meeting of key Democratic and Republican Senate leaders was arranged for January 11 with the president.[17] Roosevelt was more candid about the limits of American power than he had ever been in any public statement.]

MEMORANDUM FOR THE
SECRETARY | *January 11, 1945*
The president took the situation in the Balkans as an illustration. He reviewed the discussions at Teheran regarding the

Western Front and stated that he and Marshal Stalin had strongly taken the view that the concentration of power should be in France and that he had refused to employ American troops in Greece or the Balkans.

* * *

In brief, the president stated that although spheres of influence had been mulled over at Teheran the idea kept coming up because the occupying forces had the power in the areas where their arms were present and each knew that the others could not force things to an issue. He stated that the Russians had the power in Eastern Europe, that it was obviously impossible to have a break with them and that, therefore, the only practicable course was to use what influence we had to ameliorate the situation. In reply to a question from Senator Vandenberg, he stated that our economic position did not constitute a bargaining weapon of any strength because its only present impact was on Lend-Lease, which to cut down would hurt us as much as it would hurt the Russians.

Senator Austin asked whether the most hopeful course was not to press forward with the Dumbarton Oaks Proposals and set up that machinery as soon as possible. The president and Mr. Grew stated that this was exactly the course which the administration was following.

The president then went on to say that before the United Nations met he would make an effort to work out the unresolved points with Stalin. He thought that Stalin would yield on the request for the sixteen votes which, if pursued, would cause endless trouble and the president would have to give way on the Russian demand for unanimity in the council. The president asked Mr. Acheson to state the compromise offer. In his comments, the president leaned strongly toward the belief that unanimity was as a practical matter inevitable and might as well be conceded as a formal matter.

Senator La Follette then argued that the present Russian course would be to settle all of the questions by force of arms and elimination of opposition before the Dumbarton Oaks institutions were set up, thus leaving none of these matters for later action. The president replied that he still believed that much could be done by readjustment if the machinery could be set up and if the Russians could be brought in and could acquire confidence in it.

The president then spoke at some length about Far Eastern matters stressing the importance of turning the Chinese away from anti-white race attitudes which could easily develop. He spoke of his urging upon Churchill the turning over to China of sovereignty of Hong Kong and of Churchill's opposition.

* * *

[On January 19, after a week's rest in preparation for the arduous trip to Yalta, Stettinius met with Roosevelt for final review of the State Department position papers.]

CALENDAR NOTES | *January 19, 1945*
I first presented to the president the set of maps prepared for him for his forthcoming conference. He seemed greatly pleased and said this was exactly what he had hoped for. He then said, however, that he would want to talk with me Sunday on military zones of occupancy for the French and would I please have it available to show on Sunday. He also said he wanted a study and map prepared to be available Sunday (if he called me) on the matter of French occupancy permanently all the way to the Rhine.

I then presented to the president the memo on the Emergency High Commission for Liberated Europe.[18] His reaction was . . . that we should concentrate on the main objective of an early agreement on an international organization, that the European Advisory Commission could carry on in the meantime. I replied that while we did not have time to get into the matter thoroughly now that I felt that this was a question he would wish to analyze quite thoroughly. . . .

* * *

I then presented to the president the black binder that we had prepared for his conference.[19] He was greatly pleased; thought it was quite thorough and said he would study it with great care.

I then discussed with the president the Soviet postwar proposal set forth by Secretary Morgenthau. [The Russians had recently asked for a large loan, a proposal Morgenthau vigorously endorsed.] The president said he thought it a mistake to communicate with Russia on postwar financing and would prefer holding the whole question until he saw Stalin personally and could discuss the matter with him at that time.

* * *

Discussed with the president privately . . . the "V" matter [A-Bomb] and said that he might wish to keep this in mind in his discussion with Stalin.

[In the final week before departing for the Big Three meeting, Stettinius concerned himself increasingly with strategy for the United Nations organization. This vital subject had been the topic of intensive discussions between Pasvolsky and Ambassador Gromyko in mid-January, and Stettinius wanted to be certain the president had a clear understanding of the American position on the veto and other unsettled questions.]

CALENDAR NOTES | *January 22, 1945*

* * *

I met at Mr. Hopkins's house last night with Mr. Bohlen. We reviewed many matters. Mr. Hopkins's talk with the president on pushing for early completion of Dumbarton Oaks has taken effect and he will support us in every way at the forthcoming conference.

[Military leaders took exception to the State Department's plan for early conclusion of the United Nations charter. Stettinius discussed their objections with Stimson, Forrestal, and the joint chiefs on January 21.]

CALENDAR NOTES | *January 21, 1945*
Mr. Stimson called me this morning and said he was disturbed about trusteeships. He stated they might be discussed at this meeting. He then said he thought it was a mistake to have the United Nations conference before the end of the war. I told him I would talk with him again but the president is determined to go ahead. . . .

[At Stimson's suggestion, Stettinius went to the Pentagon the following morning for a full review of American objectives in the Pacific, the atomic bomb program, and the United Nations.]

CALENDAR NOTES | *January 22, 1945*
I went to Secretary Stimson's office today and had two hours with Stimson, Forrestal, and [Assistant Secretary of War John J.] McCloy. It started off with a half hour with Stimson and [Harvey] Bundy [adviser to Stimson] on S-1

[atomic bomb]. Bundy has given me a private note to take with me relative to X [see following memorandum] if it comes up. General Marshall will have with him an army officer named Considine who will have all the basic papers. He has been instructed to give me these papers if I ask him and he will look me up at M [Malta.]

* * *

The matter of the world organization was discussed and Stimson still thinks it is a mistake to hold a United Nations conference soon and is writing a memorandum to me that I may take and show the president.

The attached is an agenda which McCloy prepared for Stimson to take up with me.

MEMORANDUM OF FACTS FOR
MR. STETTINIUS:

1. The United States authorities did not know of the X government interest when individual X scientists were employed on a part of the [atomic bomb] project in Canada. They were so employed and thereby got some of our information.

2. Sir J. [Sir John Anderson] consented that one of these X scientists go to X and tell the leading X government scientist there some facts about the project. Sir J. stated that these scientific facts were not important to security and contended that by letting the X scientist tell the X chief scientist something it tended to keep X from urging immediate government participation in the whole project. Upon this representation, Sir J. got W. [Churchill?] to consent reluctantly to the trip to X and the disclosure. The U.S. scientific authorities think the disclosure made was prejudicial to security.

3. U.S. has now insisted that no further disclosure be made to X without consent of the committee. The committee today, while noting the danger of X pressing for participation,

219 | *Storm Before Yalta*

unanimously decided that although there was no objection to Sir J. making to the X government a statement in the following form:

> *"Since it is inadvisable to attempt detailed discussions as to arrangements with X in the field of T.A. [atomic energy] until after the termination of hostilities with the Axis powers, the government of UK is prepared, in view of this postponement, to assure X that upon the termination of hostilities with the Axis power it will discuss further with X fair treatment of any claims of X relating to commercial or industrial applications of T.A."*

Any further discussion or negotiations with the X government would have great danger to the security of the project.

* * *

Program for Discussion with Mr. Stettinius
[January 22, 1945] *Trusteeships*

We feel that the topic should not be brought up before the end of the war.

Mr. Stimson has no objection to another general Dumbarton Oaks meeting prior to the end of the war, but the subject of the trusteeships is fraught with danger because immediately it will introduce territorial discussions.

How would Mr. Stettinius care to express himself on the desirability of the secretaries of war and navy writing him their views apart from the JCS view, or would he prefer to have an overall military viewpoint stated, if it is possible to obtain it?

Germany

Is there to be a Russian controlled government set up in their area? Do they envisage a division of Germany, and to what extent? Would they destroy German industry or seek its control after its initial demilitarization? The sooner we have the answer to these questions and a determination of our own policy, the better the military will be able to plan for the occupation.

Mr. Stimson's views are that where the Russians are acting in the course of their own occupation, our line should be to interfere with them as little as possible, but where they call upon us for our action, we must consider our own traditions and our own public opinion (for example, in the matter of the delivery of Germans or others into the hands of the Russians).[20] In our dealings we should be open but entirely self-respecting in our approach to the Russians as we have as much to give them as they to give us.

As for Poland, Mr. Stimson's opinion, for what it is worth considering his lack of personal knowledge of this problem, is as follows:

(1) Curzon Line—The Russian position is understandable and we are not prepared to say it is unreasonable in the light of history—it certainly does not seem to be worth a quarrel with Russia. The Polish administration of Silesia has not been too bad and it may very well be that a carving out of some German territory to compensate for the Curzon Line adjustment on the East would be a feasible thing to do.

(2) The London Committee against the Lublin Committee— on this we haven't enough facts. It does seem as if the Russians with their possession have 99 44/100 percent of the law.

[While Stettinius was convinced of the importance of moving forward on establishing the UN, he now had the military reservations clearly in mind. Overseas bases in the Pacific would secure America's role as a Pacific power. The atomic bomb, when perfected, could be decisive in accomplishing U.S. military and diplomatic goals in the Far East. There was also the secretary's own apprehension over compatibility between Russia and America. His fears subsided during the Yalta conference, but they were destined to return with redoubled strength in the spring.]

VII
DECISIONS AT YALTA
January–February 1945

On the bitterly cold morning of January 25, 1945, Stettinius, accompanied by Freeman Matthews, Alger Hiss [Deputy Director, Office of Special Political Affairs], and several personal aides, departed from Washington's National Airport on a specially fitted military transport. During his six-week absence from the State Department he would attend both the Yalta and Mexico City conferences. His 16,000 mile odyssey was the longest any secretary of state had made up to that time.

Originally Roosevelt had wanted the secretary to accompany him aboard the *U.S.S. Quincy*, but this valuable chance for a personal review of topics was put aside so that Stettinius might fly ahead for last-minute consultations with Anthony Eden at Malta. Their discussions touched on the unresolved UN issues, the Polish question, the occupation of Germany, and the reestablishment of governments in liberated Europe. Churchill and Roosevelt arrived by February 1, and their personal friendship was still able to maintain an aura of camaraderie despite deepening differences on postwar policies. Altogether the brief sojourn at Malta repaired some of the damage from recent misunderstandings in Anglo-American relations.

The Russians welcomed their Western guests to the Crimea with a lavish hospitality, and Stalin seemed determined to recapture the spirit of unity achieved a year earlier at the Teheran conference. In some respects, the decisions at Yalta simply ratified those first outlined at Teheran. But the Crimea meeting went far beyond Teheran in the crucial area of international organization. The Big Three resolved the open issues left over from Dumbarton Oaks, and their success in this area helped to make possible agreements on Poland, Germany, and liberated Europe.

In contrast to earlier heads of state meetings, the State Department took an intimate part in the deliberations at Yalta, a change partly attributable to Stettinius's improvement of working relations between the department and the White House. The secretary conferred at length with the president several times each day. With the exception of the Far Eastern discussions, he played a significant role in deliberations leading to all of the Crimea decisions. He was instrumental in winning over Roosevelt, Churchill, and the Russians to the State Department proposals on voting in the Security Council, an agreement that in turn made possible general acceptance of the principles for an international organization. He found the pace exhausting, but he was exhilarated by the personal sense of accomplishment and by the spirit of harmony that he felt the Allies had developed at Yalta. Four years later he would look back upon these days as the "high tide of Allied unity."

[Stettinius had long regarded agreement on the UN as a paramount objective, and he devoted much of his thought immediately prior to Yalta to strategy affecting the open questions, especially the veto. The State Department was committed to a compromise formula that allowed a veto on the imposition of economic or military sanctions but did not provide for it on the discussion of peaceful settlement of disputes. Stettinius and his advisers were still pessimistic about Russian acceptance of the proposal, however, and stopping briefly at Marrakesh in Morocco, they reviewed the possible alternatives.]

CALENDAR NOTES | *January 28, 1945*
We worked most of the afternoon on papers concerning the coming conference. Matthews, Hiss, and [Wilder] Foote [Stettinius's personal aide] discussed with me the problem of voting in the Security Council at great length. We went over various alternatives and the climate of U.S. public opinion on the question. Since the Russians so far gave no indication that they will change their minds and agree to the United States formula on the voting procedure, we felt we should have at least one alternative ready in case of a deadlock. Matthews, Hiss, and Foote tentatively agreed that the alternative proposing voluntary abstention would be at least a possible solution in case of a deadlock at the conference. We also discussed the proposal to establish an Emergency High Commission for Liberated Europe. This plan has still to be put up to the president.[1]

[After a daytime flight across the Mediterranean, Stettinius met with Harry Hopkins and Ambassador Alexander C. Kirk at a villa on the outskirts of Naples. Friction with the British over Italy was the main subject of the discussion.]

NOTES ON CONVERSATION | *January 30, 1945*
Mr. Hopkins went on to say that he thought it was very important that the United States government not continue to accept the position of a mere silent partner of the British with respect to Italian policy. He pointed out that the British military authorities in Italy, as elsewhere, take their orders from the Foreign Office, whereas the American military officials do not hesitate to take a position quite independent of State Department policy. Mr. Hopkins said that he thought it was of the greatest importance that the United States should insist with the British upon the Italians being given more direct po-

litical responsibility. He said that at present the Allied military authorities in Italy are responsible for all decisions. The Italian government can do nothing, even in the most inconsequential matters, without Allied military approval. Because of the fact that the United States is participating militarily in Italy it cannot escape responsibility for these military decisions on political matters even though it is the British who really make the decisions. He said that the American military officials say that the larger military responsibility is British and that we have to agree. He said he did not think this was an adequate way of discharging American responsibility. He thought that in spite of the fact that General Eisenhower is the supreme commander in Western Europe the president should insist on an American being placed at the head of the Allied Control Commission.

[The following morning Stettinius and Hopkins discussed the UN and problems relating to occupation zones in Germany.]

NOTES ON CONVERSATION | *January 30, 1945*
Dumbarton Oaks Voting. Mr. Hopkins said that he had had several talks with Prime Minister Churchill and several with Mr. Eden on the question of Dumbarton Oaks voting procedure. He said the British Foreign Office are [*sic*] entirely in agreement with the State Department as to the advisability of the American proposal. However, Mr. Churchill made it plain that he himself is not committed to that proposal, although he approves of it. Mr. Churchill said that he will have to get an agreement at the forthcoming conference whether or not he is able to persuade the Russians to agree to the American formula. Mr. Eden told Mr. Hopkins that Lord Halifax had cabled him that the president had himself said that he was not firmly committed to our formula. Mr. Hopkins said that it

is clear that the British Foreign Office and State Department are in precisely the same situation: that both realize the importance of obtaining Russian agreement to the American proposal. At the same time, both Mr. Churchill and President Roosevelt are not firmly committed to the idea that this is a matter of major importance. Mr. Hopkins said that the British situation is complicated by the fact that the British Cabinet is not unanimous in agreement with the Foreign Office. He said Churchill had given him a copy of a memorandum by Sir Stafford Cripps [member of the War Cabinet, former ambassador to Moscow] which argues that the Soviet formula is more desirable than the American formula from the standpoint of British interests. Mr. Hopkins remarked that Mr. Eden had been irritated that the prime minister had seen fit to give a copy of this memorandum to Mr. Hopkins as it indicated a lack of unanimity within the British government. Mr. Hopkins said that Mr. Eden did not entirely accept Mr. Churchill's view that the British Parliament could be brought without much difficulty to accept the Russian formula.

* * *

Treatment of Germany. Mr. Hopkins said that the most outstanding point on this subject is the absolute lack of centralization and the final decision within the United States government [sic]. He pointed out that Mr. Winant was particularly disturbed because neither the British nor the American governments have yet formally approved the protocol on zones of occupation, although the only reason for delay is the relatively minor disagreement between the military authorities of the governments as to the degree of American control in Bremen and Bremerhaven. Mr. Winant is fearful that the Russians may reach and cross the border of their zone before formal agreement is reached, in which case they might say that they are not bound by the draft protocol since it has not been formally adopted. Mr. Hopkins said that he agreed with Mr. Winant that it was of the greatest urgency and that the president and Mr. Churchill should reach immediate agreement on this matter, if necessary leaving Bremen and Bremerhaven for settlement between the British and Americans later.

[That same afternoon Stettinius and Hopkins flew to Malta, where Anglo-American military conversations were already in progress. In the next two days, during which Roosevelt arrived, Stettinius sought to promote a common stand with Churchill and Eden on key political problems they would be covering with the Russians at Yalta. Stettinius and Eden held their first extensive discussion the morning of February 1 aboard the *H.M.S. Sirius*. The secretary stressed the urgency of Anglo-American accord on occupation zones in Germany and they agreed to press for immediate military approval of this matter. They then turned to other political problems.]

NOTES ON MEETING | *February 1, 1945*

* * *

Poland
Mr. Stettinius then brought up the subject of Poland and said that recognition of the Lublin government would cause a great uproar. He said we had hoped for some kind of a coalition government with Mikolajczyk at least invited to join it. . . . Mr. Eden said, "We couldn't recognize Lublin." He said that before he had left London Mikolajczyk had expressed some ideas about the formation of a presidential commission. . . . Mr. Eden said that this proposal would be a little complicated.[2]

Sir Alexander Cadogan said that the important thing

to aim for is the formation of a new government. He thought that perhaps the presidential commission might be a good means of arriving at what we want, i.e., a new government. He said he thought there was no use talking about a fusion of the London and Lublin governments. . . . Mr. Stettinius suggested it might be possible to get up a simple joint memorandum on Poland policy to present to the president and the prime minister for their consideration. This was agreed to.

Mr. Eden wondered whether the Russians might also agree to the United States and Great Britain being assured in some way with regard to elections in Poland. He said he realized that this would be asking rather a lot.

Mr. Stettinius said that the Polish dispute jeopardizes the participation of the United States in the world organization. He felt it important that the president and the prime minister get that fact across to Stalin. He said that he thought the joint memorandum to the president and the prime minister should bring out the importance in this matter of the large Catholic population in the United States. . . . Mr. Eden said that if the Russians did not agree to our approach to the Polish problem we will simply have to say that we have reached a deadlock and did not reach an agreement in the matter.

Iran

Mr. Eden brought up the matter and asked Mr. [Nevile] Butler [British assistant undersecretary of state] to describe the situation. . . . Mr. Eden said the Iran matter also affects the world organization.[3]

Mr. Matthews said that, concretely, we all want the Russians to cease putting pressure on the Iranians for an oil concession.

Mr. Eden wondered whether we might go further

and say that when the supply route to Russia across Iran is no longer needed, which he felt would be by June, we would be prepared by agreement to begin the removal of troops. . . . Mr. Eden said that we do not wish spheres of influence—that withdrawal of the troops is the best way of preventing that and he said that the prime minister has agreed to this approach. . . . Mr. Stettinius said he thought that the United States should make a statement similar to the British one suggested by Mr. Eden.

Mr. Stettinius then brought up the question of the traditional Russian interest in a warm water port and asked what the latest was on this subject. Mr. Eden said that the Russians had gone no further than suggesting that the Montreux Convention [4] be revised.

At this point Mr. Eden said that he had told the prime minister that we should put everything on the table at the forthcoming conference. He said that the British have so little to give that it should be pointed out in connection with all the other matters to be discussed. . . .

China

At this point, Mr. Hiss brought up the question of China and stressed the importance which the United States attaches to U.S.-British-Soviet encouragement and support for an agreement between the Comintern and the Chinese Congress [*sic*] in order to further the war effort and prevent possible civil strife. Mr. Eden said that Mr. Hopkins had said that the president has it in his mind . . . that the British want to keep the Comintern and Congress from reaching agreement. Mr. Eden said he couldn't imagine where that idea could come from. He said we all desire Chinese unity and wish to get the Russians to take the same position.

Emergency European High Commission

Mr. Hiss was asked to describe the main purpose behind this suggestion. He pointed out the desirability of unity in fact and in appearance among the great powers with respect to postwar political and economic problems in the liberated and satellite states. It is important that France participate in this work. . . . Mr. Stettinius pointed out that he did not yet know how the president would feel about this proposal . . . and he said that the prime minister should not discuss it with the president until we had an opportunity of sounding the president out. . . . He went on to say that the proposed High Commission would tie in with the idea of quarterly meetings of the foreign ministers. . . .

Dumbarton Oaks Proposals

Mr. Eden then brought up the subject of Dumbarton Oaks and said "we like your formula very much." He went on to say that the prime minister doesn't understand it and the Foreign Office has more work to do in that direction. He said that the prime minister "slips back" on that subject. Mr. Stettinius said that he and his colleagues also have work to do in this connection, "referring to the president."

* * *

Polish-German Frontier

Mr. Eden then said he would like to discuss the question of the Polish-German frontier. He said he is worried about the increasing tendency of the Lublin group to clamor for more territory. He thought that the proper western boundary of Poland should include cession to Poland of East Prussia, Silesia, and a coastal sector of Pomerania. This would include 8 million Germans and be all the Poles could swallow. There is general agreement with this view.

Mr. Matthews said that the American government also hopes that the necessary transfers of people will not be precipitate.

[At lunch Stettinius pursued the question of occupation zones.]

CALENDAR NOTES | *February 1, 1945*
I then presented the zones of occupation as not having been settled. I also presented the EAC matter, giving the State Department's action and the president's approval, and saying that there were details still left open. I said we were anxious to have the protocol signed before we had the conference with the Russians. After a brief discussion, General Marshall and [Sir Alan] Brooke [chief of British general staff] authorized Eden and myself to wire Winant and [Sir William] Strang [British representative on European Advisory Commission] on zones of occupation.[5]

[In the evening the secretary went aboard *H.M.S. Orion* for dinner with Churchill and Eden. The prime minister opened their discussion with strong statements about the December row over British actions in Italy and Greece.]

* * *

The prime minister was rather outspoken to me regarding Greece and Italy, saying that what had been going on was distressing to him. However, he warmed up and was more cordial than he has ever been. During the last two days and the many hours that I have spent with the prime minister I have had a closer association with him than ever before. The prime minister seemed encouraged on the outlook in Greece and thought that the matter would finally be settled satisfactorily. His position all along was that if they had not acted as they did they would have had a leftist communist government there and they had a definite responsibility not to permit this.

On Italy he was distressed about our statement relative to Sforza. Churchill said he was a no-good bum and he felt that he had a personal right to make this statement. I made our position clear to the prime minister, saying that if we had been consulted in advance we would have been able to say something which would not have caused resentment.

The prime minister did not seem to understand the international organization or the voting procedure in the council. He made a great feature of the new organization doing nothing other than keeping the peace and not getting into social or economic things. Eden and I talked with him about this and I told him we would be very disappointed if the social and economic council would not have an important place.

I rode back to the *Sirius* from Government House with Eden and Cadogan and had an intimate coversation with them about the prime minister's views and the International Security Organization. They cannot agree to the Russians' position on voting and our present position is the one to be adopted.

They said they would not recognize the Lublin Committee and this would not be done regardless of consequences.

* * *

During the evening we started out on the matter of the need of recognizing social and political relief for liberated populations in the wake of Germany['s surrender].

It was felt that this was a matter that the Foreign Office, the State Department, the British, and Russians had recognized, but that American officials had not recognized this yet.

They realized how desperate the course of the war was, but we would be rapidly losing what we were fighting the war for if we would allow unrecognized governments to arise as happened in Italy. It also was brought up that the matter of feeding the people and giving them transportation . . . was a matter of necessity in war as much as ammunition was. Churchill was very depressed on the outlook of the world. He said there were probably more units of suffering among humanity . . . as of this hour when we sat down to dinner, than at any time during the history of the world . . . and as he looked out on the world, it was one of sorrow and bloodshed. He said everything depended on Britian and America remaining in close harmony together at all times.

[The president arrived early the morning of February 2, and was greeted by Stettinius, Hopkins, and Harriman. The secretary reported on discussions with the British.]

CALENDAR NOTES | *February 2, 1945*
The president asked me then if there were any new developments. I told him that we had had a most satisfactory time with Mr. Eden, referring to our memorandum, and I said that generally we were seeing eye-to-eye on points. I also said I had had a long talk with the prime minister and I felt he had blown off steam and the president would have a very harmonious time with him. . . . I also explained the action we had taken yesterday on zones of occupation. He had had this on his mind and seemed greatly relieved that Winant had been instructed before the president reached Russia, and he immediately got the psychological point in connection with the advance of the Soviet army.

The president volunteered to me that he had been giving the voting procedure in the council much thought and that he had worked out a new plan during the voyage which he had not discussed with anybody yet, but wished to discuss with me at the first possible moment. (Later I asked Byrnes whether the president had discussed this with him and he said only once at dinner in a very casual way.)

[At noon that day, Stettinius and Eden lunched with Roosevelt and Churchill aboard the *Quincy*. The two world leaders shared ideas on the Atlantic Charter's relevancy.]

CALENDAR NOTES | *February 2, 1945*
. . . There was much joking and talking about the unsigned Atlantic Charter. The prime minister said he had recently read the Declaration of Independence and was delighted to find in the same book the Atlantic Charter. He was very proud of that fact. The prime minister said he still stood for what the Atlantic Charter said. The president said that he had a signed copy of the Atlantic Charter in his book, but that Roosevelt's and Churchill's names were in the president's own handwriting. The president said he hoped that perhaps on this trip the prime minister would countersign this so that the document would be bona fide, and there was much teasing and joking about the matter. The prime minister went off on a very serious vein at this point, saying that the four freedoms were all right, but the most important of them was freedom from fear. He said the president had never made clear to the world his ideal of freedom from international fear and that there were many countries on the face of the globe at the present time where the populations were in fear of their internal governments and where they were being ruled by [the] Gestapo for example. The prime minister, in a very emotional way, said, "As long as blood flows from my veins, I will stand for this." The president seemed greatly impressed and said

that this would be a matter to which he would have to give a very careful study.

* * *

The president seemed rested and calm and said he had gotten plenty of sleep on the way here. He said he had been resting ten hours every night since leaving Washington but still couldn't understand why he was not slept out.

[Their talks concluded, the American and British delegations departed from Malta in the early morning hours of February 3, for the seven-hour flight to the Crimea. At the Saki air field they were treated to a lavish banquet spread on long tables under army tents. Following a ninety-mile motor trip across the mountains, they reached the warmer resort of Yalta, ready for their more serious business on the fourth. The president kept in constant touch with Stettinius, holding reviews of developing issues several times each day. In the first of these discussions, they ranged over numerous subjects.]

CALENDAR NOTES | *February 4, 1945*
1. *Voting Procedure*
The president O.K.'d this. . . .
The secretary explained that the British are in full agreement with the formula and he suggested that the president not refer to it as "The Compromise Formula" since it is the one we like best. The president expressed agreement.
2. *Poland*
 . . . Mr. Matthews said there were two aspects of the problem—boundaries and composition of the government. They went over the boundary situation fully with the president who examined the map with some interest. The president said that if the Russians would not agree to the Poles re-

taining Lwow, perhaps they might at least agree to the Poles having the oil fields as a matter of face. He asked how important the oil fields were and Mr. Bohlen said that while they were not very important from the Russians' point of view they were important to Poland.

The president asked for figures on the area which would be transferred to Poland under the proposals. Mr. Bohlen told him that Poland would receive about one-third less German territory than she would lose of her own territory.

On the subject of composition of the government, Mr. Matthews outlined Mikolajczyk's proposals for a presidential council which the president seemed to understand thoroughly. . . . The president said that the Lublin government should not be recognized at this time.

3. *The Proposed European High Commission*

. . . The general purpose of the commission was then explained to the president who said he still felt that he did not like the name nor the idea of setting up another body anyway, in view of the way the EAC had developed. He said he thought the proposed meeting of foreign ministers would adequately take care of any situation which arose even though it meant his leaving Washington once a month. It was pointed out to the president that the secretary's duties would not permit him to absent himself so frequently and that continuity of approach to these questions would be desired. The president then said that the secretariat could furnish the continuity.

* * *

At a later talk the same afternoon with Justice Byrnes, the justice made the following points:

1. He did not think the American public and Congress would like a United States commissioner with independent authority to act as he saw fit. It was explained to the justice that the commissioner would, of course, be subject to instruc-

tions. He replied that none the less it would be much better if the objectives of the declaration, which he liked, could be carried out by the four ambassadors in any country where trouble arose, because ambassadors are approved by Congress and are directly answerable to the secretary of state.

2. Any agency tends to perpetuate where it is and this would be undesirable. He said American troops want to come home right away, and it would be unpopular if they had to remain in Europe because of this commission.

3. Most important of all, apparently, is that the United States should be loathe to inject itself with responsibility in internal matters in Europe. It was pointed out to the justice that we could hardly expect the British or Russians or French who were in occupation of any particular territory to follow our advice if we refused to accept any responsibility for it. They would be faced with an actual problem and would have to act promptly.

* * *

4. *Zones of Occupation*

Mr. Matthews pointed out the importance of getting the Russians to agree promptly to the EAC protocol on zones of occupation, saying that the Russians may soon reach and cross their zone and they might then say that since there was no formal agreement they would not restrict themselves to their zone. The president did not commit himself on this, although he indicated general agreement that it would be desirable to get Soviet agreement to the zones of occupation question. However, he brought up at this point the desires of the French to have a zone and seemed to think that the final tripartite agreement on the zones should be left until the French zone had been settled. Admiral Leahy suggested that we give the French our zone, saying that the troops want to come home promptly. The admiral was undoubtedly speaking in a light vein, but also was indicating the general attitude on American postwar commitments in Europe.

*   *   *

At the end of the 10:30 A.M. meeting today, I had a talk with General Marshall and with the president on "X" [atomic bomb]. General Marshall does not think the matter should be raised.

*   *   *

Admiral Leahy . . . sent a wire through to the State Department without my knowledge, regarding arrangements on the president's meeting with the king of Egypt, the emperor of Ethiopia, and Ibn Saud. I said, "Who the hell is the State Department?" I said, "As far as I am concerned, this is the last time a message goes to the State Department without my knowledge." I said that Eden and I had discussed this thing with the president and had been working on this matter for weeks. I told Admiral Leahy that I would greatly appreciate it if . . . no messages be sent to the State Department without my knowledge. Leahy agreed.

[The Big Three had earlier agreed that there should be no formal agenda for their talks. The discussions ranged loosely over the entire array of issues confronting the Allies, and the pace was strenuous. The foreign ministers and military staffs of the three nations met separately each day at noon. At four o'clock they joined the Big Three for plenary sessions that often lasted until after eight. Then came sumptuous banquets followed by round after round of toasts and more discussions. Stettinius concluded each day with a review of the most recent activities and with briefings on the latest cables from

Washington. He and his staff rarely got to bed before 2 A.M.

The first plenary session convened at 4 P.M. on February 4. At Stalin's request, the meeting opened with a review of the current military situation, and the Americans and British were surprised and gratified at the unusual frankness with which the Russians discussed operations on their front.]

A Soviet discussion of military action on the eastern front featured the opening plenary session. General Marshall then outlined events along the western front.

The president then invited Stalin to have his generals report on the winter campaign and the plans for the future. This consumed about the first hour of the meeting. It was a detailed discussion and very encouraging. It was a full hour's revelation of the campaign beginning three months ago and what the plans were right up to the present and into the future months to come. The Russian generals talked from maps, mentioning places, and made a complete disclosure of the Soviet army's plans in the future. This is the first time such a thing has happened in this war. During the discussion, great emphasis was put on the fact by Stalin that many people were saying he did this thing because of demands from the president and Churchill, and Stalin said he was proud he had done it on his own without any suggestions from anyone.

This was followed by Stalin's request for a complete statement on our part of our military plans for the future.

Then General Marshall made one of the most magnificent presentations I have ever heard in my life on the last sixty days' campaigning and the immediate plans for the next thirty days. He told about what the movements were, what the plans were, mentioning places, rivers, numbers of divisions, etc. This made a very favorable impression on the Russians.

It was then agreed at the end of this that the time had arrived for us to have complete collaboration on the part of our military authorities and the generals of the three countries were then ordered to meet at 10:30 tomorrow morning at the Russian headquarters for a military staff committee to coordinate the military plans of the three powers. This is the first time that such a thing has ever been done. And it was suggested by Stalin. It was immediately taken up by Churchill and the president.

[At dinner that evening, the Big Three in turn toasted the solidarity of the Great Powers. Their statements seemed to emphasize the primary role of the United States, Britain, and Russia in keeping world order, a marked contrast to the work of their own foreign ministers, which was designed to build an international organization based on the sovereign equality of member nations.]

CALENDAR NOTES | *February 4, 1945*

I attended a dinner which the president gave for Mr. Churchill and Marshal Stalin at Livadia Palace. During the greater part of the dinner the conversation was general and personal in character. But during the last half hour the subject of the responsibilities and rights of the big powers as against those of the small powers came up. Marshal Stalin stressed in his remarks his feeling that the three Great Powers which had borne the burden of the war should be the ones to preserve the peace. He said it was ridiculous to think that a country like Albania should or could have an equal voice with the United Kingdom, the United States, or the USSR. It was they who had won the war. He said he was prepared to join with the United States and Great Britain to protect the small powers but that he could never agree to having any action of any of the Great Powers submitted to the judgment of the small powers. The president and prime minister said that they agreed that the Great Powers would necessarily bear the major responsibility for the peace but that it was essential that they exercise their power with moderation and with respect for the rights of the smaller nations.

After Marshal Stalin and the president had left, I talked with the prime minister and Mr. Eden briefly on the voting question. The prime minister reiterated that he had been inclined to the Russian view on voting procedure because he felt everything depended on maintaining the unity of the three Great Powers. Without that the world would be doomed to inevitable catastrophe and anything that preserved that unity would have his vote. Mr. Eden took vigorous exception to the prime minister's statement on voting procedure and said he believed the United States formula was the minimum essential to attract the support of the small nations to the organization, nor did he feel that the British people themselves would accept a ruling of unqualified unanimity.

*   *   *

Mr. Eden, Ambassador Harriman, myself, and Mr. Bohlen all agreed that no progress was made. It seems that it is taking the course at the moment of more of a three-power alliance than anything else. Eden is very disturbed that the prime minister does not understand the voting procedure. The prime minister seems to be switching over to the position of the Russians, and Eden and the prime minister had a little difficulty over this in my presence. However, I had a long talk with the prime minister myself and I think I made progress with him when I brought up again the example of Mexico. The prime minister said, "You are entirely correct. We should stay together in the use of force, but you should never have the right to request [deny?] a vote and let Mexico make a complaint against you." I said, "That is right." Eden said to me later, "You made an extremely important point and I believe this is the first time the prime minister realized what the question is all about."

[At the second plenary session on February 5, the Big Three and their advisers discussed postwar treatment of Germany. The following day, Stettinius sought to break the deadlock on the question of voting in the Security Council.]

CALENDAR NOTES | *February 6, 1945*

* * *

. . . The president proposed that we now proceed to . . . the United States proposal on voting. . . . He said he was not so optimistic as to believe that eternal peace was yet attainable but he did believe fifty years were feasible and possible. He said that . . . he had asked the secretary of state to explain the question of voting in the Security Council.

[The secretary then read the U.S. voting proposal plus a statement illustrating how the veto might work in the Security Council on substantive issues.]

* * *

Mr. Molotov said the Soviet government attached great importance to the question of voting in the Security Council, . . . wished to study the United States proposal and . . . discuss the question tomorrow.

The prime minister said . . . he could say on behalf of the British Commonwealth that the president's new proposals were entirely satisfactory. . . . The British government would consider that they were commiting an injustice if provision were not made for small countries to frankly state their grievances. If this were not done it would appear as if the three Great Powers were trying to rule the world. . . . He felt that the three major powers should make what he termed a "proud submission."

* * *

Marshal Stalin . . . asked the prime minister what he had in mind when he referred to a desire to rule the world. He said he was sure Great Britain had no such desire, nor had the United States and that left only the USSR.

The prime minister replied that he had spoken of the three Great Powers collectively; they could build themselves so high over the others that the rest of the world would say that these three desire to rule.

* * *

Marshal Stalin said there was a more serious question than voting procedure or the domination of the world involved in all this. They all knew that as long as the three of them lived, none of them would involve their countries in aggressive actions, but after all, ten years from now none of them might be present. A new generation will come into being not knowing the horrors of the present war. He felt that there was an obligation to create for this future generation the kind of organization which would truly secure peace for at least fifty years. He said the main task was to prevent quarrels in the future between the three Great Powers and to secure their unity. The convention of the new world organization should have this as its primary objective. The great danger was conflict between the three Great Powers represented at this table. If unity could be preserved among them there was little danger. Therefore, a covenant must be worked out which would prevent conflict between the three Great Powers.

Marshal Stalin continued by apologizing for not having had an opportunity to study in detail the Dumbarton Oaks Proposals. He said that as he understood it there were two categories of disputes involved in Mr. Stettinius's explanation: (1) conflicts which would require the application of sanctions, economic, political or military, and (2) conflicts which could be settled by peaceful means. In regard to the first, the permanent members had a right to vote even if they were parties to the dispute. Under the second category, however, the parties in the dispute would not be allowed to vote. He said the Russians were accused of spending too much time on the technique of voting. He admitted this but stressed the great importance which they attached to this matter since all decisions of the council were made by votes and Russia was interested in the decisions not in the discussions. He pointed out that if China or Egypt raised complaints against England they would not be without friends or protectors in the assembly.

Both the prime minister and I persistently pointed out that under our proposal the power of the world organization could not be directed against any of the permanent members. Marshal Stalin said he feared any conflict might break the unity of the three powers. The prime minister admitted the force of that argument but did not believe the world organization would eliminate disputes between nations and the settlement of such disputes would remain the function of diplomacy.

Marshal Stalin said that his colleagues in Moscow could not forget the events of December 1939 during the Finnish war when, at the instigation of England and France, the League of Nations expelled the Soviet Union and mobilized world opinion against her, even going so far as to speak of a crusade. The prime minister replied that at that time the British and French governments were very angry at the Soviet Union and in any event such action would be impossible under the Dumbarton Oaks Proposals. Marshal Stalin replied that he was not thinking of expulsion but of the mobilization of opinion against one country by the others. The prime minister's reply to that was that he thought this might happen to any nation but he doubted very much that either the president or Marshal Stalin would lead a savage attack against Great Britain and he felt this also applied to the other two countries.

The president concluded the discussion for the day by saying that he felt the unity of the Great Powers was one of our first aims and that our proposal would promote rather than impair achievement of this aim. He said that should there unfortunately be any differences between the Great Powers—and there might well be—this fact would become fully known to the world no matter what voting procedure was adopted. In any event there was no method of preventing discussion of differences in the assembly. Full and free discussions in the council would in no sense promote disunity, in his opinion, but on the contrary would serve to demonstrate the confidence which the Great Powers had in each other and in the justice of their own policies.

During intermission . . . Mr. Churchill told me I had done a magnificent job in my presentation of the American proposal on voting and that not only Stalin but he himself, the prime minister, now really understood it for the first time. Eden seconded the prime minister's remarks and both he and Mr. Churchill thought we had made real progress and that there was a good chance that the Russians would now agree to the voting formula.

[The Americans anxiously awaited word on the Russian reaction to the voting formula. Discussion among Stettinius, Hopkins, and Byrnes pointed up the centrality of the UN in American thinking.]

CALENDAR NOTES | *February 7, 1945*
I have just had a meeting with Justice Byrnes and Harry Hopkins. They stated that they thought the Dumbarton Oaks situation was of greater importance than anything else and that when we met at noon with Molotov and Eden, I should make a statement at the opening of the meeting saying that if there are any points relative to Dumbarton Oaks which they do not understand, we should be delighted to clarify any of them. They both thought that the French zone of occupation, control, reparation, and dismemberment of Germany could wait another day for this. Therefore, they feel that we should have all of our Dumbarton Oaks papers with us and be prepared to meet any question which might arise.

[The Soviet response came at the February 7 plenary session. The Russians accepted the American proposal, but made clear that they expected something in return.]

CALENDAR NOTES | *February 7, 1945*
Molotov had nothing to report at the foreign minister's meeting on the Soviet reaction to our proposal on voting in the Security Council but at the Big Three meeting this afternoon he announced the Soviet Union's complete agreement.
He said that after hearing my full report and explanations the issue had been made clear to the Soviet delegation and the explanation was entirely satisfactory. The Soviet delegation had also followed closely Mr. Churchill's remarks. Mr. Stettinius's report and Mr. Churchill's remarks had clarified the whole matter and the Soviet government now felt that the proposals fully guaranteed the unity of the Great Powers for the preservation of peace. This had been the chief purpose at Dumbarton Oaks as it was here and since he now felt that the new proposals fully safeguarded this principle . . . agreement had now been reached on this matter.

Mr. Molotov then went on to recall that the question of the participation of Soviet republics as initial members of the organization had been raised at Dumbarton Oaks. . . . Mr. Molotov said that the Soviet government did not intend to press for inclusion of all of the Soviet republics . . . but would be satisfied with the admission of three, or at least two of the Soviet republics as original members. These three were the Ukraine, White Russia, and Lithuania. . . . He pointed out that they had borne the greatest sacrifice in the war and were the first to be invaded by the enemy. He felt the proposal that three or at least two of these republics be made original members was only fair in view of these circumstances and hoped that Mr. Churchill and Mr. Roosevelt would accept the Soviet proposal. He referred to the dominions of the British Empire having gradually and patiently achieved a place for themselves as separate entities in international affairs.

The president expressed his pleasure at the agreement of the Soviet government to our voting proposals. He thought that this was a great step forward which would be welcomed by all the people of the world. The next step was to consider the question of summoning a conference to organize and to plan the establishment of a world organization. He said he thought such a conference could be called at the end of March, although it might be physically possible to do so within the next three or four weeks.

The president then referred to Mr. Molotov's proposal regarding the Soviet republics. . . . He felt . . . that if the major nations were given more than one vote it might prejudice the principle of having one vote for each member in the assembly. . . . He therefore suggested that Mr. Molotov's proposal be studied by the foreign ministers. . . .

The prime minister said he had great sympathy with the Soviet Union's request. His heart went out to mighty Russia which though bloody, was beating down the tyrants in her path. He could understand the Soviet point of view. After all Russia was represented by only one voice in comparison with the British Commonwealth which had a smaller number of people if only white people were considered. He was glad to hear that the president had not finally turned down the Soviet proposal. However, he . . . would like to discuss the proposal with the foreign secretary and possibly communicate with the War Cabinet in London before giving final reply.

The president remarked that his proposal had been merely that the foreign ministers should study the question as well as the time and place of the conference and who should be invited.

The prime minister said he . . . frankly . . . foresaw great difficulties in attempting to hold the conference as soon as March. . . . He also wondered if the state of the world and Europe in particular would not make very difficult any United Nations conference at all at this time. . . .

The president remarked that he had only in mind a conference to organize setting up the organization and that the world organization itself would probably not come into being for some three to six months afterwards.

*   *   *

The prime minister finally said that he had no objection to the foreign ministers discussing this point. But he emphasized that this was not a technical matter but a great political decision. Marshal Stalin remarked that the foreign ministers would not make decisions but would merely report to the Big Three.

[Having settled their chief differences on the UN the Big Three next accepted Roosevelt's invitation to hold the conference in the United States. Stettinius turned his attention to selecting a site and composing a delegation to represent the United States.]

CALENDAR NOTES | *February 8, 1945*
Justice Byrnes definitely thinks the United Nations meeting should not be out West or any place. He thinks that after having called conventions and travel off in the United States, that Government travel to the West Coast or any place would give a bad impression. The president does not want Byrnes in this matter at all, and the president pushed him out of this last night. He gave a signal to me that Alger Hiss and I should handle this entirely ourselves. The president wants this outside of Washington so that he can travel to open and close the meeting.

[A little later the secretary discussed the matter with Hopkins.]

We then discussed the World Security Organization. His instinct is definitely to have it in a Middle Western city . . . He thinks the middle of April or the first of May is right. He thinks as far as the delegation is concerned Connally, Vandenberg, Bloom, and [Representative Charles] Eaton [R.-New Jersey] should go. He discussed Warren, but when I came out with the possibility of Stassen,[6] he thought that would be better. . . .

I asked him what his advice was about Mr. Hull and told him that I wanted to invite Mr. Hull to come if it would be at all possible. Mr. Hopkins said he thought that was grand and I certainly should make the gesture to the president and say that Mr. Hull should not only be a member of the delegation, but should preside over the conference. Mr. Hopkins's private view is that Mr. Hull's doctors will not let him do a single thing.

[Stettinius strongly opposed naming Hull chairman, fearing that if poor health prevented his going the British or Russians would try to grab the conference chairmanship. Seeking evidence on Hull's illness that he could use in persuading Roosevelt to name Hull only as honorary chairman, Stettinius looked up the president's physician, Dr. Ross McIntyre.]

CALENDAR NOTES | *February 8, 1945*
I went to see Admiral McIntyre this morning. . . . I explained that I had come to call on him relative to what position the president would take regarding Mr. Hull's participation in the forthcoming United Nations conference. . . . Admiral McIntyre said, "Well, Mr. Hull is coming along nicely, but if you put a burden of this kind on him, and in which he might make a supreme effort, the task might break him," . . . I said they must realize, however, that if Mr. Hull was chairman of the American delegation and could not make the grade, the chairmanship would then go to Eden or Molotov, and that Eden would move heaven and earth to get chairmanship of the conference.

[At their luncheon meeting on February 8, the foreign ministers agreed on arrangements for the UN conference.]

CALENDAR NOTES | *February 8, 1945*
I opened the meeting which was presided over by Mr. Eden, by offering an invitation to hold the conference on world organization in the United States. I said that I hoped the foreign secretaries were not shocked by the president's

mention of the month of March as the time for the conference
. . . , but I was most anxious that the conference open at the
earliest possible date. . . . I recalled that at Dumbarton Oaks
there had been considerable discussion of inviting the associated nations as well as the United Nations. I said I had now
come to the conclusion that it would be most satisfactory to
limit the invitations to those who had declared war on the
common enemy and signed the United Nations Declaration.
With respect to Mr. Molotov's proposal of admitting two or
three of the Soviet republics I felt that this question might be
given sympathetic consideration at the conference, but I had
been unable to make up my mind just how this membership
could be arranged since the Dumbarton Oaks Proposals had
specified that each sovereign state should have one vote. I said
I wished to refer the matter again to the president who had felt
that the proposal should be given sympathetic consideration.

*   *   *

Mr. Eden said he would be glad to accept the invitation of
the United States government to hold the conference in the
United States. However, if Mr. Molotov and he were to go to
the United States for the conference he hoped there would be
an early meeting of the foreign secretaries in London. . . .
After discussion it was agreed that the conference should open
on April 25 in the United States.

Mr. Eden then said that he was sympathetically inclined
toward the Soviet proposal for the inclusion of two or three of
the Soviet republics and would be ready to say so at whatever was considered the appropriate moment. Mr. Molotov
said the sooner the better. He then said that while the Dumbarton Oaks Proposals provided only one vote for each government, Canada and Australia had individual votes and the
fact that they were component parts of the British Empire did
not prevent them from having individual membership. He

said the Soviet constitution had been amended to give the Soviet republics the right to conduct foreign relations and had in
other ways increased the rights of the constituent republics.
. . . Mr. Molotov then said that if only those nations which
had signed the United Nations Declaration were invited to attend the conference this gave rise to several questions. Which
Polish government, for example, should be invited? There
were certain other countries that did not maintain diplomatic
relations with the Soviet Union who would also be invited.
He would like to check the list of states. I then gave Mr. Molotov a list of the United Nations. . . .

Mr. Eden suggested that the question of admission of the
two Soviet republics might be placed on the agenda of the conference. He was quite ready to agree to such a proposal. Mr.
Molotov suggested an amendment to the effect that the three
foreign secretaries agreed on the advisability of granting admission to the assembly of two or three Soviet republics. I
said . . . since I had not had an opportunity to discuss the
matter with the president this morning I could not make any
firm commitment. However, I expected the United States
would be able to give a favorable reply before the end of the
day. I said I would not bring up the question of Poland since I
hoped that agreement on a Polish government would be
reached during the present conference.

[Communications within the U.S. delegation now broke
down on the question of how to handle Stalin's request
for extra seats in the UN General Assembly. Stettinius
and Hiss wanted the president to stand firm against the
Soviet argument. The secretary went to Roosevelt's
apartment that same afternoon to discuss the matter, reporting that at the foreign ministers luncheon Eden had
backed Molotov's position. Just as he was about to explain to Roosevelt that he had not promised U.S. ap-

proval, Stalin entered the room and immediately inquired whether the foreign ministers had agreed on the extra seats question. Without consulting Stettinius, the president "waved his hand and told Stalin that agreement had been reached on everything." Later in the conference, Roosevelt secured Stalin's and Churchill's agreement that the U.S. could seek extra seats should that be deemed politically necessary.

In the afternoon the Big Three further discussed which nations should attend the conference.]

CALENDAR NOTES | *February 8, 1945*

At the Big Three meeting that afternoon, Mr. Eden reported our agreement . . . on world organization. . . . At that stage British and American delegates would support the proposal to admit to original membership two of the Soviet Socialist republics.

* * *

Marshal Stalin said that there were ten nations which had no diplomatic relations with the Soviet Union who would be represented at the conference. He thought it somewhat strange for the Soviet government to attempt to build future world security with nations which did not desire to maintain diplomatic relations with her. He asked what could be done about this matter. The president replied that he knew most of these countries would like to establish relations with the Soviet Union but had just not gotten around to doing anything about it. . . .

The president then recalled that three years ago the then acting secretary of state, Sumner Welles, had told some of the other American republics it was not necessary to declare war on Germany but only to break diplomatic relations. These countries felt that they had followed the advice of the United

States and were therefore in good standing. They had in fact helped us a great deal in the war effort. Speaking frankly, our advice had turned out to be a mistake and a month ago I had brought up with him the whole question. As a result the president had sent letters to the presidents of the six American countries which had not declared war urging them to do so.

* * *

Marshal Stalin said he hoped that in the recommendations it would be possible to name the Soviet republics, the Ukraine and White Russia and this was accepted. Mr. Molotov asked if it would not be better if the two Soviet republics signed the United Nations Declaration before the first of March. Marshal Stalin also returned to this point and wondered whether if they did not sign the declaration that could be used as an excuse for excluding them from the conference. The president and I both assured Marshal Stalin that this would not occur. The prime minister said he would have preferred confining the conference to the present United Nations but if others were to be added he thought the two Soviet republics should also be added. Marshal Stalin said he did not want to embarrass the president, but that if he would explain his difficulties he would see what could be done. The president replied that up to the present they had been discussing invitations to separate states but that now it was not a question of a new country but of giving one of the Great Powers three votes instead of one in the assembly. This was a matter he felt should be put before the conference and we would all three agree to support the Soviet request at the conference. Marshal Stalin inquired if a signature by the Ukraine and White Russia of the United Nations Declaration would not solve the difficulty. The president said he did not think it would. And then Marshal Stalin withdrew his proposal.

[After a final plenary session on Sunday, February 11, the conference adjourned. Stettinius and other Americans regarded the UN agreements as the major product of the meeting, but the Yalta protocols included a number of decisions on other matters that would in time become the source of great controversy. In a secret agreement, the result of private discussions between Roosevelt and Stalin, the Russians reiterated their earlier pledge to enter the war against Japan and promised to support Chiang Kai-shek's government in China. In return, Roosevelt accepted the restoration of Russia's pre-1905 status in the Far East. He further agreed to the USSR acquiring Japan's Kurile Islands, which, with the restoration of southern Sakhalin Island, placed Russia at the doorstep of Japan's northern home islands. FDR acquiesced in maintaining the status quo for Outer Mongolia, which meant that territory would continue to be dependent on the Soviet Union.

European matters proved the most difficult to resolve. The Big Three agreed on occupation zones for Germany, but they were unable to spell out the details on dismemberment and reparation and referred these problems to commissions for further study. They established the Curzon Line, with some digressions, as the eastern boundary of Poland, but dealt less satisfactorily with the future government of Poland, the most explosive issue to come before the conference. Stalin was determined to have a friendly government in Warsaw. The Western Allies were sympathetic to Russia's security interests, but mindful of public pressures, they wanted to guarantee an independent Polish government. The result was a vague agreement, later to be the source of a most acrimonious and divisive conflict, to "reorganize" the existing Lublin government "on a broader democratic basis." Stettinius never presented the State Department's plan for an Emergency High Commission for Liberated Europe. Instead, the Big Three agreed upon a Declaration on Liberated Europe, a statement of general principles promising to assist the smaller European nations toward economic recovery and the establishment of freely elected democratic governments.

Although some presidential advisers privately criticized the Polish accord and the Declaration on Liberated Europe as weak and lacking in enforcement mechanisms, Stettinius agreed with Roosevelt that the United States could not do better in view of Russia's military presence in Eastern Europe. The secretary shared the president's larger hope that tying Stalin to public promises and bringing Russia into the UN as a full partner offered the best chance for a stable peace.

The Yalta agreements and the general spirit of harmony that prevailed at the conference indeed encouraged much optimism on the part of the participants. Roosevelt and his top advisers regarded the meeting as a success, and some first-hand observers gave Stettinius major credit. Averell Harriman, who for some months had been pessimistic about U.S. relations with Russia and critical of the weakness of American policy, thought that the secretary had helped to alter the course.]

HARRIMAN TO STETTINIUS |
February 20, 1945

I feel I must take this opportunity to tell you what a gratification it was to me to see at Yalta the grasp which you have of our problems. The careful preparation which you organized for the conference and the skill with which you handled the negotiations with Molotov and Eden laid the foundation for the ultimate decisions reached there by the president with Marshal Stalin and the prime minister. Knowing Molotov and the other Soviet officials as well as I do, I can say without qualification that your frankness and fairness in these discussions have, in the brief period of the conference, materially improved our relations with the Soviet Foreign Office. The historic suspicions of the Soviet Foreign Office have been much allayed. I already sense the development of far franker relationships. There is no doubt that we will have further difficulties. On the other hand I am satisfied that your discussions at Yalta have resulted in a tremendous stride in the direction of greater mutual confidence which will stand us in good stead in future negotiations.

* * *

The peace and tranquility of the world depends [sic] on the development of intimacy between the three Great Powers who are winning the war. This is the avowed Russian policy and I believe you have seen enough to accept its sincerity.

[After departing Yalta, Stettinius made a short day-long visit to Moscow which was a combination goodwill gesture and an attempt to lay the groundwork for postwar trade relations between Russian and America. No substantive negotiations took place, and there was no mention of the Russian loan request. At a luncheon where the secretary discussed new food storage processes, Deputy Soviet Foreign Minister Andrei Vyshinski extolled the prospects of economic cooperation and peaceful competition.]

CALENDAR NOTES | *February 14, 1945*
Vyshinski then declared that he wished to propose a toast to economics. We lawyers, he said, may know nothing of its

mechanics, but we can appreciate the art of it. In wartime, not only what can be eaten with pleasure is important, but any food at all is important. He therefore proposed a toast to industry and agriculture, to the men who guide them and work in them; all those who build up the vast resources of a country, and especially to the workers and farmers and business leaders of the United States, who have created so much that is useful, not only to the United States, but to other countries as well. Vyshinski added, we do our best to learn. We have already had successful lessons. We have already mastered the art of producing many of the things for which America is famous. He hoped, he continued, that the Soviet Union would eventually not only equal but surpass the United States in production. That, he declared, is the right kind of competition—peaceful, economic competition.

[This struck a responsive chord in Stettinius who valued the potential market Russia offered to American industry. From Cairo, where he saw President Roosevelt, the secretary wrote in cordial terms to Anastas I. Mikoyan, peoples commissar for foreign trade.]

STETTINIUS TO MIKOYAN |
February 14, 1945

I was delighted to have had the opportunity of seeing you at lunch yesterday noon, after having exchanged cables and letters so often with you during my tenure of office as administrator of Lend-Lease.

The collaboration between the Soviet Union and the United States in economic affairs can become just as important as its collaboration during the war from the standpoint of keeping the peace and security of the world. Let us hope that you and I can have the privilege of playing a part in such a program.

[The secretary wrote this letter from Cairo en route to Brazil and a highly important mission to see President Vargas. He was satisfied with the outcome of the Yalta meeting and confident that the agreements reached meant the strengthening of the wartime alliance for the new challenges of the postwar peace.]

VIII

THE MEXICO CITY CONFERENCE
February–March 1945

The army transport carrying Stettinius westward from Africa toward Brazil took him into a new set of problems in some ways more difficult than those encountered at Yalta. Following a visit with President Getulio Vargas of Brazil, the chief purpose of which was to secure a long-term commitment on raw materials vital to the atomic project, he flew north to Mexico City for the opening of the Inter-American Conference on Problems of War and Peace. His primary objective was to gain Latin American backing for the Dumbarton Oaks Proposals. He arrived in Mexico confident that this could be easily achieved, but from the outset he faced serious obstacles.

Since the early months of the war, United States relations with Latin America had steadily deteriorated. As the U.S. turned its attention toward Europe and Asia, it devoted less time to hemispheric matters. Latin Americans resented this neglect of the Good Neighbor spirit and feared its implications. They had developed deep attachments to the inter-American system, and during the war sought to bind the United States closer to it through specific defense commitments against outside intervention and more precise restrictions on unilateral action within the Americas. In contrast, the Dumbarton Oaks Proposals suggested that the United States was placing global concerns above hemispheric interests and the rights of the Great Powers above those of the small nations. Latin American leaders protested that they had not been consulted on Dumbarton Oaks and feared that the Great

Powers through the international organization would effect what one commentator called a "partition of the world." [1]

Economic matters compounded their apprehension. Since the outbreak of war, the United States had provided assistance through Lend-Lease and the Export-Import Bank and had purchased huge quantities of Latin American raw materials at high prices. Yet these extraordinary arrangements were a mixed blessing. The demand for raw materials brought shortages and a spiraling inflation to the Latin American economies. Trade agreements with the United States were conditioned on low tariffs that prevented the signatories from protecting their struggling industries. Concerned that the demand for their products might end with the war, dependent upon commerce with the United States yet resentful of the restrictions imposed on them, Latin Americans looked to the future with foreboding.

Argentina provided an additional and unexpected problem at Mexico City. Unlike other hemispheric nations, the Argentines had rejected U.S. leadership during the war, refusing to break relations with the Axis and tolerating various German activities within their borders. The United States had responded by refusing to recognize the Farrell government and by applying increasing economic and diplomatic pressure. [2] Until 1945, the other American nations had generally supported United States policy toward Argentina, but by the time of the Mexico City Conference they had begun to revise their views. They distrusted Farrell and feared possible Argentine designs on neighboring nations. But they were increasingly concerned that U.S. policy toward Argentina might set a pattern for unilateral intervention in other hemispheric nations.

The Mexico City Conference was thus called at Latin American insistence, and the delegates came to the meeting determined to confront the United States with their fears and problems. They sought to amend the Dumbarton Oaks Proposals to provide greater safeguards for small nations and for hemispheric interests. They wanted commitments for continued postwar economic aid and for trade agreements which would maintain a high level of exports to the United States but eliminate restrictions against tariffs. They planned to promote reconciliation with Argentina.

Mexico City provided a stern test for Stettinius's diplomacy. He was unprepared for the strong opposition he encountered, and he was not authorized to make the economic arrangements Latin Americans desired. He desperately wanted unified hemispheric support for the Dumbarton Oaks Proposals; but the regional security concerns of the Latin Americans, endorsed in some instances by members of his own delegation, caused him serious problems. He ultimately achieved his objective, and the Declaration of Chapultepec marked a significant step in the evolution of the inter-American system. But this was not accomplished without concessions toward regionalism that would come back to haunt him at San Francisco and without radically altering U.S. policy toward Argentina, a move that would outrage liberals in the United States and provoke a major controversy with the Soviet Union.

[Before arriving in Mexico City, Stettinius journeyed to Rio De Janeiro for talks with President Vargas of Brazil. The secretary had been directed by President Roosevelt to obtain an agreement for United States purchase of all of Brazil's production of monazite sands. The thorium extracted from this mineral was critical for construction of the atom bomb. Stettinius gave no hint, of course, of this underlying significance of his trip to Brazil. He first discussed general diplomatic matters, sketching for Vargas the general outlines of the Yalta conference and the question of how the inter-American system could be tied to the UN. Only toward the close of their conversation did he raise the question of monazite sands.]

CALENDAR NOTES | *February 17, 1945*

. . . I first said . . . that there had been a few minor irritations between the Big Three . . . and . . . the president and Churchill went to the Crimea really not knowing what kind of items they would meet politically or militarily. . . . I was gratified to be able to report that they had found a high degree of cooperation on the part of Stalin. . . .

* * *

The president then wanted to know whether Stalin was a very tough man to work with. I said he was very tough but he was also very realistic. Vargas then asked about the president's health. I said it was good although he was naturally showing his twelve years of strain. . . .

I said . . . the president was confident that the Soviet Union had decided to take its place in the United Nations family as a good citizen and . . . could be completely relied upon for collaboration in the future. Vargas then asked what her policy would be relative to spreading her philosophy. I said that all this points to the fact that she has too many problems at home to spread communism throughout the world. The president then said . . . that it would be very helpful if I could give him my official advice . . . as to how we felt Brazil's position should be in relation to Russia. I immediately . . . said that no time should be lost by Brazil in recognizing Russia. . . . The president then asked, "Would it be possible for the United States to give us assurance that if we did do this that there would not be trouble in the future?" I replied there was no question that the president of the United States would be delighted to sponsor such a relationship. . . .

I then . . . said that we had made very favorable progress in the establishment of a world organization. . . .

The president then asked as to . . . "the make-up of the [security] council." I said that there had been no change since the Dumbarton Oaks discussions on that point. . . . The three big powers merely had arrived at a plan . . . to be presented to all the nations of the world, and the door at San Francisco would be wide open for any suggestion they might wish to make. . . .

The president then asked a question as to how we solved the voting procedure. . . . I then . . . stated the president's position at Yalta had been accepted. He wished to know what the president's position was. I stated concisely and clearly that as long as peaceful means were used, a party to a dispute would not cast a vote. The president seemed pleased with this decision.

The president then asked, "Please tell me for my private information what is going on in connection with getting some of our friends in this hemisphere into the war at this late date." . . . I then briefly told him that two years ago six South American countries had broken relations and [not] declared war. They received advice from the United States government that it was not necessary to declare war and that what they had done was sufficient. The Soviet Union, British, and ourselves had agreed that at this first meeting no one should attend who had not declared war. We feel a great moral obligation to our friends in this hemisphere, and the only way we could create a place at the table of the United Nations for all the members of this hemisphere except Argentina was for them to make that gesture. It was a moral obligation on our part more than anything else. I said one of the important features in our minds relative to this unanimity was that if every member of every American Republic had its rightful place in the United Nations family commencing at San

Francisco, they would have great strength in connection with solving the Argentine problem. If three or five of the American Republics were left out, there would be some danger they might, therefore, look elsewhere to leadership in this hemisphere. This made a very important impression on the president and it was a new thought of mine which had not occurred to me before.

The president then raised the Argentine situation generally. . . . He volunteered the hope that if it was possible to figure out a way in which the Argentine could join the Mexico City Conference it would be most useful and helpful. . . . To that I immediately replied . . . that I thought that idea was off beam. . . . I said we already had much evidence relative to sabotage, to smuggling, to clandestine radio activity, and we did not wish to stoop to that position at this time. . . .

The president then got on the subject of the British and the Argentine. He said the British were imperialistic and were worse than the Argentines. He said the British were not playing fair with them and they had tremendous investments and there was no question but that the British were working against the interests of the United States and Brazil in the Argentine. I stated that Britain's interest in the Argentine at the moment was one of emergency war economic needs, . . . and I was confident that as soon as her war emergency was over that Britain would fall in line. . . . It is very apparent that he distrusts the British and dislikes them immensely and thinks they are not playing fair insofar as his own country is concerned.

* * *

I then took the ball . . . regarding the matter of postwar economic collaboration. . . . I said it would be helpful for me to know what he had in mind from the standpoint of immediate economic needs in order that . . . we might . . . concentrate on his immediate needs the moment our shipping is available. This greatly pleased him and he . . . responded by saying there were three emergency needs in the future. First, gasoline and lubricating oils; second, rolling stock—possibly cars and locomotives, and three, coal. . . .

I said . . . there is a certain product "T" [monazite sands] in which you have a supply. It so happens that India has a supply of this product, and with India's low labor cost she would be able to undersell you in the world market unless you and we can make some immediate arrangement whereby you can give us an option for the next five or ten years. . . . I said it is our desire to trade with you as one of our close neighbors wherever possible. I then stated that this product was a very important one and we need it particularly from the standpoint of radio tubes, electric light bulbs, etc. . . . The president said, we have had complete agreement in the past in supplying you with raw materials in the war, and I am sure we can renew that agreement from the standpoint of your needs during the period you wish it.

[Stettinius arrived in Mexico City in the early afternoon of February 20. The conference, which was scheduled to begin the next day in historic Chapultepec Castle, was the first inter-American meeting since the 1942 Rio conference. The secretary knew that the Latin American nations were concerned about Argentina, economic problems, the future of inter-American security, and the Dumbarton Oaks Proposals. He was particularly anxious to find a proper balance between the objective of a strong United Nations and the regionalism of Latin America. He needed hemispheric support at the forthcoming United Nations conference, but he did not want the United States identified with amendments to the Dumbarton Oaks Proposals before the Great Powers agreed jointly on their own revisions. He especially wanted to

DRESS REHEARSAL

Reproduced with permission from the Chicago Daily News

avoid restoring relations with Argentina, recognizing that to do so would affront the Soviet Union.

Despite these complex problems, Stettinius came to Mexico City in a hopeful mood. Assistant Secretary of State for Latin American Affairs, Nelson A. Rockefeller, who had handled preparations for the conference, optimistically predicted success. More important, he assured Stettinius that the Argentine issue would be kept off the agenda. Mexico's foreign minister, Esequiel Padilla, had lined up support to postpone the question until other matters had been resolved. Then a committee would be appointed to study it, thus insuring indefinite delay. At dinner that evening Padilla informed Stettinius that "this has been a difficult thing to accomplish but that he had been able to do so diplomatically." [3]

As it turned out, Rockefeller and Padilla had miscalculated. Argentina was the first order of business raised in the conference steering committee.]

CALENDAR NOTES | *February 21, 1945*
The delegate for Cuba at once mentioned postponement by the Pan American Union of the meeting requested by Argentina. The Paraguayan delegate added that his government believed a preferential place should be given for discussion of the Argentine situation, pointing out that Pan American procedure provided for consultation among the republics on all important matters. Padilla commented that all the participating republics agreed the Argentine question should be discussed fully and frankly. Further remarks by the Paraguayan delegate and comments by a number of the others on this delicate situation were followed by a proposal by the Mexican delegate, Castilla Najera, that the Paraguayan motion be referred to the steering committee. While this was

approved by the Paraguayan delegate, it was rejected by the committee. Thus the agenda was approved in its original form.

[Keeping the Argentine issue off the conference agenda did nothing to lessen the tension it engendered in private discussions, and Stettinius would have to face up to it before the conference ended. At the outset, however, he found much of his attention absorbed not with conference matters but with French reluctance to sponsor the UN conference. The de Gaulle government had taken no direct part in earlier UN negotiations, and much to de Gaulle's anger, the Big Three had refused to include France in the Yalta proceedings. When the United States now sought France's concurrence in the Dumbarton Oaks Proposals and the voting formula, de Gaulle put up a series of stumbling blocks.]

CALENDAR NOTES | *February 21, 1945*
The position of the French regarding the San Francisco conference was destined to create considerable trouble for us at Mexico City. Despite active efforts of the department to expedite the matter, France had not yet expressed agreement with the Dumbarton Oaks Proposals as completed at the Crimea conference, while China had accepted the new provisions immediately. All of us at Yalta had felt consultation with France and China should be completed as promptly as possible so that the provisions for voting procedure could be published and invitations for the San Francisco conference issued with the least possible delay. We had hoped the invitations could be offered not later than the opening of the Mexico City conference, whether or not France had by that time agreed to be a fifth sponsoring power.

[Stettinius failed to impress his view on Acting Secretary Grew, who was more closely in touch with Paris and favored allowing the French more time.]

CALENDAR NOTES | *February 21, 1945*

Word came back from Grew that he had just advised the president that the French government should be allowed more time to consider acting as joint sponsor for the San Francisco conference. He recommended that issuance of invitations and public release on voting procedure should be effected on March 1. . . .

On receiving this unwelcome news, I wired back that I was in a difficult and awkward position, having been elected during the morning to be chairman of the Commission of World Organization at the Mexico conference. I said that the matter of the voting procedure was on the minds of all the delegates and that from the standpoint of frank and fair dealing I felt I should be able to discuss all angles of the world security proposals at the earliest possible moment.

I was still hoping that somehow between the evening and the following night, when I would deliver my address, that Ambassador [Jefferson] Caffery would be able to explain in Paris the fact that twenty republics were meeting to discuss the world security organization and that, as the French delay was proving most embarrassing to the United States, we ardently hoped that they would give their prompt consent.

[While he waited for news of French action, Stettinius devoted his attention to the work of Committee II on international organization. In order to prevent public discussion of amendments to the Dumbarton Oaks Proposals, the secretary suggested creating a drafting subcommittee not open to the press.]

CALENDAR NOTES | *February 22, 1945*

Venezuela and Ecuador were leading a drive for inclusion of specific items of dissent about the proposals. Padilla had time to work with the other governments in emphasizing that the U.S. was bound by a gentleman's agreement with the other three sponsoring the proposals, not to negotiate with the other states until the general United Nations conference took place. The U.S. delegates meeting concluded that we should not initiate a resolution on the proposals, since this would become a focus for all those wishing to express opposition on any point in the proposals, and since the press would make it appear that concessions and even discussions were defeats for us. Because other committee meetings would be open, Committee II should follow this rule to prevent suspicion. After a few days of general discussion, however, there should be appointed a drafting committee which would hold closed meetings, on the ground they were simply sessions for drafting at a high technical level. Matters not easily discussed in public could be handled in the course of such drafting.

[The French government soon responded, but its agreement to cosponsor the San Francisco conference contained a troublesome catch.]

CALENDAR NOTES | *February 24, 1945*

French sponsorship. During the morning Mr. Grew phoned Mr. Raynor in Mexico City . . . that the French were accepting the invitation to San Francisco and would also sponsor the meeting. However, they might wish to present amendments to the Dumbarton Oaks Proposals for consideration in San Francisco. Mr. Grew said that, while this was a strange request because any country had the right to present amendments, he and Mr. Dunn felt that in the interest of good relations we should accept the reservation. Nevertheless, before replying, we should consult the Soviets, the British, and the Chinese. Mr. Raynor phoned me at Cuernavaca to acquaint me with these developments, and I approved both the recommendations. Mr. Pasvolsky was not entirely comfortable with the reservation, feeling that psychologically it would open the San Francisco meeting to too many additional suggestions and make our job far more difficult.

[One of the crucial proposals presented at the Mexico City conference was Colombia's sponsorship of an inter-American security pact, an idea also put forward in resolutions by Uruguay and Brazil. It reflected a maturation of the hemisphere nations' view on collective defense. The trend in this direction, seriously begun in the 1930's, had been speeded by the onset of World War II. At conferences in Lima (1938), Panama (1939), Havana (1940), and Rio De Janeiro (1942) the governments of the Western Hemisphere had taken various steps which bound them together in a wartime alliance system aimed at the Axis powers. The success of this cooperation in multinationalizing the principles of the Monroe Doctrine encouraged Latin American governments to establish permanent machinery for regional security. They feared that the Dumbarton Oaks Proposals signaled a shift in United States security thinking, which would leave the Western Hemisphere open to the interference of other powers, such as Russia, through a powerful Security Council. By the terms of the Colombian treaty, each nation would be bound to render immediate assistance when a member state was attacked. The resolution presented possible threats to the supremacy of the UN over regional groups as well as to the congressional authority to declare war. American military representatives thought security of the hemisphere took precedence.]

CALENDAR NOTES | *February 24, 1945*

General [Stanley] Embick [military representative on the U.S. delegation] read a statement that the Joint Chiefs of Staff had agreed that the Colombian Resolution regarding nonaggression was entirely satisfactory because, if approved, it would constitute a regional pact which could be built into the world security system. Mr. Rockefeller suggested that the general speak with me (Stettinius) on this matter early in the following week. The meeting decided that we should persuade the Uruguayan delegation to agree to support the Colombian proposal, because the resolutions from the two Latin American delegations were similar. The point of reference during the discussion was almost entirely whether the U.S. could take immediate action if Argentina should attack a neighbor. Judge [Green] Hackworth [State Department legal adviser] said that the Colombian proposal was essentially that the American republics should work together against any active aggression, and there was a saving clause providing for modification upon the creation of a world organization. On the question whether the Colombian proposal could be made effective immediately, Dr. Pasvolsky thought Senate ratification might be necessary. General Embick said we should go to the Senate for approval, if necessary.

[Over the next several days the Americans weighed the alternatives. General Embick stuck to his position and seemed on the verge of swinging the delegation to the military viewpoint. On the afternoon of February 26 the U.S. Steering Committee ". . . discussed the importance of inter-American solidarity from a military, political, and economic viewpoint concluding that solidarity of the Americas was essential to the defense of the United States." [4] Senator Warren Austin, Vermont Republican who along with Tom Connally was a special congressional adviser to the U.S. delegation, had doubts, on constitutional grounds, about accepting the Colombian proposal.]

CALENDAR NOTES | February 27, 1945

Committee III on the Inter-American System. The previous afternoon (February 26) the greater part of the Colombian and the Uruguayan projects was combined in a draft approved by the subcommittee. Because of the subject's importance, the subcommittee had decided to recommend that the declaration be called the "Declaration of Chapultepec." The revised resolution for joint action against aggression was brought before the full committee during the morning of February 27. A move to place the committee on record as approving it by acclamation was stopped by Senator Austin who mentioned the absence of any English text, the need for opportunity to study the resolution, and the desirability of awaiting Senator Connally's arrival next day. Later, a meeting of the U.S. group for Committee III was called at the request of Senator Austin, who said that introduction of this resolution in the main committee by the rapporteur had come as a bombshell to him and the other U.S. representatives. He said the committee had agreed to postponement, only until 11:00 the following morning (February 28). However, Mr. Rockefeller undertook to say that the meeting should be postponed until March 1.

Mr. Rockefeller reviewed for Senator Austin a conversation between Ex-President Santos of Colombia and President Roosevelt and an ensuing cabinet discussion.[5] He said Mr. Roosevelt wanted to effect the guarantee of territories through a resolution. Senator Austin interrupted to point out that the contemplated measure would provide a guarantee during peacetime and not, like earlier ones, only during the war. Therefore, it would require action by Congress. In the following discussion it was the sense of the meeting that the use of economic sanctions, military force, etc. requiring legislative action in the U.S., should be brought before the Congress in connection with the World Organization rather than in connection with the inter-American system. Mr. Pasvolsky thought there might be a unilateral declaration by the U.S. under the president's war powers of our determination to assist other American republics if attacked. This guarantee under a treaty should be made at a time deemed appropriate by the Senate.

[Senator Austin reiterated his objections the next day.]

CALENDAR NOTES | *February 28, 1945*
Senator Austin reviewed the text of the Colombia-Uruguay resolutions on the use of force to repel aggression in this hemisphere. He said changes would be necessary for the U.S. Senate to approve it, since it would commit the armed forces of the U.S. and of other nations to be used anywhere in the hemisphere without providing for due consideration before military action was taken. The conference should understand that all the countries represented were bound by constitutional limitations which would have to be satisfied.

Mr. Rockefeller commented that this "Declaration of Chapultepec" showed a fear of aggression from neighboring countries, and he cited Argentina, Peru, the Dominican Republic, and Haiti as possible sources of that aggression. It was left that Senator Austin, Judge Hackworth, and the Colombian delegate would bend their efforts toward presenting the proposal so that all countries would understand we were united in the security of the hemisphere.

[The ad hoc committee devised a two-step formula for developing a new regional treaty, which was acceptable to the conference committee on inter-American security and the U.S. delegation.]

CALENDAR NOTES | *March 1, 1945*

In Committee III compromises had been made in regard to strengthening the inter-American system, along lines that would preserve the Pan American Union and Washington as the seat of the union—which were the fundamentals we had stood for. Consideration of the resolution for joint action against aggression was deferred until tomorrow so that Senator Connally would have an opportunity to crystallize his views. During the morning a meeting of the U.S. Steering Committee went over the proposal in detail with Senators Connally and Austin. Great enthusiasm for this resolution developed among the Latin American countries, partly directed against Argentina and partly as a symbol of solidarity. Now called "The Declaration of Chapultepec," the resolution was being regarded as one of the keystones of the conference.

Later, however, I was able to wire the president that, pursuant to his conversation with Ex-President Santos of Colombia, the Colombian delegation had introduced a proposed nonaggression declaration, along with similar proposals from Brazil and Uruguay. I then outlined its provisions and reviewed developments. I said that as matters then stood the proposal was in two parts—first, measures to become effective immediately, effective during the war; second, measures to be determined by treaty for the postwar period. (This treaty would be submitted for ratification during the emergency war period after San Francisco.)

I stated that the proposal appeared to conform to the president's objective as outlined in his conversation with President Santos and I believed it was essential to the success of the conference not only because of the Latin American enthusiasm for it but because it gave security against the danger of

Argentine aggression and would remove "the fear from the hearts of the people of the Americas" as emphasized by President Santos. I was able to report that the proposal had been gone over in detail and revised in accordance with suggestions of Senators Connally and Austin and had the support of all our delegation from the point of policy and from constitutional world organization viewpoints.

[In a much publicized address on February 27, Assistant Secretary of State Will Clayton set forth United States policy toward inter-American economic problems. While carefully avoiding any specific commitments, he pledged United States assistance in promoting expanded trade within the hemisphere and maintaining raw material purchases at high levels. Stettinius weighed the significance of the speech and its reception by the delegates.]

CALENDAR NOTES | *February 27, 1945*

Mr. Clayton's Economic Speech. Before a joint session of Committees IV and V Mr. Clayton presented the U.S. position on major subjects in the economic field. It was received with applause and at once made an excellent impression. The statement had been presented to American press representatives the preceding afternoon. They were thus provided full opportunity for background material and discussion. While the first reactions among Latin American representatives indicated some disappointment that Mr. Clayton had not made more substantial commitments, a more considered view crystallized and the moderation and balance of his statement were worth far more than rhetorical bombast. Mr. Clayton promised the other American republics that we would help them solve their reconversion problems, but he reminded them that the rest of the world also had reconversion problems. He emphasized his conviction that the future would see a larger volume of international trade than ever before. Press reaction was that it constituted a "simple and direct statement which avoids normal diplomatic language of international conferences," and a tendency to understate and to underpromise.

[Clayton's speech set the tone for the economic agreements that resulted from the conference. The United States would give only a vague promise of economic assistance during the reconversion period, and it continued to insist that the Latin American nations cooperate in the lowering of tariff barriers. The economic agreements provided small comfort to the Latin American delegates and did nothing to ease the settlement of other issues.

By the last day in February the secretary still awaited positive action from Paris. The next day invitations were to go out for the UN conference, and simultaneously, Stettinius was to announce the details of the voting compromise. In London, meantime, Cadogan had been holding intensive discussions with French Foreign Minister Georges Bidault. During their talks he proposed a formula whereby the invitations to the conference would be modified to allow France leeway for its amendments to be considered simultaneously with the Dumbarton Oaks Proposals.]

CALENDAR NOTES | *February 28, 1945*
Mr. Grew phoned me from Washington at 10 minutes before 1:00 in regard to Ambassador Caffery getting in touch with the French about the voting procedure. I particularly asked that Mr. Dunn and Dr. Matthews keep confidentially in mind the absolute necessity of my continuing my friendly relations with the Latin American republics here in Mexico City, as the whole French situation was very delicate. I got Mr. Dunn on the phone and said that if France should "break"

this situation suddenly, I wanted to call a special meeting of the foreign ministers within the hour, as the statement would be terribly damaging if it came out before I had a chance to tell the foreign ministers. Mr. Dunn said that the French had agreed with the Cadogan formula, that he had been told by Caffery that the French might announce adoption of this formula in order to "scoop the world. . . ."

At 5 minutes after 1:00 I phoned Dr. Padilla and told him that I had some good news. France had fallen in line and would join in the sponsoring, and there would be no trouble. We would be able to go through with the plan I had discussed with him the day before. It was good news indeed that we could all now go hand-in-hand. I couldn't promise making the announcement the next day, March 1, because we had to work out the form of invitations—both in London and Moscow. However, I felt sure everything would be ready by Friday or Saturday at the latest.

[Stettinius soon learned that instead of the French publicizing the voting formula, the first word might come from Roosevelt.]

CALENDAR NOTES | *February 28, 1945*
At 4 that afternoon Mr. Jonathan Daniels [presidential assistant] called me from the White House, saying the president wanted to announce the voting procedure tomorrow in his speech to Congress. I answered that I had advised the Latin American foreign ministers I would tell them the first moment the invitations would be made public. I said that France had only acted during the morning and we had to finish our consultation with Moscow and London. . . . France had reserved her position on the voting procedure until San Francisco. I said it would cause great difficulty in our relations with the Soviets and with the others to do it his way because it had

been agreed at the Crimea conference that the voting procedure would be in the invitation and everybody was instructed and it was agreed that the voting procedure would not be made public until the invitation was issued.

I inquired particularly whether the president was anxious to do it that way, emphasizing that "I have had one hell of a time here holding this Latin American situation together, and this very question is the most important of all." I said it was impossible for me to discuss voting procedure until the invitations were issued as agreed upon. . . .

[The secretary immediately called Washington.]

I then spoke to Mr. Dunn in the department and said I thought it would be most embarrassing to make the voting procedure public tomorrow as the president wished to do in his address before Congress. . . . I said Daniels had put a lot of pressure on me.

Mr. Dunn said, "We are under the obligation of not issuing the voting procedure until the consultation is completed. We cannot consider the consultation completed until we have heard from Moscow." Moscow would need to advise that this change in the invitation was acceptable. Therefore, it would not be in keeping with our agreement to publish the voting procedure separately. I asked Mr. Dunn how long it would take for us to hear from Moscow and when we might expect to give our answer and issue the invitation. Mr. Dunn said Friday morning.

. . . I told him I agreed with his position, that it would be damaging to our relations with the others to do this tomorrow. I said he should call Daniels right away. I wanted to do it in the manner which the president wanted, but I had made a commitment to Padilla and I had to live up to that too. I particularly asked Mr. Dunn to handle it so that something would be done tomorrow, and to let me know if the president decided to go ahead, so that I could announce it simultaneously in Mexico City.

[The Anglo-American willingness to modify the invitations to the UN conference was negated by Russia. Molotov informed Harriman that Russia considered the modification a change in the Yalta decision on invitations and could not concur. News of this setback reached Mexico City while Stettinius was at Chapultepec Castle.]

CALENDAR NOTES | *March 1, 1945*
French Sponsorship. In the late afternoon, Mr. Dunn phoned Mr. Raynor in Mexico City to say that word had been received through the British that the Soviet government would not accept the change in the form of invitations demanded by France, on the ground that this would conflict with the decision reached at the Crimea. Mr. Dunn proposed to inform Ambassador Caffery of this development by phone and instruct him to inform the French that they would either have to agree to our original text or else drop out as a sponsoring power. . . .

[The French refused to accept the Soviet answer as final and wished to continue discussions. Having already postponed announcing the invitations one day, Stettinius, heeding Eden's advice, agreed to a further delay.]

CALENDAR NOTES | *March 2, 1945*
French Sponsorship. During the morning, while I was at Cuernavaca, Mr. Raynor phoned Mr. Dunn from Mexico City and found that word had just been received at the department, through the British Embassy that the French government had refused to accept the Soviet turndown as final and

that they were instructing their ambassador in Moscow to raise the issue there.

Because of this development the British requested a twenty-four-hour postponement. Mr. Dunn explained to them that if I intervened from Mexico City, this in effect meant forty-eight hours. . . .

As soon as I reached Mexico City, Mr. Raynor referred the matter to me, and I talked it over with Messersmith, Rockefeller, Pasvolsky and Warren. We all agreed that, while there was considerable risk in postponing the announcement until Monday, it should not be disastrous and we could afford to take it. Meanwhile I tried to reach Dr. Padilla to explain this to him. . . . I asked Mr. Raynor to phone Dunn and tell him that with great difficulty we had worked out the forty-eight-hour postponement but that we had made a firm commitment to announce the invitations here at 10:00 Monday morning, and I felt this schedule must be final and unalterable. The British and French should be informed and the British should be told that the postponement was worked out by me with great difficulty as a courtesy to Mr. Eden. . . . Therefore, at the end of the day, the matter stood that we would have to receive word from the French government whether or not they would participate in the sponsorship, not later than Sunday March 4 at 12:00 noon (Washington time). Any further postponement would not, under any circumstances, be agreeable to the U.S. government.

* * *

[While they awaited Stettinius's announcement of the Security Council voting formula, the Latin American delegations worked at drafting joint amendments they wanted written into the UN Charter. They had reached a consensus by March 1.]

CALENDAR NOTES | *March 1, 1945*

Mr. Pasvolsky said that the views of the various countries on the Dumbarton Oaks Proposals were being correlated and analyzed in his committee. A summary of views as expressed by other American republics showed that only one—Haiti—had ever officially expressed complete approval of the proposals. Nevertheless, in spite of such criticism as I mentioned yesterday regarding Cuba,[6] all of the republics appeared willing to use the proposals as a basis for discussion in setting up the general international organization. The countries appeared unanimous in wanting modifications in the proposals to attain:

1. Universality of membership.
2. Changes in purposes and principles in order (for instance) to include language about international law, respect for treaties, etc.
3. Greater powers for [the] assembly.
4. Guaranteed Latin American representation on the council.
5. Greater scope for the international court.
6. Requirement that inter-American disputes be settled in the Western Hemisphere.
7. A committee for cultural cooperation.

Committee II postponed until Friday, March 2, its meeting scheduled for today . . . since I was not yet in a position to announce invitations to San Francisco and the voting procedure in the Security Council. In addition to the Cuban attack on the proposals, another difficulty arose when the Mexicans, with whom it had been arranged that they should present the U.S.-drafted resolution, actually introduced it saying that they took this action "on behalf of the United States." As this was contrary to the understanding, the resolution was withdrawn, and it was not immediately reintroduced because of differences within the Mexican delegation itself. Instead, a rather hostile resolution was introduced,[7] but Ambassador [George] Messersmith felt confident that at the right moment Padilla would come through with the resolution of approval. Another difficulty arose when Brazil received support for a proposal that the world organization should have no jurisdiction over matters in the Western Hemisphere unless they directly affected the rest of the world.

[In an effort to reassure Latin American delegates about U.S. sincerity in its proposal for a two-phase approach on hemisphere security, Stettinius invited delegation chairmen from Colombia, Uruguay, and Brazil to lunch with congressional representatives on March 2.]

CALENDAR NOTES | *March 2, 1945*
My purpose was to discuss certain parts of the Act of Chapultepec. It became apparent that the members of the American delegation disapproved of the wording of Part III [8] as it then stood. The problem was to harmonize the regional agreement with the proposed general international organization and yet overcome the fear of Latin American countries that Great Britain and especially the Soviet Union might interfere in inter-American affairs. During the argument, Senator Connally had occasion to proclaim emphatically that the United States had no intention of abandoning the Monroe Doctrine. At the end of the luncheon Senator Austin said Part III should simply be a statement that the act was a regional arrangement consistent with the purposes and principles of the general international organization when established. He then drafted a paragraph which was immediately approved and accepted by all present.

[Within the next few days, the conference moved rapidly toward conclusion. On March 5, Stettinius was able to extend invitations to the conference on international organization and to explain the compromise on voting. An arrangement had also been worked out to deal with amendments to the Dumbarton Oaks Proposals. The delegates adopted a resolution endorsing the proposals as the basis for an international organization and referred to the San Francisco conference amendments that had been sponsored at Mexico City by individual nations. The amendments, in general, attempted to strengthen the position of small nations and to provide for settlement of hemispheric issues within the inter-American system. Since they were not formally adopted by the conference, the United States was not bound to support them and indeed each nation retained freedom of action at the upcoming conference.

Shortly afterward, the conference adopted the Act of Chapultepec, which like the arrangements on Dumbarton Oaks attempted to reconcile hemispheric concerns with the proposed international organization. The declaration established a military alliance against aggression from within and without the hemisphere which was to last for the duration of the war and which would be given permanent status after the war ended. It provided for further strengthening of the inter-American system by coordination and consolidation of its various agencies and organs. At U.S. insistence, however, it was agreed that the arrangements thus outlined should be consistent with the purposes and principles of the international organization and that the relationship of the inter-American system to the United Nations was subject to revision by the San Francisco conference.

Argentina was now the only question remaining before the conference. Stettinius had come to Mexico City firmly committed to the policy of isolating the Farrell regime, but by the end of the meeting he had decided that compromise was the only feasible alternative. There was strong Latin American support for reconciliation, and with the other agreements near completion the secretary did not wish to risk delay or a major controversy over the Argentine issue. On March 3, he wired the president recommending a change in policy.]

STETTINIUS TO ROOSEVELT | *March 3, 1945*

On arrival here I found the Argentine situation boiling. The Argentines seemed prepared to desert the Axis and join the Good Neighbors. They have considerable support in their maneuvering but so far we have been able to hold the line. However, I am convinced that we should take decisive action promptly in order to maintain the initiative. As Argentina meets conditions on which I believe there is a consensus of opinion, we can insure the unity of the Americas. Otherwise, while Mexico on the surface might appear to be a success to hemispheric unity, yet basically there would be quicksands that would undoubtedly begin to shift before the conference is over.

Since our arrival I have reviewed carefully with the FBI our accounts against Argentina, and I am now confident that, while one year ago there was substance relative to Axis relationships, of recent date it had been more of an emotional feeling on the part of the American people and within our own government, rather than any substantial evidence that there is actual aid to the enemy.

[The president approved and the American delegation concurred in a formula whereby, if Argentina declared war on Germany, purged herself of fascist influence, and subscribed to the ideals of noninterference and nonaggression expressed in the Act of Chapultepec, she could rejoin the hemisphere group of nations and hope to become a member of the UN. On March 6 Stettinius reported these developments to the president.]

CALENDAR NOTES | *March 6, 1945*

As for the Argentine resolution, I had occasion to wire the president that the formula which he had approved had been presented by one of the group of American republics which prepared it, and had been rejected by Argentina. Unanimity now existed among all delegations that the only course now was to pass a resolution at the end of the conference expressing regret at Argentina's absence but indicating hope that in the interest of continental unity, Argentina would adhere to the Act of Chapultepec and to the acts of the conference, as well as qualify for United Nations membership. Padilla, by unanimous action of the conference, would be requested to bring the resolution to Argentine attention through the Pan American Union. A resolution to this effect would be adopted at the final plenary session.

[The same issue dominated the United States delegation meeting on March 7.]

CALENDAR NOTES | *March 7, 1945*

The principal uncertainty was whether it should be insisted that Argentina could not join the United Nations unless she declared war, inasmuch as some of the other Latin American nations had only declared a state of belligerency rather than a state of war. . . . This draft was milder than the one now being contemplated.

Immediately following, there was a meeting of the American delegation, which was essentially a rump session of the American Steering Committee. . . . The subject was the resolution on Argentina. After considerable debate it was agreed

. . . that the conference viewed Argentina as an integral part of the united peoples of America, that the conference hoped Argentina would place itself in a position to concur in the work of the conference, that Argentina would aim its policy so as to become a signatory to the United Nations Declaration, and finally that the final act of the conference would be open to Argentine adherence.

[This plan was accepted by the conference, and Argentina subsequently followed each step thus becoming eligible to attend the San Francisco conference. Despite declaring war on the Axis, however, Argentine leaders continued to tolerate fascist influence at home. The problem of Argentine admission to the UN conference was to cause serious divisions between Russia and the United States and arouse sharp domestic criticism from the American press and Congress.

At the final United States delegation meeting, Stettinius seemed to sense that the future might see the Latin Americans trying to form a bloc to influence the UN, especially with the way cleared for Argentina's adherence to the Act of Chapultepec.]

CALENDAR NOTES | *March 8, 1945*
Some danger existed that the other American republics might meet among themselves to establish a common policy before the San Francisco Conference, thus forming a Latin American bloc at San Francisco. I particularly charged Messrs. Rockefeller and [Avra] Warren [director, Office of American Republics Affairs, Department of State] with the responsibility of preventing such a situation.

[As the conference prepared to adjourn Stettinius was invited to the National Palace for a discussion with Mexico's President Camacho. The occasion served as an opportunity for the secretary to express his views on Mexican-American cooperation.]

CALENDAR NOTES | *March 8, 1945*

I now extended to President Camacho my appreciation for his interest in the conference and the constructive leadership which he and Padilla had given. Much of the success of the conference resulted from Dr. Padilla's able statesmanship. I referred to the increasingly good understanding between Mexico and the United States and said that a factor in this was the sound, wise, and constructive programs followed by Mexico during Camacho's administration in the field of education, hospitalization, improvement of living standards, etc. The new atmosphere in our relationships had made possible effective collaboration during wartime and the same kind of understanding should serve the postwar period.

I told the president we realized there were those in Mexico who did not favor full cooperation with the United States, just as he realized our problems at home, where some people did not fully understand the importance of our relations with Mexico. The vital importance of mutual understanding, I said, meant that future Mexican-American relationships must be further extended on the basis of present collaboration.

President Camacho replied warmly in appreciation of President Roosevelt, and of my more recent efforts, and he spoke with great emotion and he said there was no longer any need to have fears about the future relations between our two countries and our capacity to solve our mutual problems constructively.

[The secretary's chief mood was one of satisfaction no doubt, as he confided his feelings during the closing plenary session to his diary.]

The conclusion was marked by a general feeling of elation and goodwill among the delegates, who unanimously regarded the conference as successful in its major objectives. Experienced United States press and official observers saw the conference as a culmination of the Good Neighbor Policy and as an attitude pursued by President Roosevelt and his government consistently over the last twelve years.

[The secretary was right in both his caution and his high spirits. The conference instilled real hemispheric unity,

Courtesy The Washington (D.C.) Star-News

restored faith in United States leadership, and repaired the low morale that had been pervasive in inter-American relations at the close of 1944. Much of the credit for this must go to Stettinius's skillful diplomacy. On the other hand, the very unity achieved at Mexico City emboldened Latin American leaders to speak up with greater assurance at the UN conference, often to the acute embarrassment of the United States and the secretary of state.

Stettinius departed for home on March 9, already looking ahead to a full schedule of preparations for the San Francisco conference. Little did he dream just how hectic the immediate future would be or that he soon would be reporting to a new president.]

Stettinius addressing the Mexico City delegates.

Stettinius and Nelson Rockefeller at Mexico City, March,
1945

Stettinius, President Truman, and Governor Earl Warren of California in San Fran-
sco motorcade, June, 1945

IX

PREPARATIONS FOR THE SAN FRANCISCO CONFERENCE
March–April 1945

Ever since the Dumbarton Oaks conference, Stettinius had led the campaign for an early meeting of the United Nations to implement the Dumbarton Oaks Proposals. Immediately on his return from Mexico City, the Secretary plunged into the work of planning for the San Francisco meeting, providing leadership in its every facet.

Numerous other matters continually diverted him, particularly the deepening crisis with the Soviet Union. As the weeks passed, Stettinius concluded that his optimism at Yalta had been premature. While officially hopeful about relations with Russia, his private doubts multiplied as bleak dispatches piled up from American diplomats in Europe. When the USSR excluded American and British representatives from consultation while it forced a leftist government on Rumania, Stettinius invoked the promises of mutual consultation in the Declaration on Liberated Europe. He accepted the negative result, deciding it would be better to test Russia's intentions in the matter of Poland. Allied negotiations on this problem soon bogged down and before long Roosevelt and Stalin were hurling charges of bad faith at each other. Stettinius found himself listening seriously to Harriman's advice about applying economic pressure to force a change in the Soviet Union's political behavior.

The Washington mood was shifting toward distrust of the USSR as the first blooms of spring appeared, and the sudden death of Franklin Roosevelt and the advent of Harry S Truman strengthened the influence of Russia's critics. Although the new president directed Stettinius to proceed with plans for the United Nations conference, a growing nationalism came rapidly to the fore in the first weeks of Truman's leadership, its hallmark being a toughness akin to hostility. By the time V. M. Molotov arrived in Washington in late April for preconference talks with Stettinius and Anthony Eden, the atmosphere was rife with mistrust and recrimination.

At the same time, the public temper, which had grown euphoric in the days following the release of the Yalta communiqué, showed indications of a return to fear and pessimism. There was still a faith in America's UN policy, but underneath expressions of support could be found signs of a cynicism that boded ill for the future.

[Stettinius noted in his record the first signs of post Yalta friction with the Soviet Union the week after he returned from Mexico City.]

RECORD | *Section vii, pp. 1–2*
Difficulties in dealing with Soviet authorities concerning their influence on the Rumanian government already were testing some of the Yalta conclusions—for example, the covenant that in liberated areas the Big Three would see to it that there should be "governmental authorities broadly representative of all democratic elements in the population." Another situation involving our relations with Soviet Russia was the continued impasse in Poland, with the British and ourselves supporting Mikolajczyk and the London Polish government, while the Soviets were backing the Lublin regime. This conflict was sharpened by the Russian desire for Lublin Polish attendance at the San Francisco conference, while we insisted

that Poland should not be represented unless a united government were formed before or during the conference.

[The first priority in preparing for the San Francisco conference was to organize the American delegation and put it to work considering possible amendments to the Dumbarton Oaks Proposals. Stettinius had exercised the chief influence in selecting the members of the delegation. A key element was its strong congressional bipartisan flavor. In addition to the secretary of state its members were: Senators Connally and Vandenberg; Representatives Bloom and Charles Eaton [R.-New Jersey]; Commander Harold Stassen, a liberal Republican and former governor of Minnesota; and Virginia Gildersleeve, dean of Barnard College.

Government agencies and private organizations brought tremendous pressure on Stettinius to have official representation at the conference, but the secretary rebuffed every such attempt. He had discussed this problem with Roosevelt on March 12, and the president was determined to keep the delegation small.]

CALENDAR NOTES | *March 12, 1945*
I discussed thoroughly with the president the matter of attendance at San Francisco. He is adamant that he will not enlarge the delegation . . . and does not want representatives of labor or representatives of various organizations. I said . . . I thought he must let us think through a little more thoroughly for him the matter of representation of various organizations, having in mind the American Legion which would be helpful.

* * *

[Roosevelt and Stettinius discussed important issues developing out of the recent Yalta conference. At this time they still thought that the agreements reached there meant better relations with Russia. But the president was growing apprehensive about Poland, and Stettinius foresaw trouble over the extra seats for the two Russian republics.]

The president talked to me about the Polish matter last night. . . . He said he was disturbed and . . . hoped that Harriman would be able to work it out. . . .

* * *

I then told the president that I was extremely apprehensive and had . . . an intuitive feeling that it would be much better not to let the X-matter [extra seats] come up in San Francisco if we could possibly avoid it. He said he had come to the same conclusion and said he wanted me to have a talk with Leahy . . . and . . . Byrnes and see if there wasn't some way we could get around it. He said, however, if it does come up I must be able to say proportionately that I must have the same number for my country. But the president himself has made up his mind without my guiding it that he would like to get by San Francisco without that coming up.

[In response to British overtures for closer working relations with the United States, Stettinius had hit on the idea of sending Bernard Baruch to London on a special mission. Baruch was a close friend of the prime minister and enjoyed a wide circle of acquaintances in Britain. The secretary was certain that he could smooth over previous irritations. Roosevelt warmly approved the idea, and Stettinius went to Baruch's home to discuss the mission.]

CALENDAR NOTES | *March 12, 1945*

. . . Mr. Baruch stated that he did not want to do any-thing that wasn't completely in accordance with the view of the State Department and . . . would report to us in detail any conversation that he had with the prime minister. He asked me whether there were any matters that I would like him to discuss with the prime minister. . . .

I told Mr. Baruch that the prime minister was still uncon-vinced that the World Security Organization should have a social and economic council and that it would probably be helpful if he could point out the need of such an agency in the world organization. This, Mr. Baruch said he would be de-lighted to do, and felt that the world organization would fail unless it had a strong economic and social council.

Mr. Baruch stated that the president had mentioned trusteeships in his conversation and inquired as to whether or not I felt it was a matter he should discuss with the prime min-ister. I told him . . . that anything he could do to persuade the prime minister to accept the thesis of the united trustee-ship would be most helpful.

* * *

He talked at length with me relative to reparations saying that he had certain definite ideas ready to discuss with [Isador] Lubin [U.S. representative on the Reparations Commission]. He could not find that this government had a clear-cut policy. Mr. Baruch stated that before he left he would like to have a talk with us in order to get definitely in mind what our views were relative to reparations.[1]

[One of the key appointments to the American delegation was John Foster Dulles. He had taken a prominent role in shaping the foreign policy views of Dewey in the 1944 campaign and at San Francisco he was to exercise a leading role in delegation decisions. Stettinius pushed his case for appointment despite the president's antipathy toward Dulles. He informed Vandenberg that the State Department would probably appoint Dulles as a delegation adviser.[2]

Stettinius worked hard to develop a close rapport with Vandenberg, realizing that the Michigan senator exercised a potent influence on the Republican senators whose votes were vital to passage of the UN Charter. On March 15 he discussed with Vandenberg changes the senator wanted made in the Dumbarton Oaks Proposals.]

MEMORANDUM OF CONVERSATION |
March 15, 1945

I told Senator Vandenberg that I didn't want to raise the question of the use of force, that I thought it can be handled later on. It will require separate legislation. On the matter of the use of United States force, he says he is willing to cross that later on as [to the] power of [the] delegate. Our present job, he said, is to approve a charter and when we get down to the power of the delegate, he will come to me. He didn't want to make any trouble now.

Senator Vandenberg said that it is rock bottom necessity that somewhere we write into the business on the assembly and the council both that they will have the right to look backward as well as forward on conditions of the world that led to war. He referred me back to his January 8 [10] speech in which he said that a spoilsman's peace cannot be approved without an escape clause of some kind. He said that what it can be is to use some beautiful language about justness and rights and he said it would take a fellow like La Follette. It would take 60 percent of the poison out of his soul and it would eliminate half the Republican opposition if they got some general language of that kind.

I asked him how much opposition he was going to get. He said that if we can get this thing buttoned up in the way that he can go through and read it with Tom [Connally], you will only get eight votes against you on the Republican side.

* * *

I asked Vandenberg if we are going to see eye to eye and go down this thing together, and he said he had made up his mind to do it. . . . Mr. Vandenberg then said that every Polish Democratic group in Wayne County had disbanded within the last two weeks as a protest against the president's action at Yalta. This represented 250,000 Polish votes that had been for the president for his three terms.

[His work with Vandenberg was but one aspect of the secretary's effort to build close understanding with Congress. On March 16 he met with a bipartisan group of House leaders to report on the recent conferences. Stettinius's portrayal of prospects for Allied cooperation was optimistic. He found the congressmen dubious about the wisdom of allowing a veto when a great power was involved in a case before the UN.]

NOTES ON CONFERENCE | *March 16, 1945*

* * *

The secretary stated that . . . he wanted to emphasize that the agreed voting procedure . . . represented our position, and was the arrangement which we felt would be the fairest, safest, and soundest to all concerned. It was not a compromise with the Russians. Mr. [Joseph] Martin [R.-Mass.] . . . questioned the wisdom of allowing any one of the major powers to have an absolute veto. He thought that this allowed any one of the five nations to create chaos again if they [sic] saw fit. The secretary said that his feeling was that if the Big Three, Russia, the United States, and Great Britain fell out among themselves, the world organization could not keep the peace, and would be broken if it attempted to do so. Mr. Martin said that he recognized the practical aspects of the problem but still felt that the plan was poor in principle. The secretary stated that he thought a very important aspect and one which had not received sufficient recognition was that the United States naval, military, and air forces could not be called into action without the approval of the United States.

* * *

Mr. Martin said that . . . he would like to see the United States delegation propose a new formula at San Francisco even if only for the record. He suggested a formula requiring the majority of the Big Five and a majority of the smaller six nations without any individual rights of veto.

* * *

The secretary said his . . . feeling [was] that the Russians had made up their minds to take their place in the world and support the world organization. . . . The Russians were going to make a great effort to gain the confidence and respect of the peoples of the Western world. It was not true that at Yalta we had given way on all matters to the Russians. The Russians had frequently made concessions on a variety of . . . matters.

* * *

Mr. Eaton said that if the secretary could carry to San Francisco the goodwill which existed in Mexico City, we will be able to make a great contribution to the history of the world. The U.S. delegation was going to San Francisco to perform one of the greatest services possible—to establish a civilization based on law rather than force. He felt that every effort should be made to educate the American people . . . to this view.

[The secretary of state did not reveal to the congressmen one problem that especially worried him—the potential trouble France might make at San Francisco. The French had already created much difficulty over their role in the United Nations, and when Ambassador Henri Bonnet called at the State Department on March 16, Stettinius spoke bluntly.]

MEMORANDUM OF CONVERSATION |
March 16, 1945

The secretary expressed his disappointment that France had not seen fit to accept sponsorship of the conference. . . . The secretary asked the ambassador frankly whether the French government was coming to San Francisco in a spirit of cooperation and helpfulness, or whether they expected to make trouble. The ambassador stated, as his own personal opinion, that the French delegation would be fully cooperative and would not come with the intention of causing trouble and difficulty. . . .

[With representatives of fifty countries soon to converge on San Francisco, some U.S. officials saw a great opportunity to gather intelligence which might prove useful to the American government. On March 19, Stettinius received a letter from OSS chief General William Donovan on this subject.]

DONOVAN TO STETTINIUS | *March 19, 1945*

As I told you and Julius Holmes the other night, we have a sizable organization on the Pacific Coast which we would be glad to have of use to you.

We have a group of foreign experts who can be available to you on any research work you may wish to call upon us to do during the conference. In addition, I think Julius has talked to Dewitt Poole about the use of our Foreign Nationalities Branch. It would be helpful, of course, if you have in mind before the conference any particular questions upon which you would wish us to prepare studies, if you would let us know so they could be ready before the conference meets. . . .

. . . If, as quickly as they are available to you, you could let us know the names of all the delegates and the various staffs, we would do our best to prepare information on all personnel concerned.

It is [un]necessary to assure you that any way in which we can be of help, we hope you will call upon us.

[Some of Stettinius's advisers, including J. F. Green of the Office of Special Political Affairs and his chief, Alger Hiss, strongly opposed the Donovan proposal. "It seems to me," Green advised Hiss on March 23, "that this proposal should be scotched at once. . . . Revelation that officers of the OSS, which is generally known as the intelligence agency for our government, were doing espionage work at San Francisco would seriously embarrass us as host to the conference." Hiss vigorously endorsed Green's views in a note to Stettinius, and American intelligence work at the conference was sharply limited.[3]

The troublesome issue of colonialism and trusteeship absorbed much of Stettinius's attention in the weeks before the San Francisco conference. During the preceding year, the State Department had been at loggerheads with the War and Navy Departments on this problem. Following Roosevelt's lead, Hull had developed a proposal to establish a Trusteeship Council that would give the United Nations broad power to move colonial areas toward independence. But Secretaries Stimson and Forrestal feared this would undercut retention of the Pacific bases which they deemed vital to future national security. The conflict had not been settled by March 1945, and Roosevelt's determination to perfect the trusteeship system before setting policy on existing colonies made it difficult to resolve issues relating to specific regions. An important example was Indochina.]

RECORD | *Section vii, pp. 50–51*

General de Gaulle made a radio speech on Wednesday the fourteenth [of March] appealing to the United States and the other Allies to provide arms and supplies to the ill-equipped resistance forces in Indochina. In spite of the president's well-known attitude that we should take no position at present on Indochina, I sent him a memorandum on Friday, suggesting issuance of a public declaration. Not only had the French been requesting aid for resistance groups fighting the Japanese in Indochina, but they had wanted an understanding on civil affairs in connection with possible future operations in Indochina. Furthermore, we had received a cable from which it appeared that the French were preparing to blame the U.S. for weakness of the resistance to Japan in Indochina. The British also might be expected to encourage this view. . . .

In the light of our more open public relations policy, I felt that without in any way prejudicing our future position on Indochina, we could combat these developments by publicizing our desire to help. I pointed out in my memorandum that we were checking with the Joint Chiefs of Staff. But the president very promptly sent me back a memorandum signed by Admiral Leahy: "The president is of the opinion that it is inadvisable at the present time to issue the proposed statement."

On the same day that I sent the memorandum to the president, Elmer Davis [head of the Office of War Information] asked whether or not editorial comment on Indochina would be helpful. I explained to him that the whole thing was up in the air—whether it would be an international trusteeship or be turned back to France with an understanding for independence—and said we could not take any action until later. In a conversation with Mr. Charles Taussig [Chairman, U.S. Section, Anglo-American Caribbean Commission] the day before, he told me that the president had stated to him on the fourteenth that he was willing now to have Indochina trusteed to France, with the understanding that she could eventually have complete independence.

[While State Department experts continued their search for a formula that would meet War and Navy Department demands for postwar bases, Stettinius worried over Roosevelt's Yalta pledge to support admission of Byelorussia (White Russia) and the Ukraine as charter members of the UN. The secrecy surrounding the agreement particularly bothered him. On March 19 he told his personal secretary Bob Lynch that he thought the president ought to discuss this question with the delegation.]

TRANSCRIPT OF TELEPHONE
CONVERSATION | *March 19, 1945*
Stettinius: . . . As for the president's plans—we should do something during the week about the X-matter (two votes in the assembly for the new Soviet republics) or it would be too late. I thought the president probably should send for the

members of the San Francisco delegation who were in Washington (within the next few days) and tell them the whole truth about this X-matter. I suggested that the president should have Messrs. Hiss and Bohlen with him when he saw the delegates, and then he should put the question up to them, for their guidance and advice on how we ought to handle the Soviets. If the president took the delegates into his confidence . . . it would make them feel a sense of responsibility.

[Roosevelt accepted Stettinius's advice and called the American delegation to the White House on March 23. His portrayal of the agreement reached at Yalta misrepresented the strength of his promise to Stalin to support Russia on extra seats.]

REPORT ON MEETING | *March 24, 1945*
The president said he had asked the delegation to talk to them because he wished to tell them about a matter that had come up at the Crimea conference. He said that Marshal Stalin . . . had said that he wished to have six or seven (the president said he did not remember the exact number) of the Soviet republics as members of the world organization. Marshal Stalin had developed at great length the thesis of the right of these republics to have such representation because of their contribution to the war and the sacrifices they had suffered. The president said that he had announced that in that case he would have to ask forty-eight votes in the assembly and that President Vargas of Brazil would ask a number equivalent to the Brazilian provinces. After considerable discussion Stalin had reduced his request to two and had asked that the British and Americans support his proposal at San Francisco. The president said that he had replied that if he were a delegate at San Francisco that he personally would favor the Soviet pro-

posal. The president concluded by saying that that was all there was to that subject.

The delegates in general received this announcement in silence and it was not evident that they fully appreciated . . . the degree to which the United States government was committed to support the Soviet proposal.

[Word of the extra seats agreement was known by too many people to remain secret. On March 29, the *New York Herald Tribune* broke the story and soon reporters were besieging the State Department for details and asking if there had been any other secret agreements at Yalta. Confusion reigned momentarily as the White House and State Department worked on a public statement and debated whether the American government should ask for the extra representation to which Churchill and Stalin had agreed at Yalta.

Stettinius met reporters on March 30 and was confronted with a list of twenty-seven questions. He gave reporters his "personal assurance there would be no other Dumbarton Oaks matters which had been agreed to at Yalta that would cause surprise in the future," and he expressed strong confidence that the UN conference in San Francisco would be a success. Undersecretary Grew was present and felt that never had he seen a secretary of state put so much "on the spot" but that Stettinius "had handled the situation beautifully." [4]

The secretary was still troubled by Roosevelt's meeting with the congressmen, however, and discussed with Dean Acheson the strategy that should be followed.]

RECORD | *Section viii, pp. 21–23*

When I later reached Mr. Acheson on the phone, he was in Sol Bloom's office. . . . Acheson summarized the problem we faced: first we must clear up whether the president agreed at Yalta that the delegates at San Francisco should unquestionably support the Russian claim. I told him that the president had committed the U.S. government but not the delegates. Acheson said he would so inform Sol Bloom. Acheson then told me that Bloom's reaction was that the wisest course would be to omit any questions about the delegates supporting the Russian claim and their ability for putting forward a claim of their own. . . .

At my Staff Committee meeting on April 3, I reported that the press release on the San Francisco conference would be issued later that day. This touched on some highly difficult issues, I said, such as the participation of the two additional Soviet republics, the statement that there were no other undisclosed agreements made at Yalta, and the question of three votes for the United States in the General Assembly. Trusteeships were also mentioned, but it was emphasized that the "basis of the San Francisco conference remains the Dumbarton Oaks Proposals."

Carrying out my promise to the group of newspapermen, at my press conference on Tuesday April 3 I presented . . . a long, carefully prepared statement answering as many questions as possible. Owing to the rapid tempo of military and political developments I said that, far from postponing the San Francisco conference, I felt it increasingly necessary that the Dumbarton Oaks plans for an international organization should be carried out promptly. . . .

[The announcement that the United States would not request additional UN seats and Stettinius's explanation of the reasons for the USSR's request quieted much of the public outcry. In the meantime, the Argentine problem once again came into the forefront. Having promised to accept Argentina back into good standing once

it followed the steps set forth in the Act of Chapultepec, the United States soon had to make a decision.]

RECORD | *Section viii, pp. 27–31*

* * *

The most important development of the day [March 28]
was the announcement by the Argentine government that it
was ready to "put into effect the principles, declarations, and
recommendations resulting from the Mexico City conference," including a declaration of war against Japan and Germany. . . .

* * *

The governing board of the Pan American Union actually resolved at its March 31 meeting that the measures
adopted by the Argentine government were in accord with the
resolution adopted at the Mexico City conference and agreed
that Argentina might now sign the final Act of the Conference. Meanwhile our missions were informed that "if the
Argentine situation continues to develop satisfactorily" we expected the American republics would reestablish relations
with Argentina in about a week. . . .

On April 3 I signed a circular telegram to the U.S. diplomatic missions in all the other American republics, declaring
our policy that Argentine recognition would not commit us to
sponsoring Argentine adherence to the United Nations Declaration "until there was agreement that from a world as well as
a hemispheric point of view it was warranted. . . ."

* * *

I sent to the president on April 6 a memorandum telling
of our consultation with the Latin American republics "in
terms of recognition on April 9, 12:00 noon, Washington

time," and added that we were informing European United Nations governments which had "cooperated with us on the Argentine question." Reviewing the cooperative steps already taken by Argentina, I suggested that Mr. Spruille Braden "would be a good choice for ambassador to the Argentine, in view of his force, energy, and the excellent record he made in Buenos Aires." Next day a reply came back from the White House that "the president has approved the memorandum from the Secretary of State, dated 6 April, 1945" and particularly mentioning Braden's nomination.

[By late March, Stettinius had become convinced that U.S. policy toward Russia must be reconsidered, a view shared by the British and French. The Soviet Union seemed bent on building a sphere of influence from the Baltic to Turkey, and although Stettinius sought to keep an optimistic public face on Soviet-American relations, in reality he was increasingly concerned about the prospects and leaned more and more toward a tougher line with the Russians.]

RECORD | *Section viii, pp. 34–44*

On March 22 the department analyzed the recent Soviet decision to terminate their treaty of friendship and neutrality with Turkey as the forerunner to a request for modification of the Montreux Convention,[5] and part of a design to bring Turkey into the Russian *Cordon Sanitaire* of Soviet-influenced buffer states. Two days later we learned from Ambassador Harriman in Moscow, in connection with the lack of progress on the part of the Polish Commission, that although Molotov himself had suggested that the British and American ambassadors send observers to Poland, the Soviet government now greeted with amazement the idea that this be carried out.

Thus, negotiations of the Polish Commission had virtually come to a standstill. . . .

The discussions were showing that the general nature of the Yalta Declaration on Liberated Europe needed clarification. Apparently, different people were interpreting the same words in different ways. We held that the Yalta declaration had established the principle of joint responsibility, as contrasted to separate action by the three powers. By March 29 Harriman called to our attention a Soviet article to the effect that regional security relations—at least as they involve Germany and the immediate future—were more important in Soviet eyes than the world organization. News that Molotov would not attend the San Francisco conference, but that Ambassador Gromyko would head the Soviet delegation, had created by the end of March a gloomy view in the press about the accomplishments of the conference.

* * *

By April 2, we learned that Turkey expected to be subjected to violent Soviet criticism as Russia moved toward revising the regime of the Dardanelles: Turkey would rather fight than cede bases or territory. But the Turks did not view this as necessary and would not exclude bilateral conversations. During a dinner given for President Beneš in Moscow, Stalin had said that the Soviet government had no desire to promote the old Czarist policy of Pan Slavism nor to bolshevize Europe; Soviet policy had become reoriented to present conditions and the communist parties would become nationalist parties interested in their own countries. . . .

By April 3, Harriman considered that negotiations of the Polish Commission were near the breaking point and the only hope was a reply from Stalin to President Roosevelt and Churchill which would leave some loophole for future discussions. A negative reply from Stalin would force us to take a definite position upon which we would be prepared to "break" if necessary. Harriman suggested being ordered home for consultation. As for our economic relations with the Soviets, Harriman felt we should tie closely our economic assistance in Europe to our political problems with the Soviet. We and the British should take a positive line to reestablish a sound economic life for the people of Europe and so counteract the Soviet program, which was proving to be mainly totalitarian in purpose.[6]

* * *

Meanwhile British Ministers Lyttleton and Llewellin [7] had told Mr. [Ray] Atherton, our ambassador in Canada, that conditions in the bread basket of Europe under Russian control (such countries as Rumania, Poland, and Hungary, to say nothing of the Ukraine and Pomerania) "would be in marked contrast to hunger in Western Europe." They also believed that "Hungary was increasingly menaced by Russia," and we should "support the British policy of upholding democracy and Western ideas in Western Europe." They felt we were firm enough with the USSR politically, but were being too lenient with supplies.

The French Foreign Office likewise showed concern over our relations with the Soviet Union, particularly questioning how seriously we regarded the Yalta Declaration on Liberated Europe. We instructed Ambassador [Jefferson] Caffery in Paris to leave no doubt about our determination that the Yalta agreement should finally be carried out, and the French should not believe otherwise because of evidence in Poland.

[Amid this soul searching over relations with Russia, word flashed from Warm Springs of the death of Franklin D. Roosevelt. Stettinius's record of the events of April 12 provides an intimate picture of the reaction in official circles to the passing of the president and of the first hours of the administration of Harry S Truman.]

RECORD | *Section ix, pp. 2–8*

I was in my office meeting with Forrestal, Biddle, and Patterson discussing world intelligence. I received a call from Steve Early about ten minutes after five. He said to please come over to the front door of the White House immediately without being noticed. I told him I was with three Cabinet officers, but he said to come immediately and that it was an "order." I went over and was shown to the front of Roosevelt's bedroom by the head usher. Mrs. Roosevelt was there, very composed. . . . Mrs. Roosevelt took me by the hand and said it was her sad duty to announce that Franklin had died a few moments ago. . . .

Everything was completely disorganized and nobody knew exactly where to turn. I spoke up and said a Cabinet meeting should be held immediately, and Anna Boettiger [the president's daughter] asked where. I said it should be in the Cabinet Room at 6 P.M. Truman then asked me if I would make the arrangements. Anna then said she should make the arrangements for the funeral. . . . I stated I thought it would be wise for Mrs. Roosevelt and Steve Early to fly immediately with Anna and have a special train assembled there tonight and leave Warm Springs tomorrow morning, getting here Saturday morning and the services could be held at the White House Saturday afternoon. This clicked immediately and Mrs. Roosevelt said this was what Franklin would have wanted and that we could have the services at Hyde Park on Sunday afternoon. I (then) told Mrs. Roosevelt that I had lost one of the best and closest friends I had ever had in the world.

I (then) instructed the chief usher to call a Cabinet meeting at 6 o'clock, and I returned to my office, where I met Forrestal and told him of the president's death. Forrestal said that he had heard yesterday from someone in the Senate that the president was very ill and that his death was not a shock to him.

I then saw Dunn relative to proclamations.

I then returned to the Cabinet Room at 6 o'clock . . . Truman called the Cabinet to order and immediately said that it was his sad duty to announce the death of the president and all he could say was that he would carry on to the best of his ability. . . .

I spoke up and stated on behalf of the Cabinet I wished to pledge him personally our support and that we would do everything within our power to carry on in this critical moment in any way he wished us to. Stimson then pledged his support, and [Secretary of Labor] Frances Perkins throughout the entire meeting was quietly praying. Morgenthau, [Claude] Wickard [secretary of agriculture], and Forrestal slipped a note to the new president and said they would carry on as Truman wished them to. Stimson said everyone would have to send in his resignation immediately.

It was then decided that Truman should take the oath of office immediately and we asked him whom he would like to have give the oath. He said the chief justice and he was sent for. . . . Truman took me aside and asked me whether or not it would be appropriate for him to have a photograph taken as he took the oath. He said his mother was ninety-two years old and he wished she could be there. Truman said that Jonathan Daniels was pressing him to have the photograph taken, and I agreed that it would be proper. . . . Steve Early made an announcement to the Cabinet that services would be held Saturday afternoon at the White House quietly. They would then proceed by private train to Hyde Park for the burial. . . . The people present at the burial would be limited to the Cabinet, congressional leaders, heads of war agencies, and any other intimate friends in Washington who wished to make the trip.

* * *

I talked with Forrestal and Stimson about the whole situation. They want a very close liaison between State, War, and Navy at this critical moment.

* * *

After Truman took the oath, I went back into the Cabinet Room and walked over to the White House to join Mrs. Roosevelt. I was shown into the Red Room where Truman, his wife, and daughter, and Steve Early were alone. I said that it was important to announce tonight that the San Francisco conference would go on. Truman said that anything I might say would be all right. I said I would say that on the authority of President Truman I wished to announce that the San Francisco conference will not be postponed. The president asked me to please make the announcement.

* * *

During the time we were waiting for the Chief Justice to arrive I was sitting next to Truman and we had a rather intimate talk relative to the fact that he did not believe that this would happen. He was shocked and startled that he had been called upon to perform this great task. I told him that he had a job with the greatest responsibility of any one man in the world. He said he realized this and that he would do his best. I said somehow a person is given an inner strength to arise to any occasion and said that I had full confidence that the American people would rally around and see us through. I said we were well on the road to defeat of the enemy and we must win on the world organization. Truman said, "I understand thoroughly, and you will have my fullest support in everything."

I did not say anything to Truman about the Cabinet officers submitting their resignations, but left that up to him. I did mention the fact that there were a number of matters relative to San Francisco and regarding relations with the Soviet Union which it would be necessary for me to bring to his attention promptly, and Truman agreed to it. "Any time at your convenience, day or night, either at home or at the office, if you will, just call me."

My impression of Truman is that he handled himself very well. He did not get rattled and gave me the impression of being a simple sincere person, bewildered, but who is going to do everything in his power to meet this emergency. I had no feeling of weakness whatsoever. . . .

* * *

I talked with Admiral McIntire [Roosevelt's personal physician] and he said that this was a complete shock to him—it was something absolutely new and came as a complete surprise. The president's blood pressure was all right and had been for some time, and there was absolutely no apparent cause for the stroke. Henry Wallace walked with me from the office to the White House and said that from the standpoint of Roosevelt as a person in history that this was a good time for him to go. Wallace said that he had won the war and would have to go through a fight with the Senate, and he went out like Abraham Lincoln. He said it is tragic for all humanity, but from the standpoint of a person, the good Lord was looking out for him.

I left the Cabinet Room to telephone Mr. Hull, and he said what he had feared had happened. Mr. Hull said that this was the most serious blow to the world that he could imagine. I told all the details and said I would see him soon.

[The next morning Stettinius was back at the White House to brief the president about State Department operations and the recent difficulties with the USSR. Truman indicated immediately that he was prepared to take the tougher position with the Russians already advocated by many of Roosevelt's advisers.]

CALENDAR NOTES | *April 13, 1945*

* * *

I told the president that I had some items to mention to him and that it would take a few moments. He said "Take as long as you want." I then stated that we must make our definite arrangements for San Francisco. He said, "I have decided that I shall not go to San Francisco—the president has appointed a delegation, the plans are made—you will go to San Francisco and conduct the meeting with great success." He said, "If you wish me to deliver a message, I shall be glad to do so." I immediately said that would be most appropriate.

* * *

I stated I wanted to tell him as a friend that Mr. Hopkins had an extremely important and unique relationship as far as foreign relations were concerned, inasmuch as he was the one person who really thoroughly understood the various ramifications and the relations between Roosevelt and Churchill and Roosevelt and Stalin and that I hoped that in some way, certainly for a time, this knowledge could be capitalized on. The president said, "I have the greatest regard for Hopkins, he is a grand friend, and I plan to use Hopkins to the limit of his strength."

I then told the president that during the past few years there had been a good deal of confusion relative to the relations between the White House and the State Department on diplomatic matters—that each had not always been properly informed, and that the president and I had . . . agreed jointly on the appointment of Mr. Bohlen from the department to serve as liaison officer between the State Department and the White House. . . . I strongly recommended this relationship continue, as it had been worked so wonderfully in recent months. Mr. Truman's response to that was, "That is agreed—there will be no change whatsoever in that plan."

*   *   *

I then stated that I thought the president should think very seriously about an early meeting with the prime minister. He stated he had the same thought in mind and hoped it could occur very promptly. I said, "Do you wish me to take steps to push that along?" He said, "Any steps you take to encourage an early visit by Winston Churchill to this country will be a great service."

*   *   *

I then told the president that our relations with the Soviet Union since Yalta had deteriorated. He said he understood this, but asked why. I said there was no explanation other than the fact that Stalin had his own political problem within the Soviet Union and perhaps certain influences were being brought to bear on him from within his own country. He then stated, as he had yesterday, that we must stand up to the Russians at this point and that we must not be easy with them. He gave me the impression that he thought we had been too easy with them. I at this point alluded to a very tough exchange of wires between Stalin and the president last week on military matters [the German surrender in Italy], that I was sure Admiral Leahy would wish to discuss with the president at the first opportunity.

. . . Mr. Bohlen joined us and ably and briefly gave the

president the essence of the situation between Roosevelt and the Soviet Union and Great Britain on the Polish issue. . . . Truman asked us to return at 3:30 this afternoon with a draft of the cable to thrash the whole matter out.

[Even in the midst of the tragic circumstances of the president's death, Stettinius had his mind on the UN conference, now less than two weeks away. Early on April 14, while waiting to board the presidential funeral train in Washington's Union Station, he discussed the unresolved trusteeship problem with Pentagon officials.]

STETTINIUS MEMO TO DUNN
AND PASVOLSKY | *April 14, 1945*
. . . I had a private talk with Forrestal, King, and Marshall.

I told them that we must find a solution at San Francisco to compose the trusteeship issue and it was impossible for us to go into San Francisco with the policy of annexation which representatives of the armed forces had publicly enunciated.

I also said that we in the State Department were willing to meet them half-way, but we could never agree to a policy of annexation.

All three of the gentlemen listened sympathetically and obviously appreciated the importance of the point I was making.

Forrestal stated that he had drafted a memorandum on the whole subject.

Would it not be possible, before throwing the entire issue to the delegation on Monday, for our people to have a round up . . . tomorrow to see whether or not some suggestions could be made now by the army and navy which I could propose to the American delegation and which could later be endorsed by President Truman.

[The proposal which Stettinius got Stimson and Forrestal to approve recommended that certain areas of trust territories could be designated by the administering nation as strategic areas. To be used for military bases, they would be exempt from close supervision by the UN. This compromise with the Pentagon's desire for outright annexation of Japanese islands was presented to the President on April 18.]

CALENDAR NOTES | *April 18, 1945*

. . . We immediately sat down and I opened the conversation by saying that the Army, Navy, and State Department had been working many months endeavoring to find a satisfactory solution for this question of trusteeships, maintaining our strategic bases in the Pacific, and at the same time not being charged with annexation and expansionist policy. I said that the papers that I handed to him were the result of much labor on the part of Stimson, Forrestal, and myself and it had our endorsement. After he read the memorandum I thought that both Stimson and Forrestal should make statements. The president proceeded to read the memorandum very carefully and said that he thought it gave him a clear understanding of the picture.

* * *

After I finished Mr. Forrestal and Mr. Stimson talked for about five minutes. Mr. Stimson reviewed his experience as governor of the Philippines, and as secretary of state and said that it was unthinkable at this time that we give up our bases and our protection in the Pacific. Mr. Forrestal stated that this was an innocuous statement and they endorsed the statement handed to the president. Mr. Truman approved the statement and handed it back to me. . . .

Mr. Forrestal spoke up and stated he was very anxious in connection with the Pacific matters and before we agreed to final independence of the Philippines we should make agreement with them on United States bases. The president said he was seeing President Osmena tomorrow and would discuss this with him. He said he wanted the secretary of war and the secretary of navy there with him tomorrow when he saw Osmena at 12:30.

* * *

I then stated that there had been a bit of confusion on how Navy and War had been informed on political matters and the State Department on military matters; that Stimson, Forrestal, and I had a suggestion and we wished to make joint recommendation to the president. I spoke for all three of us and said that we wanted authority from him to have complete interchange on all subjects at all times and I was authorized to tell them fully about all secret diplomatic matters and they were instructed to inform me fully on military matters. As we came to the end of the war it was impossible to improvise these military and political matters and we had to have this information. He said you are now authorized to do this and I think your suggestion is a highly constructive one. Mr. Bohlen should act on this.

[Just one week before the opening of the San Francisco conference, Stettinius found his position threatened by rumors that President Truman planned to replace him with James F. Byrnes. The story first came to the secretary's attention in a conversation with Senator Connally, who informed him that he had learned that Byrnes was going to attend the United Nations conference.]

CALENDAR NOTES | *April 16, 1945*
I 'phoned Senator Connally and asked him to preside at the [delegation] meeting this morning. He said he would but he wanted to speak to me about Jimmy Byrnes. He said, "The president has appointed us. Are we to represent the United States or not?" Senator Connally then hit the ceiling and said, "Jimmy Byrnes has no business whatsoever in San Francisco. I'm for you anyway before him and if Byrnes goes out there like an FBI agent it will discredit you and me and the whole delegation. Don't let this get by you." He said, "I'm not going to raise this with the president. It's up to him to make whatever arrangements he wants."

[Stettinius immediately sought from the president reassurance about their relationship.]

CALENDAR NOTES | *April 16, 1945*
. . . The president then said, "I now have something to say to you. I am counting on you to go to San Francisco and that's your job. I'm not going. I'm counting on you. I have complete confidence in you, but from your own standpoint this whole situation must be clarified promptly." He then said he wanted me to go right ahead and finish this job as Roosevelt wanted me to do. I then said, "Well, I think that the easiest and quickest way to clarify the matter—you have had my resignation before you for three days. If you do not wish to accept my resignation, write me and say you decline to accept my resignation and that you have confidence in me and you are counting on me to go to San Francisco and head the United States delegation and represent the United States there." He said, "I'll do that." I said, "I should tell you as a friend and in confidence that Senator Connally is thoroughly aroused about this whole matter of Jimmy Byrnes going to San Francisco. . . ." He said, "Jimmy Byrnes is not going to

San Francisco, and we are counting upon you to carry through."

[The story that Byrnes would replace Stettinius continued to circulate in the press throughout April and May, and the secretary had to work during the entire conference under the handicap of rumors about his resignation. In fact, the story was correct. Truman had asked Byrnes to become secretary of state, a decision he preferred to keep from Stettinius until his work at the conference had been completed.

Despite persisting doubts about his own future, Stettinius approached the San Francisco meeting in the firm conviction that he would be taking part in a decisive moment in history. This belief found expression in a letter to Cordell Hull.]

STETTINIUS TO HULL | *April 20, 1945*

* * *

In the meantime I shall keep in constant touch with you and will be counting on your guidance throughout these important deliberations. I know I am speaking for each United States delegate in saying that we approach with great humility our tasks at this conference of United Nations, which you so justly describe as "one of the great turning points in history." I believe that all of the delegates from the United Nations, who are already assembling in San Francisco, feel this deep sense of responsibility and I share your faith that we will be successful in this great undertaking.

[Several days later, Stettinius went to the White House for a general discussion of matters pertaining to the upcoming conference. The British foreign secretary, Anthony Eden, was already in Washington for preliminary talks, and Soviet Foreign Minister Molotov was scheduled to arrive later in the day. Before talks among the three diplomats opened, the secretary wanted to clarify with the president his position on pressing matters such as Argentina, the extra seats for Russia in the assembly, and the Polish problem.]

NOTES ON MEETING, STETTINIUS AND THE PRESIDENT | *April 21, 1945*

* * *

I stated that Mr. Molotov was delayed. . . . The president said he thought it would be good psychology for him to see Mr. Molotov briefly and then he could give me my instructions by telephone and I could be just as firm with Molotov as Molotov was going to be with us.

* * *

I presented the Argentine matter to the president. I told him . . . how they had behaved in the past, the proposals that had been made to them at Mexico City and they had finally declared war and signed the Act of Chapultepec and were clearing up their situation relative to the Nazis. They had yesterday asked to establish diplomatic relations with the Soviet Union and China and appealed to us for the privilege of signing the United Nations Declaration. I said that there were commitments involved and there was a large political issue at stake with regard to which the president would have to make a decision. The president said he didn't like it at all. He said "It reminds me of a political convention where the guy fights to the last five minutes and then gets on the band wagon to qualify as an ambassador." He said it was all wrong. I said, "Mr. President, while I was away Mr. Rockefeller had a visit with the president and the president made a commitment that if they cleaned house and took these various steps they would be received into the United Nations family." He said any commitment the president made he will abide by, regardless of what the consequences are, but he hoped that with honor and with decency and fair play we could get around this matter, so that this country would not have to take the lead in advancing the proposal at this time. . . .

* * *

The president told me that he was very hazy about the Yalta matters, he had been over the Yalta minutes last night, that the agreement on Polish political as well as territorial questions was very hazy and he was amazed that it wasn't more clear cut. I said that the president had tried to get it clear cut and definite but it had been impossible to do and the president had made every effort to make it crystal clear and President Truman said that he understood that.

[Later that day Stettinius met with Eden to coordinate Anglo-American thinking on various questions, particularly how to handle Russia on the thorny Polish problem.]

MEMORANDUM OF
CONVERSATION | *April 21, 1945*

* * *

Mr. Eden said that he felt everything turned on the Polish question and that this must be discussed first. The secretary said that Ambassador Harriman advised us that Molotov did not want to come to San Francisco at all and had objected at first when Stalin suggested it. He had also made difficulties when Stalin authorized him to discuss the Polish question.

Mr. Eden said . . . Mikolajczyk had . . . accepted the Yalta compromise . . . [and] that Stalin might agree to Mikolajczyk going to Moscow. He asked the prime minister whether Mikolajczyk had agreed or would agree to the eastern boundary of Poland agreed upon at Yalta. The prime minister had replied that he would not have sent Stalin his original telegram if he had not been sure that Mikolajczyk had agreed to this. . . . The secretary advised Mr. Eden that he had discussed with President Truman the question of the United States's position on the matter of the Yalta agreement to support the Russian request that the Ukraine and White Russia should be initial members of the international organization. The president had stated that President Roosevelt's commitment would be carried out and was going to give the secretary a letter which would be made public if the question was raised. He asked what Mr. Eden's position was on the proper interpretation of the agreement to "support the Soviet request," whether this meant that we merely had to vote in favor of it or whether we had to exert other pressure. Mr. Eden stated that he felt that our position was clear, and that all we had agreed to do was to support the Soviet request. This did not mean that we had to insist on the approval of the Soviet request and break up the conference if the other nations would not go along. He felt that if we voted for the Soviet request and made a short statement of the reasons for our position that would be adequate. The secretary said we were in agreement then on this issue.

* * *

Withdrawal of British and United States forces into zones of occupation. The prime minister [had] made a proposal to the president recently that we should not immediately withdraw into our own occupation zones. . . . Mr. Dunn stated that this matter was in the hands of the Combined Chiefs of Staff. He understood that the U.S. proposal was that Eisenhower should be authorized on the basis of military considerations to make minor adjustments and withdrawals. Major withdrawals should be referred back to the Combined Chiefs of Staff for approval. The British, on the other hand, wanted Eisenhower to get previous approval before each withdrawal. Mr. Dunn stated that after all we had reached a firm agreement with the Russians on zones of occupation and that he thought it would be a mistake if we allowed it to appear that we were not prepared to live up to this agreement. If there was no military reason against a withdrawal, we felt that General Eisenhower should certainly have authority to do so. . . . Mr. Eden pointed out that in Austria the Russians were in our zones and that we might find it difficult to get them to withdraw. He thought the two matters should be adjusted together and was not suggesting that we go back on our agreement. Mr. Dunn stated that he thought a reply to the prime minister was going forward shortly on this matter.

[They discussed a meeting between Truman and Churchill. Stettinius indicated that the president would be unable ". . . to take time off from his job to visit Europe, at least until the late summer or autumn." If there were to be a meeting "during the next sixty days as seemed important" perhaps Churchill could come to Canada.]

* * *

Poland. Mr. Eden said . . . he thought some progress on this matter was absolutely essential before San Francisco if the conference was to be a success. It was impossible to expect a final solution but we may be able to make public some agreement which constitutes a step forward, giving some promise of final solution.

The secretary stated that he had discussed this matter in the morning with President Truman. The president was prepared to tell Molotov that a failure to reach agreement on the Polish question in the near future would jeopardize the conference and would have such a reaction on public opinion in the country and in the Congress that there would be little chance of a treaty carrying out the Dumbarton Oaks plan being approved by the Senate. He felt that the continued failure to settle this matter satisfactorily endangered the entire position of the United States taking its place at the world table. Mr. Eden said this was fine. He said he thought our position should be to stand on the general lines of the joint message from the president and the prime minister.[8] He hoped that the Russians would agree that the Poles referred to in that message should be called immediately to Moscow and that Harriman and Clark-Kerr should go back right away for the discussions. We should bear in mind that even with this we cannot wait very long for further steps to be taken, otherwise public opinion will suspect another breakdown.

* * *

[Molotov arrived in Washington the following day, April 22, and was soon received at the White House. He told the president of his great admiration for Roosevelt and of the Soviet Union's hopes for continued friendship with the United States. Truman soon cut through these amenities to speak of the Polish problem. In blunt terms, he stated that Poland was symbolic of the Allies' ability to work cooperatively, and he expressed hope that the foreign ministers might resolve the question during their Washington talks.

In the evening of April 22 and again in the morning of April 23, Stettinius, Eden, and Molotov held extended discussions on the Polish issue. The United States and Britain insisted that the Yalta declaration required the creation of a new and broadly based Polish government and pressed Molotov, as a first step, to invite representatives of the various political factions within and outside Poland to Moscow for consultations on the formation of a new government. Molotov, maintaining that the Yalta agreement provided only for the addition of new members to the existing Warsaw government, objected that he must secure the approval of the leaders of that government before anyone could be invited for consultations. In the meantime, he added, the Warsaw government should be invited to attend the San Francisco conference. Neither side was willing to budge from its position, and the talks got nowhere.

The foreign ministers' deadlock over Poland stiffened the determination of the Truman administration to deal firmly with the Russians. At a meeting with his advisers in the afternoon of April 23, the president himself complained that thus far U.S. relations with the USSR had been a "one way street and that could not continue; it was now or never." Truman observed further that he intended to "go on with the plans for the San Francisco conference and if the Russians did not wish to join us they could go to hell." With the exception of Secretary of War Stimson, who thought the Russians "were being more realistic than we were in regard to their own security," the president's advisers endorsed his position. At a final meeting with Molotov later in the day, Truman curtly informed the Russian that the United States could not be a "party to the formation of a government which was not representative of all Polish democratic elements," and demanded that the USSR carry out the Yalta agreement. "I have never been talked to like that in my life," the shaken Russian replied. "Carry out your agreements and you won't get talked to like that," Truman tartly informed him.[9]

Wings Over The Golden Gate

Courtesy Richmond Times-Dispatch

Reproduced with permission from the Chicago Daily News

Despite this inability to resolve one of the basic problems, the Allies went ahead with their plans for the United Nations conference. To millions of people across a war-weary world, April 25, 1945, seemed like the dawning of a new hope, the beginning of the fulfillment of their dreams for an era of peace. For the moment, at least, even such a serious disagreement as the Polish question, must move aside for the grand task at hand. The next two months were to prove a period of excitement and intense work for Secretary Stettinius, a time when his talent at compromise was tried to the limit.]

X

SAN FRANCISCO: POWER BLOCS AND THE UNITED NATIONS
April–May 1945

For two months beginning on April 25, 1945, the battles of war shared their gory headlines with more hopeful reports of the proceedings of the United Nations Conference on International Organization. The delegates of fifty allied countries possessed a detailed guide in the Dumbarton Oaks Proposals, but faced the herculean task of incorporating many competing amendments into a UN Charter that would command universal support. The eventual success of the charter writers was a tribute to their patience and skill as negotiators in the face of arduous circumstances.

Relations among the Great Powers were at a wartime low as the conference opened. The Yalta spirit of unity had crumbled into protracted, bitter wrangling on many of the major problems, notably over creating a new Polish government. Western suspicions of Soviet expansion had risen, and Anglo-American leaders began to fear that communism might overwhelm Western Europe as well as the nations bordering Russia. Stalin harbored his own suspicions, accusing the Western Allies of trying to impose hostile regimes in Eastern Europe. On the eve of Germany's surrender, he still believed the West was trying to turn Germany against Russia, as evidenced by his stinging attacks over the surrender of German forces in Italy. Germany's surrender on May 8 removed the one common wartime bond uniting Russia and the West.

If there remained an identity of interests in the nether

world between war and peace, it lay in San Francisco where Molotov, Eden, and Stettinius daily rubbed elbows with foreign ministers from around the world. Peace, or more precisely, the creation of functional machinery to head off future wars was the new cement linking East and West. Aware of Germany's V-1 and V-2 rockets, the new jet aircraft, and predictions of futuristic push-button warfare, the statesmen at San Francisco fully appreciated the significance of their work. It was generally assumed, and often expressed, that the world could neither afford nor would civilization survive another global conflict.

Yet so pervasive were the suspicions of small nations toward the Great Powers, so great the aspirations of the major powers themselves, and so deep their ideological differences that the conference became a kind of battleground itself, with diplomats maneuvering and fighting across a field of green while elsewhere men shed their blood for peace. The confrontations at the conference ranged from organizational disputes to substantive problems affecting the basic powers of the United Nations.

Throughout the conference the most significant trend was the shift away from a powerful international organization. The high point of "universalism" had occurred during the Dumbarton Oaks conference. Erosion set in thereafter, correlating closely with the deterioration in relations among the wartime Allies. At the San Francisco conference, the forces of regionalism gained strength, emerging with Article 51 of the UN charter which later became the legal basis for the alliances of the cold war. In addition, the Russians previewed their attitude in the UN by efforts to extend the use of the veto in the Security Council and in their demands to limit the scope of the General Assembly. Finally, the Great Powers jointly secured adoption of a trusteeship system that bolstered their global ambitions by providing strategic areas that would be exempt from UN scrutiny.

Beyond this weakening of the UN fabric was the more significant accomplishment of achieving consensus on the Charter. It advanced beyond the covenant of the League of Nations in its greater flexibility, clearer delineation of security functions, and broader commitment to economic and social issues. While the covenant had been drafted without Russian participation, the UN Charter was created by full consultation among the USSR and other powers.

Dozens of technical committees and commissions rendered yeoman service in drafting and reconciling smaller issues and the plenary sessions passed on major reports and the Charter itself, but many of the crucial decisions came in the conference Steering Committee. Composed of delegation chairmen this committee voted on all substantive issues. Yet even its actions were often based on decisions reached earlier in meetings of the Big Five chairmen and private talks with key delegates of smaller nations.

Much of the conference's inner decision-making occurred in Stettinius's penthouse suite atop the elegant Fairmont Hotel. Here the U.S. delegation and the chairmen of the Big Five nations met once or twice each day. In addition the secretary held countless private conversations with other leaders, and often when not otherwise occupied, he could be found at the phone conversing with Truman, Hull, Vandenberg, Eden, Gromyko, and others. Without question this conference marked the apex of Stettinius's diplomatic career. His contribution lay in the decisiveness with which he operated and the unfailing strength of his conviction that the conference would succeed despite every obstacle.

His activities became a focal point of the conference, yet, unlike Wilson at Versailles, Stettinius cooperated fully with the U.S. delegation. He sought advice but he always kept final authority in his own hands and frequently acted on his own initiative to resolve a question. Even with the pressures, Stettinius's energies seemed to increase as the days passed. His confidence in his abilities had never been greater, and many of his earlier self-doubts had been overcome. All of this was ironic, since he worked amid press speculation that Truman would replace him as secretary of state at the conclusion of the conference.

[The first challenge he faced was Russia's proposal that the chairmen of the sponsoring nations (U.S., Britain, Russia, and China) share the presidency of the conference. Also at stake was the seating of Byelorussia and the Ukraine. Evidently, Molotov thought that with an equal voice in running the conference, Russia would be able to secure more favorable decisions. Stettinius discussed these topics by phone with the president.]

CALENDAR NOTES | *April 25, 1945*
. . . I told him that the delegates had decided to support all the way the Soviet voting proposal [on seating Byelorussia and the Ukraine] and he said it was entirely agreeable and he agreed that the letter could be made public. I told him that Molotov would go home if they did not get the two republics admitted as initial members of the organization and he said go down and put it across. I explained that it was not certain whether or not the Soviets would raise tomorrow the question of these republics participating in the San Francisco conference. I told him about the Soviet proposal for four equal presidents and he said that that was absurd and we should maintain our position of a single presiding officer.

[The struggle over the conference presidency came to a decision in the Steering Committee the following morning.]

DIARY | *April 26, 1945*

A serious argument developed over the appointment of the permanent chairman of the conference. Foreign Minister Molotov of the USSR had been full of questions. After Mr. Eden had proposed me as a permanent president of the conference, I recognized Mr. Molotov who began by saying . . . he believed there should be four presidents of the conference whose authority would rotate from day-to-day. . . . Anthony Eden proposed a compromise by which there would be four presidents so as to preserve in public the unity of our sponsorship, but as the chairman of the host delegation I would act as plenary chairman of the four presidents whenever they met together, and also as chairman of the Steering Committee and the Executive Committee of the conference.

Meanwhile my friend Padilla, foreign minister of Mexico, advanced most eloquently the position that I should be president of the conference. This step, he said, should be taken, if for no other reason than as a tribute to the United States as host nation. The delegation chairmen of the other sponsoring powers would be vice-presidents of the conference. Any opposing views among the four sponsors would be reconciled among themselves.

* * *

Molotov stuck to his position, threatening that if the United States chairman were to be sole president of the conference, the Soviet Union would no longer act in a sponsoring capacity but only as any other participating nation.

* * *

In presenting his compromise, Foreign Minister Eden said, "I believe the British are supposed to have something to do with compromise"—which brought laughter. As the hour was getting very late, I decided to put on some pressure, and said, "Gentlemen, we must reach a decision on this promptly so that we can get on with our solemn task. The only desire of the United States, I assure you, is to make a success of the San Francisco conference."

Finally Molotov agreed to the Eden compromise but insisted on deferring action until the following day. I leaned across Mr. Hiss and the Russian translator at my left and made a personal plea face-to-face with Molotov. (The translator put my words into Russian.) After some further discussion by the committee, I had occasion to repeat my attempt at personally persuading Mr. Molotov. Finally I got a really friendly, cordial smile from him and we shook hands on the proposition that we would work things out.

[That evening the secretary discussed the issue with Truman. Stettinius believed that Molotov's suggestion would set a bad precedent for UN leadership.]

TRANSCRIPT OF TELEPHONE
CONVERSATION | *April 26, 1945*

Mr. Stettinius: . . . We got to the president of the conference and ran into a deadlock. . . . Molotov arose and gave a long speech on equality of four equal authorities. The British did not carry through as they had indicated and we expected. General Smuts,[1] Mackenzie King,[2] and Eden made other speeches along the lines of having four presidents of the conference with the host representative acting as chairman of the Steering Committee and of the Executive Committee.

I told Eden we couldn't accept—in accordance with my agreement with the president I could not agree. Eden said the four foreign ministers could agree that one of the four act as chairman.

Finally when that was put to the test Molotov refused even to have the American representative act as presiding officer over the four presidents, so we adjourned the Steering Committee meeting to resume that discussion tomorrow morning at 10:30. . . .

Query: Should I give in and agree to four presidents of the conference with your representative being named chairman of the Steering Committee and chairman of the Executive Committee, or must I stick to my guns and insist that I am to be the presiding officer and we must accept the four presidents representing China, USSR, UK and U.S., but the American must be the presiding officer over the four chairmen?

President Truman: I think we ought to insist on presiding over the conference, don't you?

Mr. Stettinius: The delegation is firmly of that opinion.

President Truman: That is my opinion.

Mr. Stettinius: It is a precedent. There never has been an international conference where the host is not presiding officer. There are two dangers not apparent on the surface—if the Russians ever get the chair they can stall; second, when we lay the pattern they can insist on four chairmen for the new Security Council. If they were in for a year or even for a month they would dominate the situation.

President Truman: Stick to your guns.

[Molotov accepted the British compromise. With Stettinius's authority intact, the Steering Committee considered seating of certain disputed delegations.]

DIARY | *April 27, 1945*

We next considered the appointment of Commissions and Committees. This of course was the subject which we knew would raise the question of membership of two additional Soviet republics, Poland, and Argentina. Molotov at once asked to be recognized by the chair and . . . explained that White Russia and the Ukraine each had a million men in the Red Army and their countries had borne the main burden of the German attack. He referred to my mention of the juncture of the Allied armies and said that of all who rejoiced, that White Russia and the Ukraine were the *most* glad of this.

* * *

There was no doubt but that the success of secondings of Mr. Molotov's proposal produced a cumulative dramatic effect upon the meeting. But . . . one could not help [but] feel that there was a kind of conspiracy of unreality or hypocrisy on the part of committee members in apparently disconnecting Mr. Molotov's request from the proposal for three Soviet votes which had produced such loud American protest not many weeks earlier. Nevertheless the motion was unanimously carried. After it, I reached across and shook hands with Mr. Molotov and he greeted the whole group with his usual wave that was also a salute.

* * *

The question of Polish representation at the conference was introduced by Mr. Masaryk [3] "as a neighbor of Poland." He proposed that the solution of this problem be carried through as recommended at the Crimea conference. Molotov urged that this be done. Leaving no doubt about the firmness of my stand I said "the United States government cannot accept Mr. Molotov's proposal . . . until the Crimea decisions are carried out." Mr. Eden said his government's position was exactly the same as ours.

* * *

I said that this committee having decided faithfully to support the Crimea agreements, must support all the Crimea agreements. And I left no room for doubt as to how strongly we felt on this point. Mr. Molotov again insisted that Poland be invited at once to the conference, and Mr. Eden again backed up my position.

* * *

Later I learned that before I joined the meeting of the U.S. delegates that night, Vandenberg had said to those present in the conference room: "By God, I saw something today—something that made me proud to be an American. Our secretary took hold of the situation and by God, he just put it through! The way he did it, I was proud of America and proud of Ed Stettinius today."

[Unable to agree on Poland, the Steering Committee deferred action over the weekend hoping the sponsoring powers might reach agreement. In the meantime, the seating of Argentina had created added tensions.]

DIARY | *April 27, 1945*

The Argentine problem was growing acute. President Truman was [not] in favor of having Argentina represented at the conference. Nelson Rockefeller undoubtedly had been responsible for bringing the situation to the point where the nineteen Latin American republics probably would not vote for the two new Soviet republics being seated until Argentina was also admitted to the conference.[4] On the other hand, the USSR would not engage in voting on the commission and committee chairmen until the two republics were seated. This had produced a deadlock in which the questions of Argentina and the two republics would have to be settled before the conference could proceed to do its principal work of drafting a charter for world organization.

[There was no dissension among the Great Powers on admitting the two Soviet republics, but opposition did come from the Latin American delegations who threatened to block the Soviet republics unless Argentina were admitted. Stettinius realized the need of Latin American backing for seating the Soviet republics; thus, it might be necessary to drop U.S. opposition to accepting Argentina. Stettinius discussed this prospect with Truman.]

TRANSCRIPT OF TELEPHONE
CONVERSATION | *April 27, 1945*
Mr. Stettinius: . . . The only thing that can come up is the question of the timing of letting the Soviet republics and Argentina come to San Francisco without any of them being members of the United Nations. We are going to have to make a deal on that and my guess is that we are going to have to do it a little bit earlier than I indicated to you last night.
President Truman: You make it any day. You have to get that thing going.
Mr. Stettinius: The issue in your mind is that as a matter of principle we don't want to accept Argentina into the United Nations family, but if the conference votes that they can come and take a place at this conference without being one of the United Nations, you won't object?
President Truman: That is right.

Mr. Stettinius: And even if that comes pretty soon? I think we are going to have an issue either Monday or Tuesday when the two Russian republics and Argentina are allowed to be here to take part in this conference, although none of them would be

If You Regret It Later—

Courtesy Reg Manning, Arizona Republic

allowed to join the United Nations. I think that public opinion would stand that.

President Truman: I think so too, and you can be as tough as you want to before you come to a conclusion and I will back you up.

Mr. Stettinius: I was very tough on Poland today and I took Tom [Connally] and Van [Vandenberg] into the Steering Committee with me and had them sit by my side as my advisers and they went along every step of the road and are in complete accord. I think you have reason tonight to be encouraged that we are off to a good start and we are going to come home with the bacon.

President Truman: I am going to take a drink and really sleep tonight.

[Over the next several days maneuvering proceeded on seating the disputed delegations, and tempers began to mount in the Conference Executive Committee.]

DIARY | *April 30, 1945*

After action had been taken on the two Soviet republics and on Poland, Foreign Minister Padilla proposed discussion on seating Argentina, and Fernandez of Chile [5] followed him in urging the move.

Molotov immediately objected on the grounds that the cases of Argentina and White Russia and the Ukraine were different, and that inviting Argentina while Poland still remained outside would not be understood.

I had my agenda cards before me, in a black ringed binder notebook which I leaned on the gavel. From this I read the statement of the U.S. delegation backing up Padilla and Fernandez. Mr. Evatt, of Australia,[6] spoke for amending the statement unfavorably for the seating of Argentina. Mr. Molotov objected that he had not heard of the Argentine resolutions. However, I countered that the Soviet delegation had been fully informed by us.

Padilla arose to thank me for my "vigorous efforts on behalf of unity of the continent." He said that Poland was a matter that should be entirely in the hands of the four sponsoring powers. His position on Argentina was that the people themselves were democratic, while the government was not, but it should be encouraged in that direction. . . .

Molotov next moved that the matter of Argentina be referred to the four sponsors, and Masaryk, of Czechoslovakia, seconded the motion. Mr. Eden took issue with this view, saying that originally invitations of course were the responsibility of the four sponsors, but that now the conference was in session, invitations were the responsibility of the conference as a whole. He emphasized that the committee should "take the decision" and added that we should make as many decisions as possible during the conference.

There followed a rather petty discussion whether Argentina should receive only *permission* to join the conference or should be tendered an outright invitation.

Cutting through this argumentation I referred back to the Padilla motion and asked for a show of hands. This motion was carried 9–3 (with Dr. Soong not voting).

*   *   *

After the Padilla motion was carried Mr. Molotov moved that the whole matter be referred to the four sponsors before going to the Steering Committee and to the conference in plenary session. I called for a vote on this by show of hands, as had been done in the case of Padilla's motion, and as the hands went up Mr. Molotov looked around speculatively at each representative who was voting, as he had during the Padilla vote. It was 8–3 against Mr. Molotov's motion and a real defeat for him.

[The U.S. was willing for Poland to attend the UN conference if the Great Powers agreed on a new government. Stettinius, Eden, and Molotov held numerous talks on this matter, with the West urging a renewed role for former Polish premier Mikolajczyk.]

SUMMARY OF TELEPHONE CONVERSATION | *May 2, 1945*

Stettinius told the president he had met with Eden and Molotov on Poland this morning. Molotov informed them that Mikolajczyk, as an individual, could go to Moscow immediately for consultation. Stettinius said that Harriman and Sir Archibald Clark-Kerr [7] would return to Moscow and start consultations with the various Polish leaders; that if they could agree on a new government, that government could take its seat in San Francisco. Stettinius remarked that Molotov's manner as a whole has changed; that all day today he had been bending over to try to be nice.

[This arrangement deferred a final decision on Poland and allowed the delegates to turn to other matters. Argentina quickly became the most controversial problem. The American press had reported no real transformation of the Buenos Aires regime, and the public could not grasp why the conference admitted Argentina while denying representation to Poland. Former Secretary Hull was outraged, and privately lambasted Stettinius for poor leadership.[8] Two staunch UN supporters in the Senate, Carl Hatch and Joseph Ball, sent a sharply critical telegram to the secretary of state charging that the U.S. had connived in ". . . a cynical repudiation of the whole cause of Democracy and freedom for which we are fighting this war against the Axis." [9]

The secretary, conscious of the support Hatch and

Ball could provide the administration in lining up Republican votes for the UN charter, enlisted Senator Vandenberg's aid.]

VANDENBERG TO HATCH AND HILL, TELEGRAM | *May 1, 1945*

This will reply to you and Ball. Fully understand how you feel about the Argentine decision. It was unavoidable to hold twenty South American republics in line following pledge of Chapultepec. I do not like it any better than I like the White Russian and the Ukraine decision. But this conference will have to be judged by its ultimate product and I respectfully suggest that if I am willing to withhold my judgment until the finish you ought to withhold yours. Roosevelt started a chain of events at Yalta which I hope is now liquidated. . . . This comment is personal and confidential to you and Ball. No single event of the past week can be judged by itself. What we have done is to save the conference from disintegration and to give the peace organization a fair chance.

[The secretary also directed Nelson Rockefeller, who had returned briefly to Washington, to confer with the senators. When they understood the dilemma and realized that the delegation had acted out of necessity, Hatch and Ball dropped their criticism. Writing to Stettinius on May 3, Hatch said they believed "that the delegation met a practical situation in a practical way." [10] That same day the president relayed word to San Francisco that he was "eminently satisfied" with the job Stettinius was doing and that he was with him "100 percent right down the line." [11]

During the struggles over conference organization the sponsoring powers were working on their amendments to the Dumbarton Oaks Proposals. Stettinius had planned to announce them on May 5, but the talks were incomplete by that date. The main issue was Russia's request to exempt its security treaties with France and England from control by the Security Council. The Big Five discussed it in a meeting on May 4.]

* * *

Mr. Molotov said, "I thoroughly believe in such an organization, but I don't know how soon we can set it up. . . . It will take time and study. . . . Germany has been a great aggressor over twenty-two years and will do everything to build up her strength. After the international organization has built itself up strongly, that will be different, but meanwhile the Anglo-Soviet and Franco-Soviet treaties must stand. . . ."

This dilemma produced silence for a while. . . . Feeling the need for the American delegation to collect its thoughts, I suggested a short intermission of about fifteen minutes. The American members of the group adjourned to my bedroom, where . . . after everyone had agreed that the proposed exception on treaties in the original amendment was such as to protect our interests, Governor Stassen made a very strong statement pointing to a "grave defect" in the position which would cut us out of a share of control over enemy countries. He said it was "unthinkable" to agree to this amendment. He added that repetition of the language in another part of the Dumbarton Oaks Proposals . . . regarding action against enemy states would cure the defect. Sensing another delay in our already lagging schedule, I urged that Dr. Pasvolsky's language was probably adequate in view of the nature of the surrender terms, with which Commander Stassen was not familiar.

[Unable to reach agreement after examining numerous drafts of a proposed amendment covering security treaties, the sponsoring powers decided to submit joint amendments on other points but separate statements on the unresolved question.

The split among the Great Powers over the role of regional treaties in the UN provided the opening the Latin American countries needed to put forward their claim for an exemption for the inter-American system. Pasvolsky canvassed key Latin American foreign ministers on May 5, and then warned Stettinius to expect trouble. They "want the regional arrangement to be completely free of the world arrangement." [12]

Earlier that evening, Rockefeller, who had just returned from the capital, dined with Senator Vandenberg. Rockefeller stressed the need to safeguard the inter-American system. Immediately realizing that he had slipped up in not pressing earlier for a clear statement excluding the inter-American system, Vandenberg wrote to Stettinius.]

VANDENBERG TO STETTINIUS | *May 5, 1945*

I am greatly disturbed lest we shall be charged with a desertion (1) of our Pan American obligations at Chapultepec and (2) of the Monroe Doctrine. The former is a threat to the Pan American solidarity which becomes increasingly indispensable to our own safety. The latter is a threat to confirmation of the entire San Francisco charter by the Senate of the United States. . . . I am quite willing to continue it for the very good reason that we can't expect our Allies to depend upon an untried peace league for their defense against a resurgent Axis until it has demonstrated its adequate capacity to serve this defense function.

But what can we say in defense of our action in requiring at the same time that Pan America must depend upon this new peace league (before it has demonstrated its adequacy) and must abandon its primary reliance upon inter-American relationships which are fifty years old and which were vigorously reasserted (under our auspices) at Mexico City within the last two months?

We have all been troubled about this phase of the matter . . . we have been deterred by our fear that an exemption of our inter-American "Regional Agreements" might be an invitation to the rest of the world to divide itself up into similarly immunized blocs and regional balance of power groups. . . .

I have come to the definite conclusion that it is possible to protect our status without endangering the general objective and in a fashion to which none of our associated sponsoring powers can object because none of their interests will be involved.

[Vandenberg proposed an exemption for the inter-American system identical to the one Russia had proposed for its European security treaties. This would preserve the Act of Chapultepec and the Monroe Doctrine and prevent a Security Council veto regarding "Western Hemisphere self-defense." The senator denied his proposal would encourage other regional blocs.]

* * *

I call your attention to the fact that this does not rob the Security Council of any authority in respect to the maintenance of peace and security. It merely temporarily suspends the power of the Security Council to prevent the American states from exercising their traditional functions of self-defense.

[Angered at the prospect of new delays in presenting amendments to the full conference, the secretary pointedly asked Rockefeller if he had written Vandenberg's letter. Rockefeller answered that he had not, although he conveniently overlooked his part in inspiring the senator. Stettinius realized how vital Vandenberg's assistance would be in the Senate, so he reluctantly brought the regional question before the U.S. delegation on May 7.]

DIARY | *May 7, 1945*

. . . Senator Vandenberg's letter . . . proposed an additional change in the regional arrangements section to protect the Monroe Doctrine and the Act of Chapultepec. Vandenberg requested an opinion from Rockefeller, who said the Latin Ministers were upset, feeling the Big Four had made a deal on amendments and the leading foreign ministers were going home and only nominal discussions henceforth would take place in the technical committees.

Governor Stassen spoke powerfully against . . . destroying the world organization—"We might as well as say in Chapter I, Section 1, 'we are *not* setting up a world organization.' " Mr. Notter [13] also felt strongly that an amendment along the lines of the Vandenberg proposal would "wreck the world organization." Mr. MacLeish also supported this position, while Mr. Rockefeller furnished the main support for Vandenberg. Messrs. Dulles and Dunn gave a balanced exposition of the situation, with Mr. Dunn tending to take the worldwide rather than the regional viewpoint.

[Unable to develop a response to Vandenberg's questions, the delegation continued deliberation in an evening session.]

DIARY | *May 7, 1945*

As for our newest problem that was emerging, I said, "We have to reach a very quick decision" on Latin America and the original amendment. I said that I was very concerned about opening up this whole question, with Molotov under the impression that he had finished his job and was ready to go home. I asked Harriman to speak on this subject. He argued for our approaching Molotov in company with the other three powers, in the interest of definiteness and clarity of approach; we must realize also Molotov's determination that European problems should be handled by European countries. . . . He added that Molotov was anxious to get us out of Europe.

* * *

Dr. Pasvolsky in a brilliant exposition clarified the Act of Chapultepec as being in its origin consonant with the Dumbarton Oaks Proposals: "If we open the way anywhere to regional action, the world organization is finished. . . . There will be four or five armed camps consisting of groups of nations . . . and another world war."

In arriving at his position, Senator Vandenberg obviously was thinking of the problem of ratification of the world organization in the Senate. He frequently would say something like: "When Senator Wheeler [14] asks me on the floor of the Senate . . . what am I to say to him?"

On the other hand, Dr. Pasvolsky insisted on the world viewpoint: "When good faith fails in the Security Council, the world organization is through."

The senators and congressmen demanded to know whether the Monroe Doctrine would be protected under the terms of the proposed amendment and the discussion grew intense. . . .

Mr. McCloy [15] reported on a talk with certain Latin Americans. On the whole he expressed the military opinion that the British and French armies and navies were more valuable than the armies of Latin America—but he believed *both* valuable to us.

[While U.S. experts groped for a way to safeguard the inter-American system without undermining the UN, Stettinius decided to discuss the problem frankly with the Latin American delegation chairmen. They met in his penthouse early on May 8.]

DIARY | *May 8, 1945*

* * *

After my introduction to the subject, Victor Andrade, Bolivian ambassador to the United States, . . . said . . . that some of the Latin American representatives had held a meeting the night before and talked over the present "threat to the Monroe Doctrine" and to the inter-American system with a history extending over fifty-two years—all by an untried organization. He said that peace . . . emanated from the example of the Western Hemisphere. He sympathized with the need of the United States to intervene in Europe. But . . . in making a choice in favor of the world organization to the detriment of the inter-American system, the United States would be gaining an intangible vague power, and losing the solid inter-American cohesion.

* * *

Dr. Padilla said that threats to the American continent would be not so much from armies as from ideas, and that our system as defined in the final Act of Chapultepec consisted of much more than a regional scheme.

Ambassador [Ramirez] Belt of Cuba argued a little differently. Control by the Security Council would destroy the inter-American system because each Latin country would seek favor and support from one or another of the Big Five—the permanent members on the council. He said the Latin American nations would not vote for the Soviet regional amendment unless a similar exception were made in their favor. . . .

I pleaded with the Latin American gentlemen that we must have enough ingenuity to find a formula satisfactory to the American countries and to the Soviets also.

[At this point Colombian Foreign Minister Lleras Camargo bluntly expressed Latin American fears of postwar communist penetration of the Western Hemisphere. His comments are more completely recorded in a memorandum of this meeting than in Secretary Stettinius's diary.]

STETTINIUS-LATIN AMERICAN FOREIGN MINISTERS, MINUTES OF MEETING |
May 8, 1945

Any country seeking to attack the United States in the future would attack through the weakest point which is in South America. The next war will be between Russia and the United States, not between any two countries in Europe. [An] attempt will be made to [out]flank the United States through South America. Penetrations would be made in South America, similar to the ones made by Germany in this war, when she planted the seeds of fascism in surrounding countries by utilizing small minorities. We must retain the independence of action of the inter-American system, particularly with reference to the veto in the Security Council which will [preserve] this freedom of action.

* * *

[Stettinius replied by appealing to the ministers' statesmanship.]

DIARY | *May 8, 1945*
I concluded emphatically that no U.S. delegation member had ever had any idea of weakening the inter-American system—but wanted on the contrary to preserve the system and keep the peace of the world at the same time.

[Although Stettinius had listened in quiet exasperation to the regional views of the Latin American ministers, he strongly believed that the Western Hemisphere nations must subordinate their own regional interests for the sake of creating a strong international organization. His irritation was evident in the U.S. delegation meeting that afternoon.]

DIARY | *May 8, 1945*
. . . I asked Mr. Rockefeller pointedly, "What has happened to the Latin Americans during the past two weeks to destroy their faith in the international organization?" Mr. Rockefeller said that they had been upset by the Soviets' behavior toward Padilla and Bidault (in the Steering Committee meetings), that in general they feared the Russians, and that they felt bewildered by the death of President Roosevelt and felt fearful that his Good Neighbor policy might not be vigorously followed.

The delegation advised me to call to Mr. Molotov's attention the attitude of the Latin Americans, in a very general way. I would reassure him actually that we would fight for *his* rights and *other* bilateral treaty rights. In connection with this whole difficult Latin American problem which had just arisen afresh when it seemed as though our chief difficulties had been surmounted, it was reported that the Arab states—with five

356 | EDWARD R. STETTINIUS, JR.

votes—had approached the Latin Americans to form a combined bloc, and that the Latin Americans had turned them down.

There were low points during the conference when it was difficult to see how without a spirit of high courage and confidence any worthwhile charter could be written. This was one of those times. It was a curious coincidence that just then after the cathedral clock had struck six, the chimes in the tower played the hymn "Eternal Father, Born to Save." Indeed there seemed a need for prayer at this moment of controversy and danger for the success of the world undertaking.

* * *

[After he left the delegation meeting, the secretary phoned President Truman and advised that the regional issue might require "a very far-reaching decision of foreign policy" and it might be necessary for him to fly to Washington.[16]

Later that evening Stettinius and Molotov met for their final talk before the Russian foreign minister departed for Moscow. Stettinius put forward Latin American views in a careful, low-key statement, comparing them to the Russians' desire for temporarily exempting their treaties from the authority of the Security Council. Stettinius emphasized that the U.S. would continue to support the Russian exemption and implied he expected a similar USSR gesture on the inter-American system. Molotov offered no encouragement, and the Russian position on the inter-American system remained unclear.[17]

The struggle over regional blocs coincided with a major review of Soviet-American relations. Molotov's unbending stand on Poland, in particular, had convinced many U.S. officials that the time had come to deal more firmly with the Russians. The end of the war in Europe on May 8 required alteration of all Lend-Lease programs, and U.S. officials were especially eager to modify policies for aid to Russia that since the beginning of the war had enjoyed a unique status. Before Harriman had left for San Francisco, it had been agreed that the Soviet protocol arrangement, which committed the United States to supply the USSR a specified volume of supplies over a one-year period, should be abandoned after V-E Day. Henceforth, the United States would approve only those Russian requests which could be demonstrated to be essential to prosecution of the war. This change would satisfy Congress, which insisted that Lend-Lease be reduced to the bare minimum. It would also make possible the use of Lend-Lease as an instrument to extract political concessions from the Soviet Union.

On May 9, Harriman and Stettinius discussed the proposed changes in Lend Lease policy. They agreed that alterations should be made, but they advised caution in implementing them lest abrupt changes anger the Russians and disrupt the conference.]

MEMORANDUM OF CONVERSATION |
May 9, 1945

Ambassador Harriman said before he returned to Washington to talk to President Truman he wished to know what the State Department's view was on the extent to which the Polish question was a real issue affecting our general relations with the Soviet Union. He said this brought in the question such as Lend-Lease, postwar credits, etc. After some discussion, it was decided:

1. That on the Polish issue, we should impress upon Stalin the gravity of this question for our future relations—no specific acts of pressure or retaliation should be suggested or considered until the end of the San Francisco Conference.

2. That the needs of Western European countries should receive top priority over Russian desires under the fourth protocol and that we should curtail Lend-Lease shipments to Russia on a purely supply basis but without any hint of relationship with the Polish or other political problems with the Soviet Union.

[Harriman flew to Washington that same day to oversee the execution of these recommendations. The following day Stettinius talked with Truman about the changes in Lend-Lease policy.]

TRANSCRIPT OF TELEPHONE
CONVERSATION | *May 10, 1945*
President Truman: I saw Harriman and had a very pleasant talk with him.
Mr. Stettinius: You like the suggestion of him going to Moscow?
President Truman: Yes.
Mr. Stettinius: And of course the other one of getting tough on Lend-Lease shipments?
President Truman: I agree with that entirely.

[On May 12, 1945, officials in the War Department and Foreign Economic Administration executed a presidential directive on aid to Russia. Misinterpreting the order, they cut off all shipments to the USSR and even called back a number of ships at sea loaded with supplies for the Russians. This move, which Stettinius later described as an "untimely and incredible step," [18] produced great shock in San Francisco and in Washington, and though the order was later revised to permit shipments intended for Soviet use in the war against Japan, it left a lasting impression on Stalin and exacerbated Soviet-American relations at a critical period. [19]

In the meantime, Stettinius and his advisers [20] had been working frantically to find a compromise that would protect the inter-American system without undermining the United Nations Organization. Increasingly, they focused on the concept of "self-defense." The essential idea was that each nation enjoyed an inherent right to self-defense, and that countries in a region ought to be able to resort to this if the UN failed to meet an act of aggression. After an all-night drafting session on May 10, Dulles presented to Stettinius a memorandum that the secretary used as a basis for discussion in the American delegation meeting the following afternoon.]

DIARY | *May 11, 1945*
. . . I explained to the group that there was the utmost need for speed because Anthony Eden had to return home almost immediately . . . owing to the delicate political situation at home.

Mr. Dunn had phoned Assistant Secretary of War McCloy regarding our new proposal, and McCloy was to report reactions from Washington. Just after this Mr. [Artemus] Gates, assistant secretary of the navy, joined the meeting, having just arrived from Washington. He gave an account of a meeting held in Washington the day before with Stimson, Forrestal, General Marshall, Admiral Edwards (for King),[21] and others on the subject of regional arrangements. I told the group that I had phoned Mr. Hull, who wanted further time for consideration.

When I asked General Embick [22] and Admiral Fairchild [23] about their views, they said that "personally" they favored our new draft. However, when Admiral Hepburn [24] joined the meeting a little later, he reported the final action in Washington had been adverse, as there was a feeling the new regional paragraphs threatened the integrity of the world organization.

It was explained that the basis of . . . the Act of Chapultepec was:

1. defense (attack against one is attack against all)
2. security council for the American continent.

The French proposal on regional arrangements,[25] like the League of Nations, allowed a country to take defensive action if the league failed to act; the problem was, *when* does the league fail?

Breaking through this discussion I said, "the time has arrived when we must not be pushed around by a lot of small American republics who are dependent on us in many ways—economically, politically, militarily . . . we must provide leadership."

* * *

While Mr. Dulles in an interpretation of our latest draft emphasized that it dealt with *self-defense* and *not* regionalism, he was very intense about the discussion and drew pictures on a yellow pad.

* * *

Governor Stassen, who all along had insisted on a broad, worldwide approach, said that subject to military and presidential approval, he would vote for the present draft. He complimented our advisers in having devised in the form of this drafting means to accomplish our regional objectives without undermining the world organization. Mr. Rockefeller added that he was enthusiastic about the draft.

* * *

Mr. MacLeish suddenly broke in: "This will be regretted as long as the memory of this conference lasts." He said he was unhappy about our new draft because it was based on defense, "which was the way this war started, using defense as an excuse."

* * *

[Stettinius left to telephone Washington.]

On my return . . . I reported that I had consulted Stimson, Forrestal, and Grew, all of whom thought that our draft overemphasized the hemisphere at the expense of the world organization. Mr. McCloy felt a specific hemisphere exception would be better, but . . . was satisfied with our draft from the point of view of the hemisphere military situation and thought we had clearly improved the language. Considering everything, I felt it safe to say that we would have definite authority given into the hands of the delegation by the war and navy secretaries by the following morning.

[The next day Stettinius discussed the compromise on regionalism with the president.]

TRANSCRIPT OF TELEPHONE
CONVERSATION | *May 12, 1945*
Mr. Stettinius: It reads as follows—Should the Security Council not succeed in preventing aggression and should aggression occur by any state against any [UN] member state such member state possesses the inherent right to the necessary measures for self-defense; the right to take such measures for self-defense against armed attack shall also apply to understandings or arrangements like those embodied in the Act of Chapultepec under which all members of a group of states agree to consider an attack against one of them as an attack against all of them.
Mr. Truman: That sounds perfectly all right, good.

Mr. Stettinius: The taking of such measures should be immediately reported to the Security Council and shall not in any way affect the authority and responsibility of the Security Council under this charter to take any action as it may deem necessary to maintain international peace and security.

Mr. Truman: I don't see a thing wrong with it. It sounds very good to me. It covers the world situation supreme and maintains our situation here as we want it.

Mr. Stettinius: We can act immediately if the Security Council doesn't act and we have the inherent right of self-defense.

Mr. Truman: That's what we want.

[With U.S. officials agreed on an amendment to safeguard the inter-American system, Stettinius presented it to the other Big Five powers. He had moved hastily summoning Gromyko (who had replaced Molotov), Eden, Koo, and Bidault without bothering to circulate the U.S. proposal first.[26] Although Eden knew the tenor of what Stettinius would request, he reacted angrily during the meeting.]

DIARY | *May 12, 1945*

Opening our main agenda matter of regional agreements, I said that our latest statement was based on the French suggestion. Gromyko at once brought up the question of treaties, suspiciously, and I assured him quickly, "That had nothing to do with your matter, Andrei." I then read from the typed copy of our draft.[27]

Mr. Eden declared immediately, "I am frank to say I dislike it intensely. . . . It makes me extremely unhappy. Either we have a world organization or we don't. There would be regional organizations all over the world. How do you define aggression. . . . I would rather not sign the charter. . . . That this should come so late in the day!"

Gromyko, as usual, said that the Soviets would have to "study" it. . . .

Senator Vandenberg kicked back hard at Eden, alluding to the reservations on which the British had insisted for their own treaties. Senator Connally in more measured language explained our problem, largely in terms of Senate ratification and our delicate inter-American position.

Nevertheless, Eden apparently was still in a temper. "We didn't come here with this in view," he said.

Commander Stassen helped to get the situation in hand by . . . a calm analysis of our "underlying approach." He said, there would be three stages: (1) peaceful settlement, which could be local; if this proved inadequate, then (2) enforcement would be undertaken on a world scale; if this proved inadequate, then (3) "self-defense" would come into play, as a local right.

* * *

Stassen further elaborated, "This does *not* give the regions freedom of action . . . or right of enforcement of action."

Anthony Eden, visibly in a better mood, leaned forward and gesticulated to give his views. He felt we must not lay down a principle for a regional system "as a way to do things"; this would be too much of an open invitation to repetition. Nevertheless, Eden acknowledged our problem [regarding the inter-American system].

[At Eden's suggestion the meeting recessed. The British foreign secretary wanted to pursue the American proposal—but in private. Eden expressed British concern over Russia's expansionist aims in Europe and the Mediterranean and wanted to make certain that they devised a broader article empowering regional action.

After drafting by British and American experts the term "collective self defense" was inserted in the proposal. The whole matter was then presented to the reconvened Big Five meeting, where Gromyko asked for time to study it.

Anticipating agreement on the regional formula by the sponsoring powers, Stettinius decided to call another meeting with Latin American foreign ministers. They gathered two days later in his penthouse in "an atmosphere of suspense and expectancy."]

DIARY | *May 14, 1945*

I opened the meeting by saying that . . . we had been working night and day and . . . I would shortly hand to them in confidence a paper on the regional question. I emphasized strongly the need for security and absolute privacy from the press, because of our negotiations which would have to follow with the British and Soviets.

* * *

I told the meeting that this matter was as important to us as to any of the Latin American countries, but the U.S. had been in a particularly difficult position because others at the conference had been charging us with "becoming isolationists and abandoning Franklin Roosevelt's policy for a world organization to keep the peace. We must make the world organization succeed—we can *always* have the inter-American system, because that can never be hurt."

* * *

Senator Vandenberg, alluding to what he called his well-known sympathy for the Latin American point of view, told the group that he had "reluctantly" come to the conclusion that the words "Act of Chapultepec" should be eliminated from the [amendment] language. If this were done, he guaranteed that the Senate Foreign Relations Committee would "specifically spell out . . . collective action" to mean to us "chiefly the Pan American Union and everything else connected with it." . . . If we should try to include the Act of Chapultepec in this amendment there would be many other pacts of less validity which others would also attempt to insert. Finally he shouted, "The Senate of the United States will nail this down so nobody on earth can misunderstand it."

I indicated my complete agreement with the sentiments expressed by Senator Vandenberg.

Lleras Camargo, the Colombian foreign minister, apparently altogether unimpressed began immediately to talk in Spanish—very quietly and coolly . . . Mr. Rockefeller translated Lleras Camargo's remarks; definite mention of the Act of Chapultepec in the amendment would be the only possible way to tie the inter-American system effectively to the world organization. Future regional systems, said Lleras Camargo, should be admitted to similar relationship with the world organization.

I pressed Dr. Lleras Camargo on his position, referring to his "small hemispheric view" as opposed to "world leadership." But . . . he feared that unless the whole question were agreed upon at present, the world organization might fail to give its approval later to the inter-American system.

* * *

Just about this time a general murmur of conversation broke out among little groups all over the room and I went along the line of Latin Ministers bending over talking to each one and giving them a little fight talk on the importance of working out a compromise along the lines of our latest position. I talked to about four or five of the delegation chairmen in this manner. Calling the meeting to order again, I suggested that the Latin Americans get together and discuss the new suggestions, and that we meet again later. I especially called attention to the distress being caused in other delegations and the danger involved in allowing this problem to drag along as an obstacle to the conference created by a Latin American bloc. "We cannot let the success of San Francisco," I said, "be jeopardized by these discussions we're having."

* * *

Pleading for Latin American acceptance of the new documents, Vandenberg explained that the U.S. delegation unanimously interpreted "collective action" as meaning "Act of Chapultepec" and that this interpretation would be set down in black and white . . . by the Senate Foreign Relations Committee.

[Stettinius's veiled threats and Vandenberg's strong assurances combined to win grudging consent from the Mexican, Brazilian, Peruvian, and Cuban delegation chairmen, thus undercutting any solid Latin American stand that Colombia's Lleras Camargo might have hoped to sustain. They adjourned at 3:40 A.M., having agreed to seek a common ground on the regional formula.

One of the ideas which had emerged was to convene a Western Hemisphere meeting sometime after the San Francisco conference to draft a regional security treaty. The U.S. delegation discussed this possibility at its morning meeting on May 15, with Stettinius modifying his initial opposition.]

DIARY | *May 15, 1945*
. . . I reported on the work which had been done during the previous night on this question, including the development of a proposal that during the San Francisco conference

President Truman should call a meeting of Latin American nations for the following autumn to make the Act of Chapultepec into a formal treaty. Senator Vandenberg believed the Latin view was that they must have us: (1) identify the Act of Chapultepec specifically in the Charter, or (2) guarantee the implementation of the Act of Chapultepec.

Nobody seemed to have any clear ideas on pulling together a good plan and there was considerable defeatist talk, and for the first time during the conference I told the delegation, "I am getting a little discouraged."

Senator Vandenberg made some rather explosive remarks about our stopping the Latin Americans and others from "pushing us around. . . ."

I said that the idea of calling a conference of Latin American nations during this San Francisco conference "gives me a cold shock," and I mentioned "pointed questions" which the consultants [28] had asked during the preceding evening—questions which indicated slipping faith in the world organization.

In spite of the obvious hazards to the world organization Mr. Rockefeller kept tenaciously and exclusively advocating the limited Latin American viewpoint.

Finally the idea of a treaty conference several months after San Francisco began to appear to advantage in my mind and I realized that this would mean we would not have to go so far in keeping satisfaction of the Latin American demands during the San Francisco conference. After I expressed these sentiments, Commander Stassen said that my sense of timing was right, and he thought it would be healthy to let the Latin ministers face their problems at home for a few weeks after their return. The basic idea of a treaty conference, however, was a matter of national policy only the president could decide.

Vandenberg turned to me and said, "You must personally take charge of this for a couple of days and work it out with President Truman as his first secretary on the line of basic national policy."

* * *

In order to be perfectly clear, I said, "For the record, I am completely opposed to having a proclamation during the San Francisco conference calling for a meeting of this hemisphere."

Mr. Rockefeller protested that he was interested primarily in the welfare of the United States and the world organization.

* * *

At this point I read a message just received from Mr. Hull, who warned that if the individual national ideas continued to strengthen, the international organization "will gradually fade away."

Later Vandenberg referred to his attitude toward the Latin American countries: "Didn't I tell them off yesterday, speaking in favor of the world organization?" I told the senator that he had, but asked if I hadn't done the same. He replied, "But I am talking about *me*, because I am the old isolationist."

[Following the delegation meeting, Stettinius phoned President Truman to discuss a future inter-American conference.]

TRANSCRIPT OF TELEPHONE
CONVERSATION | *May 15, 1945*
Mr. Stettinius: . . . Remember the other day you approved the text about the regional arrangement—nothing would impair the right for self-defense in the event that the Security Council does not prevent aggression. We have come

to the conclusion in the delegation that it would be a mistake to mention the Act of Chapultepec, which you will recall we mentioned in the draft that you approved.

Mr. Truman: I believe you have come to the right conclusion.

* * *

Mr. Stettinius: . . . Dr. Padilla . . . should write me a letter recognizing, or requesting what plans the United States government would have later on. . . . I would say to him we aim to continue the Good Neighbor policy started by Roosevelt, successful for these twelve years. We are going to carry the sound Good Neighbor policy and everything that goes with it. We are going to stick by the Monroe Doctrine and continue to stick by it. We would be favorable to a treaty providing that an attack against any American state from within or without should be considered [as an attack] against all of them.

Mr. Truman: Nothing wrong with that.

Mr. Stettinius: To get by with it I would have to assure these fellows that they will be invited to come some time in the summer to a conference in Washington [or], autumn, to agree on the treaty and we would have a treaty to send to the Senate that would line up the American republics.

Mr. Truman: I'd be glad to do that.

Mr. Stettinius: You think that's all right? That's in the Act of Chapultepec, in Mexico. It called for war powers after the present [ones] had expired—that we would get together. The only question would be whether this exchange of notes should take place while this conference was going on or afterwards.

Mr. Truman: It would be better afterwards, then Russia couldn't find fault.

Mr. Stettinius: I'll send you a two-page digest of what we have been talking about so you can understand all the lines. Meanwhile, it is perfectly all right for me to assure the Latin American ambassadors we will go along on the Good Neighbor pol-

icy; we will be friendly toward the treaty; and arrange a meeting in the autumn?
Mr. Truman: That's right.

[Armed with the president's approval, the secretary called the Latin American chairmen into session two hours later.]

DIARY | *May 15, 1945*

I then said that I was changing my role and was now speaking as the secretary of state of the United States rather than as head of the United States delegation at the San Francisco conference. In a purposely dramatic style, I said that I had just spoken to President Truman and could authoritatively say that there would be no weakening in the inter-American system but that instead it would be strengthened, partly by implementing the Act of Chapultepec by treaty, next autumn. . . .

After a murmur of consultation had broken out among small groups of the Latin ministers, Senator Connally was suddenly on his feet, starting off quietly on a speech in terms of forty-nine nations rather than twenty-one nations. His dark gray suit was buttoned up close to his black bowtie and gold shirt studs, and he seemed so neatly turned out and was so quietly grave behind his great tortoise shell glasses that he seemed like a Sunday school boy speaking a piece. At the beginning it had that kind of set-speech quality. He reminded the group how very greatly we need to depend on confidence in each other, and, he said, "You know the United States is not going to let *any* nation interfere in the Western Hemisphere." Gradually gaining momentum his voice became louder and he gestured dramatically, as if he had forgotten that he was talking in a living room in San Francisco to a small group but was on the Senate floor or perhaps at a political rally. He hammered his ideas, first turning toward the Latins and then to the American delegation. His face grew red with effort, and he made an unforgettable picture of a senator in action, against the background of the huge Gobelin tapestry.

"I appeal to you, 'Trust us!' " he proclaimed. "*We* are in the Western Hemisphere just as much as you are. We *can't* do it alone—You've got to help us—harmonize this with the international system." He had been more operatic than any of the Latins during the conference; they appeared to appreciate the speech and greeted its conclusion with sustained applause, as Senator Connally, having shut off his stream of oratory as if it could be controlled like a faucet of water, quietly walked back to his chair and sat down.

I said, "Senator Connally has spoken from his heart."

Ambassador Belt asked, "I have faith in the United States, but *when* can I tell my people about your treaty proposal?" I said that I did not know and then Senator Connally followed up, "We also have *our* people to report to."

[While pleased with the United States proposal, the Latin American delegates wanted an immediate public announcement of the proposed conference as an additional indication of good faith. Stettinius's misgivings about the wisdom of doing this were allayed following discussions with the other sponsoring powers. After the U.S. delegation concurred, the secretary again talked with President Truman who agreed that it was wisest to make a public statement.

With this accomplished there still remained final approval by the sponsoring powers of the language on regional arrangements. Gromyko caused further delay while he consulted Moscow on the new wording. This irritated Vandenberg who, as the U.S. representative on the technical committee on regional arrangements, had met many objections over repeated postponement of its work.]

DIARY | *May 17, 1945*

It was announced that a Big Five meeting scheduled for 3:00 that afternoon had been canceled because Ambassador Gromyko had not heard from Moscow regarding the new language for the regional amendment. . . . Senator Vandenberg took exception sharply that the meeting had been canceled and "we were knuckling under to the Russians." At one point he went so far as to give an ultimatum that if we did not make a decision the next day, regardless of Soviet instructions being received, he would withdraw from the Regional Committee, because "I will not any longer be humiliated on behalf of my country and myself." After I had tried to explain to Senator Vandenberg the purely technical nature of the delay, Mr. Dunn undertook to assuage the feelings of the senator: "If we were in Moscow—we would feel we were being pushed around." Vandenberg: "We are being shoved around all over the world by these Russians."

[News that Russia would accept the regional compromise opened the way for final Big Five approval. By May 21 it was submitted to the technical committee, which approved, without change, the language of what became Articles 51 and 52 of the UN Charter.

The enhancing of regional blocs at the UN conference represented a shift away from a powerful international organization, and over the next few years the founding nations used Articles 51 and 52 to justify their alliance systems. These agreements, such as the OAS, NATO, and the Warsaw Pact became the nuclei of security to the detriment of the UN. Given the suspicion in

Allied relations by the time of the San Francisco conference, this was a predictable development.

An even more serious challenge to the UN—the veto
crisis—arose in the wake of the regional problem, and
brought out even more clearly the growing distrust
among the Great Powers.]

XI

SAN FRANCISCO: THE VETO
DISPUTE
May–June 1945

No sooner had the regional bloc controversy been resolved than the question of voting in the Security Council emerged as the major issue before the San Francisco conference. From the start of negotiations for the world organization, this problem had caused great difficulty. The Soviet Union's demand for an absolute veto in the council had produced a deadlock at Dumbarton Oaks. After months of arduous and highly technical discussions the Big Three foreign ministers had finally worked out a compromise position that had been accepted at the Yalta conference. This so-called "Yalta formula" provided that the veto should apply on decisions pertaining to enforcement through economic or military sanctions, but that it would not apply on the investigation and consideration of peaceful settlements of disputes.[1] Certain of their agreement on the Yalta compromise, Stettinius, Eden, and Molotov had not brought it up or given it much additional thought in the early sessions at San Francisco.

The Yalta agreement had provoked strong opposition from other quarters, however. Critics in the United States and other Western nations had protested that its all-inclusiveness would cripple the United Nations. The forty-five small nations represented in San Francisco objected that the Great Powers had not consulted them in formulating the veto arrangement and had not replied to their suggestions for modification. They feared that the Yalta accord would enable the

Great Powers to dominate the world organization, and desired that some of its ambiguous features be clarified. Thus when the issue came up in committee on May 17, critics of the Yalta agreement submitted a list of twenty-three questions probing every aspect of the practical operation of the veto power.[2]

In the early stages of the dispute, the Great Powers were aligned against the small nations. Some U.S. delegates privately sympathized with criticisms of the Yalta accord and wished to see the veto power narrowed. But the delegation was primarily anxious to maintain Great Power unity, and there was some resentment that the small nations should attempt to undo something that had been settled after great effort. The United States therefore stood firmly with Britain and Russia in opposition to changes in the Yalta compromise.

As the debate continued, however, the Great Powers became divided among themselves. In response to one of the questions submitted by the small nations, the Soviet delegation insisted that the Yalta formula allowed the use of the veto to prevent an issue from coming before the council for discussion. The American and British delegations flatly rejected the Russian interpretation, and the conference soon reached a dangerous impasse. It appeared for a time that the dispute might prevent the delegates from writing a charter, and the deadlock was only resolved by a direct appeal to Stalin through Harry Hopkins, who was then in Moscow.

Resolution of the veto issue cleared the way for completion of the conference. The delegates finished drafting the Charter by June 18, and with great ceremony approved it in a final session on June 26. For Stettinius it was a moment of personal triumph, the culmination of a sustained effort beginning at Dumbarton Oaks. He was not able to savor his victory, however, for even before the conference had ended he learned that President Truman had decided to appoint James F. Byrnes secretary of state.

[The American delegation discussed the Yalta voting formula frequently in the week following May 17. Many delegates personally sympathized with the smaller powers' desire to limit the veto beyond the provisions of the Yalta agreement. But they reluctantly agreed that unity with the Soviet Union must take priority and there was even some irritation that the small nations, particularly the Latin American nations should challenge the leadership of the Great Powers. Senator Tom Connally was especially vocal, and Stettinius concurred that they must suppress any challenge to Great Power unity, even if they had to use a heavy hand to bring small nations into line.]

DIARY | *May 22, 1945*

He [Connally] expressed great concern over the trouble we were having with the Soviet delegation on the interpretation of the voting formula. "We're right up against the buzz saw on this," he said, complaining that the "latinos," whom we had given all kinds of assistance, were now not cooperating well in our hour of need. Senator Vandenberg joined the hue and cry against the Latin American countries, and Mr. Rockefeller said "Why did I ever come to this meeting!"

* * *

This was a serious matter and I did not hesitate to say that the Latins must be brought into line. And I found it necessary to remind Mr. Rockefeller of this very forcefully.

* * *

Governor Stassen added . . . that, where we ran into trouble, we must not drive the Latin Americans but appeal to them for their cooperation.

Senator Connally again attacked the attitude of the Latin

Americans, and Mr. Rockefeller protested that they would "go along with us where we tell them the success of the Charter is involved." Mr. Rockefeller seemed to have taken Senator Connally's remarks almost personally, and the senator told him good humoredly, "I was not speaking of you, only of your satellites." Commander Stassen repeated, "Don't try to drive them or anyone else until you work out these interpretations of the text. It is the worst thing you can do."

I myself felt that we had done a great deal for the small countries, especially the American republics, and we should have some recognition of our efforts . . . when we needed it. "Here we've been in San Francisco a month," I said, "and we haven't begun to swing our weight around yet. . . ."

[On May 22, Stettinius flew to Washington to confer with President Truman. He arrived at the White House prepared to review a wide range of policy matters, but the president restricted their discussion primarily to the United Nations.]

CALENDAR NOTES | *May 23, 1945*

The president greeted me with great warmth. He again complimented me on the fine job I had been doing in San Francisco and he thought I looked particularly well in view of the great strain I had been through.

* * *

On voting in the Security Council, the president said he had studied this and thought that it would be much better if the veto powers did not apply to peaceful settlements, but, if the Russians insisted upon the Yalta interpretations applying, of course we had no choice and he would abide by the decision of the delegation in this respect.

378 | EDWARD R. STETTINIUS, JR.

[Truman had earlier decided to send Harry Hopkins to Moscow and former ambassador to Russia, Joseph Davies, to London, for top-level talks with Stalin and Churchill. During his conversation with Stettinius, the president expressed great optimism about the two missions.]

I had a frank talk with the president relative to Harry Hopkins's mission and the Joe Davies mission. He said he had great confidence that Harry would be able to straighten things out with Stalin. He stated that he got a three hour answer [reply within three hours] from Stalin saying that he would be delighted to receive Hopkins. He stated that he had hopes now that the Hopkins mission was going to unravel a great many things and that by the time he met with the Big Three that most of our troubles would be out of the way. He said that he was not worried about things in Europe. . . .

* * *

He then said that he thought sending Hopkins, an ultraliberal, to Stalin and Joe Davies, an arch-conservative, to Churchill would be helpful at this moment. . . .

[Upon returning to San Francisco, Stettinius found his advisers increasingly confused and divided over the veto issue. Caught in between the demands of the small nations and the insistence of the Russians upon standing by the Yalta formula, the American delegation struggled to establish its own position.]

DIARY | *May 26, 1945*
Senator Connally said, "We've got to face a lot of these things and the best way to face them is by hitting them on the nose"; we should liberalize our interpretation of voting as much as possible while respecting Roosevelt's agreement at

Yalta. "We've got to rely on the Latin Americans if we can catch them at a moment when their intellects and consciences are alive."

Mr. Rockefeller at once shot back: "You've got to catch them when they're asleep if you want to get this one by them." Governor Stassen asked that the U.S. position be made clear first, and only then should we compromise with others among the Big Five powers. Senator Connally . . . spoke in favor of a more compromising approach than Stassen's. But Stassen maintained, "There never has been a U.S. position on the *interpretation* of the Yalta formula."

* * *

I said, "I can tell you now Gromyko and I have talked about this in the last several days, and Gromyko cannot deviate from the Yalta formula without instructions from home. . . . It must be done by a wire from me to Molotov or from President Truman to Stalin."

Governor Stassen commented, "The small powers are trying to jockey us around into a reactionary position." Senator Connally pointed out that not only Soviet Russia, but China and the United Kingdom were against any change in the formula, and he concluded: "If you aren't going to get it changed, why not hit it in the nose and say we're for it?"

[The discussion continued after lunch.]

Dr. Pasvolsky reported on his morning meeting with the Committee of Five and presented a new draft of the joint interpretation statement of the Yalta voting formula.

* * *

I summarized that "this is a statement by the Four Powers on the reasons why the Yalta voting formula is necessary. . . ."

Congressman Bloom cut into the discussion with "What are we to gain and what are we to lose by this thing?" Dr. Pasvolsky answered him "This is an attempt to answer a *challenge* . . . on the inclusion in the charter of the Yalta formula"—It represented a compromise between a simple majority vote in the council and complete unanimity—the latter alternative would "stymie" the organization.

When someone questioned him, Dr. Pasvolsky answered, "I am *thoroughly* satisfied to take the Yalta formula." Senator Vandenberg followed, rather cynically, "I am taking the Yalta formula because I have to take it . . . What I don't understand is why do you have to have a unanimous vote to inquire and investigate." Pasvolsky told him that some of the other nations, who had gained more experience with these things than we, believed this was necessary.

* * *

Mr. Notter cautioned that this document should not give the appearance of a four-power ultimatum. Dr. Pasvolsky took a different point of view. "This is one case where we have to . . . say 'Take it or leave it.' "

* * *

[Turning to Russia's view of the Yalta voting formula, Stettinius spoke emphatically.]

. . . I made clear that the Russian position was, "The Yalta agreement was a firm commitment made by a dead president." This was expressed plainly in two talks I had with Molotov, and I got the same thing from Gromyko. Someone asked whether the Yalta agreement would continue to bind us into the indefinite future. I replied that "After we get this organization started and we are off to the races, then Roosevelt's commitments come to an end." Someone again spoke of the shortened precipitous nature of the Yalta conference, and I explained that regarding the formula for voting agreed upon in Yalta, "It was a thing that developed gradually from August to January—not done in a hurry." I found it necessary also to remind the group that a complete veto was supported by Stalin, and Churchill "wavered in that direction for three minutes." Mr. Dulles remarked that Ambassador Gromyko recently had told him the voting formula represented a big compromise from the Russian point of view. "I'm glad you said that," I responded to Mr. Dulles. Another good reminder was put forward by Mr. Notter: "Agreement on this formula alone made this conference possible."

In answer to a suggestion that the matter be reopened by the president, I said, "I think nothing can be answered by this delegation raising this matter on a higher level. President Truman has put the matter up entirely to this delegation." I asked General Fairchild his opinion, and he stated that the existing compromise on voting in the Security Council was the favored position of the military as taken before Dumbarton Oaks. I then urged upon Mr. Rockefeller the need for Latin American votes in supporting our position. But Mr. Rockefeller felt that we would have sufficient votes without complete unanimity among the American republics, and some division among them would "look better," avoiding the appearance of a solid bloc.

[On the evening of May 26, the Big Four delegation chairmen met in Stettinius's apartment to discuss the paper their technical experts had drafted in reply to the twenty-three questions from the other delegations. A serious division broke out at once over Question 19: "In case a decision has to be taken as to whether a certain point is a procedural matter, is that preliminary question to be considered in itself as a procedural matter or is the veto applicable to such preliminary questions?" This question raised the basic issue whether the veto could be used to stop *discussion* of problems in the council and seriously intensified the voting crisis.]

DIARY | *May 26, 1945*

Sir Alexander Cadogan talked long and rather obscurely on the procedure in the Security Council for determining what would be procedural and what would not be procedural. He seemed to succeed in adding confusion to the already difficult situation.

Gradually a cleavage seemed to develop between the Soviet group and the others on the subject of whether or not the veto would apply to a vote on a question of a matter being procedural or not procedural.

Mr. Dulles, who had had a haircut since the afternoon meeting and looked neat and trim for an evening of relaxation rather than another difficult meeting, said, "A fool can ask more questions than ten wise men can answer. . . ." Gladwyn Jebb [3] countered: "But some fool *has* thought up *this* question."

[Gromyko refused Stettinius's plea that they "find a way to get on with this matter," insisting that he must consult with Moscow to get instructions. For the next five days the conference came to a standstill. In the meantime, Acting Secretary Grew informed Stettinius of the president's desire to bring the proceedings to a successful conclusion as quickly as possible. On May 31, Stettinius met privately with Gromyko, and the ambassador informed him that he expected to have word from Moscow the next day. [4] The chairmen of the Great Power delegations gathered on June 1 in an atmosphere charged with anxiety and expectation.]

DIARY | *June 1, 1945*

Ambassador Gromyko raised the question of voting procedure and announced, "I'm in a position to give you at this meeting the final position of the Soviet delegation on this question. . . . I wish to state that we have to stick to the Crimea decision as it stands." This he interpreted to mean that a qualified vote [5] was necessary for all matters before the Security Council, and would even be necessary for bringing matters up for discussion. . . .

[At another session the following morning, Stettinius vigorously set forth the U.S. position on this issue.]

DIARY | *June 2, 1945*

I said that we could not agree to the Soviet interpretation presented the night before. We had interpreted the [Yalta] formula at Mexico City [6] and "it would be utterly impossible for us to join an organization" holding veto power against introduction of measures for discussion only. Lord Halifax followed my lead, saying, "It is unacceptable to my government. . . ."

While Gromyko admitted that he would, of course, consult with his government, he said that the Soviet position was "definite and clear in this matter: for the Crimea decision with no revising." As for any earlier interpretation, such as that given at Mexico City, he said this was "without agreement" by the Soviet, and it represented a "retreat from the spirit" of Crimea. I quickly replied to Gromyko that the U.S. policy was to follow the Crimea decisions in every way and that I regretted he had used the word "retreat" as entirely "out of keeping" with the existing situation.

Tension in the room was extreme and Gromyko was about to speak. At this key point the French interpreter became formal again and interrupted Gromyko at the beginning of his remarks. After another protest by Gromyko, I said, regarding his new interpretation, "It is not in keeping with the Dumbarton Oaks Proposals and something which the United States government cannot accept."

* * *

Ambassador Gromyko started to read from the Dumbarton Oaks language to support his point. . . . I broke in to say that we had stated our position and our efforts would result in no Charter at all if the Soviet view should prevail. I did not mince matters at all at this point but talked to the Soviet representative in as firm, emphatic, and unmistakable terms as possible so that the importance of our stand could not be misunderstood.

Senators Vandenberg and Connally each said that the Soviet interpretation would mean that the Charter would not pass the Senate, with its tradition of free debate. Vandenberg was particularly emphatic on this point, and Senator Connally concluded that on this basis, if members applied to the Security Council for help it would be better to "send 'em to the deaf and dumb asylum instead."

[Aware that his arguments were having little effect on Gromyko and determined to cut through the normal procedure of waiting for the ambassador to communicate with the Kremlin, Stettinius tried a direct appeal of his own. Taking up an idea suggested earlier by Lord Halifax, he decided to urge Harry Hopkins to raise the issue directly with Stalin. The secretary secured President Truman's approval of the plan and then drafted a strong note which was dispatched by Acting Secretary Grew to Harriman in Moscow. Referring to the "very serious crisis" in San Francisco, Stettinius detailed the essence of the dispute.]

GREW TO HARRIMAN | *June 2, 1945*

With the president's approval I am bringing this matter to your attention urgently. I know that in the past Marshal Stalin did not know himself of some of the decisions that were being taken and communicated to us. I feel therefore that it would be most helpful if you and Harry could meet with Marshal Stalin as soon as possible and ask him whether he realized fully what the instructions sent to Gromyko mean and what effect the Soviet proposal would have upon the character of the world organization we are trying to work out. Please tell him in no uncertain words that this country could not possibly join an organization based on so unreasonable an interpretation of the provision of the Great Powers in the Security Council. Please tell him that we are just as anxious as he is to build the organization on the foundation of complete unity among the Great Powers but it must be unity of action in the light of a maximum of free discussion. At no stage in our discussions relative to the creation of the world organization at Dumbarton Oaks or at Yalta or at any other time was a provision ever contemplated which would make impossible freedom of discussion in the council or the assembly. This is a wholly new and impossible interpretation.

Please let me know when you think you can put this up to Stalin and when you can give me some word as to his reaction since we will have to take the necessary steps to wind up the conference here if we have nothing favorable from you in this regard.[7]

[At this critical juncture, James Reston of the *New York Times* published a story outlining the details of the veto deadlock and blaming the Russians for it.[8] Stettinius was greatly annoyed by the leak, which threatened his behind-the-scenes attempt to resolve the voting dispute, and feared its implications for the conference. He immediately consulted with Pasvolsky to explore ways to repair the damage.]

TRANSCRIPT OF TELEPHONE
CONVERSATION | *June 3, 1945*

Mr. Stettinius: If we can't move them [the Russians] on this business what's the next course?

Mr. Pasvolsky: The trouble is that we have put them into a position in which they can't move except forcing them to publicly. We have now taken a position from which we cannot withdraw and we have put them in exactly the same position. Reston says this. That's a hell of a way to negotiate. We have to find another solution—so that it won't be theirs and it won't be ours. I have been racking my brains—we have to put it another way.

Mr. Stettinius: Is it possible to go ahead and write a charter and sign a charter and leave this up in the air?

Mr. Pasvolsky: No.

Mr. Stettinius: The small nations will never vote for the voting procedure?

Mr. Pasvolsky: They will vote for it, but I don't know when the organization will recover from that blow. This article has done us more harm than anything else—it throws doubt into the organization if we sign a charter now. . . .

* * *

[Reston's article had provoked some speculation that the conference might have to be adjourned, but Stettinius and Pasvolsky agreed that this was unthinkable.]

Mr. Pasvolsky: . . . this thing of adjourning the conference. . . .

Mr. Stettinius: We can't do that.

Mr. Pasvolsky: We can't possibly do that, but this is mentioned—if the Russians don't come through we have to adjourn the conference. That's being said.

Mr. Stettinius: We aren't going to adjourn the conference. We are going to have a charter and we are going to find an answer and I have complete confidence.

Mr. Pasvolsky: All I have confidence is that we have to do a lot of hard work. . . .

[To many delegates and observers, it seemed as though the San Francisco conference was rushing toward disaster. The frustrations over delays and the pessimism of radio and news stories cast a gloom over the proceedings. Public confidence had noticeably declined, and an increasingly skeptical attitude toward the United Nations was becoming more apparent daily.[9]

Under this strain, the bonds of bipartisan political cooperation threatened to break. Senator Vandenberg, who knew nothing of the administration's effort to resolve the veto crisis through Hopkins, feared an American "surrender" to the Soviet Union, and along with Dulles and Stassen, concurred that the Republican party would have to dissociate itself from such a step.

Stettinius soon learned of the Republicans' uneasiness. He had invested too much hard work in developing cooperation with the Republican leaders to risk its dissipation now. Aware that Vandenberg's support was necessary to secure Republican votes for the United Nations, he decided to consult with the Michigan senator.]

CALENDAR NOTES | *June 4, 1945*

I have had a very frank talk with Senator Vandenberg. . . . He stated that he had talked to three members of Congress and they say that confidence is going down hourly.

We should definitely do something to make our position clear, particularly on the veto question.

They feel the Russians are running things and stalling everything, and there is a fear we will give in to them.

Vandenberg stated that the one-page statement we had Saturday night should be given out and promptly.

He said he wanted a meeting of the American delegation to discuss the matter, but then withdrew his point, saying that he didn't think it was necessary for the American delegation to meet if I would be willing to issue the statement after clearing it with the president. . . .

Vandenberg said he and Stassen and Dulles had had a very frank talk and exchange of views this morning and are very disturbed about their own positions in this matter. If we don't do something ourselves quickly, he said, the Republicans are certainly going to do it.

[To head off a Republican revolt, the secretary called President Truman and asked that he be permitted to inform the delegates about Hopkins's approach to Stalin. The president reluctantly agreed. Stettinius immediately showed Vandenberg and Stassen his telegram to Hopkins.

Stettinius's revelation restored Vandenberg's faith in his abilities as a negotiator. "I was amazed," the senator wrote in his diary. "It was magnificent in its unqualified assertion of our position. It would not have been stronger if I had written it myself." [10]

While waiting for news from Moscow, Stettinius and Pasvolsky continued private discussions with Gromyko in hopes of finding a basis for agreement.]

MEMORANDUM OF CONVERSATION |
June 4, 1945

In opening the conversation, the secretary said that it would be helpful if he and Ambassador Gromyko could have a frank exchange of views. He said he felt sure there was nothing in anyone's mind at the conference but that the proposed international organization should be a success from the very start. However, he said, certain facts in the present situation had to be squarely faced. . . . The four sponsoring governments had come to San Francisco with the understanding that they would maintain in principle the Dumbarton Oaks Proposals and the Yalta agreements on the voting formula in the Security Council; to that end, at the beginning of the conference, the four had quickly arrived at the amendments which they felt strengthened those proposals and had shown great unanimity of purpose and action.

During the last two weeks, however, the secretary stated, it was being said by many of the delegations at the conference that the three major powers could not work together. . . .

The secretary said that he felt that we were facing a critical situation; that public confidence in the United States was falling, and something had to be done quickly to revive it. He said that this growing feeling of uneasiness was also being reflected in the Senate of the United States and it was necessary to correct this impression if the United States were to go forward as a full participant in the world organization.

* * *

In his general reply to the secretary's opening statement, Ambassador Gromyko said that he agreed fully with the secretary that neither the conference nor the proposed world organization could be successful without the unanimity of the Big Five. He said that the position of the Soviet delegation on the question of voting procedure was the decision of the Crimea conference, and . . . that his delegation viewed the current attempts to interpret the Crimea decision not as an attempt to change the Crimea language but rather as a change in the spirit of the Crimea decision. He said that the position of the United States delegation—that no veto should be allowed on the first step of the chain of events leading to enforcement measures—was not right; that such first step might ultimately lead to war, and that experience in this war had shown that complete unanimity was necessary from the first step onward. . . . He said that, in his view, if agreement could not be reached on this important point of interpretation of the Yalta voting formula, it would have a very serious effect on the conference.

The secretary said that at Yalta the United States had agreed that the veto would apply on enforcement measures, but that former President Roosevelt had never agreed that the veto would apply on the question as to whether a particular case should be discussed by the council.

. . . The secretary . . . read from the minutes of the Yalta meeting the president's statement and explanation of the formula on voting procedure. He emphasized the president's statement that every nation would have the right to present its case to the council; and that unless there was full and free discussion in the Security Council, the international organization that it proposed to establish would be different from the one contemplated by the United States government. He pointed out that there were two major points in the president's voting formula, namely, unanimity among the Great Powers and the right of full and free discussion. He said that the president was always clear that any nation could bring its problem to the Security Council for hearing and discussion without the necessity of a vote.

The secretary pointed out to Ambassador Gromyko that the question at issue between the two delegations seemed to be such a little thing. Ambassador Gromyko said that if it was such a little thing, why did not the U.S. delegation agree with the Soviet interpretation of the voting formula? Furthermore, Ambassador Gromyko added, the statement that the secretary had read was not the Crimea decision but was in itself an interpretation of the Crimea decision.

Mr. Pasvolsky inquired as to how the Security Council would be able to vote unless it had heard a case. Ambassador Gromyko said that the Crimea decision does not prevent free discussion in the Security Council once it has been decided that such discussion should proceed; but that the first stage of discussion was often the most important link in the chain of events leading up to final enforcement action. The secretary also inquired as to how it would be possible for the Security Council to vote unless the facts had been presented to it. Ambassador Gromyko replied that it would be an exceptional and rare case in which a permanent member would use a veto to stop discussion; but that such right of veto should be exercised when necessary to save the prestige of the international organization; and that it was a power that would not be abused, as had been emphasized in the proposed Soviet interpretation.

* * *

[With the issue still deadlocked in San Francisco, everything now rested on Hopkins in Moscow. The suspense ended two days later when Hopkins wired that Stalin, over Molotov's protest, had accepted the American interpretation.[11]

Stettinius learned of the breakthrough before Gromyko, and he excitedly called the Soviet ambassador to his penthouse to inform him of a decision by his own government! The secretary explained that he had taken that step "because . . . I feel I owe it to you in all friendliness to tell you immediately. . . ."[12]

Thus when the Big Five delegation chairmen gathered in the afternoon of June 7, Stettinius immediately turned the floor over to Gromyko so that he could announce his surprise.]

DIARY | *June 7, 1945*

. . . I was able to open this meeting with the knowledge that the log jam on this question had at last been broken. I said, "Ambassador Gromyko has a statement to make." In silence charged with expectation the meeting waited for Gromyko's remarks.

The Soviet ambassador . . . read slowly and distinctly: "The Soviet government continues to consider that Yalta prevents deviation from unanimity. But in interest of unanimity of [the] four sponsoring powers" the Soviets would permit a change in the interpretive document of May 26 as an exception.[13] One of the Soviet delegation members then distributed a few typewritten carbon copies of the changes suggested by the interpretive document.

* * *

This was a moment full of tension, and the rattling of papers, as everybody consulted the interpretive document and other pertinent exhibits, was louder than the murmur of comment from the various groups. There was a feeling of high significance.

* * *

The buzz of the conversation continued; it had been going on nearly twenty minutes when I called the meeting back to order, at 3:25 P.M. I recalled to the memory of the group the long hours of work spent on the paper of May 26 by Dr. Pasvolsky's committee of five, and I asked Dr. Pasvolsky now to comment on the paper just presented by Ambassador Gromyko.

* * *

During the rather long exposition on this question Mr. Dulles rather characteristically wandered about the open center of the floor across the elaborately figured oriental rug, with his hands jammed into his pockets, his head bowed a little, especially as he bent over to consult with me or someone else among the U.S. delegates or advisers. As he listened during these little interchanges of consultation, he blinked slightly through his dark glasses.

"Provided we reach an understanding of the way to meet the question of the further determination of matters which would be subject to procedural vote," Dr. Pasvolsky said, "I think this statement meets our views as it stands."

Gromyko nodded in a restrained manner, but [he was] apparently relieved and appreciative of our agreement with the Soviet statement.

* * *

I informed the meeting that Ambassador Gromyko and I had held a noon conference and decided that a Steering Committee meeting should be called immediately to prevent misunderstanding, and we had drafted a public statement on the subject of the veto decision. I then read the proposed release. While I read it, Dr. Pasvolsky sat on the little chair by the window quietly smoking his pipe.

* * *

When I requested the views of M. Paul Boncour [French delegate] on the whole matter, he agreed not only on the revised text of the interpretive statement . . . , but also on the proposed public release as well. Dr. [Wellington] Koo [Chinese delegate] with his usual finesse agreed in general and expressed his appreciation of the "efforts of our Soviet colleagues," but he questioned how well the changes would fit in with the draft of the interpretive document as a whole.

Passing around the circle, I asked Lord Halifax for his views. He said that the public statement was agreeable to the British delegation if acceptable to the Soviet ambassador. He said, "It's a fine statement. . . . It appeals to the heart as well as to the head."

"We need that at this point," I said.

Gromyko wanted a key phrase omitted from the public release, and I talked with him privately. "I can't take that out . . . that would take the heart right out of it," I told him. He was being as literal about the public release as if it were part of the Charter draft itself. "But, Andrei, that's awfully small," I protested, "you can't find fault with that."

. . . Finally, quite suddenly, Gromyko yielded and gave his approval to the statement. I patted him on the shoulder and laughed with him, and he began smiling and laughing too. . . .

[Shortly after this meeting, Stettinius announced to the press the agreement ending the veto crisis. He hailed it as offering "a new and heartening proof of the will and ability of the United Nations . . . to construct, upon the strong foundation of their wartime collaboration, a workable and effective and lasting peace. . . ." [14]

The high tension of recent days now yielded to elation. Stettinius phoned the president to report that the news of the agreement had produced an "electrifying effect" in San Francisco. In a jubilant mood, he and his secretary, Bob Lynch, went out "to cut the cable," dining at Amelio's "spaghetti joint" where the proprietor opened a "great magnum of Three-Star Hennessey" and treated everyone.[15]

Little time could be devoted to such pleasures, however, for much hard negotiating remained. Very soon after the resolution of the veto crisis, the Great Powers became divided on the question of freedom of discussion in the General Assembly. The Soviet delegation insisted that the assembly should be concerned only with questions of peace and security and should not discuss matters touching upon domestic problems of member nations. The other powers favored allowing the Assembly to function, as Vandenberg described it, as a "town meeting of the world." They examined the problem at a Big Five meeting on June 13.]

DIARY | *June 13, 1945*

Agenda point no. 3—discussion in the General Assembly—had been put on our agenda at the request of Ambassador Gromyko, who wanted . . . limits placed on the discussion in the Assembly. Taking exception to his view, I pointed out that . . . we had only made a small unimportant concession as a gesture to the small countries. At my request Vandenberg described how no substance was involved because the five-power amendment already allows the Assembly to discuss "any subject," etc. Any change now, he said, to restrict discussion in the "town meetings of the world" would cause a "revolution in Committee II/2, especially on top of today's big-power victory on the veto procedure." [16] Paul Boncour at once agreed with Vandenberg.

Halifax quizzed Gromyko about his *reasons* for wanting the change. Gromyko's point of view was that the world organization was only for the purpose of "peace and security" and therefore activities of the assembly should not be unlimited. . . .

At this difficult juncture I reminded the meeting, "We still have a very high hurdle to take at this conference . . . unanimity of the five powers in voting on amendments . . . and we'll need all our strength for that." I appealed to the good sense of everyone that we should not waste our energy elsewhere.

* * *

Meanwhile Halifax was trying to be especially friendly to Gromyko talking and smiling directly at him. While agreeing with us, Halifax suggested to Gromyko that there might be some possibility of handling this question as we did the last one. Gromyko did not budge. He would raise this question at the Executive and Steering Committee meetings.

"I have made my position clear," I said, "and if this is raised at the Executive and Steering Committees by the Soviet delegation, I cannot associate myself with the Soviet position. The British, French, and Chinese delegation heads immediately agreed with me. "Is there anything else to do," I asked, "but in good spirit agree to disagree?"

[Part of the Russian position on limiting the role of the General Assembly went back to the Kremlin's view that the Great Powers alone possessed the strength to assure peace. The Russians also believed the Great Powers were making too many concessions to the smaller countries.]

DIARY | *June 16, 1945*

. . . Gromyko was incredulous that other members of the Big Five should be so easy going with the small countries.

He asked in amazement whether we thought we should have made "three concessions in one day?" [17]

* * *

Senator Connally clearly and eloquently pointed out that the vote in the General Assembly was relatively unimportant because we still had our veto in the Security Council. . . . Gromyko stood firm on the position that he still wanted only one concession to be made by the Great Powers. He thought that was enough of a gesture to the small countries.

* * *

Finally Gromyko said that, as for the view expressed by Senator Connally and some of the others, he would not talk against it and would probably abstain from voting. . . .
Connally rose from his seat and walked over toward Gromyko's chair. As he moved along, he started making a speech. "This is for ourselves," he explained to Gromyko, "this is not for a concession." He warmed up to his topic: "The veto is the whole insides of this—it's the heart and the stomach and the liver"—as he referred to these organs he pointed to his own vitals and brought laughter and applause. During this performance Gromyko sat looking grave and unperturbed, directly at Connally. But Novikov,[18] sitting beside Gromyko and usually of a stern and unmoving countenance, smiled and chuckled at the show put on by the senator. Astonishingly enough, Gromyko agreed, and Connally shook hands with him amid acclamation. The senator concluded, "We ought to take time out to baptize the ambassador." Mr. Hickerson,[19] sitting in a back row, said in an aside: "God, how awful!"

[By June 18 most open questions had been resolved. Having already made tentative arrangements for President

Truman to address the closing session, Stettinius decided to prod the Russians from two directions. He warned Gromyko that should the Big Five allow the General Assembly discussion issue to go into the Executive Committee, the Russians would surely suffer a defeat. Simultaneously, he called Harriman to raise the problem with Molotov. Further drafting sessions in San Francisco, more telegrams and discussions in Moscow over the ensuing forty-eight hours produced the desired result. On June 20 Harriman cabled that Moscow accepted language that permitted the assembly to "discuss any questions or any matters within the scope of the charter . . ." [20]

Agreement on the "town meeting" question paved the way for the final plenary session. San Francisco came alive with a holiday mood. The president arrived to cheering throngs and the conference concluded its work in a fanfare of publicity and brave rhetoric about how the United Nations organization would ensure peace.

It was a moment of personal triumph for Stettinius, but, ironically, it was at this time that he learned what he had long suspected: Truman intended to name James Byrnes his new secretary of state. White House aide George Allen made a special trip to San Francisco to lay the groundwork. On the morning of June 21, Stettinius and Allen talked for nearly an hour in the handsome pine-panelled meeting room of the penthouse. Allen flattered the secretary on his accomplishments at the conference, and suggested that he "might be president of the United States someday." Regardless of his future, the signing of the United Nations Charter would "be the biggest day of your life." Allen then moved awkwardly toward the point of his visit.]

CALENDAR NOTES | *June 21, 1945*

I don't know what the situation is relative to the president making a change as secretary of state, but if he has made a commitment, I want to be prepared to talk to him. It's very important . . . that if any change is made it is done just right. You have done a magnificent job here and the only thing that can happen to you is to be something bigger than secretary of state. . . .

[Allen briefly alluded to the post of ambassador to Great Britain, but this, he said, would be a "demotion and the public would say Stettinius got a kick in the tail."]

He then stated that . . . if the president has made a commitment—the one thing would be the head man of the United States in the new world organization. . . . I said, "George, . . . what are you talking about?" He said, "I'm talking about the foreman—of your being the United States delegate on the World Security Council—that's specifically what I mean." He then repeated, "I don't know if the president has made any commitment or not, you know he was flirting with Jimmy Byrnes." I said I knew that. I said this was a new thought. . . .

[Stettinius stressed to Allen that he had "no other desire than to serve my country in this emergency," but added that from the "standpoint of knowing the substance of the world organization and knowing the world personalities," the idea made sense. Allen mentioned other possibilities, Joseph Davies and Postmaster General Frank Walker, but insisted that there really "isn't anybody else."]

I then stated that I thought that it was very important from the standpoint of the administration to clear this thing

up—that either I was going to be secretary of state or somebody else was. There was no use postponing a week or a
month. . . . If the president was thinking . . . of me as the
world security man there was no use taking me to Berlin,[21] he
should leave me in charge of the legislation, get the bill
through the Senate, and also the Preparatory Commission was
meeting in London and . . . whoever was going to be used for
this ought to go to London with the rank of ambassador for a
few weeks to work on that Preparatory Commission. He said
he thought that was a point. I then said I thought that to make
the appointment as delegate of the United Nations before the
legislation was passed creating the position of representative
on the World Security Council might be very difficult and no
matter what the president did now would be a kick in the
pants or a kick upstairs. He said, "Well, I think this thing
could be presented in such a way as to be convincing. . . ." I
said, "We can't fool around any longer. I've either got to say
I'm going to be secretary of state or somebody else." He said,
"I agree 1,000 percent. . . ."

> [Not yet ready to commit himself, Stettinius nevertheless
> suggested that if he accepted the post the president might
> use the Charter signing ceremony to announce it.]

George Allen said that would be dramatic. I said, "One
thing is sure—if the president is going to make a change and
wishes to do it now he had to do it in a very careful, adroit
way because it won't hold water unless it is done in an extremely careful, convincing way." Allen said he agreed. . . .
At the end of the conversation he and I went to the window. I
said, "Tell me one thing—do you think the president has
made a commitment to Byrnes?" He said, "I think he has." I
said, "So do I." I said, "If he has, the sooner the better." I then
also said, "When the president sent you out here for this damn

parade and receptions did he have in mind your talking to me about this matter?" He said, "No. I don't think he did. . . ." I said, . . . "I entered the government service because of the love of my country. I don't like public life. I am loyal to Truman and this administration, and I will be the easiest man to deal with that Truman ever dealt with. I'll step aside tomorrow and still be his friend. I will continue as secretary of state although I preferred not to be when I was appointed. I said I would think this matter out but I couldn't make any commitment as to whether this would be agreeable to me or not. . . ." He wanted to know if I was absolutely certain about not wanting political life. I said yes, that Harry Byrd had talked to me about being a senator from Virginia. He said that would be a terrible comedown. He said if I went over to London I would be humiliated—that I could come back in two or three years and be the natural presidential candidate in 1948. I said, "That's absurd. Nothing could persuade me to stay in public life."

[When word leaked out that Truman was replacing Stettinius with Byrnes, the secretary's friends rallied to his defense. *New York Times* columnist Arthur Krock called to say that if Stettinius wished to remain in his post Bernard Baruch and Harry Byrd would go to Truman and "have a showdown on this thing," with the idea that Stettinius should remain secretary of state "indefinitely." Stettinius expressed gratitude for Krock's support, but his reply betrayed his weariness. "As a matter of fact," he confessed, "I just forgot about myself on this thing. We're coming out of it but there have really been some months." [22]

During the next few days, Stettinius and his staff busied themselves with final preparations for President Truman's arrival in San Francisco and the Charter ceremony. On June 25, the secretary greeted the president at Hamilton Air Base and then rode with him along a parade route to the Fairmont Hotel.]

DIARY | *June 25, 1945*

The president's plane gleamed into sight from the north, circled the field very low, and as it taxied to a standstill, the president could be seen hatless, sitting at the rather large square window toward the rear of the fuselage. Then he appeared at the door of the plane in his gray western Stetson with narrow ribbon. . . .

A twenty-one-gun salute was fired at rather short intervals from a small field base beyond the tail of the plane. This began as I was shaking hands with the president, and the blue smoke drifted lazily through the bright sunlight toward the standing cars. The president was sunburned, healthy, and smiling and he greeted each chairman of the foreign delegations as I introduced them and they filed by. . . .

The whole countryside seemed somehow influenced by the honor of the occasion in which the president of the United States passed by. . . .

Suddenly over the shoulder of a hill, there was a view of the mystic white city across the bay—San Francisco, with just a soft touch of sunlight upon it. Apparently the sun had itself decided to have a look at President Truman and the festivities. A huge banner bearing the word "welcome" had been fastened to a cross piece of one of the towers of the Golden Gate Bridge. Fog hung heavily a little distance above the dark sea, and a tanker was just coming in through the gate headed for the bay.

[The people of San Francisco gave the president a most enthusiastic welcome, and that evening Stettinius held a reception at the Fairmont. During a private moment before dinner, Truman candidly discussed with the secretary his appointment as U.S. representative to the United Nations.]

CALENDAR NOTES | *June 25, 1945*

We entered the living room and there were my twenty-six guests. He [the president] did not shake hands with anyone but had to meet everybody. . . . I took him to the end of the living room and started to tell him about the historic setting. As we walked down to the end of the room Sol Bloom pushed in and said "That's Eden's chair, that's Molotov's chair. . . ." I jumped in and took the ball. I sat in my chair. I explained the whole thing and the whole setting. Cocktails were passed. He took an old-fashioned and I took a martini. . . .

The president said, "Well, you certainly have done a grand job out here. Are you satisfied with what I am planning?" I said, "We can have a leisurely talk tomorrow." He said, "You have got to be satisfied—I want you to be." I said, "There are three important matters on my mind. First I want you to know that I respect you and I think you are a straight shooter. But I have three things in mind. First of all, I am very concerned as to whether I can have the same happy relationship with Jimmy Byrnes and that crowd in the State Department that I could have with you. He and I used to be old friends but since I have been in the State Department things have been different." He said, "I can guarantee that. Jimmy Byrnes will work with you harmoniously and satisfactorily and I shall insist upon it. That will be part of the understanding."

I said, "The second point is that I personally entered the government service for the war and cannot commit myself to a public career under any circumstances." He said, "There are only two people in the country for this job—you and Mr. Hull, and he can't do it. You know all the international personalities and circumstances from Dumbarton Oaks on as no other American." I suggested Joe Davies and Frank Walker and he said they couldn't touch it. He said, "You are the only one I can turn to to carry this thing." I said, "If I do it it's got to be on the basis that I can knock at the door after the ship is out to sea." He said, "All right, to the end of my term." I said, "No, before that." He said, "We will cross that bridge when we come to it." I said, "I am making no commitment as to time." He said, "Well, that's all right."

I said, "The third point, Mr. President, is this: I can understand this great honor and that this is really and truly one of the great jobs in the world that any American can have, but it will be a great job only after the Senate has ratified and approved the position of member of the Security Council and a man could move directly into the job. Unless you dress this thing up so that my prestige can be preserved I won't be effective in the new work." He said, "It could be done if it could be presented right. Don't you have full confidence in Charlie Ross? [23] Don't you trust him?" I said, "Yes." He said, "There is no question that it can be presented in a way that makes it the biggest job in the world today for an American outside the United States." I said, "Well, if you do this thing, are you going to make it clear I have succeeded as secretary of state?" He said, "Yes, you have done a magnificent job and I shall say so." I said, "Mr. President, do you really believe that you can do this thing and put Byrnes in without its appearing publicly like a kick in the pants for me?" He said, "I sincerely believe it can be done that way."

* * *

[On June 26, 1945, the delegates gathered in the Veterans Auditorium for the signing of the United Nations Charter. The hall was filled with guests in the downstairs center section and with spectators in the upstairs. The

Courtesy Fort Worth Star-Telegram

Courtesy Reg Manning, Arizona Republic

stage was draped in blue; at its center the Charter rested on a blue-draped table; behind was a semicircle composed of flags of the member nations. Each delegation entered and signed in alphabetical order, the chairman sitting in a small oak chair, originally owned by Daniel Webster.

The United Nations Charter, so painstakingly drafted, so intensely speculated about in the press, so hopefully portrayed in cartoons and so prayerfully watched over by war-weary millions, contained the broadest expression of international political, social, and economic powers ever agreed upon by sovereign nations. Considering the conflicts among the sponsoring nations and the differences between the Great Powers and smaller nations the delegates found a remarkable area of agreement.

The Charter preserved the essential organs agreed upon at the Dumbarton Oaks conference. Major changes included agreement on the Security Council voting procedure, a broader grant of authority to regional bodies, and the completion of agreements for a trusteeship system. The Charter also contained a stronger commitment to humanitarian principles as a result of the San Francisco conference. The imperfections of the organization would be manifest in time, but on June 26 the delegates could well take pride in their accomplishments. It was a proud moment for Stettinius, in particular, for the completion of the Charter was to a large extent the result of his unswerving faith, his tireless effort, and his tactful negotiating. On his last night in the city, the secretary stood silently looking out from his penthouse window across the city lights to the Golden Gate and quietly reflected on the words pronounced by Lord Halifax at the final ceremony: ". . . we may all feel that we have taken part, as we may hope, in one of the great moments of history."] [24]

XII

LAUNCHING THE UNITED NATIONS
August–October 1945

On September 1, 1945, Stettinius arrived in London to represent the United States on the Executive Committee of the United Nations Preparatory Commission. The commission had been appointed by the San Francisco conference to make arrangements for the first meetings of the General Assembly and the Security Council, to choose a site for permanent United Nations headquarters, and to select a secretary general for the world organization. Stettinius would be absorbed in its work until a severe illness forced him to return to the United States in October.

The commission opened against a background of continuing enthusiasm for the new international organization. The United States Senate had approved the United Nations Charter on July 28 after only a perfunctory debate and with only two dissenting votes. The birth of the atomic age at Hiroshima and Nagasaki had reinforced in the minds of thoughtful people around the world the importance of an effective international peace-keeping body, and the sudden end of the war against Japan underscored the urgency of getting the United Nations organized as quickly as possible.

Stettinius was especially encouraged by his initial contacts with President Truman and James Byrnes. He had been momentarily rankled by the appointment of Byrnes as secretary of state, but his early discussions with the two men apparently removed his doubts. Truman repeatedly affirmed his support for the UN and concurred with Stettinius's view that it offered the best device for controlling the awesome military potential of atomic energy. The president and Byrnes assured him of their unqualified commitment to make his new position a vital one. He was given an office in the White House, and he began his work certain that his position would be accorded a status coequal to that of the secretary of state. One of his aides even suggested before his departure for London that as a leader of the UN in its formative years, Stettinius could establish himself in the public mind as the "Eisenhower of the peace." [1]

Almost as soon as he arrived in London, however, the U.S. representative encountered serious difficulties. That close Anglo-American cooperation which had sustained the United Nations through trying days at Dumbarton Oaks, Yalta, and San Francisco, did not carry through to the London meeting. The new Labour government of Clement Attlee was preoccupied with the economic crisis at home, and its faith in the United States had been shaken by the Truman administration's abrupt cessation of Lend-Lease on V-J Day. Stettinius found the British indifferent to the immediate fate of the United Nations. He had difficulty working with the new foreign secretary, Ernest Bevin, whom he considered abrasive, and the British representative to the Preparatory Commission, Philip Noel-Baker, who was limited by his preoccupation with the defunct League of Nations.

The work of the Preparatory Commission was also affected by the breakdown of the Foreign Ministers conference which met simultaneously in London. The meeting, which was designed to draft peace treaties for the liberated German satellites, quickly degenerated into a shouting match. The American delegation peremptorily rejected draft treaties prepared by the USSR for Hungary, Rumania, and Bulgaria, and Molotov denounced U.S. interference in Eastern Europe. Secretary Byrnes, on the other hand, angrily rejected Molotov's demand for a greater voice in the occupation of Japan. The conference broke up without accomplishing anything, and drastically increased tensions among the former Allies. The utter failure of the meeting proved a psychological impediment to the early work of the United Nations.

The commission thus got off to an extremely slow start. The delegates could not agree on a site for the United Nations, the British and French preferring a European location, the Russians favoring the United States, and the Americans themselves divided. Nor could they agree on a secretary general. With strong support from Andrei Gromyko, Stettinius drove the conferees to complete preliminary recommendations by mid-October, but this limited victory could not assuage his growing concern about the fate of the world organization. His misgivings increased when he returned to the United States and found its leadership and its people increasingly preoccupied with the emerging Cold War and less interested in the United Nations.

[From his first days in London, Stettinius encountered discouraging conditions. He managed to renew many of his wartime acquaintances and to partake of modest social engagements, but he found the atmosphere of postwar London depressing. The city seemed crowded, living conditions chaotic, and the people worn thin after their long years of discipline and sacrifice. His reception by British officials contrasted sharply with that of his mission to London in the spring of 1944. His initial discussions with Noel-Baker were frustrating and barren of accomplishment.[2] He found Bevin a marked and crude contrast to the urbane, experienced Eden. On September 5, he lunched at 10 Downing Street with Prime Minister Attlee. He was heartened by Attlee's obvious enthusiasm for the United Nations, but disturbed by the prime minister's determination that the organization should be located in Europe.]

CALENDAR NOTES | *September 5, 1945*

The prime minister and I stood by the fireplace and exchanged general views. He emphasized the importance to the world of getting the Security Council organized promptly and that that was the most important thing in his mind at the present time.

I explained my idea of speeding up of the work of the Executive Committee and the meeting of the assembly taking place as soon as possible this autumn if the ratifications justified. He stated he agreed wholeheartedly with this plan and hoped I could carry through on it. He then said, psychologically, from the standpoint of public reaction it was vitally important that immediately after the meeting of the Assembly, the Security Council take up its work to keep the momentum going—from Dumbarton Oaks to San Francisco to London to somewhere else. He stated that this was essential. . . .

I then stated that the all-important decision . . . was the permanent site of the world organization. He stated that he, likewise, attached great importance to that. He . . . said . . . frankly he felt, after due consideration, that the site of the organization should be in Europe. . . .

[The two men sparred briefly about Copenhagen as a site—Stettinius concluding in his diary notes:]

. . . There is not a question in my mind but that . . . the British have definitely determined the world organization seat must be in Europe, and they will stand out for that.

I then stated to the prime minister that . . . we might choose a temporary seat . . . but I did not get a favorable response from him as to whether or not it would be wise to consider the United States as the temporary site.

The prime minister then mentioned the great contribution I had made to the war in the administration of Lend-Lease. I told him I would always be proud of that record. I said I was very sorry over the recent misunderstandings relative to the termination of Lend-Lease.[3] He said, to his mind, it was a tragedy . . . he recognized that Lend-Lease had to come to an end, but if it had been possible for him and the president to have made a joint announcement . . . it would have gone down well with his people. He said the way it had been done had caused great resentment in this country.

[The contradictions between British officials about speeding up the Preparatory Commission worried Stettinius and on September 7 he sought out Ambassador Halifax, an old and valued confidant. Their talk touched on British politics and Lend-Lease, as well as UN matters. Halifax agreed that nothing was more important than bringing the UN into being "quickly."]

CALENDAR NOTES | *September 7, 1945*
. . . I told Lord Halifax that I did not sense that Bevin felt the urgency as much as Attlee did. Halifax stated that Cripps [4] was a great power within this government and felt it was very important for me to have a talk with him without delay.

* * *

Lord Halifax then inquired as to what our views were now relative to the functions of the World Security Council. I told him of Hull's and Roosevelt's idea that it should stand on its own feet and should not be a body where the chairs are occupied on the official level, and where foreign ministers took their places when important business was up. For example, the recent disturbance in Lebanon and Syria,[5] should have been a matter to be handled almost overnight. I told him we were thinking in terms of [a man of] his stature [to represent Britain]. . . . Halifax said . . . it was highly important that I continue to talk aggressively to the British government on this line and must get this story across to Bevin and Attlee during the coming weeks.

* * *

Halifax asked me what I felt about general domestic affairs in England and I told him that after many conversations since my arrival, it all added up to the fact that it was probably best that the [political] change had taken place from the standpoint of the 45 million people in England who were tired and discouraged and badly housed, clothed, and fed, and if the Conservatives had gone back in, they would probably have had minor social unrest which would have been felt throughout the world, like coal strikes and so on. Halifax said "You are entirely correct and I am convinced it is the best thing for England and the world. . . ."

Halifax stated that Pudge Ismay [6] had seen Churchill immediately within an hour after he had received the returns of the election, and said he likened the situation to a person who slams his finger in a door—he howls and carries on in a normal way when one is hurt, but a man who receives a hard body blow is bewildered and can't express himself in a rational way. Churchill seemed to be mortally wounded. His first reaction was "I have no automobile; no place to live—what shall I do?" Churchill seemed to be stunned and couldn't believe this had happened to him. . . .

We discussed Lend-Lease and Halifax said . . . he thought it was a great tragedy that after all the goodwill Lend-Lease had generated throughout the world, the release had generated such a bad odor here, and it would have been much better to have done it in a joint way. He asked how on earth it could have happened in our government. I told him it was impossible for me to explain but that it happened as a result of a conference between Truman, Byrnes, and Crowley,[7] and I had been told . . . that the abruptness was a Crowley recommendation to Truman. Halifax stated he thought Truman's pronouncements since Lend-Lease had ended had been helpful and useful. . . . I told him in confidence that the job Winant [8] would want was secretary general and that he was asking for it. Halifax said this would be awful; that Winant was the worst organizer he had ever known and he had no confidence whatsoever in his ability for this job; that he had no penchant for organizing and could imagine nothing more inappropriate.

Halifax then stated he would miss me as we had had such a frank relationship at all times and could talk as brothers. Likewise, he felt free to talk with Mr. Hull and he was not at all sure he could ever have the same relationship in the State Department again from the standpoint of complete frankness at all times and in all things.

Halifax ended up by saying that . . . what I was doing was the most important thing to be done in the international field at the present time . . . and that . . . unless I carried the ball we really would never get the United Nations off the ground. . . .

[The Preparatory Commission negotiations afforded Stettinius a further opportunity to work closely with Andrei Gromyko. The Soviet ambassador to Washington had been assigned to the commission, doubtless because of his earlier role at the Dumbarton Oaks and San Francisco conferences. On the evening of September 7 the two men dined at Gromyko's apartment in the Park

Lane Hotel. Their conversation lasted late into the evening and touched on numerous UN issues.]

CALENDAR NOTES | *September 7, 1945*

During the four years that I have worked with Gromyko in a most intimate manner, from Lend-Lease on, I have never found him as completely frank in discussing any subject that arose. He displayed an extremely cordial feeling for me personally. . . .

Gromyko stated he . . . thought that the time had arrived when someone had to pick up the ball and carry it along or the work of the United Nations Preparatory Commission would last for many months. He said he would back me up wholeheartedly at all times in driving through and accomplishing our task in London this autumn as quickly as possible.

* * *

He then stated that he thought I was making a mistake by pressing for a meeting of the Assembly in London following the full meeting of the commission. This undoubtedly was the big point he had in mind discussing with me at the time he invited me for dinner. He stated that . . . if the Assembly were held here . . . the work of the United Nations Organization would become entrenched in Europe. . . . He stated he thought this would be a great mistake, that the center of political and economic affairs in the world had moved away from Europe and it was logical and reasonable to look to the Western Hemisphere as halfway between Asia and Europe [and] as a logical place for the permanent headquarters of the UN.

* * *

[Gromyko proceeded to quiz Stettinius in detail about potential UN sites in the United States. They next

416 | EDWARD R. STETTINIUS, JR.

turned to the relationship between the Security Council and the Council of Foreign Ministers.]

I told Gromyko of the British conception of the council as being a body on which individuals on the official level would sit and important business would be done from time to time by meetings of the foreign ministers who would sit representing their countries on the Security Council.

The ambassador stated that this was absolutely contrary to their views as they had always regarded the council as a body on which high-level representatives would sit . . . continuously the year around, and who would be in the position to act on instructions from their governments immediately in an emergency, and that the whole conception of the UNO, as worked out at Dumbarton Oaks and at San Francisco, would be destroyed in the event the Security Council was not given such a status.

* * *

I inquired as to whether his government had given any thought to a person who would take the position of secretary general. He said he had not given this matter a thought. . . .

He volunteered however that if the constituent assembly were held in the United States this autumn, and we were not in a position to select in London the permanent secretary general, he would be very happy to see Alger Hiss [9] appointed temporary secretary general as he had a very high regard for Alger Hiss, particularly for his fairness and his impartiality.

* * *

He emphasized several times during the evening that the Soviet Union attached paramount importance to the early establishment of the UNO. He said this was a turning point in international affairs and that his government was relying heavily on the effective action of the UNO in years to come.

[While the Preparatory Commission was carrying out its tasks, the Council of Foreign Ministers also convened in London. This body was designed to provide a means of regular high level discussions among the major wartime Allies, and had been assigned the job of negotiating peace treaties for liberated nations. Secretary of State Byrnes had worked aboard the *Queen Elizabeth* making final preparations for the London meeting.

The council proceeded stormily from its September 11 start, and was marked by intense arguments over Molotov's demand that the United States grant Russia an occupation role in Japan and support his bid for a Soviet trusteeship in North Africa.

The following day Byrnes arranged to see Stettinius in his apartment at Claridges. The two men spent a half hour reviewing UN developments.]

CALENDAR NOTES | *September 12, 1945*

I told him [Byrnes] that on my arrival here I had lunch with Mr. Attlee and found Attlee had his heart in the United Nations organization and felt that a speedup was essential and seemed to understand all aspects of the problems we were facing.

I said that in my first meeting with Bevin, I did not find Bevin as interested in the United Nations movement as Attlee, and [he] had said to me rather frankly that the main thing he was interested in was world security and felt that the rest of the matters we were working on were not of such great importance. Bevin thought the emphasis would be more on power politics of the world in the immediate future than anything else.

Mr. Byrnes interrupted at this point saying that he had gathered from the Russians that they were most interested in the role of the Security Council and had not displayed as much interest to him on economic and social matters.

I stated that this was contrary to the impression I had gotten; that the Russians were attaching great importance as far as I could gather from my conversations with them from Dumbarton Oaks to the present, to all matters relating to the social and economic council. . . .

[Stettinius explained that Noel-Baker was insisting that there be a final meeting of the Assembly of the League of Nations in Geneva in December to be followed by the first UN Assembly in January in the same city. Stettinius expressed vigorous opposition to this plan as it would delay the start of the UN's work.]

Mr. Byrnes then interrupted the conversation on United Nations affairs and said the lack of drive and progress did not surprise him. He said, "I am facing a similar set of conditions."

Byrnes said they couldn't get the British to move on anything. Their meeting (the foreign ministers) yesterday and this morning had been completely wasted. . . .[10] They didn't know their own minds and the Russians were welching on all the agreements reached at Potsdam and at Yalta, and he was very discouraged.

I had come to see him at a moment when he was very blue and downcast, and he said he didn't know whether he could make anything out of this conference or not. He thought the Russians might take the position that unless we gave in to their desires on the Balkans, Austria, Hungary, Yugoslavia, and Rumania, they might go back on the Italian Treaty, which was the very first thing on the agenda.[11]

* * *

I told Mr. Byrnes that after I had been here for another two weeks or so, I felt it important for him, the department and the president, that I return to the States and spend some leisurely hours with him and the president, because they had not been intimately associated with the evolution of the United Nations, and it was very important that they get fully imbued with all aspects of the problem, both past and the forecast of the future. Mr. Byrnes thought this was excellent and stated that after this council was over, and he got home and settled down, it would be a very appropriate time for him and myself and the president to have some long periods together.

[The next evening Stettinius, accompanied by his chief assistant Adlai Stevenson,[12] and Ambassador Winant, dined with Noel-Baker and other British UN experts. Their working session was aimed at reconciling basic differences about the timing of the first General Assembly session. Stettinius pressed the British to agree to London as the Assembly site. He argued that this would expedite setting a date since the purpose of the Assembly would be chiefly organizational and so many of the people who would be involved were already in the British capital. He stressed the "prestige" this would bring to the United Kingdom.

Some of the British concurred with the American arguments, but Noel-Baker, who had long experience in League work and favored Geneva as the site for all UN functions, stuck to his guns.]

MEMORANDUM OF CONVERSATION |
September 13, 1945

. . . He pointed out that he had referred several times to the wholesome possibilities of the concluding meeting of the League, both as a means of wooing the Russians with apologies for the past,[13] inviting world attention to the success of the League, as well as its failures, and the hopes for the new organization emerging from the ashes of the old. He finally agreed, however, to pointing toward the first meeting in London in December. . . .

We left the dinner party with little doubt that this program would prevail, and Mr. Winant felt on the whole, that it had been a constructive achievement.

[Hoping to break through the plodding procedure of the full Executive Committee, Stettinius arranged an informal gathering of the Big Five representatives for the afternoon of September 17. He explained that this device, which he had employed so successfully in the past, would promote "a friendly and frank spirit to exchange views and if possible reach a general line of agreement on various problems." Hardly had he started before Noel-Baker spoke out against such secret diplomacy.]

MEMORANDUM OF CONVERSATION |
September 17, 1945

. . . Mr. Noel-Baker expressed the view that these meetings would be useful to exchange views, but objected to Big Five agreements. . . . He did not want to enter into a binding agreement among the Big Five on these questions. He said that his experience with the League was that such a system did not work and that agreements among the permanent members ahead of League Assembly meetings had provoked resentment among the others. . . . He indicated further that debate in the various organs of the United Nations would very likely change his mind on certain matters, and he wanted to be free to do so. . . .

Ambassador Gromyko . . . referred to the experience in San Francisco, and said that no one could tell whether we would ever have had a charter if the Big Five had not reached agreements. He said that the smaller powers had understood the reasons for this, and in fact had been thankful that the Big Five had done this. Noel-Baker expressed doubt as to this.

* * *

Mr. Stettinius said . . . that the United Nations were looking to the Big Five to provide leadership and that in order to do so, they had to have informal talks to understand each other and reach common solutions where possible. He said that we should not attempt to reach unalterably binding agreements among ourselves and then attempt to dictate decisions to the rest of the United Nations. He said that he also would want an opportunity to discuss matters with all of the other United Nations, and particularly the Latin American countries, but that these meetings would not preclude this any more than our meetings in San Francisco had.

* * *

[There ensued discussion of how to divide responsibilities among various member countries and procedures to employ in elective posts and selecting members of councils, such as the Economic and Social Council. Most important was choosing the secretary general.]

Mr. Stettinius said that the terms of the Charter require that the Big Five should reach agreement on the person to be nominated as secretary general. It was therefore most appropriate for them to discuss this together in advance. . . . It was also generally agreed that the secretary general must be a man of the highest qualifications. Ambassador Gromyko said that he felt that it was necessary to consider also the nationality of the candidate for this office, as he, for example, would not be willing to agree on a representative from Argentina no matter how capable he was.

It was also agreed that it was of the utmost importance that there should be no debate in the General Assembly over the nomination, and that it would therefore be necessary to discuss informally any proposed nominee with the individual United Nations, so that we would be certain that any nominee would be acceptable. It was felt that the Security Council should nominate only one man, rather than several from whom the Assembly might choose. . . .

[This informal diplomacy soon brought results, and Stettinius was able to wire the State Department on September 20 that the Executive Committee had approved his goal of the full Preparatory Commission convening early in November. They would hold an organizational meeting of the Assembly and councils in December in London.[14]

On Tuesday of the following week, Stettinius and his family drove to Anthony Eden's home near Chichester in Sussex. Stettinius was captivated by the beauty of the countryside. He found Eden recovering from an ulcer. Stettinius suggested to Mrs. Eden that they would enjoy a winter vacation in the Caribbean and described new plane service which would cut the flying time from London to eleven hours.

Stettinius and Eden then excused themselves for a stroll and talked of politics and the UN.]

CALENDAR NOTES | *September 25, 1945*

* * *

Walking through the yards and over the fields after tea, Anthony and I had ample opportunity for private talks. He stated frankly that he felt the change in the government had saved him. It would not have been possible for him, he said, to go on any longer the way he was going, which was taxing his strength to the point of exhaustion.

Eden also thought there was no question that it had been the best thing for the country to have a change in government at this time as the Conservatives could never have held the line, and that now Labour had its chance. He said eventually there would be a swing back, but during the coming generation it was a good thing for Labour to be in at this time.

* * *

He stated he felt the San Francisco conference would have never gone off successfully if it hadn't been for me, and he admired tremendously my stand on the two big Russian issues.[15]

He stated he thought that I had come out in international affairs better than anyone; that I had kept my standing and prestige and was in a very strong position. He thought Roosevelt, Hull, and he, with Churchill, had started the United Nations organization movement in 1942, and he thought it was perfectly excellent that I was the one now who was carrying their dream through to realization. I told him I would rather do what I was doing than anything else in the world at the present time.

* * *

We exchanged views relative to . . . the foreign ministers. He seemed greatly discouraged and was placing great hopes on the Security Council. He stated Bevin called him from time to time for advice and consultation. He stated he thought Bevin was a strong man and that he was the best possible person for that post.

. . . He stated he liked Noel-Baker personally and he was a very sincere man, but did not feel he was a practical person as he was a dreamer and not a doer. . . .

* * *

Eden talked a great deal about Churchill and said he thought Churchill would settle down now to an easy life, probably spending about half his time as the leader of the opposition in Parliament, and that he, Eden, didn't know as yet as to how much time he would actually spend, but Churchill had said he thought he and Eden should divide the time between them.

Eden was very relaxed and seemed to be a normal healthy person for the first time since I have known him, and was not high-strung as usual. He was chopping wood and sawing wood; working in the garden, shooting quail and rabbits, and was feeling wonderful and better than he had for ten years.

[By the time Stettinius had returned to London, the Foreign Ministers conference was more deeply mired in controversy. Bevin and Molotov spent much time exchanging verbal blasts and insults. The United States had rejected Molotov's demands on trusteeships and a Russian role in the occupation of Japan, and had refused to recognize the Soviet-sponsored governments of Eastern Europe.[16] After two weeks of discussion, the conference had made no measurable progress.

The trusteeship question particularly embarrassed Byrnes, because during the debate Molotov had quoted a letter from Stettinius to Gromyko which pledged American support for the Soviet Union as a trustee nation.[17] Instead of working with Stettinius on this question, Byrnes handled it himself. It was not until September 28 that he discussed with his predecessor the deadlock in the Foreign Ministers conference and his impressions of U.S. relations with Russia.]

CALENDAR NOTES | *September 28, 1945*

Secretary Byrnes called me on the telephone at Claridges at 8:15 P.M. . . . Before I could say anything, he said "don't worry about that letter you wrote to Gromyko about Russia being eligible for trusteeship. That was perfectly proper and the Russians have just tried to make something out of it and take advantage of the situation. . . ." I then asked him when he was getting away. He said "the Lord only knows. We haven't even written a communiqué yet. I would think Monday, certainly Tuesday. . . ."[18]

[Stettinius went up to the secretary's suite and found Byrnes "cordial . . . frank and candid."]

He started the conversation by returning again to the question of the letter to the Russians on trusteeship. He said, "I want you to know I mean everything I say. You have no reason to feel in any way embarrassed about the letter. Talking strictly within the family, I think it would have been a little better not to have said 'we will support you in becoming a trustee.' It would be better to limit it to eligibility." He then inquired as to who drafted the letter. I replied that Gerig [19] had drafted the letter but Stassen had carried on the negotiations on trusteeships. Secretary Byrnes then said, "Well, I think it's important that we keep Stassen in the picture, so to speak, because if there is ever any difficulty about that letter, I want you and me to say Stassen had carried on the negotiation

426 | EDWARD R. STETTINIUS, JR.

and was responsible for the letter." I said, "That's an accurate statement." Byrnes asked me whether it would be agreeable to me to have the text of my letter published. He thought that if this was done, it would clear up the whole matter. I said I hoped he would, and that I was sorry he hadn't done it before this. He said at his first press conference in the United States somebody would ask a question. He would have a copy of the letter and give it out; would make a comment and say the letter was appropriate. . . .

Secretary Byrnes then told me generally the state of affairs that he was faced with in the Council of Foreign Ministers. They were at a deadlock on most everything they discussed. They were getting nowhere and it was most discouraging. . . .

Secretary Byrnes then stated there was no question but that we were facing a new Russia, totally different than the Russia we dealt with a year ago. As long as they needed us in the war and we were giving them supplies, we had a satisfactory relationship, but now that the war was over, they were taking an aggressive attitude and stand on political and territorial questions that was indefensible.

* * *

Byrnes then stated, "Well, what are your troubles? What can I do to help you?" I said . . . while the work isn't going as fast as we would like, we have had extremely good cooperation from all sides and it appears we will be able to finish our work with the Executive Committee in the course of three weeks. We would have a meeting of the Preparatory Commission in November and a short constituent meeting sometime in December. He said, "that's splendid, I congratulate you, and the Lord knows we need the United Nations. . . ."

I then told him the difficulty we were having with Noel-Baker being so much interested in the League. . . . He said that this was too bad and . . . that our only interest in the League would be to liquidate it as fast as possible and take over some of its personnel records. We then touched on the matter of the resentment that was being caused by the United States attempting to run the world, as some were putting it. He had from all sides heard criticisms of our policy toward Japan by not taking our Allies in on control of Japan. He thought the president's statement of last Sunday [20] had not been drafted in quite as expert fashion as it could have been. Australia, the Chinese, and the British were all being offended. We were going off in a unilateral way as the Russians were going off in the Balkans.

* * *

[They reviewed in detail American personnel for various UN posts and discussed strategy for locating the permanent headquarters in the United States. Toward the end of their talk, Stettinius raised the question of control of atomic energy.]

Just before we broke up I told Mr. Byrnes that there was one important thing I hoped he and the president would put their minds to rather promptly and that was what our policy would be on the atomic bomb. The moment the Security Council was organized in December that question would arise. He said, "yes, I agree with you. We have to get to grips with this." He said, "of course I have been studying this atomic bomb thing and some of the scientists came down to Spartanburg [South Carolina] where I was resting and spent a day with me down there. I'm worried about the way people are saying things about the atomic bomb." He said, "the best scientists I have talked to say it is true the Russians will be able to unravel the scientific secret within three or four years but that it would take them many years to create the production facilities, if ever, inasmuch as so much of the equipment is of a highly technical nature, comparable to a chemical plant or oil refinery and his best information indicated that no matter how fast they moved they couldn't produce the thing before about eight years." If that was true, in view of the way the Russians were behaving now, as emphasized in this Council of Foreign Ministers, he would be opposed to giving the secret to anybody at the present time. He had thought Molotov would have raised the matter here in these talks but he had not. If he had raised the question of the atomic bomb, Byrnes would have said to Molotov that General Marshall had tried on many occasions during this war to exchange military secrets with Russia and Russia had always refused. The United States has a secret process that we haven't given to anybody else. This was just another kind of bomb. He would have said, "I can pledge to you that the United States will never use this bomb at any time unless it is within the United Nations Charter signed at San Francisco and we will only use it in the case of an aggressor to keep the peace. You don't exchange scientific secrets with us and until we can have a complete arrangement we won't give this out." He said, "it is true we must think ahead and determine our policy but I think it ought to be something along the line that we have joined the United Nations organization, we sit on the Security Council and we won't use this bomb unless we are asked to call out our forces, and that if we are asked to call out our forces to keep the peace, we will come with our forces and the atomic bomb to stop an aggressor." I then asked whether or not he [had] thought of allowing the other four of the Big Five to have a veto power on the big bomb. He said, "no more veto on the use of the bomb than on any other thing." [21]

[The next evening Stettinius talked with John J. McCloy, assistant secretary of war. He regarded McCloy as one of his most valued friends—"a man of great intelligence" and "fine character." They discussed the problem of maintaining public enthusiasm for the UN and the tendency of the military to downgrade the importance of the international organization in national security.]

CALENDAR NOTES | *September 29, 1945*

McCloy stated that he was very anxious to find out about the United Nations work. He stated that there was a tendency in the Army, particularly in the War Plans Division, to think more of hemispheric defense than of world defense; that in a recent War Plans paper they had placed the United Nations fifth on the list. McCloy said he battled this through with Marshall and the others and emphasized to them the importance of placing our military interests in the world at the top. He stated that Embick [22] was still having a bad influence in the Army of thinking in narrow terms of the defense of the Western Hemisphere rather than of the world. . . .

McCloy stated that at home the people had forgotten San Francisco; had forgotten the United Nations; were saying "Where was the United Nations?" "What has happened to Stettinius—we know he is in London, but what is he doing?" The publicity has been very scanty and . . . had practically no value. People were thinking of the failure of the Council of Foreign Ministers, fear of the Russians, strength of the atomic bomb, and were forgetting about the machinery that we were setting up to keep the peace.

* * *

He stated that things in Washington were very chaotic; . . . that there was not the planning that there had been; that the whole atmosphere at the top did not have the high tone either from the standpoint of personalities or programs that it did a year ago. . . . I told him that I was extremely pleased to be doing what I was doing; that I had an inspired feeling of carrying the United Nations through to actual existence. He then inquired as to my plans for the future. I told him that I had no plans other than to make the United Nations a success and that I was going to stay with it as long as necessary . . . because . . . if we didn't give it the drive and the leadership, I was fearful that things might bog down.

* * *

McCloy had great hope for the United Nations. He feels that it is the only thing that we can do from an international standpoint and that if we should fail in that we would be up against a condition of world chaos. . . .

[On October 1 Stettinius had lunch with John Foster Dulles, whom Byrnes had appointed to the American delegation for the foreign ministers conference. Byrnes made a shrewd choice: Dulles had proven a valuable adviser during the San Francisco Conference, and his presence in London preserved bipartisan cooperation in foreign affairs. Dulles found the negotiating atmosphere in London an unhappy contrast to the San Francisco experience.]

CALENDAR NOTES | *October 1, 1945*
I found Mr. Dulles discouraged and unhappy about the foreign ministers meetings. He said matters of substance had gone astray and there had been a display of bad blood. . . . He was particularly critical of Bevin. Mr. Dulles said Bevin had become ugly on occasions and had used abusive language after which he would feel penitent in order to heal the wounds he had caused. Mr. Dulles . . . had watched Molotov operate during the course of the meetings and frequently Molotov

would arouse Bevin purposely knowing that in the end Bevin would lose his temper and eventually give in on the substance.

* * *

[Dulles reported that the foreign ministers had nearly broken up the previous day but decided on a final effort at the suggestion of China. Dulles thought "there was a 90–10 chance that they will break up without a communiqué and everyone would go home tonight."]

Mr. Dulles . . . said Mr. Byrnes was extremely nervous, was tired out and exhausted, and facing this failure of his first mission on his own was getting under his skin.

* * *

Dulles referred to the nerve and guts I showed at San Francisco, not to be satisfied with a paper victory and having been willing to face the music of a complete failure at San Francisco rather than to have given in to the Russians on the two big points we made an issue on; namely freedom of discussion and others.

Dulles said he was still telling all the Republicans of the excellent manner in which we had faced the music, as he put it, at San Francisco.

* * *

Dulles then stated it was very distressing to him to be associated with a failure of this kind.

* * *

Dulles stated that if we cannot cement international relations among nations through the various organs of the United Nations organization, the hope of civilization is gone.

Dulles then stated that he knew for an established fact

that the first atomic bomb which was dropped on Japan was twenty thousand times as strong as TNT; and that the United States actually had manufactured, and the bomb was in existence, which was XM [*sic*] times TNT rather than twenty. Why on earth they had manufactured the bomb he doesn't know, as now they are scared to death to use it, for if they drop it in the ocean, the scientists are convinced it would stir up a tidal wave that might wreck New York and perhaps Europe and, moreover, some of the scientists feel a bomb of that strength might "set off" atmospheric elements on this continent immediately which would just burn the oxygen up on this planet and leave the earth in the state of the moon.

Dulles then stated he was convinced now that the Russians could not be controlled, which was evident from the meetings of the foreign ministers, and he wanted to say to me that all depended on the success or failure of the United Nations organization. He said, "I mean just that." He continued, "With Roosevelt and Hull gone, the leadership will not come from anyone but you. You put this thing across and I am perfectly serious when I say I believe that others will find not only the technique, but also the manufacturing possibilities of atomic energy, and everything depends upon the United Nations organization."

[Dulles's prognosis on the foreign ministers' collapse proved correct, as the meeting adjourned that very day without even agreeing on a communiqué. With the October 15 target date for completing the Executive Committee's work, the Big Five delegates still had to agree on a permanent site as well as a candidate for the secretary general post. While the rancor of the foreign ministers meetings was absent from the Executive Committee sessions, it did have some indirect effect on the discussions over UN headquarters.

On October 3 the Executive Committee had voted to give first priority to the United States for a site. The next day, at a luncheon for the delegates, Noel-Baker came up to Stettinius and asked for a private talk "immediately."]

MEMORANDUM OF CONVERSATION |
October 4, 1945

Noel-Baker said he was very unhappy with the vote of yesterday; that Beneš and [Jan] Masaryk [23] had both told him that they wanted Europe; that the Yugoslavs wanted Europe but that they had voted for the United States under an ultimatum from the Russians. . . .

Noel-Baker then stated, "I am convinced that if we go to the United States it means that Russia will have a free hand in Europe and her power politics will make it difficult for the rest of us. . . .

[Stettinius sidestepped the political element in Noel-Baker's remarks, but he believed the difficulties in relations among the Great Powers made it necessary to get the UN functioning quickly. As yet some nations, including Russia, had not deposited their ratifications of the UN Charter. On October 11, Stettinius chided Gromyko, and got him to promise to cable Moscow about the need for action.]

I then stated "Andrei, you and I have gone a long way together since Dumbarton Oaks, Yalta, San Francisco, and now London and our child is beginning to walk." I said, "And before long it will begin to talk." He then said, "But how long will it be before our child has teeth that can be used effectively?"

[Uncertainties in Great Power relations following the foreign ministers' failures undercut Stettinius's drive to conclude agreements on crucial UN questions. At tea with Canadian Prime Minister Mackenzie King on October 12, he complained that he had come to London ". . . with a program to put the United Nations into existence before Christmas, . . . but the British and French had made things very difficult." King thought that British reticence was due to the pressure of postwar domestic problems. Stettinius attributed the British and French lassitude to "difficulties with the Russians."]

MEMORANDUM OF CONVERSATION |
October 12, 1945

He (Stettinius) said that we felt strongly that this should not delay the beginning of the United Nations and that there was all the more reason for pushing ahead to get the various organs into being. The prime minister said . . . he was very much concerned over the Russians' position and the developments which were rapidly unfolding in regard to their policy. He thought perhaps it might be wiser to take a little more time.

There was a long discussion concerning the policy of the Russians. The prime minister said he did not understand the Russian point of view. He thought they must realize that they were building up opposition in the entire outside world by their present tactics. He spoke of the relationship between Stalin, Molotov, and the rest of the party. He thought Stalin was probably really interested in collaboration with the outside world. He had certainly earned a high place in history and could hardly have any great personal ambition left. He felt Molotov was a bad influence.[24] He was concerned at the development of communistic activities in all the democratic countries and foresaw even greater difficulties in this respect in the future. He asked Mr. Stettinius whether the Russians had deposited their ratification. Mr. Stettinius said they had not, although the government had ratified and Gromyko had informed him that the deposit would be made shortly. . . . The prime minister said he hoped the Russians would not use this as a bargaining weapon on the issues which had broken up the foreign ministers conference.

* * *

The prime minister said that one of the many matters which he was concerned with himself on his trip was the atom bomb. Ever since Hiroshima, he had been obsessed with the necessity of taking drastic action to prevent the world from destroying itself. He said he was convinced that the secret of the bomb would be available to other nations in a very short time. Even though it was at the present a very expensive process to manufacture, he felt quite certain that within the next few years other countries than Britain, Canada, and the United States would have bombs capable of doing enormous damage.

[Three days later a gall bladder attack interrupted Stettinius's activities. Doctors warned him that the condition, which he had suffered periodically for several years, required surgery and that afterward he would have to curtail his efforts for at least two months. Thus, a quirk of history intervened to sideline the man who was the chief proponent in the late fall of 1945 of international control over the atomic bomb. It removed him from action also, at the moment when the State Department was wrestling with questions about timing the opening UN sessions as well as the permanent site problem.

Bowing to the inevitable, he left London on October 21, having arranged to see Truman and Byrnes the following day to bring them up to date on UN preparations and to underscore his ideas on atomic control. Stettinius was chagrined to find that, after his careful lobbying on an American site for the UN headquarters, a schism still existed in the State Department over whether to locate UN headquarters in Europe or the U.S.[25] When Stettinius told Byrnes that it would be "very embarrassing" for the U.S. to shift to a European site now, Byrnes replied that "after having looked into the situation [he] had some doubts" about locating the UN in America. The secretary cited two reasons. "Several sources" reported the Russians "were most anxious to get us out of Europe" to have a free hand there. Further, "some people" feared that "verbal squabbles" between Congress and UN representatives would embarrass the U.S. owing to "high-speed American news coverage." [26]

That afternoon Stettinius reported to the president. Describing his efforts to stimulate action by the Executive Committee, Stettinius noted the general impression that it made "little difference" whether the UN started soon. The picture from the San Francisco conference was "completely different." Stettinius criticized the British and French for arguing that the UN should take a back seat until the Great Powers had resolved their problems. He acknowledged that the break-up of the Foreign Ministers conference "may have had something to do with" this attitude, but he insisted he had gotten excellent relations with Gromyko and Russia should deposit its ratification of the Charter soon.

Stettinius emphasized the need for American leadership.]

CALENDAR NOTES | *October 22, 1945*

He told the president that it was absolutely vital that the United States give real leadership and drive to UNO. If they didn't, it was unlikly to succeed. He said that Mr. Hull and President Roosevelt had given the organization its original impetus; it was their leadership which had made it possible to hold the San Francisco conference last spring. The United Nations was definitely our baby and it was up to us to teach it to walk and talk. Mr. Stettinius made a very impassioned plea to the president to give the United Nations his full support. It was the hope of the world and it simply couldn't be allowed to fail. . . .

The president said very earnestly: "I am with you a hundred percent. You say the word—I'll give you anything you ask for. I'm with you all the way." He said that he felt strongly that the United Nations must be made to work and we would *make* it work. He said that he was not seriously concerned with the suspension of the Foreign Ministers' conference. He said this was almost bound to happen at the end of the war. During the war, we'd been able to work with the Russians because of the overwhelming military necessity. All the real difficult problems had been postponed until the end of the war; now we were running into them. It was inevitable that we should have real difficulties, but we should not take them too seriously. It was perhaps better to happen out in the open at this stage. He said we did have some real problems with the Russians but we had every hope that we could work them out amicably if we gave ourselves time. He thought the United Nations could play a big part in this process. One of our jobs was to use it to work out our difficulties with the Russians. He said we had to make the United Nations effective in this respect. The only alternative was a bitter armament race with the Russians.

* * *

Mr. Stettinius said that there were indications in London that led him to believe that at the first meeting of the General Assembly, some countries would very likely raise the question of the control of atomic power; that there was the possibility the United Nations might want to set up some international machinery to study the problem. He said this was a problem in which the United Nations could not fail to be vitally interested and that he hoped the United States policy would be sufficiently settled by the time the Assembly convened so that the United States could give the United Nations some real leadership on this issue from the start.

The president said he agreed and had every hope that he would be in a position to make some definite proposals to the United Nations in December or January.

The president said Prime Minister Attlee and Prime Minister Mackenzie King were coming to Washington on November 11 to see him about the atomic bomb. Prime Minister Mackenzie King had been in London for several weeks seeing Attlee about this, and had dropped in to see the president before having left. Mackenzie King was terribly upset about the problem of the atom bomb. The president said he hoped the three of them could come to some conclusion.

The president said that he disagreed with the popular view in the United States that we had a "precious secret" which we could withhold from other countries; that this was not the case. The scientific knowledge was public information and the only thing we had which other countries did not was the industrial and engineering know-how. Any other country with a large and advanced industrial organization and with the materials could learn by trial and error, in the same way we did, in from four to ten years. It took us four years from the time we started. He said it was a very expensive process. The cost of the first bomb had been two hundred million dollars per pound. There were not many countries who had the national wealth or industrial power to present any danger. Russia, of course, was one of the countries which had the industrial power and probably the scientific knowledge to produce atom bombs. We don't know for sure whether they have the necessary materials, but they probably have some. There are indications that the Russians have been doing some research in this field. They will probably acquire the necessary know-how within the next few years, if they haven't it now.

The president said he . . . thought it was definitely the number one problem of the world at the present time. We had perhaps from four to ten years . . . to work out international arrangements to assure the appropriate control of atomic power in the interests of world peace. The president said he hoped to work out detailed proposals with the two prime ministers [27] and then discuss the matter with the congressional leaders. He emphasized the importance of the use of atomic power for useful purposes under international controls. He said that his present thinking was that we ought to be able to outlaw the use of the atomic bombs in the same way we outlawed the use of gas. He said that any bombs we had would be placed at the disposal of the United Nations Security Council.

* * *

[They concluded the conversation by discussing rumors of Stalin's illness. Stettinius thought there might well be something to it and Truman recalled Stalin's complaint at Potsdam about getting old and feeble.]

. . . The president said, of course, it would be a real catastrophe if Stalin should die at the present time. If this happened, there would be no telling what might happen inside Russia. There was a possibility that the army might get control and in any case there was a real possibility that there would be, at some period of time, a division between various cliques. He said he thought that Stalin was a moderating influence in the present Russian government.

The president said that he thought the Russians must be having real problems of their own at home. He said that we certainly had our internal problems and they were bad enough. He had concern that a new form of isolationism might be growing which would seriously plague us. He thought that probably in the same way the Russians were having very real problems at home and that this might explain some of the things that they had been doing.

[The rising tensions among the former Allies and the specter of an uncontrollable arms race and an atomic war overshadowed the progress made by the UN Preparatory Commission. Adlai Stevenson ably represented the United States in Stettinius's absence. The commission was still unable to agree on a site and a nominee for secretary general, but it did complete final arrangements for the Assembly to open in London in January 1946, and the council to hold an organizational meeting simultaneously. Despite these accomplishments, conflict between the Great Powers mounted during the remainder of 1945, ensuring that the United Nations would commence its operations under troubled circumstances.]

XIII

THE UNITED NATIONS IN ACTION
January–June 1946

During the autumn of 1945, conflict between the Soviet Union and its former Allies increased to ominous proportions. The utter failure of the London Foreign Ministers conference in September had raised tensions on both sides, and the breach widened still further in the days that followed. Soviet occupation policies in Korea, Manchuria, and Iran angered and deeply disturbed British and American officials, strengthening their suspicions that the USSR harbored global ambitions and hardening their opposition to further concessions. Russian fears were aroused by continued Anglo-American protests against Soviet domination of Eastern Europe.

In the first months of 1946, spokesmen for the Big Three nations talked in increasingly threatening terms. When Secretary of State Byrnes agreed at the Moscow conference in December 1945, to recognize the governments of Bulgaria and Rumania, Truman reacted sharply, privately complaining that he was tired of "babying the Soviets." Unless they were faced with an "iron fist and strong language," he affirmed, "another war is in the making." In a speech on February 9, 1946, Stalin warned of the implacable hostility between capitalism and communism, and called upon his people to develop the industrial and military capacity to ensure against any "accidents." One month later, former Prime Minister Churchill spoke in Fulton, Missouri, and with Truman on the platform denounced the "iron curtain" that the USSR had drawn across

Europe and called for an Anglo-American military alliance to stave off the communist menace.[1]

The first sessions of the UN Security Council, which met in London in January and again in New York in March, were deeply affected by rising East-West hostility. The Big Three had difficulty agreeing on a secretary general, the Russians sponsoring a Yugoslav and the British and Americans a Canadian. More important, the London and New York meetings were dominated by the Iranian crisis, the first showdown of the Cold War, which erupted in 1945 and continued into late 1946.

Stettinius was sufficiently recovered from surgery to take a part in the stormy birth of the international organization. He helped to arrange a compromise on the appointment of Trygvie Lie as secretary general, and he was deeply involved in behind-the-scenes negotiations on Iran. In addition, he spent much time mediating often acrimonious discussions among officials of the UN, the United States government, and the city of New York, trying to arrange suitable facilities for the world body.

By the late spring of 1946, however, he found his position untenable. As leaders in Washington became preoccupied with the Cold War, they placed less faith in the United Nations. President Truman did not live up to his promise to make the Security Council representative "the biggest job in the world today for an American outside the United States." He did not consult Stettinius on appointments to key UN posts or on major policy decisions. Stettinius's relations with Byrnes became strained when the secretary of state insisted on handling the U.S. case on Iran before the Security Council. Exhausted from his physical disability, frustrated by his isolation from the centers of policy making, he resigned his post in June and retired to private life.

443 | *The United Nations in Action*

[Stettinius boarded the *Queen Elizabeth* on January 1, 1946, and during the voyage and after his arrival in London he worked with the U.S. delegation preparing for the opening of the Security Council. James Byrnes had arrived in London by mid-January, and Stettinius, disquieted by the secretary of state's presence, sought him out to discuss their respective roles in the initial sessions of the United Nations.]

CALENDAR NOTES | *January 13, 1946*

I then stated that the Security Council was scheduled to meet tomorrow for its first meeting, and I thought it would be wiser—to avoid any misunderstanding—for Byrnes and me to discuss the procedure for handling Security Council matters. . . . "You will recall the legislation, Jimmy, the president or the secretary of state can always represent the United States in any organ of the United Nations." He said, "Yes, I do—I think that that was put in to meet emergencies and when vitally important matters were up, and when others of that rank attended. You go right ahead and sit on the Security Council and handle it—it is your job and the only thing I have in mind is perhaps when you get to the matter of the election of the secretary general, I might like to fool around with that a little bit." He did not say whether in "fooling around" he meant to discuss with me and to keep in touch or whether actually he would like to come to the meeting. I explained that this would be in executive session, and he said naturally you can't discuss the qualifications of any man before the world.

* * *

[The two turned to discussion of a deputy for Stettinius, and the more complex problem of selecting a secretary general. When Stettinius referred to the boom for General Eisenhower, Byrnes snappishly said he opposed the nominee being from the Big Five nations and that his mind was "closed" on any military candidate. The secretary reacted negatively to Eden because Bevin had told him it would cause embarrassment for a Labour government to advance a Conservative's name. It was agreed that Stettinius would continue to back Canada's ambassador to the United States, Lester B. Pearson.

Stettinius left the secretary's apartment satisfied with their working relationship. He later wrote in his diary "Byrnes was most cordial, was most frank throughout the discussion, confiding in me in a number of matters, and I feel my personal relations with him are just as good now as they ever have been and they have always been excellent."

One of the few cordial ties remaining in Soviet-American relations was the friendship between Stettinius and Gromyko. On January 17, Stettinius phoned the Russian and invited him to dinner, as "we had not seen each other for a long time." Their conversation the following evening touched on a number of UN matters and revealed Gromyko's thoughts on his future plans.]

CALENDAR NOTES | *January 18, 1946*

* * *

I then asked Gromyko what his personal plans were for the future. At some length and with great candor and frankness, he discussed his personal situation with me. He said his mother was ill, his wife not well and his two children were being raised in Washington in a foreign country without a father. He stated that he did not know his government's plans relative to the Soviet Embassy in Washington or the membership on the Security Council, but he said he must admit to me as a friend that he would welcome the appointment on the Security Council. I conveyed the fact that it would be a mistake to have the same man occupy both posts. He agreed and said he also thought that it would be a mistake and he was sure his government did not have that in mind. I am convinced he does not know himself what is to be done with him, but it is very clear that his ambition is to sit on the Security Council.

Gromyko then asked me a great many questions relative to the new Washington personalities, feeling that it was very strange we should have a complete change of people with the same administration. I told him Mr. Stimson had had a heart attack and we were greatly concerned about his health. I said Harry Hopkins was desperately ill and he showed genuine and deep concern over this. It was rather interesting to me to note a real reaction of distress and sympathy on the part of Gromyko over Hopkins's illness in contrast to the rather cold reaction from men like Churchill, Harriman, and Bohlen, all of whom were devoted friends of Hopkins, for when I told them of Hopkins's desperate condition I did not feel anywhere near as great a concern or as warm a feeling as I did from Gromyko.

Gromyko stated that Stalin's health was excellent and he could tell me this as a definite fact that Stalin's two months' rest in the Crimea had cured him of the fatigue from which he was suffering.

* * *

[Gromyko inquired about American thinking on a secretary general. Stettinius expressed disbelief that the USSR was serious in promoting the Yugoslav Foreign Minister, Stanoje Simic. He was an "unknown person." Gromyko protested that with the UN headquarters in the United States it was "very important that the secretary general be from Eastern Europe." Instead of rejecting

Pearson, Gromyko suggested they have a five-power consultation.

They briefly discussed the location of the United Nations, Gromyko suggesting "Privately to you Ed, we believe that New York is the best solution. . . ."]

Gromyko then stated that there would be a great effort on the part of the British to keep the secretariat of the organization in London after the Assembly [adjourned] for some time. He asked me how we felt about this and I said we would be violently opposed to it and would make a very firm stand against that taking place. Gromyko was pleased we felt that way because that was his exact reaction.

* * *

[Toward the end of their discussion, Stettinius raised the increasingly volatile Iranian problem. In 1942, Britain and the Soviet Union had agreed to a joint occupation of Iran to prevent a German takeover of that oil-rich nation and to protect the Persian Gulf supply route to Russia. Their agreement stipulated that all occupation troops would be withdrawn at the end of the war, and while the British had complied the Russians still remained in Northern Iran in early 1946. London and Washington suspected the USSR of using its military presence to extort oil concessions from Iran, and their fears of Soviet designs were increased when tribesmen in the northern Iranian province of Azerbaijan presumably with Russian backing, launched an independence movement. In late 1945, Britain and the United States pressed the Soviet Union to remove its troops from Iran, but the Kremlin had refused, and the Iranian government made known that it would bring the issue before the United Nations.[2]]

I then asked him if there was anything he could tell me privately relative to the Iranian situation. Gromyko said, "No, there is nothing I can tell you. I cannot read the Iranian mind nor can I understand their motives. I can assure you, however, that the presence of the Soviet armies in Iran has nothing to do with the present situation. The present matter with which we are faced is a spontaneous democratic movement." Gromyko then said that I must always remember that the permanent site would not have been in the United States without the influence of the Soviet Union. I said, "Andrei, we owe you nothing for that—we are entirely sincere in our statement that we are willing but not seeking [it] and would go any place in the world and we had no preference."

* * *

[To take the glare of publicity off its actions in Iran, the Russian government had accused the British of illegally maintaining troops in Greece and Indonesia. Since it could not be denied that the British presence in these areas bolstered a political status quo favorable to London, it was awkward for the West to point a finger at Moscow's aggressiveness toward Iran.

Stettinius and Byrnes discussed these problems on the evening of January 23.]

CALENDAR NOTES | *January 23, 1946*
We then discussed in detail the appeals to the Security Council by Iran, Greece, and Indonesia. On Iran Mr. Byrnes said he had talked privately to Vyshinsky [3] about it the day he arrived and that Vyshinsky told Byrnes the matter was going to be settled without any difficulty. He indicated that the Russians were going to make an arrangement and the Iranians

were going to withdraw their request. Byrnes is convinced that the problem will not be on us. I said our position should be willingness to hear the case and if an investigation is necessary we should sponsor it. He said he agreed entirely with this position.

On Greece he stated he talked to Bevin about that and Greece is prepared to come out and say the British troops are there at their request and they want them to remain there.

On Indonesia he said that the British can prove that the British troops are there as a result of surrender terms on [General Douglas] MacArthur's orders. He thinks that if we have a hearing on these two cases Bevin will blow the Russians out of the water.

[During the last week of January, a flurry of backstage maneuvering took place on these major issues. Vyshinsky used the Chinese delegate, Wellington Koo, to relay word to the Western powers that bilateral talks between the Soviet Union and Iran might produce a settlement. Stettinius, in charge of the U.S. delegation after Byrnes's departure from London, bluntly told Koo that he was opposed to dropping the Iranian complaint because the matter was before the council and "it was of paramount importance at this moment to keep world confidence and world respect for the Security Council." They discussed Greece and Indonesia, Koo arguing that the Russians were convinced that Britain was suppressing "democratic processes" in Greece and that Indonesia was only a minor problem. Koo speculated that the Russians were trying to weaken the British Empire, but they were nevertheless "showing a very friendly spirit toward the United States." [4]

The next day, Stettinius called at the Foreign Office to discuss the Iranian issue with Bevin. The British foreign secretary reported that Russia was trying to pressure Britain into recognizing Rumania and Bulgaria, Vyshinsky promising that if this were done he would drop charges on Greece and Indonesia. Bevin had rejected such a deal, but he was still optimistic that the problems could be worked out and he felt that Vyshinsky was more flexible and compromising than in days past.]

Bevin stated that Vyshinsky had spent the evening with Cripps on Thursday night, as they had been friends in Kuibyshev. . . . [Vyshinsky] had broadened his outlook and he realized Russia had been wrong in the past with respect to many of her policies, and he was extremely anxious for Russia to get on with England and the United States, making sure of United Nations collaboration.

At this point, Bevin stated that he had a definite feeling that Vyshinsky was winning Stalin's confidence more and more and he was confident that Stalin was pushing Vyshinsky ahead. Bevin said, "You know that Molotov is the nigger and that Stalin is a reasonable person, and I think Vyshinsky is also a reasonable person. . . ."

[One major breakthrough occurred in the midst of the preoccupation over Iran when the Big Five agreed on a secretary general. The choice fell on Norway's Foreign Minister Trygve Lie, a compromise candidate selected after Byrnes had made it clear to Vyshinsky in a Big Five executive session on January 20 that the United States strongly opposed a secretary general from Eastern Europe. With Russia opposed to Lester Pearson, over whom the American delegation was split, and the British undecided, the way was open for the selection of a neutral candiate. Byrnes and Vyshinsky agreed on Lie in a phone conversation on January 24.

A week later Lie called on Stettinius to express his thanks and to discuss his role as secretary general.]

CALENDAR NOTES | *January 31, 1946*

* * *

He stated he . . . had always felt a very friendly feeling toward President Roosevelt, Harry Hopkins, and myself, and said that he could always trust what we three told him. He said he was nonpolitical and he would rely heavily on me in all matters as he had complete trust and confidence in me and my motives.

* * *

Lie stated he was very bewildered and didn't quite know where to turn. I told him I would help in every way. . . .

* * *

Lie was most cordial and friendly. It is perfectly obvious to me, however, from the forty minutes I spent with him that he will need a tremendous amount of help and guidance and that he will rely upon us in a very heavy way.

[Behind-the-scene efforts to resolve the Iranian crisis remained stymied into February, and the acrid debate in public sessions of the Security Council threatened to discredit the UN in world opinion. At an evening meeting on February 5, council chairman Norman Makin of Australia called an executive session in an effort to find a solution to East-West countercharges on Iran, Greece, and Indonesia. Bevin and Vyshinsky brought their bitterness into Lie's office, but toward the end of the secret session Stettinius suggested a compromise both sides agreed to work on.]

RECORD OF SECURITY COUNCIL
SECRET SESSION | *February 5, 1946*

* * *

Vyshinsky all of a sudden stated, "Well, Mr. Bevin, if we can't agree on this matter, [Greece] let's send a commission to Greece to investigate the situation and whatever the commission says we will abide by. . . ." Bevin said, "I will have no commission of any kind go to Greece. I am either a decent citizen, and my people are decent citizens, or we aren't."

Vyshinsky then stated, "I resented very much what you said the other day, Mr. Bevin, relative to the fact that you could not sit with me any longer if this matter was not solved immediately." Bevin made an unsatisfactory explanation of this matter, in which he did not clarify exactly what was said. I broke into the conversation and said, "Gentlemen, I remember exactly what Bevin said and it was if these charges are correct he wasn't fit to sit with any member of the Security Council. It did not relate at all to his sitting with the USSR." My explanation was concurred in by all present.

Vyshinsky went on to say that it was a great pity that such a discussion had to take place. He said they could not have won the war alone, and Britain could not have won the war alone—they needed each other then as they needed each other now. He then said, "We want to stay friendly with you and we must find a way." Bevin said something pleasant about his great desire to stay friendly.

* * *

Makin during all this time tried to act as chairman but every time he spoke or even opened his mouth he just wasn't listened to. It was really a tragic performance.

* * *

I then became quite aroused for . . . I felt that a great mistake had been made for Makin to adjourn for five minutes and allow us to be out for almost two hours. I felt that since it was a discussion among the five, it should be held in public and generally I felt very unhappy about the whole thing. I finally just couldn't contain myself any longer and made a three or four minute statement.

I said that the . . . exchanges which had taken place this evening had been very disturbing. Civilization as we know it depended upon not only the success of the United Nations but specifically the success of the five countries here represented finding a solution to their problems. . . . I then stated that I felt personally that they should both be satisfied with having the chairman make a statement something along the following lines—that we should take note of the declarations of the representatives of the Soviet Union, the United Kingdom, and Greece, and we should also take note of the views expressed by France, China, the United States of America . . . with regard to the situation in Greece which had come about as a result of the presence of British troops, and all of these declarations and statements should be published in the official records and that the matter should be closed. I said something of that kind certainly should satisfy the situation particularly in view of the fact that the day before yesterday we had a vote and the vote was nine to two stating that a threat to the peace did not exist.

I then said that I now wished to make very clear to Mr. Vyshinsky in making this proposal that I link what I said to the declaration of the U.S. made the day before yesterday . . . that we did not believe a threat to the peace existed as a result of the presence of British troops in Greece and, moreover, I placed great emphasis on the fact that the overwhelming majority of the council had already publicly so stated.

Bevin again stated that "We must get a clean bill of health

from the council." I said, "Ernie, I don't think you're going to get it without one of the big powers exercising their veto."

Vyshinsky spoke up and said he wanted a copy of the text. I said, "I have no text—I said it out of my own head." Vyshinsky said, "You have a good head." I replied, "I was in Moscow a year ago and while I was there I had some good vodka and I still have the effects of it." Vyshinsky smiled at that, but said "This is very interesting but I must consult my government." Bevin stated, "I will have to discuss this with the Cabinet."

Lie then came up to me and said, "For God's sake, move along and continue in the way you're going and you can put this across tonight."

I asked Vyshinsky if he could not consider this as it was a clear-cut thing. Vyshinsky said, "I must talk to my government." I said, "I have heard that at Dumbarton Oaks and at San Francisco and in most cases *you* were 'the government.' Who is 'the government' this time you have to take it up with?" Vyshinsky said, "You are perfectly correct. If you wanted me to say I have to have more time or I don't understand you, I can say that." He got a great kick out of this.

[Stettinius's formula opened the way for resolution of the Security Council deadlock. The Russians dropped their charges against British actions in Greece and Indonesia, and the Western powers allowed time for further negotiations between Iran and the Soviet Union on withdrawal of Russian troops. The council then adjourned, and Stettinius returned to the United States, arriving in New York on February 19.

Still not completely recovered from his recent surgery, he planned a Florida vacation in the interim before the next UN session convened in New York. He first reported to Secretary Byrnes and President Truman.

His conversation with the secretary of state focused on the appointment of personnel to key United Nations positions. Both men were tired, and the discussion got nowhere.[5] Stettinius then crossed the street to the White House, chatted briefly with reporters, and was shown into the president's office.]

CALENDAR NOTES | *February 28, 1946*

The president looked remarkably well. He had put on weight, his color is better, and he seems more relaxed and the pouches under his eyes are less pronounced than they were ninety days ago.

He opened the conversation by saying he had reports from several people that I had done outstanding work in London and he wanted me to know that he generally appreciated it and was very pleased. I replied by saying that I had my heart in the United Nations and it could not fail, that the United States would have to give it leadership and if we did not . . . I would be very apprehensive as to what might develop in the next five years. I said when I spoke of leadership I spoke of you, not Byrnes, or anybody else, that he was the person who would carry the flag at the head of the parade.

He said I appreciate it and stand ready to do whatever you ask. I said the way to kick it off is by your agreeing to come to New York on September 3, [for the General Assembly] which will be a world event and make a broadcast to the world in the United Nations of the United States [sic]. He said, sold, I agree.

* * *

[They talked briefly about personnel for UN posts. Truman said that he wished never to make an appointment to United Nations positions "not agreeable" to Stettinius.

Stettinius then raised some of the problems involved in locating the UN in New York, and Truman reacted strongly.]

* * *

He said I have something privately to [tell] you. I don't like what's been done and am very concerned and unhappy about it. He said it was perfectly ridiculous to let foreigners come over here and pick out areas not wanted, expensive land, when five communities offered land free of charge—Asheville, North Carolina ("where the Biltmore place is"); Chicago; Denver; San Francisco; and Philadelphia, all of whom want the United Nations and have said they are willing to give the free land. He said what can we do about it now? Frankly, I guess I made a mistake by not jumping in and advising them where to go after deciding on the United States. He said it would have caused difficulties politically but thought we should have done it and said what we can do now, I don't know.

I said that I thought it was too late to do anything other than to use our influence on New York authorities to make the thing go in New York City. . . .

* * *

The president was about ready to take some aggressive action and I said, well, I have discharged my conscience by telling you that I think they will do a great many things to make this thing go. He said there was nothing to do but continue to study it and perhaps find an answer later on.

I then asked the president what his desire was relative to my consultations. He said it was important that we keep in close touch—this is the most important thing going on in the world and I want to see you as often as you think it necessary to come down.

[Stettinius had been concerned about lack of bipartisan coordination among the U.S. delegation in London. While he did not raise this with the president, he apparently felt freer to discuss it with former secretary Hull. He found that Hull shared his apprehensions.]

CALENDAR NOTES | *March 1, 1946*
. . . We had trouble with the Russians using the Security Council as a sounding board. . . . Van[denberg] is pretty sore on not being taken into camp a little bit more, not only in London but in Washington too. He and Jimmy are not getting on at all well. . . . I think it is a two-edged sword. Van always talks collaboration. He says collaboration at the present time is just being told about it the night before it goes into the newspaper. . . . In his private talks he doesn't think well of Truman but he blames Jimmy about this lack of cooperation. . . .

When he finished, Mr. Stettinius said that Mr. Hull had said, "When a certain man [Byrnes] took over where I used to be, [Secretary of State] I just want you to know privately that I ain't been consulted a bit."

[During the two weeks Stettinius was vacationing in Florida, the Iranian issue flared up into a major crisis. Russian troops remained in Iran, and the Soviet government ignored a firm American note demanding their withdrawal. U.S. diplomats then reported extensive Soviet troop movements toward Iran and Turkey, and Washington began to suspect that the Iranian crisis might be but one part of a Russian offensive to gain the upper hand in the eastern Mediterranean. By this time the Truman administration had decided to "get tough" with Russia, and a minor war scare pulsed through the Pentagon, State Department, and White House. Protests and warnings, coupled with naval movements in the Mediterranean, conveyed to Moscow the firmness of U.S. opposition. These developments ensured that Iran would occupy a prominent place on the agenda when the Security Council convened in New York on March 25.[6]

When Stettinius returned to begin preparations for the meeting, he found that his position was being increasingly undermined by Washington. During his absence, Truman had named John G. Winant, former ambassador to Great Britain, as U.S. representative on the Economic and Social Council, and Bernard Baruch to represent the United States on the United Nations Atomic Energy Commission, an organ created by the Moscow Conference in December 1945, to develop proposals for international control of atomic energy. Both appointments had been made without consulting Stettinius, and it was unclear whether Winant and Baruch would report to him as chief of the U.S. delegation to the United Nations. In the meantime, Byrnes had decided to go to New York to speak for the United States during the Security Council debate on Iran.

Angered by these decisions, Stettinius went to the State Department on March 20. He immediately questioned whether the secretary wanted him at the table when he argued the Iranian case.]

CALENDAR NOTES | *March 20, 1946*
He said, Ed, I leave the whole thing to you to work out. The only thing I have to say is that I feel I should personally argue the Iranian case. He said I have spent a lot of time on it and I feel that's important. I said that's entirely satisfactory with me.

. . . He said, Mr. Stettinius, you should be at the table as the representative to attend to all the formal business, but when the Iranian case is presented I will represent the United States. I said, do you wish to take the place at the time the Russians answer? He said I think I ought to take the place as I would in court, from beginning to end. I said, I agree. I then said, what is your desire when you take my place at the table—what would my role be? He said, your role would be as my principal adviser to sit with me and you and I will run the performance together.[7] I said, we will work that out. I will sit with the advisers. He said, no, you will sit with me.

* * *

I said that leads to the next question. . . . I am the easiest, most cooperative person in the world but Baruch was appointed without my knowledge or coordination and now you tell me about Winant. I said, to what degree am I to act? I explained that without proper coordination it would be difficult and that we had to see eye to eye. I said, let's have no misunderstanding, all I am interested in is the success of the United Nations.

[Byrnes then indicated that Baruch would answer only to the president through the secretary of state, but his budget would come from funds allocated to Stettinius. Stettinius protested vigorously, and said that this was a "fundamental matter," but Byrnes's secretary reminded him of another appointment and their conversation ended abruptly. Stettinius left the State Department greatly dissatisfied, but there was little he could do except appeal to the president, and he chose not to do this perhaps realizing that forced to make a choice Truman would support Byrnes.

In New York two days later, Stettinius went for a walk along Fifth Avenue. He soon encountered Bernard

Baruch, and the two men strolled into Central Park and discussed a number of matters with the greatest candor.]

CALENDAR NOTES | *March 22, 1946*

Mr. Baruch stated he was still unhappy that I wasn't in the State Department. I told him I was happy I wasn't, that I was doing at the present time exactly what I preferred to do most. He stated that he was very concerned about Byrnes, that Byrnes would not take any advice, that Byrnes and the president had a very serious clash a couple of months ago relative to Byrnes's autonomy—that [Fred M.] Vinson [secretary of the treasury] and Byrnes have Truman terrorized for some reason and he didn't know where to turn. He thought that Truman and Byrnes made a tragic mistake in appointing Winant to the Economic and Social Council, that he was impractical, dreamy, and wouldn't tell anyone what he was doing. . . . Mr. Baruch stated he did not think Byrnes could stand the strain physically. He had known him for thirty years and he was very concerned. He stated that he remembered after Yalta a private talk with Roosevelt when Roosevelt said it would take about eight years to make the peace, that he couldn't go on and he was training young men "like Ed Stettinius" to carry on. He said "I'm going to tell Truman this some day." He said "when Byrnes drops out Truman has only two choices, either to put you back in or Marshall. Marshall is too old." I replied that I had entered the government service for the war period, that I had no desire to stay in public life, that I was sticking with the United Nations now because of the burning urge in my soul and as soon as I saw the ship fully manned and operating and on the high seas after a trial run I felt that I should have a free conscience and under no circumstances would I like to remain indefinitely in government service. I added "of course I'm not a politician anyway and sometimes politicians are wanted." He said, "that's absurd. You've got an asset that Truman can't lose at this time. People know that you are a man of principle, that you are religious, that you stand for something and behind your pleasant smile is some seriousness of purpose and some ability that most people don't recognize."

[As the March 25 opening of the Security Council drew nearer, the Iranian crisis continued to occupy the attention of the UN delegates. On March 24, Moscow radio announced that Soviet troops would evacuate Iran within six weeks, and Gromyko sought to get the issue taken off the council agenda. Byrnes refused to accept the Russian proposal, informing Stettinius that he wanted an investigation of the Iranian situation and that it was vital to "nail down the Russians to a promise to the Security Council to withdraw in six weeks." [8] With strong backing from the U.S., the Iranian delegate indicated he would place the issue on the agenda.

Gromyko then urged Secretary General Lie to postpone the opening of the council until April 10, and Lie called Stettinius to his quarters in the Waldorf Astoria for consultation.]

He then stated that he had seen Gromyko at 6:30 and Gromyko had advised that he had firm instructions to move at the opening of the meeting tomorrow postponing to April 10. . . . Furthermore, if the council did not grant his request he would refuse to sit from now until April 10.

Lie said he and I must find some way over this hurdle and I . . . stated that Mr. Byrnes was very firm and we were meeting tomorrow presumably the year round and no one country had the right to move that the council not meet for one day or one month—we might have an emergency tomor-

row morning which we [would have] to meet on a minute's notice. I then told Lie I thought that owing to Mr. Byrnes's feeling . . . we should go see him immediately. I phoned Mr.
Byrnes, and Lie and I went up in a cab. Byrnes became quite
aroused and stated that he had nursed the Russians the last
time, that Gromyko could make his motion, he would do it on
the radio before the world and he, Byrnes, would answer
before the world at the table and would move that he had
declined the recommendation.

[At a luncheon the next day, Stettinius found Gromyko
jumpy and snappish. When he asked if a short postponement would help, the Russian snapped, "I don't need any
help." Stettinius responded calmly, "Now, Andrei, you
would not have gotten through Dumbarton Oaks or San
Francisco without my help." Gromyko warmed somewhat, but the deadlock remained.[9]

In the ensuing debate, the council voted to leave the
Iranian issue on the agenda, and Gromyko angrily
walked out. At the end of the week and after hours of
debate, the council adopted a compromise position, voting to continue the Iranian complaint until April 10.[10]

During the next two weeks, Stettinius was increasingly preoccupied with the question of United Nations'
facilities. Postwar reconversion had been chaotic in New
York, and when the delegates arrived in March they encountered shortages of housing and office space and an inadequate transportation and communication system. City
officials had provided Hunter College in the Bronx as a
temporary site for the assembly and council meetings,
but the other UN agencies as well as the fifty delegations,
were scattered across Manhattan.

The situation worsened in the first weeks of the UN
session. The delegates repeatedly complained of the incon-

veniences they suffered. Stettinius took the complaints to New York city officials who blamed the incompetence of UN officials. Numerous delegates suggested that the UN should leave New York for another location, and at a meeting of the Council on April 10 several members criticized the United States government for not doing more to resolve the difficulties. This brought a strong rejoinder from Stettinius.[11]]

CALENDAR NOTES | *April 10, 1946*

I had a part in deciding on the location of Dumbarton Oaks, San Francisco, and even London, all of which were eminently successful, and the present confusion is a great heartache to me. . . . Our position has always been that we . . . were willing to accept the United States if it was their desire to come here. You will recall that in London during the autumn many communities of the United States appeared and made presentations relative to their facilities. . . . I wish to remind you that New York City was selected based on an invitation from the mayor of New York without any presentation as to interim temporary facilities, and as I recollect you decided to come to New York without making any inquiry relative to such facilities. . . . You may be assured that the United States government stands ready to help in every way possible.

Then a question was asked as to whether or not there were any federal laws or state laws that would make it possible to take over a place such as Rockefeller Center or the Waldorf Astoria. I stated in reply that I did not know of any such powers and moreover, if there were, a long period of litigation would ensue and that would not answer the immediate emergency problem with which we are faced. . . .

* * *

I further referred to the fact that I had many private conversations with the mayor and Mr. [Robert] Moses, [head of UN site commission] bringing pressure on them to do everything within their power to meet the needs of the United Nations.

My estimate of the situation is that the great majority of the members of the Security Council now recognize that an error was made in deciding to come to New York for temporary headquarters. They are greatly concerned with the frustration and confusion with which they are faced. Several representatives indicated that if nothing suitable could be found they might be prepared to consider moving away from New York.

[During the remainder of his stay in New York, Stettinius worked to promote better cooperation among U.S., UN, and New York officials to find suitable facilities for the international organization. Largely through his mediation, an agreement was reached to hold the September General Assembly meeting at Flushing Meadows and to provide living quarters for the delegations in Manhattan hotels. This arrangement did much to keep the United Nations in New York permanently. Later in the year, after Stettinius had retired to private life, John D. Rockefeller, Jr., and the city of New York gave adjoining tracts of land to the United Nations, and several years later the United States Congress appropriated funds to assist in the construction of permanent headquarters.[12]

In the meantime, the council had resumed consideration of the Iranian case. On April 3, it voted to delay formal debate again, this time until May 6, and in the interim that followed the USSR counterattacked. Through the Polish delegate, it demanded an investigation of the Franco government in Spain which was allegedly harboring Nazis and threatening the government of France. Then on April 15, the Iranian government instructed its ambassador, Hussein Ala, to withdraw Iran's complaint from the council. Ala suspected that Prime Minister Qavam was yielding under pressure from Moscow and confided his fears in Stettinius.]

CALENDAR NOTES | *April 15, 1946*
He . . . stated that he had just received ten minutes ago a cable from Qavam which stated that because of new assurances that had been received and the full agreement had been signed Ala was now instructed to request [of] the Security Council that the matter be dropped from the agenda and he was not to add one word or any interpretation to this fact.

Ala then said he was considering cabling to Qavam stating this was contrary to [the] interests of Iran and he was sure this was being done under great pressure and he could not carry out these instructions and Qavam could appoint anyone he desired to represent him before the Security Council. Ala stated he was calling upon Sir Alexander Cadogan to review the matter and would call upon me at my apartment as soon as he had seen Sir Alexander.

[Frantic maneuvering continued throughout the day. While Ala checked with Cadogan, Stettinius called council President Tai-chi Quo to plot how they could retain the Iranian complaint on the council agenda despite Prime Minister Qavam's clear instructions to withdraw it.]

TRANSCRIPT OF TELEPHONE
CONVERSATION | *April 15, 1946*
Mr. Stettinius: Here is the situation that I can give you privately—you are the only person I am telling. He [Ala] has

instructions to withdraw the case. We have to find some way to play for time. It would be terrible for us to make these new charges [13] and then for Iran to come in and withdraw. I am wondering if we shouldn't postpone the whole thing until we can play for time. We might be able to find an excuse not to have the meeting today. I don't want to make that suggestion, but I wanted to tell you that was in my mind. Don't do anything about that now. I am going to see Ala in a few minutes again and then I will tell you if I have any suggestions to make. . . .

Dr. Quo: This is very bad.

Mr. Stettinius: Yes, this is very bad. See you later.

[On returning from his talk with Cadogan, Ala told Stettinius that the British advice was to inform Secretary General Lie of Qavam's withdrawal request and then privately to line up the necessary seven votes to reject his own government's request.

Ala left on his little mission. Stettinius phoned Secretary Byrnes and they considered the prospects of this strategy.]

TRANSCRIPT OF TELEPHONE
CONVERSATION | *April 15, 1946*

Mr. Stettinius: . . . He feels he should not say he can carry out these instructions. He is going to write Lie a letter quoting the cable he has just received from Qavam saying Qavam wants the matter withdrawn and he has been so instructed to advise the Security Council and he is not to appear or interpret or anything else and leave the whole matter to the Security Council to decide. He thinks everybody is on his side with the exception of Brazil and China. . . .

Mr. Byrnes: The burden's on him. He's got to get the 7. There is no use in stalling—let him take it up.

Mr. Stettinius: Our course is to let nature take its course—let it come up this afternoon and hit it hard when it comes.

Mr. Byrnes: He gave no explanation? He just changed his view?

Mr. Stettinius: . . . He did say that Alec [Cadogan] told him if he just washed himself out of the picture everybody would say all along "you haven't represented the Iranians. You haven't been doing what Qavam wanted you to do" and [Cadogan] thought it was important he stay in the picture.

Mr. Byrnes: You can't do a thing about it but let nature take its course.

[Twice on April 15, Stettinius and Cadogan discussed how they could best coordinate action on the Iranian and Spanish problems. By this date, they knew that they would have to formulate a stand on Spain; but the views of their governments were dissimilar, as the following discussions show.]

CALENDAR NOTES | *April 15, 1946*

I called upon Cadogan at his apartment this morning at 11 o'clock . . . We first discussed Iran. We reviewed all aspects of the matter. While Cadogan has no instructions from his government at all, he feels that under no circumstances can he possibly agree to the matter being taken off the agenda. . . .

We discussed Spain. Cadogan had yesterday morning in Washington a long conversation with Secretary Byrnes on Spain. . . . Byrnes said he would insist on Spain being allowed to come to the table and present its case. I asked Cadogan as to his view on this matter and he said, "well of course Spain cannot come to the table unless there is a dispute and if Franco says it is not a dispute Spain cannot come to the table and if it is a situation Spain cannot come to the table." [Since Spain was not a UN member, there would be no way for it to appeal directly to the Security Council.] In any event Cadogan would not oppose Spain being put on the agenda and would vote on it being included in the agenda and would wait and see what evidence Poland produced. However, he could not allow at any time for the council to interfere with internal conditions in Spain. If the council was going to attempt to unseat Franco as a result of pressure from communists he would fight them.

[Late that evening Cadogan and Stettinius met again at the Savoy Plaza.]

CALENDAR NOTES | *April 15, 1946*
Sir Alexander Cadogan called upon me this evening in my apartment at ten o'clock at his request. . . . He had just received a cable from the Foreign Office on the Spanish matter, that he wanted to tell me about promptly. . . . He read parts of the cable to me; the first paragraph stated that they did not agree at all with Secretary Byrnes's suggestion of calling the representative of the Spanish government to the table, that they did not see how this could be done technically and even though it could be they thought it would be wrong tactics as it would give the Polish and Soviet representatives an opportunity to delve into matters relating to the Spanish regime, that it would be quite embarrassing and would accomplish no useful purpose. He stated that his instructions were to be willing to have the Spanish matter come on the agenda, to have an open mind, but that if no new evidence was presented that was convincing that he should state he did not feel that the existence of the present Spanish regime was a threat to the peace and move that no action should be taken; that he was instructed to discuss this matter with Byrnes or myself and attempt to persuade us to take the same line.

He stated that he did not think it was likely that the Pole

would be able to bring new evidence relative to Nazi activities in Spain, that the British representative at Madrid was giving constant reports to the Foreign Office which he thought were quite convincing. For example, there were 1,500 Nazis who have been corralled that were waiting to be sent back to Germany at the present time. An American boat was scheduled to take them soon.

I told Cadogan that we would be working this evening on the Spanish matter and that after we had our position thoroughly determined I would be happy to advise him of it before taking action in the council.

* * *

I then inquired as to what was going through his mind relative to the Iranian matter and he stated that he had thought he would go into detail and answer [Oscar] Lange [14] and Gromyko but that he had come to the conclusion now that if Quo could be persuaded to say that we have heard everyone, is there a motion? If we could vote Gromyko down promptly he would be perfectly willing not to speak again and call it a day. I told him that I could not take this course as I felt the charges were quite serious and for the record I was planning to make a short statement even though a quick vote was forthcoming.

[During the next few weeks, the Security Council debated the Spanish question. The Russian and Polish delegates bitterly denounced the Franco regime while the United States and Britain tried to head off any action. In the end, the council voted to refer the problem to the fall meeting of the General Assembly—a victory of sorts for the West.

As the May 6 deadline for Iran approached, the U.S. government kept close watch on internal developments in that country. Byrnes and Stettinius were particularly concerned that the Russians might achieve by internal subversion what they had thus far failed to do by military pressure. On April 24, Stettinius and Ala discussed the situation in Iran.]

CALENDAR NOTES | *April 24, 1946*

He then stated that . . . the action taken by Qavam was not the desire of the Persian people, that Qavam had been under extreme pressure, and serious threats had been made to him relative to Soviet activity in Iran, and that he did not believe, under the circumstances, that Qavam had any other alternative than to take the action he did.

The ambassador then stated that the coming elections in June would decide the fate of Iran; if the communists (Tudeh party) won additional seats that would bring about complete political domination over Iran by the Soviet Union. . . . The ambassador then inquired as to whether it would be feasible or possible for us to consider having the UN send to Iran a commission to supervise the elections this June. He referred to the Australian suggestion of the council needing "more facts" and said this might be done by a procedural vote in the council. I replied that while I would need time to study the matter that on first flush it would seem to me it would have to be a substantive vote which might give the Soviet Union a veto. Moreover, I felt it would be very difficult to have the council take such action unless the Iranian government asked the council to send such a commission. I also pointed out that it might not be wise for the Security Council to get into a question of . . . domestic jurisdiction. . . .

[Upon the arrival of the May 6 deadline, the Iranian problem again threatened a major crisis. There was no indication that Soviet troops had been withdrawn, and when the Iranian government sent forces toward the capital of Azerbaijan they met resistance from rebel troops. Civil war broke out and Prime Minister Qavam dispatched a commission to determine possible Russian involvement.

Just as the State Department was preparing to ask the Security Council to send an investigating team to Iran, the crisis broke. On May 20, Qavam informed Ala that his investigations had turned up no evidence of Soviet troops or equipment in Azerbaijan. The British continued to push for UN action, and Ala went before the Security Council on May 22 and charged that Russia was still interfering in Iran's internal affairs. But the United States, feeling that to press the matter further would accomplish no good purpose and exacerbate relations with Russia, agreed to back Qavam. The Security Council subsequently accepted Qavam's report and dropped the question. The UN had weathered its first major crisis.[15]

The lull following the resolution of the Iranian crisis gave Stettinius the opportunity to make a decision he had been pondering for some time. From the opening of the London session in January, he had felt increasingly uncomfortable with his status in the Truman administration. Byrnes's insistence upon presenting the United States position on major issues troubled him, and he was further disturbed by columnists' reports picturing him as an errand boy for the secretary of state. He was frustrated that Truman had not given him the backing he had promised, and he deeply resented the president not consulting him on major UN appointments. Tired from more than six continuous years of public service and uneager to continue under trying circumstances, he submitted his resignation to the president on May 30.

In his letter of resignation, Stettinius did not refer to

his growing dissatisfaction with his job. He simply stated that the UN was now functioning, he had fulfilled his commitment and he now wished to return to private life. At a conference with Byrnes on June 4, however, he openly expressed his complaints.]

CALENDAR NOTES | *June 4, 1946*

. . . The secretary was waiting for me. . . .

Byrnes . . . stated, "Well Ed, the real reason I wanted to see you today was to find out how hell-bent you were on resigning. We are very anxious for you to continue. We feel that you have done an excellent job and we would have great difficulty in finding anyone who could be appointed in your place."

. . . He then said, "Well, couldn't you stay on for a while until the present matters are cleared up?" I replied that there was nothing pending before the Security Council that was vital, that the Iranian matter was over and . . . that the Spanish matter was not of great consequence. Mr. Byrnes said, "Well, I agree that there is nothing that is vital."

I then added that if I felt I were really needed I would, of course, be willing to stay, but there was nothing to be accomplished by my staying on, particularly in view of the fact that the atomic energy committee and ECOSOC [Economic and Social Council] and the Trusteeship [Council] etc., were all set up independent of the "Representative" [to the] Security Council.

Byrnes then referred to my letter to him of the eighteenth, saying that he thought it was excellent, that he agreed with my logic and that, of course, the whole matter of coordination of the work at the headquarters could be fixed up to my complete satisfaction. I stated that my resignation had no relationship to that letter, that I would have written that letter whether I was going to stay or whether I was going to resign. . . .

* * *

We then talked about the matter of coordination of United Nations work within the State Department. I pointed out the extremely inefficient and ineffective manner whereby no one person was responsible for the United Nations affairs. We had all the . . . offices . . . dipping in here and there. He said that he was amazed to hear this, that he was holding [Dean] Acheson individually responsible for all relationships with the UN organization.[16] I said, "Well, it is not working that way . . ." I then told Byrnes that I felt it was best for him and best for the United Nations and best for me that he make a change, that I did not feel that I was on the inner circle, so to speak, and being a part of the policy-making group, and that I had done what I had promised Truman to do, that I had always played fair with him, that I had told Roosevelt that I thought that he, Byrnes, ought to be secretary of state before I was made secretary, that after San Francisco I stepped aside and I had been loyal throughout. He said, "You have been wonderful and I couldn't ever ask for anything finer."

[When Stettinius arrived at the White House, Secretary Byrnes was already there. In a few minutes the two men were shown into the Oval Office.]

CALENDAR NOTES | *June 4, 1946*
The strain of the last month or two is beginning to show in the president's face. He is grayer and more strained, and not as exuberant as he was months ago. The president started the conversation by saying that he was extremely sorry that I was thinking of leaving the United Nations, that I had been in

the movement since the very start, had done such satisfactory work that he couldn't bring himself to accept the fact that I was leaving, and wouldn't it be possible for me to reconsider, as he would be willing to make any adjustment necessary for me to remain.

I stated that the reasons for my desiring to resign were fully stated in my letter to him. . . . The president then stated, "Wouldn't you be willing to stay on until Jimmy completes the negotiations (meaning in Paris)?" [17] I stated, "I would be willing, Mr. President, to stay on a week or a month or a year, if I felt that I were really needed, but I am not needed. With atomic work being handled by one group and social and economic and trusteeship work by another, and the State Department determining policy on Security Council affairs, I am just not needed."

At this point, the president turned to Byrnes and Byrnes stated that he agreed entirely with me, that there was nothing to be gained by my staying thirty days or sixty days and that, of course, he, Byrnes, wanted me to stay on indefinitely, but if I couldn't do that, we might as well make a break now. The president then referred to the fact that he had been disturbed by the rumors of difficulties and frictions, and said that Drew Pearson had helped stir things up. The president then stated that two senators had come to see him one morning. It was a private conversation, and the next day Pearson had the verbatim record of the conversation. Byrnes said that he recently had an incident where Pearson had gotten a message from Bedell Smith [18] of the most highly explosive and secret nature, and that it appeared immediately in Drew Pearson's column even before he could tell the president about it—that he, Byrnes, had immediately called in the FBI to investigate, that two days later Drew Pearson had sent him a message saying not for him to waste his time, that he was on the wrong track, that he had never even gotten the information from the State

Department at all. Byrnes said he thought that was the height of impertinence and Truman said that he, Pearson, was completely unreliable.

The president then leaned back and took his glasses off and said, "Well, this is awfully bad—every time I get a good man in a good place and everything begins to click, then he wants to up and leave me." I looked squarely at the president and said, "Well, Mr. President, if things had worked out as you and I had planned them in San Francisco a year ago, I would not be here today resigning." To this the president made no reply and neither did Byrnes. I then stated, "Of course, there are many ways in which we must strengthen our representation at the United Nations. You will recall, Mr. President, that on several occasions I have spoken to you about leadership, that it had been supplied by Roosevelt and Hull, and that unless the driving leadership is continued by the United States, such as was supplied at Dumbarton Oaks and Yalta, Chapultepec, and San Francisco, the United Nations is not going to be successful because that leadership is not going to be supplied by the British or the Russians or the French or the Chinese or any of the little countries. It's vital that we have one man at the headquarters who has your confidence and Jimmy's confidence, who will be charged with the responsibility of seeing that United States policy is carried out in all branches of the United Nations, and this must be a man just as big as you are or Jimmy, from a standpoint of personal stature and be able to have the respect of all the nations of the world. This must be a man of the caliber of Cordell Hull or a General Marshall, and unless that is done we are running great jeopardy in putting the United Nations on the rocks."

I added that this was particularly true in view of the fact that we had made a mistake in picking a dud as a secretary general, that there was nothing else we could have done, that if we had not picked Lie in London, we would not have been able to pick a man at that time. The president said, "Yes, I agree with you completely, but what are we going to do now?" I said, "There are many things that we can do. . . ."

I then referred to the fact of the need of coordination of the work of the military, social, trusteeship—that all these activities were one and inseparable, and that it could not be departmentalized, and the directing head of each group should at all times be kept informed as to activities in each other group.

The president then said, "Well, I am terribly sorry." I replied, "Well, Mr. President, this is an extremely sad moment for me, because I have had my heart in this work." He said, "I know you have." I said, "I think from your standpoint, Mr. President, to avoid any more unfavorable and embarrassing speculation, it is vitally necessary that you clean this matter up immediately." He said, "I agree. It will be done today."

[Stettinius left for New York where he devoted the next two weeks to winding up his affairs and smoothing the transition to his temporary successor, Herschel Johnson.[19] By July, he was back at his beloved Horseshoe in Orange County, Virginia. The hectic pace of Washington and New York, the conferences and crises, the endless efforts to resolve seemingly insoluble problems, were all behind him. His government service ended, he was free to relax for the first time in over six years.]

EPILOGUE

Immediately after resigning the UN post, Stettinius moved his family to their country home, Horseshoe, and advised well-wishers that he planned to take life easy. But he was still only forty-five, and the relentless drive which had taken him to the pinnacles of power would not permit him to retire. There was speculation that he might enter politics—indeed the powerful Harry F. Byrd appeared ready to back him for the Virginia Senate seat vacated by the death of Carter Glass. Stettinius had no taste for political life, however, and he gave his backers little encouragement. Instead he busied himself with various public service activities until a fatal illness struck him down in 1949.

Since his student days, he had been devoted to and closely associated with the University of Virginia, and when he was offered the position of Rector in 1946 he readily accepted. His chief official function was to preside over monthly meetings of the Board of Visitors, but, characteristically, he did much more. He maintained a close personal interest in beautifying the grounds, even donating magnolias and boxwoods to plant along the lawn and near the rotunda. More important, he directed a massive development campaign which sought to restore Thomas Jefferson's university to national eminence. He persuaded his old friend, war hero Admiral William "Bull" Halsey, to become chairman of the drive, and brought in an outside firm experienced in fund-raising. He attached particular importance to expanding the graduate business program and upgrading the law and medical schools. Under his guidance, the University established a Woodrow Wilson School of International Affairs which he hoped would become an "academy" for the training of American diplomats.

During these same years, Stettinius also spearheaded an early attempt to promote economic development in the emerging nations. Inspired by the vision of Franklin Roosevelt, he was convinced that the United States must use its wealth and know-how to help less fortunate peoples attain decent living standards. He had visited Monrovia, Liberia, shortly after the Yalta conference, and he and Roosevelt agreed that this African nation, founded by the American Colonization Society as a haven for freed slaves, might be an ideal testing ground for United States humanitarianism. Thus, in 1947, Stettinius established a New York based corporation which would pool American private capital and talent to assist in the modernization of Liberia.

Throughout 1947 and 1948, he devoted much attention to the project. His corporation, the Stettinius Associates, was capitalized at one million dollars and attracted the talents of many engineers, businessmen, and lawyers who had been associated with him during the war years. In September, 1947, the corporation negotiated a long-term agreement with Liberian Secretary of State Eugene Dennis. It received the right to exploit certain Liberian agricultural and mineral resources. In return, it would supervise the construction of a modern transportation system, the development of sewage facilities, and the establishment of electric power plants. Stettinius and Liberian President William Tubman took a special interest in education, and the Stettinius Associates sponsored a Liberian Educational Foundation to help prepare Liberians to take roles in a modern society.

The American press hailed the venture as a great "new departure," and for a time it promised significant achievements. With his usual excitement and attention to detail, Stettinius traveled back and forth between Virginia and New York, consulting with the corporation's staff and bombarding them with all sorts of ideas, ranging from the development of a village handicraft industry to the whitewashing of Monrovia's government buildings. When the former secretary of state led his aides on a visit to Liberia in the spring of 1948, the project seemed well grounded.

By the end of the year, however, the experiment was in trouble. The corporation encountered delays getting subsidiary companies to undertake specific projects, and it failed to secure from the United States government the Export-Import Bank loan upon which financing depended. Within Liberia itself, there was unexpected suspicion of the influx of American capitalists, and political intrigue complicated an already difficult situation. Stettinius worked desperately to overcome these problems, but he enjoyed little success, and a severe heart attack in March 1949, forced him to sever connections with the Liberian project.

In his last months, Stettinius was able to do little more than oversee the completion of *Roosevelt and the Russians*, a memoir of the Yalta conference. He had intended to write a complete account of his government service, and in 1947 had secured the assistance of Walter Johnson, a young historian from the University of Chicago. The onset of the postwar anti-communist hysteria gave a sense of urgency to his task and led him to focus on Yalta. By 1948, the nation was coming under the sway of a revisionism which charged Roosevelt with responsibility for losing the peace and made Yalta a byword for treason. A wily, deceitful Stalin had allegedly duped the innocent Roosevelt into selling out American interests to communism, and some of Roosevelt's advisers, including Stettinius's close State Department aide, Alger Hiss, had allegedly been Soviet agents.

Stettinius explained in the introduction that he had written the book out of "a deep respect for the memory of President Roosevelt and unshaken faith in the rightness of his foreign policy," and he defended the president against these many reckless accusations. He pointed out that the United States did not enjoy freedom of action at Yalta—at the time it was thought that Russian cooperation would be essential in the war against Japan; in any event the Soviet Union had made more concessions than the United States at Yalta; and the fault was not with the Yalta agreements themselves but with Stalin's failure to abide by them. The book was released on November 3, 1949, just three days after Stettinius's death.

The last months of the former secretary of state's life were filled with disappointment and despair. Forbidden by his physicians from engaging in the active life he had always known, aware that his dreams for Liberia were collapsing, forced because of financial difficulties to sell his beloved Horseshoe, he spent the summer of 1949 in virtual isolation, talking only with close relatives and hoping for a recovery which never came. He died on October 31, 1949, while visiting his brother-in-law, Juan Trippe, in Greenwich, Connecticut.

After his death, Stettinius was widely eulogized, but in the drastically altered milieu of the Cold War he was quickly forgotten. The United Nations, his major contribution, never attained the vital role as a peace-keeping body that he and Franklin Roosevelt had envisioned. His optimistic view of Soviet-American relations, the conventional wisdom during World War II, had become unfashionable, even treasonable in some quarters, before his death. His idealism and "do-goodism" were out of place among the "tough-minded realists" of the postwar era. Those historians who mentioned him often did so only in a contemptuous way. Herbert Feis dismissed him as "affable but often inept." With characteristic arrogance, Dean Acheson ridiculed the Stettinius style. Even the more temperate have presented him as well-meaning but inexperienced and shallow, a man who contributed very little to the great events of his times.[1]

Some of the criticisms are justified. Stettinius did not dominate the shaping of foreign policy as did Acheson, John Foster Dulles, or more recently Henry Kissinger. He was not a man of great intellect, nor did he have the great personal strength of a George Marshall or even Cordell Hull. Too often he failed to discriminate between matters of real substance and inconsequential details. He was inclined to press on for decisions and agreement without carefully pondering the implications or possible consequences of his actions. His idealism and boyish optimism do frequently come off as naive. And inside the man there was a constant war between his unrelenting drive for achievement and nagging uncertainties about his ability.

Yet he was a talented man, and even though he served only briefly he made significant contributions to American foreign policy. He was intelligent, articulate, and persuasive. He brought to every task he undertook a firm sense of morality, a patriotism which placed the welfare of his country over selfish personal ends, and a deep compassion for other people. He was a gifted administrator. Veteran government officials such as Henry Stimson and Joseph Grew appreciated the smoothness and efficiency he brought to State Department operations, and in a very short time he did much to restore that moribund agency to a central place in the making of U.S. foreign policy. Despite his lack of diplomatic experience, he effectively handled the major assignments given him. At Dumbarton Oaks, Yalta, and San Francisco, he played an instrumental role in negotiations on the UN Charter. His informality, charm, and grace established a solid personal basis for Great Power discussions. His dedication to the UN ideal helped to overcome conflicts of national interest. His timely intervention saved the Dumbarton Oaks and San Francisco conferences from breaking on the rock of Great Power division. His brief diplomatic career was in fact dedicated to the ideal of international cooperation, and he can lay just claim to the title architect of the United Nations. The world organization has not met up to the expectations of its creators and Edward R. Stettinius, Jr. has been largely forgotten. But the objectives he sought and his unbending personal commitment to the ideal should live as inspiration to those who seek an alternative to strife and war.

NOTES

INTRODUCTION

[1] *University of Virginia Alumni News*, XII (September, 1923), 32, XII (February, 1924), pp. 154–155.

[2] Thomas M. Campbell interview with John Lee Pratt, June 5, 1962.

[3] *Journal of Commerce*, November 30, 1942; General Motors Corporation, *Twenty-fifth Annual Report*, May 1, 1934; Alfred P. Sloan, Jr. to General Managers, October 30, 1930, The Edward R. Stettinius, Jr., Papers, Alderman Library, Charlottesville, Va.

[4] Edward R. Stettinius, Jr., "Back-to-the-Land Scrapbook," Stettinius Papers; Campbell interview with Robert J. Lynch, November 5, 1962; S. J. Woolf, "Teagle Puts the Case for Job Sharing," *New York Times Magazine*, October 30, 1932; Share-the-Work Movement, *Report . . . Second Federal District*, ca. February 1934; "General Motors Scrapbook," Stettinius Papers.

[5] Stettinius to R. S. McLaughlin, July 28, 1933, Stettinius Papers; NRA, Industrial Advisory Board Minutes, October 5, November 9, 1933; George C. Herring interview with Willard Kiplinger, March 23, 1965; all in Stettinius Papers; Arthur M. Schlesinger, *The Coming of the New Deal* (Boston, 1959), pp. 114–118.

[6] "U. S. Steel Scrapbook," Stettinius Papers; U. S. Steel Corporation, "Functions of the Control Committee," memorandum, April 21, 1936; Ford, Bacon, and Davis, Report No. 1, November 1, 1937; Stettinius Papers; *Pittsburgh Press*, January 16, 1937.

[7] Stettinius-Taylor correspondence, 1937–1938, Stettinius Papers; William E. Leuchtenburg, *Franklin D. Roosevelt and the New Deal* (New York, 1963), pp. 247–257.

[8] Perkins to Stettinius, May 28, 1938, Stettinius Papers.

[9] William Langer and S. Everett Gleason, *The Challenge to Isolation* (New York, 1952), pp. 270–271.

[10] Stettinius to Roosevelt, June 20, 1940; "Amortization of Cost of Defense Facilities . . . ," n.d.; Stettinius–Harold Moulton, summary of phone conversation, July 8, 1940; Stettinius Calendar Notes, July 27, 1940, Stettinius Papers.

[11] Exhibits on aluminum, June 1940–June 1941; Marion B. Folsom to Stettinius, November 28, 1940; LaMotte T. Cohn to Stettinius, December 30, 1940, Stettinius Papers; *New York Herald-Tribune*, November 29, 1940.

[12] Minutes of meetings, Priorities Division, OPM, July 10–31, 1941, Stettinius Papers.

[13] On the establishment of OLLA, see Robert E. Sherwood, *Roosevelt and Hopkins* (New York, 1948), p. 278, and Edward R. Stettinius, Jr., *Lend-Lease: Weapon for Victory* (New York, 1944), pp. 105–108.

[14] George C. Herring, "Experiment in Foreign Aid: Lend-Lease, 1941–1945" (unpublished Ph.D. dissertation, University of Virginia, 1965), pp. 105–110.

[15] *Ibid.*, pp. 105–106, 114, 117, 121–128.

[16] *Ibid.*, pp. 143–150.

[17] London Trip Diary, August 7, 1942, Stettinius Papers.

[18] Herring, "Experiment in Foreign Aid," pp. 161–163; Marquis Childs in *St. Louis Post-Dispatch*, April 17, 1943.

[19] Herring, "Experiment in Foreign Aid," pp. 388–389; also E. R. Stettinius, "Lend-Lease Works Both Ways," *Saturday Evening Post* (September 15, 1942): 11, 117–118, and Stettinius, *Lend-Lease: Weapon for Victory*.

[20] *Congressional Record*, 78 Cong., 1 Sess. (1943), 1652.

[21] Krock in *New York Times*, March 12, 1943.

Chapter I
UNDERSECRETARY OF STATE
October 1943–March 1944

[1] "Unprepared for Victory," *New Republic* 109 (August 16, 1943): 211.

[2] John Crider, *New York Times*, August 4, 1943. For comment on the Crider report, see Blair Bolles, "Foreign Policy Wanted," *Nation* 48 (August 14, 1943): 174–75; "The State Department," *Life* 15 (August 23, 1943): 32; *Newsweek* (August 16, 1943), p. 42.

[3] James F. Byrnes, senator from South Carolina, Supreme Court Justice, after 1942 Director of War Mobilization.

[4] Bernhard Knollenberg, deputy Lend-Lease administrator; John Lee Pratt, General Motors executive and close friend of the Stettinius family; General George C. Marshall, army chief of staff and a personal friend of Stettinius.

[5] Apparently Lewis Douglas, then war shipping administrator.

[6] Refers to the arrangement of September 1940, whereby Roosevelt through an executive agreement transferred to Great Britain fifty destroyers

in exchange for American rights to lease bases on British territories in the Western Hemisphere.

7 Rumors had circulated in Washington that Welles had made advances toward a porter on a train. Hull had conveniently used these rumors to persuade Roosevelt to accept Welles's resignation as undersecretary of state.

8 Senators Lister Hill [D.-Alabama] and Carl Hatch [D.-New Mexico]. Along with Republican Senators Harold Burton of Ohio and Joseph Ball of Minnesota, Hill and Hatch had spearheaded a bipartisan drive in the Senate to commit the United States to participation in an international organization.

9 Claude Pepper [D.-Florida].

10 Refers to a House resolution, sponsored by Democrat J. William Fulbright of Arkansas, which expressed approval of American entry into an international organization. The House approved the resolution by an overwhelming 360 to 29 vote on September 21, 1943.

11 Alben Barkley [D.-Kentucky], Senate majority leader.

12 The Papers of Edward R. Stettinius, Jr., Alderman Library, Charlottesville, Va.

13 General Edwin M. "Pa" Watson, the president's appointments secretary.

14 Representatives John McCormack [D.-Massachusetts] and Sam Rayburn [D.-Texas] Democratic House leaders.

15 Refers to Hull's difficulties in getting the Russians to agree to China's adherence to the Moscow declaration.

16 The European Advisory Commission was a body proposed by the British in July 1943 and agreed to by the United States and the Soviet Union at the Moscow conference which was to formulate the terms of surrender for the Axis nations and to plan the implementation of them.

17 Probably refers to Stalin's message of November 10, 1943, agreeing to meet Roosevelt at Teheran in late November. For the text of the message, see Ministry of Foreign Affairs of the USSR, *Stalin's Correspondence with Roosevelt and Truman* (New York, 1965), p. 105.

18 Stettinius Calendar Notes, October 6, 1943, Stettinius Papers.

19 A detailed description of the reorganization plan as well as the organization chart is in *Department of State Bulletin* 10 (January 15, 1944): 43–67. For contemporary comment on the plan, see *Time* 43 (January 24, 1944): 16. See also Dean Acheson, *Present at the Creation* (New York, 1969), p. 47; and Robert E. Sherwood, *Roosevelt and Hopkins* (New York, 1948), p. 757.

20 Quoted in Sherwood, *Roosevelt and Hopkins*, p. 804.

21 Refers to the Declaration of the United Nations, signed by twenty-

six nations in Washington on January 1, 1942. For the drafting of the declaration, see *ibid.*, pp. 446–53.

[22] Stettinius's book, *Lend-Lease: Weapon for Victory*, was published in early 1944.

[23] Probably refers to a dispatch from London printed in the *New York Times* of January 17, 1944, which reported that "heavy new increments of German agents" had been "pouring" into Spain in an "obvious effort by Germany to save what she can of a situation that has gone badly against her. . . ."

[24] Churchill's dispatch, dated January 23, 1944, indicated that Britain would support the United States in taking firm action with Argentina, but urged the president to consider the possible consequences of a complete break, in particular the hardship it would cause the United Kingdom which received one-third of its meat supply from Argentina. See Cordell Hull, *The Memoirs of Cordell Hull*, vol. II (New York, 1948): 1412–13.

[25] This declaration, agreed upon at the Moscow Conference, stated that the annexation of Austria by Germany in 1938 was null and void and pledged the Allies to reconstitute Austria as an independent nation.

[26] Hull, *Memoirs*, vol. II: 1394.

[27] For a discussion of the criticism of U.S. foreign policy in the spring of 1944 see Robert A. Divine, *Second Chance: The Triumph of Internationalism in America During World War II* (New York, 1967), pp. 192–95.

[28] Refers to a statement issued by Foreign Secretary Anthony Eden in September 1941 pledging that the United Kingdom would not re-export Lend-Lease supplies. For the text of the so-called Eden "White Paper," see *New York Times*, September 11, 1941.

[29] The Atlantic Charter was a statement of principles issued by Roosevelt and Churchill at the conclusion of their conference off Argentina, Newfoundland, in August 1941. This statement of Anglo-American war aims is one of the key documents of World War II. For the text, see *Foreign Relations of the United States, 1941* 1: 368–69.

Chapter II
MISSION TO LONDON
March–April 1944

[1] Press release, March 17, 1944, *Department of State Bulletin* 10 (March 18, 1944): 256.

[2] London Mission Diary, March 10, 1944, The Papers of Edward R. Stettinius, Jr., Alderman Library, Charlottesville, Va.

³ *Ibid.*, March 17, 1944, Stettinius Papers.

⁴ Wendell L. Willkie, Republican presidential candidate, 1940, leading candidate for the nomination in 1944 until he withdrew after a crushing defeat in the Wisconsin primary on April 4.

⁵ For a discussion of the attacks on Hull, see Robert A. Divine, *Second Chance: The Triumph of Internationalism in America During World War II* (New York, 1967), pp. 193–94.

⁶ Churchill had acted forcefully to put down the mutiny in the Greek army. He instructed his agent in Cairo to round up the mutineers by "artillery and superior force and let hunger play its part." British troops had subsequently moved in on the Greeks, whom Churchill described as "banditti," arresting the leaders of the mutiny and imprisoning 20,000 of those who supported it. Suppression of the mutiny did not, however, solve the Greek problem, which would erupt again in December 1944, and would require further use of British force. Gabriel Kolko, *The Politics of War* (New York, 1969), pp. 178–79.

⁷ Roosevelt flatly rejected Eisenhower's proposal, apparently fearing that combined Anglo-American zones of occupation might place American troops in France, Italy, and the Balkans. For further documentation of the Roosevelt-Eisenhower exchanges on this issue, see Alfred Chandler, ed., *The Papers of Dwight D. Eisenhower: The War Years*, vol. III (Baltimore, Md., 1970): 1721–22, 1726.

⁸ Cadogan was also favorably impressed by Stettinius, whom he described as a "dignified and more monumental Charlie Chaplin," and this meeting began a long association that would develop through the Dumbarton Oaks and San Francisco conferences. David Dilks, ed., *The Diaries of Sir Alexander Cadogan* (New York, 1972), pp. 617–18.

⁹ Phillips, a career diplomat and close friend of the president, had gone to India in 1942 on a fact-finding mission. He had returned convinced that the United States must intervene to get the British to grant independence to India. When Phillips later discussed the matter with Churchill in the British Embassy in Washington, the prime minister flew into a rage, and both Roosevelt and Phillips concluded that it was hopeless to press the matter further. See William Phillips, *Ventures in Diplomacy* (Portland, Me., 1952), pp. 377, 388. At the time of the Stettinius mission to London, Phillips was serving as American political officer on Eisenhower's staff.

¹⁰ Reference is to the United Nations Food and Agriculture Conference held at Hot Springs, Virginia, May 1943, to discuss means of expanding and distributing the world food supply after the war. The press had been excluded from the conference, and had responded by blasting this

"secret diplomacy." In addition, writers had sharply criticized the sumptuous meals served the delegates and the plush surroundings in which the conference had been held. Divine, *Second Chance*, p. 116.

[11] Refers to Article VII of the Anglo-American Lend-Lease agreement of February 23, 1942, which committed the two nations to cooperate in the "elimination of all forms of discriminatory treatment in international commerce, and to the reduction of tariffs and other trade barriers."

[12] Roosevelt agreed with Churchill's stand on defining unconditional surrender. See his memoranda to the Joint Chiefs of Staff, April 1, 1944, *Foreign Relations of the United States, 1944* 1: 501, and to Hull, April 5, 1944, *ibid.*, p. 592, and Hull to Roosevelt, April 17, 1944, *ibid.*, p. 509.

[13] Refers to Roosevelt's cable to Churchill, February 23, 1944, printed in *Foreign Relations, 1944* 2:16.

[14] Roosevelt's directive is printed in Harry L. Coles and Albert K. Weinberg, *Civil Affairs: Soldiers Become Governors* (Washington, D.C., 1964), pp. 667–68. For Hull's speech of April 9, 1944, see *Department of State Bulletin* 10 (April 15, 1944): 337.

[15] Hull to Winant and Stettinius, April 18, 1944, *Foreign Relations, 1944* 1:31–32.

[16] London Mission Diary, April 26, 1944, Stettinius Papers.

[17] Thomas E. Dewey, governor of New York, and John Bricker, governor of Ohio, were leading candidates for the Republican presidential nomination.

[18] Report to Secretary of State by Under Secretary of State on His Mission to London, April 7–29, 1944, *Foreign Relations, 1944* 3:15–16, 21.

Chapter III
TRANSITION FROM WAR TO PEACE
May–August 1944

[1] Drew Pearson column, *Washington Post*, May 12, 1944.

[2] Armour to Hull, May 26, 1944, *Foreign Relations of the United States, 1944* 17:273–74.

[3] Record of conference, Stettinius and Mikolajczyk, June 6, 1944, *Foreign Relations, 1944* 3:1274–76.

[4] Roosevelt was apparently referring to two cables received from Stalin, one dated June 5, the other June 6. Both are printed in Ministry of Foreign Affairs of the USSR, *Stalin's Correspondence with Roosevelt and Truman* (New York, 1965), p. 145.

⁵ Beneš had concluded a treaty with Stalin on December 12, 1943, in which each nation promised that it would assist the other in the war, that it would not enter pacts directed against the other, and that it would respect the independence and sovereignty of the other. At the same time Beneš reached an understanding with the Russians that his government would be reorganized and one-fifth of the places would be given to Czech Communists.

⁶ In January 1944, the Russians indicated that they would be willing to conclude a treaty with the Polish government-in-exile similar to the one they had already concluded with Beneš if the London government would drop those of its members who were most violently anti-Russian and if it would accept the Soviet position on a boundary between the two nations.

⁷ The Curzon Line was a boundary line between Russia and Poland originally formulated at the Paris Peace conference and later endorsed by the British secretary of state for foreign affairs, Lord Curzon, as a means of resolving the boundary clash between the two nations. Through force of arms, the Poles had subsequently forced the Russians to accept the Treaty of Riga, 1921, which provided for a boundary considerably east of the Curzon Line. Russia reclaimed much of the lost territory in the Nazi-Soviet partition of 1939, and when the boundary dispute was revived after the German invasion of the Soviet Union in 1941, the Russians insisted upon a postwar boundary roughly corresponding with the Curzon Line and the Poles demanded a return to a line approximating that in the Treaty of Riga.

⁸ *Foreign Relations, 1944* 3:1283.

⁹ Henry Morgenthau, Jr., secretary of the treasury, and Leo T. Crowley, foreign economic administrator.

¹⁰ On June 15, Roosevelt had announced that negotiations with Britain, China, and Russia on international organization would begin in Washington in August.

¹¹ The White Paper was a statement issued by British Foreign Secretary Anthony Eden on September 14, 1941, pledging that the United Kingdom would not re-export supplies received under Lend-Lease in competition with American merchants. It had proven extremely difficult to administer, and in the winter of 1943–44, the United States had sought to open negotiations to work out a new arrangement on re-export of Lend-Lease materials.

¹² Ernest Bevin, British trade union leader and minister of labor and national service in the War Cabinet; W. Citrine, trade union leader.

¹³ Clement R. Attlee, Labour party leader and deputy prime minister

in the War Cabinet; Herbert Morrison, Labour party leader and member of the War Cabinet, 1942–45; Sir Stafford Cripps, Labour party leader until he was expelled in 1939, British ambassador to the Soviet Union, 1940–42, minister of aircraft production in the War Cabinet.

[14] Reston was true to his word. At the Dumbarton Oaks conference which began in August, he secured confidential information from the Chinese delegation and published a series of articles which infuriated the State Department and won him a Pulitzer Prize.

[15] In the summer of 1944, former Undersecretary of State Sumner Welles had published a book, *The Time for Decision*, which discussed the problem of international organization.

Chapter IV
THE DUMBARTON OAKS CONFERENCE
August–October 1944

[1] The American delegation consisted of Isaiah Bowman, special adviser to the secretary of state; Benjamin V. Cohen, general counsel to the Office of War Mobilization; James C. Dunn, director of the State Department's Office of European Affairs; Henry P. Fletcher, special adviser to the secretary of state; Joseph C. Grew, former ambassador to Japan; Green Hackworth, legal adviser to the secretary of state; Stanley Hornbeck, special assistant to the secretary of state; Breckinridge Long, assistant secretary of state; Leo Pasvolsky, special assistant to the secretary of state; Edwin C. Wilson, director of the Office of Special Political Affairs, Department of State; Admiral Arthur J. Hepburn, chairman of the General Board of the Department of the Navy; Lt. Gen. Stanley D. Embick, member of the Joint Strategic Survey Committee of the Joint Chiefs of Staff; Vice-Admiral Russell Willson, member of the Joint Strategic Survey Committee of the Joint Chiefs of Staff; Major General Muir Fairchild, U.S. Army Air Force; Major General George V. Strong, member of the Joint Post-War Committee of the Joint Chiefs of Staff; Rear Admiral Harold C. Train, U.S. Navy.

[2] Fuller discussions of early U.S. planning for international organization may be found in Department of State, *Postwar Foreign Policy Preparation, 1939–1945* (Washington, D.C., 1949); Robert A. Divine, *Second Chance: The Triumph of Internationalism in America During World War II* (New York, 1967); and Ruth Russell, *A History of the United Nations Charter, the Role of the United States 1940–1945* (Washington, D.C., 1958).

[3] Thomas M. Campbell, *Masquerade Peace, America's UN Policy, 1944–1945* (Tallahassee, Fla., 1973), pp. 35–38.

[4] *Ibid.*, pp. 39–40; Department of State, *Postwar Foreign Policy Preparation*, pp. 299, 317.

[5] Stettinius Diary, August 21, 1944, The Papers of Edward R. Stettinius, Jr., Alderman Library, Charlottesville, Va.

[6] *Ibid.*

[7] *New York Times*, August 23, 1944. At the time, Stettinius and other Americans blamed the leaks on the British, but Reston revealed some years later that he had gotten his information from the Chinese, who were annoyed at being excluded from the first stage of the conference. Divine, *Second Chance*, p. 221.

[8] Stettinius Diary, August 27, 1944, Stettinius Papers.

[9] The "associated" nations were nations who although they had not declared war on the Axis were nevertheless helping the Allies in a number of ways.

[10] Refers to the Kiplinger publication, *Changing Times*, and to the *Whaley-Eaton Newsletter*.

[11] Senator Walter George [D.-Ga.], an influential member of the Foreign Relations Committee.

[12] Cadogan Diary, August 29, 1944, David Dilks, ed., *The Diaries of Sir Alexander Cadogan* (New York, 1972), p. 659.

[13] The question was whether the council should reach decisions by a majority or two-thirds vote.

[14] The delegations generally agreed that some sort of committee should be created to advise the council on military matters, but differed on the composition of the committee.

[15] Roosevelt's cable, dated September 1, is printed in Ministry of Foreign Affairs of the USSR, *Stalin's Correspondence with Roosevelt and Truman* (New York, 1965), p. 158.

[16] According to Cadogan, Gromyko was "obviously terrified of departing a hair's breadth from his instructions." Dilks, ed., *Cadogan Diaries*, p. 656.

[17] *Ibid.*, p. 659.

[18] The Russians had pressed to empower the assembly to suspend or expel any member who violated the principles of the charter.

[19] Vice-Admiral Russell Willson, Joint Chiefs of Staff representative on the American delegation.

[20] Roosevelt and Churchill were scheduled to meet at Quebec to discuss grand strategy.

[21] James A. Farley, postmaster general and political adviser to Roosevelt during the first two administrations.

²² From the standpoint of domestic politics, the question of the use of force was the most difficult the administration encountered. Hull preferred that the president should be given the authority to commit American armed forces to the international body without having to secure the approval of Congress. But many senators, both Republicans and Democrats, opposed this principle vigorously, arguing that Congress must approve any use of U.S. troops for collective security. In mid-September, Hull worked out a compromise that in effect postponed a final decision on this issue. The Dumbarton Oaks Proposals included only a statement that each nation would agree to provide the council with a quota of troops, and it was left for future settlement whether Congress had to give its approval on each occasion when troops were actually committed to the organization.

²³ Patrick J. Hurley, secretary of war in the Hoover administration, was serving Roosevelt as a roving ambassador and had recently been dispatched to China to try to resolve differences between the communists and Chiang Kai-shek's government.

²⁴ Roosevelt's cable, dated September 9, is printed in *Stalin's Correspondence*, p. 159.

²⁵ Stettinius Diary, September 8, 1944, Stettinius Papers.

²⁶ Dilks, ed., *Cadogan Diaries*, p. 663.

²⁷ Stalin's message, dated September 7, 1944, and printed in *Stalin's Correspondence*, pp. 158–59, made clear that he "attached the utmost importance" to the X-matter, and that he intended to take it up with the president in the future.

²⁸ Joseph C. Grew, former undersecretary of state and ambassador to Japan, had been secretary of the United States Commission to the Paris Peace Conference in 1919. Edwin C. Wilson was a former ambassador to Panama.

²⁹ Stalin to Roosevelt, September 14, 1944, *Stalin's Correspondence*, p. 160.

³⁰ Stettinius Diary, September 18, 1944, Stettinius Papers.

³¹ For the role of military thinking at this point, see Thomas M. Campbell, "Nationalism in America's UN Policy, 1944–1945," *International Organization* 27 (Winter 1973): 25–44.

³² Stettinius Diary, September 19, 1944, Stettinius Papers.

³³ *Wilson*, a motion picture based on the president's life, opened in New York on August 1, 1944.

³⁴ Arthur Vandenberg (R.-Mich.), the Republicans' leading spokesman on foreign policy.

³⁵ Stettinius Diary, September 20, 1944, Stettinius Papers.

[36] *Ibid.*, September 27, 1944.

[37] For the Chinese phase of the conversations, see Stettinius Diary, September 29 through October 7, 1944, Stettinius Papers, and Department of State, *Postwar Foreign Policy Preparation*, pp. 328–34.

[38] The Dumbarton Oaks Proposals are conveniently printed in Department of State, *Postwar Foreign Policy Preparation*, pp. 611–19.

[39] Stettinius Diary, September 27, 1944, Stettinius Papers. Roosevelt's statement is quoted in Divine, *Second Chance*, p. 226.

Chapter V
ACTING SECRETARY
October–November 1944

[1] Harriman to Hull, September 20, 1944, *Foreign Relations of the United States, 1944* 4:933.

[2] Reference is to the Soviet supply protocols, annual agreements in which the United States and Britain committed themselves to make available to the USSR a specified volume of supplies over a twelve-month period. In presenting their requests for aid during Stage II, the British sought an arrangement similar to these protocols.

[3] In October 1942 Willkie had written an article for *Life* magazine, based on his recent visit to the USSR, which had discussed Russia's intentions toward neighboring states. *Pravda* had responded with a vicious attack on Willkie which had been interpreted in the United States as evidence that the Soviet Union had expansionist aims in Eastern Europe. See *Foreign Relations, 1944* 4:825.

[4] Refers to the president's speech, October 21, 1944, to the Foreign Policy Association in New York on the question of international organization.

[5] Churchill had gone to Moscow in early October for discussions with Stalin on the disposition of British and Russian power in liberated Europe.

[6] Ambassador of Poland to acting secretary of state, October 27, 1944, *Foreign Relations: Yalta*, pp. 207–8.

[7] A message along these lines was sent on November 1, 1944. For the text, see *Foreign Relations, 1944* 3:1330.

[8] Stettinius's conversation with the Swedish minister is recorded in *Foreign Relations, 1944* 4:659.

[9] Dr. Stephen S. Wise and Rabbi Abba Hillel Silver, cochairmen of the American Zionist Emergency Council, and Dr. Nahum Goldman, American Jewish leader.

[10] Charges had been made during the campaign that Truman had once been a member of the Ku Klux Klan.

[11] The memorandum of November 3 stated that the United States had made no "final decisions" on the future status of the colonial areas in Southeast Asia and that it expected to be consulted by the British, French, and Dutch regarding their plans. See *Foreign Relations, 1944* 3:780. The "action" Stettinius referred to involved Indochina. In an effort to further their hopes of reestablishing their empire in Indochina, the French in 1944 had attached a military mission to the headquarters of the Southeast Asia Command. In November, intelligence reports to Washington indicated that some U.S. army and navy officers with the command had given tacit recognition to the mission. Roosevelt, who was adamantly opposed to the restoration of French imperialism in Indochina, immediately issued a directive advising that the French mission did not have official United States recognition.

[12] Patrick J. Hurley, formerly secretary of war and a roving ambassador for FDR, would subsequently be appointed ambassador to China.

[13] The cable sent to Mikolajczyk on November 17, 1944, simply reaffirmed the president's earlier position on the Polish question. Again, Roosevelt refused to make any commitments on frontiers, advising that such action would be against the "traditional" policy of the United States. *Foreign Relations: Yalta*, pp. 209–10.

[14] The cable was sent to Churchill on November 18 and is printed in *Foreign Relations, 1944* 7:365.

[15] Under the usual procedure, supplies were approved for Lend-Lease on the basis of strategic necessity. No long-range commitments were made, and although quarterly programs were drawn up these were always subject to modification on the basis of changes in the strategic situation.

[16] A memorandum of the conversation is in *Foreign Relations, 1944* 5:467.

[17] *New York Times*, December 9, 1944.

[18] The report, dated November 25, 1944, is in *Foreign Relations 1944* 3:77–78.

[19] Churchill advised Roosevelt in a cable of November 26, 1944, that Britain would continue to buy Argentine meat on a month-to-month basis for the next six months. See *Foreign Relations, 1944* 7:365–66.

Chapter VI
STORM BEFORE YALTA
December 1944 –January 1945

¹ William L. Clayton, Texas businessman, head of Anderson, Clayton & Co., cotton exporters, assistant secretary of commerce since 1942; Nelson A. Rockefeller, president of Rockefeller Center, coordinator of Inter-American Affairs since 1940; Dean G. Acheson, Washington attorney, assistant secretary of state, 1941–1944; Archibald MacLeish, poet, librarian of Congress; Julius Holmes, brigadier general, U.S. Army; James C. Dunn, career diplomat, adviser to the secretary of state on political affairs since 1937.

² For background on the Palestine question, see Chapter V.

³ The senators present were: Arthur Capper [R.-Kansas]; Bennett Champ Clark [D.-Missouri]; Guy M. Gillette [R.-Iowa]; Theodore Francis Green [D.-Rhode Island]; Robert M. La Follette, Jr. [Progressive-Wisconsin]; Elbert D. Thomas [D.-Utah]; Arthur H. Vandenberg [R.-Michigan]; Wallace H. White, Jr. [R.-Maine].

⁴ In the letter to Senator Wagner, October 15, 1944 (printed in *Foreign Relations of the United States, 1944* 5:615–16) Roosevelt expressed his "satisfaction" that the Democratic convention had endorsed the creation of a "free and democratic Jewish commonwealth" and his assurance that efforts would be made "to find appropriate ways and means of effectuating this policy as soon as practicable."

⁵ Fearing a political takeover in Greece by the National Liberation Front (EAM), Churchill in late November had sent thousands of troops to Greece to back up the British-sponsored government of Georges Papandreou. On December 4, heavy fighting broke out between British forces and the ELAS, the military arm of the liberation front.

⁶ For Stettinius's statement, see *Department of State Bulletin* 11 (December 10, 1944): 713.

⁷ Calendar Notes, December 8, 1945, The Papers of Edward R. Stettinius, Jr., Alderman Library, Charlottesville, Va.; *New York Times*, December 12, 1945.

⁸ Record of meeting in the secretary's office, December 11, 1944, Stettinius Papers.

⁹ *Washington Post*, December 12, 1944.

¹⁰ Alexander C. Kirk, career diplomat, political adviser on the staff of the Supreme Allied Commander, Middle Eastern Theater.

[11] Summary of telephone conversation, December 15, 1944, Stettinius Papers.

[12] MacLeish to Stettinius, December 15, 1944; Stettinius to MacLeish, December 15, 1944, Stettinius Papers.

[13] For the text of the release, see *Foreign Relations: Yalta*, pp. 217–19.

[14] The cable is printed in *ibid.*, pp. 224–25.

[15] Roosevelt's memorandum to Stettinius, dated January 1, 1945, stated flatly, "I do not want to get mixed up in any military effort toward the liberation of Indochina from the Japanese." The memo is printed in *Foreign Relations, 1945* 6:293.

[16] After the Dumbarton Oaks conference, the State Department had worked out a compromise formula to try to break the deadlock on voting in the Security Council. According to the proposal, the decision and recommendation for peaceful settlement of disputes would not be subject to the veto, but a Great Power would be able to veto the application of economic or military sanctions. In early December, Roosevelt had proposed this formula to Stalin, but after a delay of nearly a month, the Russian leader rejected it, insisting that an absolute veto was necessary to maintain the principle of unanimity of the Great Powers. At this point, the president himself began to retreat, indicating on several occasions that it might be necessary to give in to the Russian position. On January 2, the secretary sent Roosevelt a cable from Harriman, dated December 28, which analyzed the Soviet position on the veto and recommended that the United States take a "very firm stand with the Russians." *Foreign Relations: Yalta*, pp. 64–66.

[17] Present at the meeting were Senators Connally, Barkley, White, Austin, Vandenberg, La Follette, and Thomas.

[18] Stettinius to Roosevelt, January 18, 1945, *Foreign Relations: Yalta*, pp. 97–98. The Emergency High Commission for Liberated Europe, to be composed of representatives from the United States, Britain, the Soviet Union, and France, would be charged with responsibility for the establishment of "popular" governments and the handling of emergency economic problems in the liberated nations. It was designed by the State Department in part to reassure American opinion and in part to assure the U.S. a voice in administration of liberated areas under British and Soviet control.

[19] The "black binder" contained position papers and memoranda on the major issues confronting the Big Three at the conference.

[20] Parenthetical material in original.

Chapter VII
DECISIONS AT YALTA
January–February 1945

[1] See Chapter VI.

[2] Mikolajczyk's proposals, summarized in *Foreign Relations, 1945* 5:119, called for the establishment of a presidential council, composed of the most respected Polish leaders in politics, religion, and science, to summon a conference to meet in the presence of representatives of the Big Three nations to establish a new government for Poland.

[3] "Iran matter" refers to the dispute which developed between the USSR and Iran in November 1944 over oil concessions. When the Iranian government granted concessions to the United States and Britain, the Russians began to exert heavy pressure for equal rights. See Chapter V.

[4] The Montreux Convention of 1936 governed access to the Turkish Straits. Stalin was dissatisfied with its provisions, particularly the authority given Turkey to close the straits in time of war or even when there was a possibility of war, and sought its revision.

[5] The cable to Winant, printed in *Foreign Relations, 1945* 3:179, notified him of Anglo-American approval of the protocol on zones of occupation in Germany. For the text of the protocol, see *United States Treaties and Other International Agreements* 5, Pt. 2:2078.

[6] Earl Warren, prominent Republican, elected governor of California in 1942; Harold Stassen, former governor of Minnesota, dark-horse candidate for the Republican presidential nomination in 1944, subsequently an aide to Admiral William Halsey.

Chapter VIII
THE MEXICO CITY CONFERENCE
February–March 1945

[1] Quoted in Federico G. Gil, *Latin American-United States Relations* (New York, 1971), p. 190.

[2] For background on Argentine-U.S. relations, see Chapters I, III, and V.

[3] Calendar Notes, February 20, 1945, The Papers of Edward R. Stettinius, Jr., Alderman Library, Charlottesville, Va.

[4] Calendar Notes, February 26, 1945, Stettinius Papers.

[5] In a memorandum of January 9, 1945, Ex-President Santos of Colombia had expressed concern that the increasing flow of arms within the hemi-

sphere could lead to internal aggression and suggested that the only remedy was a mutual guarantee of borders. President Roosevelt had agreed and expressed general support for the proposal. See *Foreign Relations of the United States, 1945* 9:25n.

[6] On February 28, Gustavo Gutierrez, a member of the Cuban delegation, had attacked the Dumbarton Oaks Proposals. U.S. observers, convinced that the Cuban delegation was not functioning as a unit, interpreted the criticism as a "purely individual performance." See *Foreign Relations, 1945* 9:133.

[7] The Mexican proposal was that the Mexico City conference adopt a common ground on certain amendments to the Dumbarton Oaks Proposals and recommend their adoption by the UN conference in San Francisco. Developments from noon, February 28, 1945 to noon, March 1, 1945, Stettinius Papers.

[8] Part III then read: "This declaration and recommendation provide for a regional arrangement for dealing with matters relating to the maintenance of international peace and security as are appropriate for regional action in the Western Hemisphere and said arrangements . . . shall be consistent with the purposes and principles of the general international organization when formed." Act of Chapultepec, Draft of Mar. 2, 1945, Stettinius Papers.

Chapter IX
PREPARATIONS FOR THE SAN FRANCISCO CONFERENCE
March–April 1945

[1] For Baruch's account of his trip to London and his report to Truman, see Bernard M. Baruch, *Baruch: The Public Years* (New York, 1960), pp. 347–49, 357–58, and Baruch to Truman, April 20, 1945, The Papers of Edward R. Stettinius, Jr., Alderman Library, Charlottesville, Va.

[2] Calendar Notes, March 13, 1945, Stettinius Papers.

[3] J. F. Green to Alger Hiss, March 23, 1945; Hiss to Robert Lynch, March 23, 1945, Stettinius Papers.

[4] Record, Section VIII, pp. 21–23; Minutes, Secretary's Staff Committee, March 31, 1945, Stettinius Papers.

[5] The Montreux Convention of 1936 governed usage of the Turkish Straits. Russia wanted changes to allow her naval vessels the right of passage in time of war as well as in peacetime.

[6] For the texts of Harriman's cables, see *Foreign Relations of the United States, 1945*, 5:817–24.

⁷ Oliver Lyttelton, president of the British Board of Trade and minister of production; John J. Llewellin, minister of food.

⁸ On April 16, 1945, Truman and Churchill sent a message to Stalin, challenging the Russian claim that the Warsaw government should have the right to approve which Polish leaders were invited to Moscow for consultations on forming a new government. They also suggested a list of men who ought to be invited, and warned of the dangers to Allied unity if the Polish dispute were not resolved. For the text of the message, see *Foreign Relations, 1945*, 5:219–21.

⁹ The Molotov, Eden, Stettinius, discussions, as well as Truman's conversations with Molotov and his advisers, are in *Foreign Relations, 1945*, 5:235–55; see also, Harry S. Truman, *Memoirs*, (New York, 1955), vol. I: 75–82.

Chapter X
SAN FRANCISCO: POWER BLOCS AND THE UNITED NATIONS
April–May 1945

¹ Field Marshal Jan C. Smuts, prime minister of South Africa and chairman of the South African delegation to San Francisco.

² William Lyon Mackenzie King, prime minister of Canada and chairman of the Canadian delegation.

³ Jan Masaryk, chairman of the Czechoslovakian delegation.

⁴ Rockefeller, a strong advocate of regionalism, had used his post as assistant secretary of state for Latin American affairs to promote hemispheric interests. See Thomas M. Campbell, *Masquerade Peace, America's UN Policy, 1944–1945* (Tallahassee, Fla., 1973), pp. 115–16; Stettinius notes on meeting with the president, April 18, 1945, The Papers of Edward R. Stettinius, Jr., Alderman Library, Charlottesville, Va.

⁵ Joaquin Fernandez, Chilean minister for foreign affairs and chairman of the Chilean delegation.

⁶ Herbert V. Evatt, Australian minister for external affairs and Australian delegate.

⁷ British ambassador to the Soviet Union.

⁸ Arthur Krock, *Memoirs, Sixty Years on the Firing Line* (New York, 1968), pp. 209–10.

⁹ Carl Hatch and Joseph Ball to Stettinius, May 1, 1945, Stettinius Papers.

¹⁰ Hatch to Stettinius, May 3, 1945, Stettinius Papers.

[11] Summary of phone conversation, Stettinius and Rockefeller, May 3, 1945, Stettinius Papers.

[12] Summary of phone conversation, Stettinius and Pasvolsky, May 5, 1945, Stettinius Papers.

[13] Harley A. Notter, adviser to the State Department and to the U.S. delegation.

[14] Senator Burton K. Wheeler (D.-Montana).

[15] John J. McCloy, assistant secretary of war.

[16] Summary of phone conversation, Stettinius and Truman, May 5, 1945, Stettinius Papers.

[17] Memorandum of conversation, Stettinius and Molotov, May 8, 1945, Stettinius Papers.

[18] Edward R. Stettinius, Jr., *Roosevelt and the Russians: The Yalta Conference* (New York, 1949), p. 318.

[19] George C. Herring, Jr., *Aid to Russia, 1941–1946: Strategy, Diplomacy, the Origins of the Cold War* (New York, 1973), pp. 201–06.

[20] Those involved were: James Dunn, Isaiah Bowman, Hamilton Fish Armstrong, Leo Pasvolsky, and John Foster Dulles.

[21] Vice Admiral Richard S. Edwards, deputy chief of naval operations.

[22] Lt. General Stanley D. Embick, adviser, U.S. delegation.

[23] Major General Muir S. Fairchild, adviser, U.S. delegation.

[24] Admiral Arthur J. Hepburn, adviser, U.S. delegation.

[25] For the text see: *UNCIO Documents*, vol. III: 385.

[26] Stettinius was most anxious to secure Big Five agreement before Eden returned to London.

[27] For text see, *Foreign Relations, 1945* 1:691–92.

[28] These consultants were drawn from a cross-section of American life, and though they were not members of the U.S. delegation, Stettinius and other officials met frequently with them during the conference.

Chapter XI
SAN FRANCISCO: THE VETO DISPUTE
May–June 1945

[1] The "Yalta Formula" contained the following provisions: "1. Each member of the Security Council should have one vote. 2. Decisions of the Security Council on procedural matters should be made by an affirmative vote of seven members. 3. Decisions of the Security Council on all other matters should be made by an affirmative vote of seven members, including the concurring vote of the permanent members; provided that, in decisions

under Chapter VIII, Section A, and under the second sentence of paragraph 1 of Chapter VIII, Section C, a party to a dispute should abstain from voting." Section A empowered the council to investigate any dispute or situation which threatened or appeared to threaten international peace. The sentence in Section C directed the council to encourage settlement of local disputes through regional arrangements or agencies. For a full discussion of negotiations on the Yalta formula, see Thomas Campbell, *Masquerade Peace, America's UN Policy* (Tallahassee, Fla., 1973), Ch. IV.

² Ruth Russell, *A History of the United Nations Charter, the Role of the United States 1940–1945* (Washington, D.C., 1958), pp. 720–29, provides the most detailed summary of the emergence of the veto dispute in the week between May 17 and May 23. The twenty-three questions are printed in *UNCIO Documents*, vol. II: 699–709.

³ Gladwyn Jebb, member of the British delegation to the conference.

⁴ Transcript of phone conversation, Stettinius and Grew, May 31, 1945; summary of phone conversation, Stettinius and Gromyko, May 31, 1945, The Papers of Edward R. Stettinius, Jr., Alderman Library, Charlottesville, Va.

⁵ By "qualified vote," Gromyko meant a vote subject to the veto power.

⁶ For Stettinius's statement at Mexico City, see Robert E. Sherwood, *Roosevelt and Hopkins: An Intimate History* (New York, 1948), p. 875, and *Department of State Bulletin* 12 (March 25, 1945): 479.

⁷ *Foreign Relations of the United States, 1945* 1:118–19.

⁸ *New York Times*, June 2 and 3, 1945.

⁹ Campbell, *Masquerade Peace*, pp. 182–85.

¹⁰ Arthur H. Vandenberg, Jr., ed., *The Private Papers of Senator Vandenberg* (Boston, 1952), p. 204.

¹¹ *Foreign Relations, 1945* 1:1171n.

¹² Calendar Notes, June 6, 1945, Stettinius Papers.

¹³ For the text of the May 26 document, see San Francisco Chronological File, Folder I, May 26, 1945, Stettinius Papers.

¹⁴ UNCIO Press Release No. 24, June 7, 1945, Stettinius Papers.

¹⁵ Summary of phone conversation, Stettinius and Truman, June 7, 1945, Stettinius Diary, June 7, 1945, Stettinius Papers.

¹⁶ Committee II/2 was concerned with the political and security functions of the General Assembly.

¹⁷ The three "concessions" referred to by Gromyko were on provisions for amending the charter, the procedures for ratifying the charter, and the proposal to hold a conference to revise the charter after ten years.

¹⁸ Kirill V. Novikov, chief of the British Department of the Soviet

Foreign Office and secretary-general of the Russian delegation to the conference.

[19] John D. Hickerson, European Division, Department of State.

[20] *Foreign Relations, 1945* 1:1353–55, 1387–88.

[21] Stettinius was referring to the meeting of the Big Three which was to be held at Potsdam, outside Berlin, in July.

[22] Transcript of phone conversation, Stettinius and Krock, June 21, 1945, Stettinius Papers.

[23] Charlie Ross was the president's press secretary.

[24] Calendar Notes, June 26, 1945, Stettinius Papers.

Chapter XII
LAUNCHING THE UNITED NATIONS
August–October 1945

[1] Louis K. Hyde to Stettinius, August 13, 1945, The Papers of Edward R. Stettinius, Jr., Alderman Library, Charlottesville, Va.

[2] Calendar Notes, September 3, 1945, Stettinius Papers.

[3] For a full discussion of the termination of Lend-Lease to Britian at V-J Day, see George C. Herring, Jr., "The United States and British Bankruptcy, 1944–1945: Responsibilities Deferred," *Political Science Quarterly* 86 (June 1971):274–80.

[4] Sir Stafford Cripps, president of the Board of Trade in Attlee's cabinet, was a veteran Labour party left-winger and had been ambassador to Moscow.

[5] France had used military force to try to reassert control over these countries which it had originally held as League of Nations mandates. Open warfare had broken out in May 1945, and had ceased only after Churchill had sent an ultimatum to de Gaulle threatening British intervention.

[6] General Sir Hastings L. Ismay, chief of staff to the minister of defense.

[7] Leo T. Crowley, Wisconsin banker and utilities executive, had been foreign economic administrator from 1943–1945 and played a key role in the termination of Lend-Lease at the end of the war.

[8] John Gilbert Winant was ambassador to Great Britain.

[9] Alger Hiss, State Department official and specialist on international organization, had accompanied Stettinius to the Yalta and San Francisco conferences.

[10] Ellipses in original.

[11] The Potsdam conference had referred to the Council of Foreign

Ministers the task of drafting a peace treaty for Italy, but on this issue as on others the London conference accomplished nothing.

[12] Adlai E. Stevenson had been in the Navy Department during the war and had been brought into the State Department by Stettinius in 1945 to assist Archibald MacLeish in handling press and public relations. He had attended the San Francisco conference on Stettinius's staff and was his top adviser at the London Preparatory Commission.

[13] The "apologies" were for the expulsion of the Soviet Union from the League in 1940 for its attack on Finland.

[14] The meetings did not formally get underway until January 1946. See Chapter XIII.

[15] Eden was referring to the veto and the question of free discussion in the General Assembly.

[16] On the London Conference, see John Gaddis, *The United States and the Origins of the Cold War* (New York, 1972), pp. 263–67.

[17] See Gromyko to Stettinius, June 20, 1945, and Stettinius to Gromyko, June 23, 1945, *Foreign Relations of the United States, 1945* 1:1398–99, and 1428–29.

[18] Calendar Notes, September 28, 1945, Stettinius Papers.

[19] Benjamin O. Gerig, chief, Division of Department Area Affairs, Department of State, had been one of the primary technical experts with the U.S. delegation at the San Francisco conference.

[20] Probably refers to Truman's statement regarding policy for Japan released on September 22. The message is printed in *Public Papers of the Presidents of the United States: Harry S. Truman, 1945* (Washington, 1961), pp. 332–40.

[21] The early discussions on postwar handling of atomic energy are well covered in Gaddis, *United States and the Origins of the Cold War*, pp. 273–81.

[22] Lt. Gen. Stanley D. Embick had represented the Joint Chiefs of Staff at the Dumbarton Oaks, Mexico City, and San Francisco conferences.

[23] Eduard Beneš and Jan Masaryk, president and foreign minister of Czechoslovakia.

[24] The view that Stalin was a reasonable, approachable person while Molotov was obstinate and difficult was widespread among U.S. and British officials throughout the war and in the early postwar period. See Charles Bohlen, *Witness to History* (New York, 1973), p. 227.

[25] See *Foreign Relations, 1945* 1:1440, for the State Department division on location of the UN.

[26] Memorandum of conversation, Stettinius and Byrnes, October 22, 1945, Stettinius Papers.

[27] Attlee and King were coming to Washington on November 11 for discussions on the control of atomic energy.

Chapter XIII
THE UNITED NATIONS IN ACTION
January–June 1946

[1] These events are analyzed in John Gaddis, *The United States and the Origins of the Cold War* (New York, 1972), pp. 282–304.

[2] Herbert Feis, *From Trust to Terror: The Onset of the Cold War* (New York, 1970), pp. 66–70.

[3] Andrei Y. Vyshinsky, assistant peoples commissar for foreign affairs, USSR.

[4] Stettinius was upset with Koo's behavior, telling the American delegation that evening that Koo "was acting very strange and it appears that the Russians have him in their pocket." Calendar Notes, January 27, 1946, The Papers of Edward R. Stettinius, Jr., Alderman Library, Charlottesville, Va.

[5] Calendar Notes, February 28, 1946, Stettinius Papers.

[6] Feis, *Trust to Terror*, pp. 81–83; *Foreign Relations of the United States, 1946* 7:339–65.

[7] Stettinius later told Alger Hiss that "this, of course, would not be possible."

[8] Calendar Notes, March 24, 1946, Stettinius Papers.

[9] Calendar Notes, March 26, 1946, Stettinius Papers.

[10] *Foreign Relations, 1946* 7:388–93.

[11] Earlier discussions on difficulties related to holding the UN sessions in New York may be found in Stettinius's Calendar Notes, March 20–April 10, 1946, Stettinius Papers.

[12] For the discussions leading up to the decision to meet at Flushing Meadows, see Calendar Notes, May 10, 14, 1946, Stettinius Papers.

[13] These "charges" were to be put before the Security Council to justify keeping Iran's complaints on the council agenda. See *Foreign Relations, 1946* 7:420–22.

[14] Oscar Lange was Poland's representative on the Security Council.

[15] For a summary of these developments, see Calendar Notes, May 21, 1946, Stettinius Papers, and *Foreign Relations, 1946* 7:466–74.

[16] Acheson was then assistant secretary of state for political affairs. For his criticisms of Byrnes's organizational methods, see Dean Acheson, *Present at the Creation* (New York, 1969), p. 163.

¹⁷ The Council of Foreign Ministers meeting in Paris had recessed on May 16 and was to reconvene on June 15.

¹⁸ Walter Bedell Smith was then U.S. ambassador to the Soviet Union.

¹⁹ Later in the year, Truman appointed Warren Austin, Republican senator from Vermont, as permanent U.S. representative to the Security Council.

EPILOGUE

¹ See, for example, Herbert Feis, *Between War and Peace* (Princeton, 1960), p. 35, Dean Acheson, *Present at the Creation* (New York, 1969), pp. 88–91, and Richard W. Leopold, *The Growth of American Foreign Policy* (New York, 1962), pp. 547–48.

INDEX

525 | *Index*

Lebanon, 211; 1945 fighting in, 413
Lend-lease, xix-xxiii, 2, 5, 17, 20, 44-45, 204, 494; Act amended (1945), 180; Anglo-American agreement, Article 7, 55, 60-61, 68, 488; Churchill statement on British debts, 61; Eden "White Paper," 32, 92, 489; to Latin America, 261; as political weapon against USSR, 357-358; question of re-export of supplies, 32, 36, 92, 155, 175, 176; to Soviet Union, xxi, 214, 357-358; Stage II discussions, 154-155, 161, 174-176, 178-179, 180; statistics, xxi, 58, 175; Stettinius as Administrator of, xxxiii, 4, 65, 258, 412; termination of, 180, 409, 412, 413-414
Leningrad, 72
Liberian aid project, 478-479, 480
Lie, Trygve, 442, 449-450, 453, 460-461, 465, 474
Lima Conference (1938), 272
Lindsey, Sir Ronald, 39
Lippmann, Walter, 98-102
Lithuania: fear of USSR, 25-26, 197; UN seat asked for, 247
Llewellin, John J., 312
London: Foreign Ministers Conference of 1945, 409, 417, 424-426, 430-431, 432, 436, 437, 441; 1944 mission of Stettinius to, xxvi-xxvii, 20, 31-34, 35, 36-71; Polish government-in-exile, 26-28, 43, 76-88, 157, 161-162, 200, 220, 227-228, 295; postwar atmosphere in, 410; as site for

first UN meeting, 415, 419-420, 422, 440, 442, 443; UN Preparatory Commission in, xxv, 400, 408, 409-410, 412, 414-417, 440, 462
Long, Breckinridge, 9, 13, 139-140
López, Alfonso, 18-19
Lubin, Isador, 298
Lublin Government, Polish, 162, 183, 200, 209, 220, 227-228, 230, 232, 236, 255-256, 295
Lwow, Poland, 162, 236
Lynch, Robert, 75, 305, 394
Lyttleton, Oliver, 312

MacArthur, General Douglas, 168, 448
McCabe, Thomas, xxi
McCloy, John J., 90, 217, 218, 352, 359, 361, 428-430; interest in UN, 428-429, 430
McCormack, John, 14
McDermott, Michael, 74, 106-108
McIntyre, Admiral Ross, 250, 316
MacLeish, Archibald, 185, 198-199; cartoons, *ill.* 186, *ill.* 195; at San Francisco Conference, 351, 360
McNutt, Paul V., 169
Makin, Norman, 450, 451-452
Malay Peninsula, 40
Malta, pre-Yalta Anglo-American talks at, 222, 227-235
Manchuria, Soviet occupation policy in, 441
Marrakesh, pre-Yalta talks at, 223-224
Marshall, General George C., 5, 49, 90, 218, 231, 359, 428, 459, 474, 481; and UN, 429; at Yalta, 238, 239